enVision® Algebra 2
Assessment Resources

SAVVAS
LEARNING COMPANY

Copyright © 2024 by Savvas Learning Company LLC. All Rights Reserved. Printed in the United States of America.

This publication is protected by copyright, and permission should be obtained from the publisher prior to any prohibited reproduction, storage in a retrieval system, or transmission in any form or by any means, electronic, mechanical, photocopying, recording, or otherwise. The publisher hereby grants permission to reproduce pages, in part or in whole, for classroom use only, the number not to exceed the number of students in each class. Notice of copyright must appear on all copies. For information regarding permissions, request forms, and the appropriate contacts within the Savvas Learning Company Rights Management group, please send your query to the address below.

Savvas Learning Company LLC, 15 East Midland Avenue, Paramus, NJ 07652

Savvas® and **Savvas Learning Company®** are the exclusive trademarks of Savvas Learning Company LLC in the U.S. and other countries.

Savvas Learning Company publishes through its famous imprints **Prentice Hall®** and **Scott Foresman®** which are exclusive registered trademarks owned by Savvas Learning Company LLC in the U.S. and/or other countries.

enVision® and **Savvas Realize®** are exclusive trademarks of Savvas Learning Company LLC in the U.S. and/or other countries.

Unless otherwise indicated herein, any third party trademarks that may appear in this work are the property of their respective owners, and any references to third party trademarks, logos, or other trade dress are for demonstrative or descriptive purposes only. Such references are not intended to imply any sponsorship, endorsement, authorization, or promotion of Savvas Learning Company products by the owners of such marks, or any relationship between the owner and Savvas Learning Company LLC or its authors, licensees, or distributors.

ISBN-13: 978-1-4184-0207-5
ISBN-10:   1-4184-0207-9

1 22

Contents

enVision® Algebra 2

Algebra 2 Readiness Assessment

Progress Monitoring Assessments

Topic 1 Assessments and Lesson Quizzes

Topic 2 Assessments and Lesson Quizzes

Benchmark Assessment 1

Topic 3 Assessments and Lesson Quizzes

Topic 4 Assessments and Lesson Quizzes

Benchmark Assessment 2

Topic 5 Assessments and Lesson Quizzes

Topic 6 Assessments and Lesson Quizzes

Benchmark Assessment 3

Topic 7 Assessments and Lesson Quizzes

Topic 8 Assessments and Lesson Quizzes

Benchmark Assessment 4

Topic 9 Assessments and Lesson Quizzes

Topic 10 Assessments and Lesson Quizzes

Benchmark Assessment 5

Topic 11 Assessments and Lesson Quizzes

Topic 12 Assessments and Lesson Quizzes

Benchmark Assessment 6

ASSESSMENT GUIDE
CONTENTS

Activity

Clear and purposeful assessment is at the heart of effective instruction. This Assessment Guide offers general information about assessment as well as specific information about assessment resources in **enVision® Algebra 2** The Assessment Guide is divided into the following parts.

Page
- vi **Why and When to Assess**
- viii **What to Assess**
- xi **How to Assess**
- xii **Assessment Data**

ASSESSMENT GUIDE
WHY AND WHEN TO ASSESS

enVision® Algebra 2 offers the most important key to success on standards-based assessments: daily core instruction that has the same rigor as the assessments. A hallmark of the program is the formative assessment integrated into core instruction through high-cognitive-level, question-driven classroom conversations.

> "enVision® Algebra 2 offers the most important key to success on standards-based assessments: daily core instruction that has the same rigor as the assessments."

Type of Assessment	Why and When to Use This Assessment	Instructional Outcomes Informed by Assessment Results
Diagnostic Assessment	Why: **Diagnose students' readiness** for learning by assessing prerequisite content When: **Before** instruction	• Develop individual study plans. • Make grouping decisions. • Prescribe specific activities to fill gaps in understanding of prerequisite content.
Progress Monitoring Assessment	Why: **Measure students' growth across time** toward specific learning goals When: **Before** the start of instruction of grade level content and **anytime** during the year to measure growth	• Determine students' level of understanding and mastery of grade-level concepts and skills. • Inform instructional activities on the content. • Determine efficacy of curriculum.
Formative Assessment	Why: **Monitor students' progress** on learning content When: **During** daily lessons	• Prescribe specific remediation or enrichment activities on the content. • Provide alternative instruction (reteach). • Alter the pace of instruction. • Adjust the instructional plan for a topic.
Summative Assessment	Why: **Measure students' learning** of the content When: **After** a group of lessons	• Provide specific remediation activities on the content.

All of the assessments listed below are available as both print and digital resources. Most of the digital assessments are auto-scored.

	enVision® Algebra 2 Mathematics Resources	
Progress Monitoring Assessment	At the START of the YEAR, DURING the YEAR, and/or at the END of the YEAR	✓ **Progress Monitoring Assessment, Forms A, B, and C** Assess students' conceptual understanding and procedural skill and fluency with on-level content. Establish a baseline from which growth can be measured.
Diagnostic Assessment	At the start of the YEAR	✓ **Algebra 2 Readiness Assessment** Diagnose students' areas of strength and weakness; results can be used to prescribe differentiated intervention.
	At the start of a TOPIC	✓ **Topic Readiness Assessment** Diagnose students' proficiency with topic prerequisite concepts and skills; results can be used to generate personalized study plans.
Formative Assessment	During a LESSON	✓ **Try It!** Assess students' understanding of concepts and skills presented in each example; results can be used to modify instruction as needed. ✓ **Do You Understand? and Do You Know How?** Assess students' conceptual understand and procedural fluency with lesson content; results can be used to review or revisit content.
	At the end of a LESSON	✓ **Lesson Quiz** Assess students' conceptual understanding and procedural fluency with lesson content; results can be used to prescribe differentiated instruction.
Summative Assessment	At the end of a TOPIC	✓ **Topic Assessment, Form A and Form B** Assess students' conceptual understanding and procedural fluency with topic content. Additional Topic Assessment with ExamView® ✓ **Topic Performance Assessment, Form A and Form B** Assess students' ability to apply concepts learned and proficiency with the Mathematical Thinking and Reasoning Standards.
	After a group of TOPICS and At the end of the YEAR	✓ **Benchmark Assessments** Assess students' understanding of and proficiency with concepts and skills taught throughout the school year; results can be used to prescribe intervention.

ASSESSMENT GUIDE
WHAT TO ASSESS

The assessment resources in **enVision® Algebra 2** assess all aspects of the program, from content and skill to practice and process expectations.

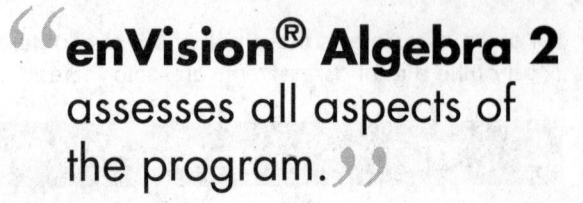

" **enVision® Algebra 2** assesses all aspects of the program. *"*

What to Assess	enVision® Algebra 2 Resources
Math Content • Conceptual understanding • Procedural skill and fluency • Applications	• **Lesson Quizzes** • **Topic Assessments** • **Topic Performance Assessments** • **Benchmark Assessments** • **Progress Monitoring Assessments**
Math Practices and Processes	• **Performance Assessments** • **Habits of Mind** in the Teacher's Edition and Student Companion
Cognitive Complexity • Depth of Knowledge (DOK)	• **Item Analysis Charts** include a "DOK" column that identifies the DOK level for each item.

Cognitive Rigor Matrix for Mathematics

Depth of Knowledge (DOK)

TYPE OF THINKING	DOK LEVEL 1 Recall and Reproduction	DOK LEVEL 2 Basic Skills and Concepts	DOK LEVEL 3 Strategic Thinking and Reasoning	DOK LEVEL 4 Extended Thinking
Remember	• Recall conversions, terms, facts.			
Understand	• Evaluate an expression. • Locate points on a grid or number on number line. • Solve a one-step problem. • Represent math relationships in words, pictures, or symbols.	• Specify, explain relationships. • Make basic inferences or logical predictions from data/observations. • Use models/diagrams to explain concepts. • Make and explain estimates.	• Use concepts to solve non-routine problems. • Use supporting evidence to justify conjectures, generalize, or connect ideas. • Explain reasoning when more than one response is possible. • Explain phenomena in terms of concepts.	• Relate mathematical concepts to other content areas, other domains. • Develop generalizations of the results obtained and the strategies used and apply them to new problem situations.
Apply	• Follow simple procedures. • Calculate, measure, apply a rule (e.g., rounding). • Apply algorithm or formula. • Solve linear equations. • Make conversions.	• Select a procedure and perform it. • Solve routine problem applying multiple concepts or decision points. • Retrieve information to solve a problem. • Translate between representations.	• Design investigation for a specific purpose or research question. • Use reasoning, planning, and supporting evidence. • Translate between problem and symbolic notation when not a direct translation.	• Initiate, design, and conduct a project that specifies a problem, identifies solution paths, solves the problem, and reports results.
Analyze	• Retrieve information from a table or graph to answer a question. • Identify a pattern/trend.	• Categorize data, figures. • Organize, order data. • Select appropriate graph and organize and display data. • Interpret data from a simple graph. • Extend a pattern.	• Compare information within or across data sets or texts. • Analyze and draw conclusions from data, citing evidence. • Generalize a pattern. • Interpret data from complex graph.	• Analyze multiple sources of evidence or data sets.
Evaluate			• Cite evidence and develop a logical argument. • Compare/contrast solution methods. • Verify reasonableness.	• Apply understanding in a novel way, provide argument or justification for the new application.
Create	• Brainstorm ideas, concepts, problems, or perspectives related to a topic or concept.	• Generate conjectures or hypotheses based on observations or prior knowledge and experience.	• Develop an alternative solution. • Synthesize information within one data set.	• Synthesize information across multiple sources or data sets. • Design a model to inform and solve a practical or abstract situation.

Developed by Hess, Carlock, Jones, & Walkup (2009) and adopted by the Smarter Balance Assessment Consortium. Integrates Webb's Depth-of-Knowledge Levels with a modified Bloom's Taxonomy of Educational Objectives shown in the first column.

Assessment Guide

ASSESSMENT GUIDE
HOW TO ASSESS

enVision® Algebra 2 offers a variety of assessment tools that help teachers evaluate student understanding.

Observational assessment in math is especially important for English language learners or students who struggle with reading and writing.

> "**enVision® Algebra 2** offers a variety of assessment tools that help teachers evaluate student understanding."

How to Assess		enVision® Algebra 2 Resources
Observational Assessment	Walk around and observe as students do work in class. Listen as students reply to questions in class.	• **Try It!** is in-class assessment right after instruction to check whether students understand Example content. • **Do You Understand? Do You Know How?** is in-class assessment to see if students are ready for independent practice. • **Guiding questions** in the Teacher's Edition give students a chance to explain their thinking in whole-class, small-group, or individual settings.
Portfolio Assessment	Collect samples of student work.	• **Written assessments** that show representative samples of student work can be especially helpful during parent-teacher conferences.
Performance-Based Assessment	Assign tasks that assess complex thinking and ask for explanations.	• **Performance Assessments** are complex, multi-part tasks and ask for explanations. Topic Performance Assessments and Practice Performance Assessments are online and in print.
Program Assessments	Measure students' understanding of lesson, topic, and grade-level content using paper-based and online assessments.	• **Program assessments**, available in print and online, use items like those found on the state assessment to assess students' understanding of concepts and skills.

Assessment Guide

enVision® Algebra 2 provides resources to facilitate data-driven decision making.

Online assessments at SavvasRealize.com generate a variety of helpful reports and provide ways to group students and prescribe differentiation.

> "**enVision® Algebra 2** provides resources to facilitate data-driven decision making."

	Assessment Data Resources in enVision® Algebra 2
Collecting Assessment Data	• **Data from online assessments** include a variety of class and individual reports that show results for an item, an assessment, or a group of assessments. Also available are individual and class reports on standards mastery. • **Data from other assessments** can include more than students' scores. Examine and discuss students' work on assessments to gain and record valuable insights into what individual students understand and where they are still struggling.
Using Assessment Data	• **Form groups** based on assessment data for the purposes of making instructional decisions and assigning differentiated resources. • **Assign differentiation** based on assessment data. Differentiation is assigned automatically after students complete online Lesson Quizzes, Topic Assessments, and Benchmark Assessments.

Assessment Guide

Name _____

Algebra 2 Readiness Assessment

1. Which expression is not equivalent to a rational number?
   - Ⓐ $\sqrt{\frac{100}{9}} \times \frac{13}{5}$
   - Ⓑ $\sqrt{\frac{25}{4}} \div 8\frac{1}{3}$
   - Ⓒ $\sqrt{\frac{81}{3}} \div 9\frac{1}{4}$
   - Ⓓ $\sqrt{\frac{52}{4}} - \frac{3}{13}$

2. Which inequality is represented by the graph?

   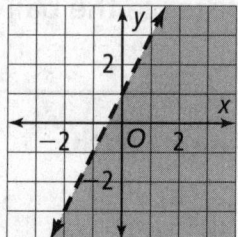

   - Ⓐ $y \leq 2x + 1$
   - Ⓑ $y < 2x + 1$
   - Ⓒ $y \geq 2x + 1$
   - Ⓓ $y > 2x + 1$

3. Akira notices that the mileage on her car follows an arithmetic sequence. Which sequence could represent the mileage on Akira's car?
   - Ⓐ 1000, 1500, 3000, 3500, 5000, ...
   - Ⓑ 1200, 1500, 1900, 2400, 3000, ...
   - Ⓒ 1000, 2000, 4000, 8000, 16,000, ...
   - Ⓓ 1200, 2300, 3400, 4500, 5600, ...

4. Gabriel is running a race. The function $f(x) = a|x - 20|$ represents his distance in miles from the water stop, where x is minutes. The graph of f includes the point (10, 1). Which of the following is true?
   - Ⓐ The y-intercept represents the time Gabriel passes the water stop.
   - Ⓑ The vertex of the graph represents the time Gabriel passes the water stop.
   - Ⓒ The x-intercept represents Gabriel's distance from the water stop at 0 minutes.
   - Ⓓ The function is decreasing over the interval $10 < x < 30$.

5. The data set 60, 68, 105, 78, 80, 81, 84, 70 shows several players' scores after bowling ten frames. Which box plot represents the data?

   Ⓐ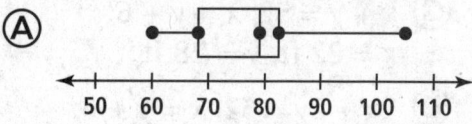

   Ⓑ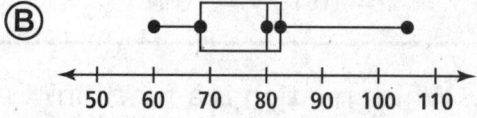

   Ⓒ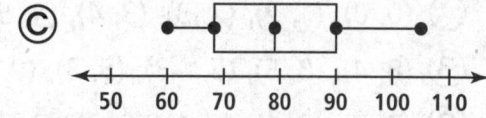

   Ⓓ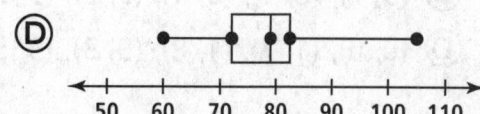

6. A pizzeria charges $6.99 for a cheese pizza plus $1.25 for each additional topping. Their costs are approximately $2.50 for each cheese pizza and $0.60 per topping. Which function models how much the pizzeria earns on a pizza with x toppings?

Ⓐ $P(x) = (6.99 + 1.25x) + (2.50 + 0.60x)$

Ⓑ $P(x) = (6.99 - 1.25x) + (2.50 + 0.60x)$

Ⓒ $P(x) = (6.99 + 1.25x) - (2.50 - 0.60x)$

Ⓓ $P(x) = (6.99 + 1.25x) - (2.50 + 0.60x)$

7. A room has a perimeter of 52 ft. The length x is 6 ft greater than the width y. Which shows the correct system and the dimensions of the room?

Ⓐ $2x + 2y = 52$; $x + 6 = y + 6$; $x = 10$ ft, $y = 16$ ft

Ⓑ $2x + 2y = 52$; $x + 6 = y$; $x = 16$ ft, $y = 10$ ft

Ⓒ $x + y = 52$; $x = y + 6$; $x = 22$ ft, $y = 28$ ft

Ⓓ $2x + 2y = 52$; $x = y + 6$; $x = 16$ ft, $y = 10$ ft

8. Which relation is a function?

Ⓐ (0, 0), (1, 2), (2, 3), (3, 4), (4, 5)

Ⓑ (8, 4), (8, 5), (5, −3), (5, 3), (0, 0)

Ⓒ (3, 7), (8, 1), (6, 1), (5, 2), (3, 2)

Ⓓ (0, 0), (1, 7), (1, 8), (5, 3), (3, 5)

9. The function $f(t) = -16t^2 + 100$ models the height of a ball in feet, dropped from a 100-foot rooftop at time t in seconds. What is the average rate of change for the function over the interval $0 < t < 2$? What does it represent in the context of the situation?

Ⓐ 36 ft; the height of the ball above the ground at 1 second

Ⓑ −32 ft/s; the average change in altitude of the ball each second over that interval

Ⓒ 32 ft/s; the average change in altitude of the ball each 2 seconds

Ⓓ −64 ft; the distance the ball fell in 2 seconds

10. What is the value of x in this equation?

$\frac{1}{4}x - 1 = \frac{1}{3}\left(9 - \frac{3}{2}x\right) - \frac{1}{4}x$

Ⓐ 4

Ⓑ 8

Ⓒ 2

Ⓓ $\frac{32}{5}$

11. What are the solutions to $2x^2 + 9x - 18 = 0$?

Ⓐ $x = 6, -\frac{3}{2}$

Ⓑ $x = -6, 3$

Ⓒ $x = -3, 6$

Ⓓ $x = -6, \frac{3}{2}$

12. Naomi invests $4,000 at an interest rate of 3%, compounded quarterly. How much will her investment be worth in 4 years?

    Ⓐ $4480.00
    Ⓑ $4502.04
    Ⓒ $4507.97
    Ⓓ $6418.83

13. Mason needs 50 hours of behind-the-wheel driving practice to get his driver's license. He gets 6 hours of driving practice per week. Which function represents the hours of practice he still needs in terms of x, the number of weeks?

    Ⓐ $f(x) = -50x + 6$
    Ⓑ $f(x) = 6x + 50$
    Ⓒ $f(x) = -6x + 50$
    Ⓓ $f(x) = 50x + 6$

14. The table shows the number of pages and the time in minutes that it takes for Sasha to complete her reading assignments. Which statement is not true?

Number of Pages	8	15	10	11	18	7
Time (min)	6	17	15	24	29	13

    Ⓐ If a trend line is drawn, the data show a positive correlation.
    Ⓑ There is likely to be a causation between the number of pages and the time it takes to complete a reading assignment.
    Ⓒ If a trend line is drawn, the slope will be positive.
    Ⓓ If a trend line is drawn, the data show a negative correlation.

15. For the data in Item 14, what does the slope of the regression line $y = 1.497x + 0.115$ represent?

    Ⓐ The average length of a reading assignment
    Ⓑ The average number pages Sasha can read in one minute
    Ⓒ The time to complete an assignment
    Ⓓ The average time to complete an assignment

16. The cost of renting a canoe for one hour is $25. Each additional hour is $6 more. Which pair of explicit and recursive formulas represents the situation?

    Ⓐ Explicit: $a_n = 25 - 6n$;
       Recursive: $a_n = a_{n-1} - 25$, $a_1 = 6$
    Ⓑ Explicit: $a_n = 25 + 6n$;
       Recursive: $a_n = a_{n-1} + 6$, $a_1 = 25$
    Ⓒ Explicit: $a_n = 25 - 6n$;
       Recursive: $a_n = a_{n-1} - 6$, $a_1 = 25$
    Ⓓ Explicit: $a_n = 25 + 6n$;
       Recursive: $a_n = a_{n-1} + 25$, $a_1 = 6$

17. Find the product.

    $(x - 3)(x + 3)(2x - 1)$

    Ⓐ $2x^3 + 13x^2 - 24x + 9$
    Ⓑ $2x^3 - 11x^2 - 24x + 9$
    Ⓒ $2x^3 - x^2 - 18x + 9$
    Ⓓ $2x^3 + 9$

18. How does the graph of $g(x) = 2 \cdot 5^x$ differ from the graph of $f(x) = 5^x$?

    Ⓐ It is translated up 2 units.

    Ⓑ It is compressed vertically by a factor of 2.

    Ⓒ It is translated right 2 units.

    Ⓓ It is stretched vertically by a factor of 2.

19. Which value of c makes $x^2 - 16x + c$ a perfect square trinomial?

    Ⓐ −8

    Ⓑ −16

    Ⓒ 64

    Ⓓ 256

20. What is the formula for volume of a cylindrical container, $V = \pi r^2 h$, written in terms of h?

    Ⓐ $h = \frac{V}{\pi r^2}$

    Ⓑ $h = \frac{\pi r^2}{V}$

    Ⓒ $h = V - \pi r^2$

    Ⓓ $hr^2 = \frac{V}{\pi}$

21. Daniela works after school. Each day she earns a set amount, plus an hourly wage, as shown in the table. Write a linear function f that Daniela can use to determine her pay.

Time (h)	1	1.5	2	2.5	3
Pay ($)	25	32	39	46	53

    Ⓐ $f(x) = 25x$

    Ⓑ $f(x) = 14x + 25$

    Ⓒ $f(x) = 11x + 14$

    Ⓓ $f(x) = 14x + 11$

22. Which is a reasonable range for the function in Item 21?

    Ⓐ all real numbers

    Ⓑ $0 < y < 8$

    Ⓒ $0 < y < 24$

    Ⓓ $0 < y < 123$

23. In Item 21, assume Daniela works from 3:30 P.M. to 7:00 P.M. How much does she earn?

    Ⓐ $60   Ⓒ $46

    Ⓑ $53   Ⓓ $39

24. The two-way frequency table shows results of a survey.

    Language Preference

	French	Spanish	Totals
Grade 11	34	75	109
Grade 12	29	62	91
Totals	63	137	200

    What percentage of students in Grade 12 preferred Spanish?

    Ⓐ 32%   Ⓒ 68%

    Ⓑ 46%   Ⓓ 45%

25. Each Saturday, Cameron runs 2 miles. He records his time each week to see if he is improving. Which equation would represent the best trend line for the data if it was plotted?

Week	1	2	3	4	5
Time (min)	25	21	20.5	19	18

    Ⓐ $y = 1.6x + 25$

    Ⓑ $y = 25 - x$

    Ⓒ $y = 18 + 1.5x$

    Ⓓ $y = -1.6x + 26$

26. Riley spends time every day for a week swimming laps in the pool. Her progress is shown in the table below.

Day	1	2	3	4	5
Laps	11	13	17	24	30

She models her data with the linear function $f(x) = 3.5x + 7$. What are the residuals for x-values 1, 2, 3, 4, and 5?

Ⓐ 0.5, −1, −0.5, 3, 5.5

Ⓑ −0.5, 1, 0.5, −3, −5.5

Ⓒ 10.5, 14, 17.5, 21, 24.5

Ⓓ 11, 13, 17, 24, 30

27. A study found a strong positive correlation between the time spent on the phone while driving and the chances of having an accident. Which r-value could match this data?

Ⓐ $r = 0.0125$

Ⓑ $r = -0.9734$

Ⓒ $r = -0.0125$

Ⓓ $r = 0.9734$

28. Researchers study the population of an animal in a certain forest. In 2016 they estimated the population was about 2,450. Each year since, the estimated population has increased by 370. Does this represent an exponential function? Why or why not?

Ⓐ No; there is not a constant difference.

Ⓑ Yes; there is a constant ratio.

Ⓒ No; there is not a constant ratio.

Ⓓ Yes; there is a constant difference.

29. Write $\sqrt[5]{6} \cdot \sqrt{36}$ using rational exponents.

Ⓐ $6^{\frac{6}{5}}$

Ⓑ $36^{\frac{1}{5}}$

Ⓒ $6^{\frac{1}{6}}$

Ⓓ $30^{\frac{7}{6}}$

30. A scientist needs 30 liters of a solution that is 15% acid for an experiment. She has a solution that is 10% acid and another solution that is 25% acid. Let x represent the number of liters of 10% solution. Which equation could she solve to find how many liters of the 10% and 25% solutions she should mix to get the 30 liters of solution she needs?

Ⓐ $30 = 0.10x + 0.25(30 - x)$

Ⓑ $(0.15)(30) = 0.10x + 0.25(30 - x)$

Ⓒ $(0.15)(30) = 0.10x + 0.25x$

Ⓓ $0.15 = 0.10x + 0.25(30 - x)$

31. What is the domain of $f(x) = \sqrt{45 - 9x}$?

Ⓐ $x > -5$

Ⓑ $f(x) \geq 0$

Ⓒ $x \leq 5$

Ⓓ All real numbers

32. The populations of three bacteria samples are shown below. The functions $f(x) = 12x + 7$, $g(x) = 4x^2$ and $h(x) = 3^x$ model the three populations. Which statement is not true?

Bacteria Populations

Week	Sample 1	Sample 2	Sample 3
1	19	4	3
2	31	16	9
3	43	36	27

Ⓐ Based on the models, the populations of all samples will continue to increase as the week x increases.

Ⓑ The population of Sample 3, modeled by the exponential function, will not exceed the other two populations in week 4.

Ⓒ The population of Sample 2 will be larger than the population of Sample 1 in week 4.

Ⓓ The population of Sample 3 is modeled with a constant ratio.

33. What is $g - f$ when $f(x) = 3x^2 - 18$ and $g(x) = x^3 + 5x - 4$?

Ⓐ $(g - f)(x) = 3x^5 + 15x^3 - 22$

Ⓑ $(g - f)(x) = x^3 - 3x^2 + 5x - 22$

Ⓒ $(g - f)(x) = x^3 - 3x^2 + 5x + 14$

Ⓓ $(g - f)(x) = -2x^2 + 5x + 14$

34. Tom has 60 feet of fencing to enclose a rectangular garden. Let x represent the length of the garden. Which functions describe the area of the garden written in standard form and factored form? What information does factored form give you?

Ⓐ $f(x) = x^2 - 30x$; $f(x) = x(x - 30)$; The roots of the equation are 0, 30. 0 ft < x < 30 ft

Ⓑ $f(x) = -x^2 + 60x$; $f(x) = x(60 - x)$; The roots of the equation are 0, 60. 0 ft < x < 60 ft

Ⓒ $f(x) = x^2 - 30x$; $f(x) = x(x - 30)$; The maximum area of the garden is 30 ft².

Ⓓ $f(x) = -x^2 + 30x$; $f(x) = x(30 - x)$; The roots of the equation are 0 and 30. 0 ft < x < 30 ft

35. Anne and Kate can make 24 tacos in 8 minutes, working together. Anne can make 12 tacos in 6 minutes working alone. How many minutes would it take Kate to make 10 tacos?

Ⓐ 6 minutes

Ⓑ 10 minutes

Ⓒ 12 minutes

Ⓓ 5 minutes

36. If $\sqrt[3]{7}$ is defined as the cube root of 7, which of the following is not true?

Ⓐ $\left(7^{\frac{1}{3}}\right)^3 = (7^3)^{\frac{1}{3}}$

Ⓑ $\left(7^{\frac{1}{3}}\right)^3 = 7$

Ⓒ $7^{\frac{1}{3}} \cdot 7^{\frac{1}{3}} \cdot 7^{\frac{1}{3}} = 7^1$

Ⓓ $3\left(7^{\frac{1}{3}}\right) = 7^1$

Name _____

Progress Monitoring Assessment Form A

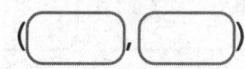

1. The graph below is translated 3 units right, and 2 units down. What is the equation of the new graph?

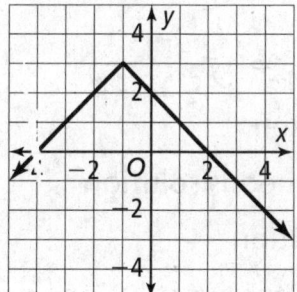

   Ⓐ $y = -|x - 2| + 1$
   Ⓑ $y = -|x + 3| - 2$
   Ⓒ $y = -|x - 4| + 3$
   Ⓓ $y = -|x + 2| - 1$

2. Select all solutions to the system of equations.

   $y = (x + 2)^2 - 4$
   $2x + y = -8$

   ☐ A. no solution
   ☐ B. $(-4, 0)$
   ☐ C. $(0, -4)$
   ☐ D. $(-4, -2)$
   ☐ E. $(-2, -4)$
   ☐ F. $(-1, -1)$

3. Which of the following is equivalent to the expression $(2i + 1)(5 - i)$?

   Ⓐ $3 + 9i$ Ⓒ $7 + 9i$
   Ⓑ $3 - 9i$ Ⓓ $7 - 9i$

4. The graph of a quadratic function $f(x)$ has a vertex at $(-3, 5)$. What is the vertex of $g(x)$ if $g(x) = f(x + 1) + 2$?

   (☐ , ☐)

5. The height above sea level of a gannet diving for fish is modeled by the function $f(x) = x^4 - x^3 - 16x^2 + 16x$.

   Select all the x-values where the bird enters or exits the water.

   ☐ A. -4 ☐ D. 1
   ☐ B. -2 ☐ E. 3
   ☐ C. 0 ☐ F. 4

6. Solve $-x^2 - 3x = 4$ over the set of complex numbers.

   Ⓐ $\frac{3 + 5i}{2}, \frac{3 - 5i}{2}$
   Ⓑ $\frac{-3 + 5i}{2}, \frac{-3 - 5i}{2}$
   Ⓒ $\frac{3 + i\sqrt{7}}{2}, \frac{3 - i\sqrt{7}}{2}$
   Ⓓ $\frac{-3 + i\sqrt{7}}{2}, \frac{-3 - i\sqrt{7}}{2}$

7. Tuning standard A has a frequency of 440 cycles per second, or Hertz. The frequency of a musical note, in Hertz, can be given by $f(x) = 440(2^x)$, where x is the number of octaves above the tuning standard A. How many octaves above the tuning standard A is a note that has a frequency of 1,397 Hertz? Round the solution to the nearest tenth. x is approximately ☐ octaves.

8. Divide $x^3 - 3x^2 + 4x + 1$ by $x - 2$. Complete the quotient using the choices provided.

x	$-5x$	$-x$	2
6	4	$\frac{-3}{x-2}$	$\frac{5}{x-2}$

$x^2 + \boxed{} + \boxed{} + \boxed{}$

9. **Part A** Solve. Check for extraneous solutions.

   $\sqrt{x+17} + 3 = x$

   (A) $x = 1$ only
   (B) $x = 8$ only
   (C) $x = 1$ or $x = -8$
   (D) $x = -1$ or $x = 8$

   Part B Which step could lead to finding extraneous solutions?

   (A) Subtracting 3 from both sides
   (B) Squaring both sides
   (C) Using the distributive property
   (D) Factoring the trinomial

10. The function $f(x) = \sqrt{x+6}$ represents the profits of a company after x years in business. Which function represents the number of years as a function of the profits?

    (A) $f^{-1}(x) = (x+6)^2$, for $x \geq 0$
    (B) $f^{-1}(x) = (x+6)^2$, for $x \geq -6$
    (C) $f^{-1}(x) = x^2 - 6$, for $x \geq 0$
    (D) $f^{-1}(x) = x^2 - 6$, for $x \geq -6$

11. What is the average rate of change for the function $f(x) = -4x^2 + 1$ over the interval $-\frac{3}{2} \leq x \leq 0$?

    (A) -9
    (B) -6
    (C) 6
    (D) 9

12. Simplify.

    $5\sqrt{96} - 7\sqrt{54} + 6^{\frac{3}{2}}$

    (A) $-5\sqrt{6}$
    (B) $-\sqrt{6}$
    (C) $5\sqrt{6}$
    (D) 192

13. **Part A** Solve the equation for a and check the solution to determine whether it is an extraneous solution.

    $\frac{5}{a-4} + \frac{2}{a+1} = \frac{-31}{a^2 - 3a - 4}$

    (A) 4; solution
    (B) 4; extraneous solution
    (C) -4; solution
    (D) -4; extraneous solution

    Part B If the value -1 was a solution, why would it be an extraneous solution?

    (A) Both sides of the equation would be equal to 0.
    (B) The left side of the equation would be equal to 0.
    (C) At least one denominator would be equal to 0.
    (D) The right side of the equation would be equal to 0.

14. Solve the equation $-4 \ln(6x) = 2$.

    (A) 0.101
    (B) 0.275
    (C) 3.639
    (D) 67.238

15. The augmented matrix $\begin{bmatrix} -1 & 6 & | & 14 \\ -5 & 4 & | & -8 \end{bmatrix}$ represents a system of equations. Find the solution to this system of Equations.

    (A) $(3, 4)$
    (B) $(-3, 4)$
    (C) $(4, 3)$
    (D) $(4, -3)$

16. Where will the discontinuities occur in the graph of the rational function?

$f(x) = \dfrac{x^2 + 6x}{x^2 + 4x - 12}$

Ⓐ at $x = 2$

Ⓑ at $x = -6$

Ⓒ at $x = 2$ and $x = -6$

Ⓓ at $x = 0$, $x = 2$ and $x = -6$

17. The values of the following finite arithmetic series represents how much money Jackie made each day in the summer. Which describes the sequence?

$35 + 32 + 29 + \ldots + 5$

Ⓐ $a_n = 35 - 3(n - 3)$

Ⓑ $a_n = 35 - 3(n)$

Ⓒ $a_n = 35 - 3(n - 1)$

Ⓓ $a_n = 35 - 3(n + 1)$

18. The values of the following finite geometric series represent the rise in water depth each year for a lake near Sean's house, in inches. How much has the lake risen in total?

$3 + 4.5 + 6.75 + \ldots + 34.171875$

Ⓐ 48.257813 in.

Ⓑ 48.421875 in.

Ⓒ 96.515625 in.

Ⓓ 130.101563 in.

19. Which of the following is true for the graph of $y = -\dfrac{1}{16}x^2$?

Ⓐ The equation of the directrix is $y = -4$.

Ⓑ The focus is at $(0, -4)$.

Ⓒ The parabola opens to the left.

Ⓓ The vertex is at $(0, -4)$.

20. You are conducting a survey to compare the popularity of different sports at your school. You survey the first 50 students that arrive at that week's football game. Is the sample likely to be biased? Why or why not?

Ⓐ No; the sample is representative of the whole student body.

Ⓑ Yes; all the students surveyed do not play any sports.

Ⓒ Yes; all the students surveyed are likely to enjoy watching football.

Ⓓ No; the students being surveyed know more about sports than the other students.

21. The scores for the midterm test in a physics class are displayed in the box. The teacher tells the class that everyone who scores above the 80th percentile will receive a grade of A. Which of the given scores is the lowest to receive an A on the test?

45	95	67	50	70
81	63	83	55	72
78	62	59	74	68
70	91	75	88	68

Ⓐ 80 Ⓑ 81 Ⓒ 83 Ⓓ 90

22. Monisha has a bag of 24 tiles, numbered 1 through 24. Her friend draws a tile from the bag at random. What is the probability the tile shows a number that is a multiple of 3 or a multiple of 4?

Ⓐ $\dfrac{1}{2}$

Ⓑ $\dfrac{13}{24}$

Ⓒ $\dfrac{1}{12}$

Ⓓ $\dfrac{1}{24}$

23. The number of people attending a local movie theater has been increasing over the last several days. On Monday, 400 people attended. On Tuesday, 450 people attended. And on Thursday, 550 people attended.

    Part A Is the sequence that represents the attendance arithmetic? If it is, choose the recursive formula for the sequence.

    ☐ A. No; the movie attendance cannot be represented by an arithmetic sequence.

    ☐ B. Yes; $a(n) = 450 + n$

    ☐ C. Yes; $a_1 = 400$, $a_n = a_{n-1} + 50$

    ☐ D. Yes; $a_1 = 400$, $a_n = a_{n+1} + 50$

    Part B If the trend continues, how many people will attend on Saturday?

    ☐ people

24. Use a graph to solve $|x - 1| = -(x - 1)^2 + 2$.

    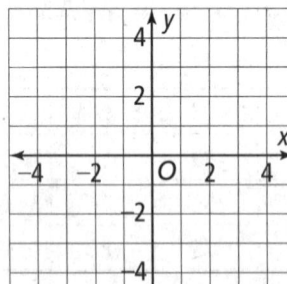

    $x = $ ☐, $x = $ ☐

25. A school's enrollment is represented by the function $P(t) = 527(1 + 0.02)^t$, where t is time in years since 2018. Rounded to the nearest student, what will be the school's expected enrollment in 2022?

    ☐ students

26. Select the solutions to the equation $x^2 = -49$.

    ☐ A. 7   ☐ E. -7
    ☐ B. 7i   ☐ F. -7i
    ☐ C. 24.5   ☐ G. -24.5
    ☐ D. 24.5i   ☐ H. -24.5i

27. Simplify $(x^2 + 2x)(x^2 + x + 5)$.

    Ⓐ $x^4 + x^3 + 5x^2$
    Ⓑ $x^4 + 3x^3 + 7x^2 + 10x$
    Ⓒ $2x^5 + 2x^4 + 10x^3$
    Ⓓ $9x^2 + 3x^3 + 10x$

28. Use a graph of the polynomial function $f(x) = x^3 - 2x^2$ to complete the following:

    The zeros of f are ☐ and ☐.

    As x decreases, $f(x)$ ☐ increases.
    ☐ decreases.

    As x increases, $f(x)$ ☐ increases.
    ☐ decreases.

29. A bee colony has a population of 30,000. The population is increasing at a rate of 10% per year. How can you write an exponential growth function to find the monthly growth rate?

    Ⓐ $y = 30,000(1.00797)^{12t}$
    Ⓑ $y = 30,000(1.010\frac{1}{12})^t$
    Ⓒ $y = 30,000(0.00833)^{12t}$
    Ⓓ $y = 30,000(1.10)^{12t}$

30. Three percent of the students at Douglas High play football, 6% are in the National Honor Society, and 2% are in both. If a student is selected at random, what is the probability that the student plays football or is in the National Honor Society?

   Ⓐ 6%
   Ⓑ 7%
   Ⓒ 8%
   Ⓓ 9%

31. For the triangle below, what are the values of $\cos\theta$ and $\tan\theta$?

   ⬚ 85   ⬚ $6\sqrt{85}$ ⬚ 11
   ⬚ $\sqrt{85}$ ⬚ 5   ⬚ $\sqrt{157}$

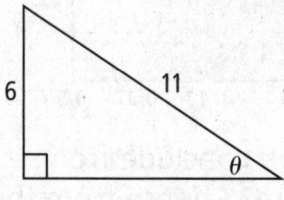

   $\cos\theta = \dfrac{\square}{\square}$, $\tan\theta = \dfrac{\square}{\square}$

32. A merry-go-round has radius 15 ft. To the nearest foot, how far does someone at the edge of the merry-go-round travel as it rotates through $\frac{5\pi}{6}$ radians?

   ⬚ ft

33. The mean SAT score of students at a school is 1020. In a random sample of students at the school, the mean SAT score is 1035. Which word best describes the figure 1035?

   Ⓐ parameter   Ⓒ variable
   Ⓑ statistic   Ⓓ sample

34. Solve $x^2 + 2x - 2 = 0$ by completing the square. Use the choices provided to complete the solution.

   ⬚ 1   ⬚ −1   ⬚ 2   ⬚ −2
   ⬚ $\sqrt{2}$ ⬚ $\sqrt{3}$ ⬚ $\sqrt{5}$

   $x = \square \pm \square$

35. Select the properties of logarithms used in each step to rewrite the expression shown below as the sum of three logarithmic expressions.

   $\log \dfrac{3x^2}{y}$

   (1) $= \log 3x^2 - \log y$
   (2) $= \log 3 + \log x^2 - \log y$
   (3) $= \log 3 + 2 \log x - \log y$

   1. ☐ Quotient Property
      ☐ Product Property
      ☐ Power Property

   2. ☐ Quotient Property
      ☐ Product Property
      ☐ Power Property

   3. ☐ Quotient Property
      ☐ Product Property
      ☐ Power Property

36. Jill has $500 to give to charity. She has ranked her favorite charities in a list. She gives 10% of her money to the first charity, then 10% of what is left to the second, and so on. How much money does she have left after giving to ten charities? Round to the nearest dollar.

   $ ⬚

37. What constant do you add to each side of the equation to solve by completing the square?

$2x^2 - 3x = 1$

Ⓐ 9

Ⓑ $\frac{9}{2}$

Ⓒ $\frac{9}{4}$

Ⓓ $\frac{3}{2}$

38. You roll a standard number cube six times. Which of the following results would make you most likely to question whether the number die was fair?

Ⓐ 6, 6, 3, 2, 5, 2

Ⓑ 1, 2, 2, 5, 4, 3

Ⓒ 1, 4, 4, 1, 4, 4

Ⓓ 3, 4, 3, 1, 5, 6

39. A precision tool manufacturer requires that its tools be within 0.5 grams of a target weight. They tested five lots of tools and reported the mean, $\bar{x}$, and standard deviation, s, of their weights. A lot is rejected if more than 5% of tools are greater than 0.5 grams over or under the target weight.

Which of the following lots would be rejected?

☐ A. target weight = 13 g
$\bar{x} = 13.1$ g; $s = 0.2$ g

☐ B. target weight = 10 g
$\bar{x} = 10$ g; $s = 0.15$ g

☐ C. target weight = 15 g
$\bar{x} = 14.8$ g; $s = 0.4$ g

☐ D. target weight = 8 g
$\bar{x} = 7.95$ g; $s = 0.18$ g

☐ E. target weight = 20 g
$\bar{x} = 20.5$ g; $s = 0.25$ g

40. A company tests a new type of laptop battery that they have designed to last longer than older versions. The table shows the battery life for the old batteries (Group A) and the new batteries (Group B).

| A | 8.1 | 8.2 | 8.6 | 8.2 | 8.1 |
| B | 8.5 | 8.7 | 8.5 | 8.8 | 9.0 |

What is the difference of the means of Group A and Group B?

☐

The data are resampled 200 times and a histogram of the difference of the means is shown below.

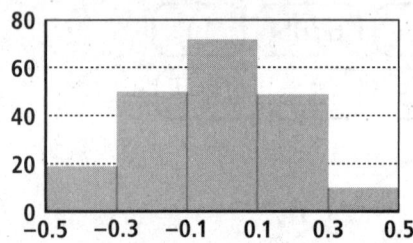

What can you conclude from the histogram? Choose from the phrases below to complete the sentences.

| less than | greater than |
| support | do not support |

A large majority of data in the histogram is ☐ than the difference of the means of the original samples. The data ☐ the hypothesis that there is a meaningful difference between Group A and Group B.

41. Select all functions whose graph has a vertical asymptote at $x = 2$.

- A. $f(x) = \ln(x - 2)$
- B. $f(x) = \log_2 x - 2$
- C. $f(x) = \log(x - 2) + 2$
- D. $f(x) = 2\ln x - 2$
- E. $f(x) = \log 2x$

42. A point $P(a, b)$ lies on the unit circle. It corresponds to angle θ. Select all of the statements that are true.

- A. $\cos\theta = b$
- B. As θ increases, the value of a decreases.
- C. $a^2 + b^2 = 1$
- D. If the radian measure of the angle is $\theta = 2$, then the distance along the circle from $(a, 0)$ to point P is 2 units.
- E. As θ increases, the absolute value of b increases then decreases in a cycle.

43. The function f has domain $[0, \infty)$. Select the functions that have domains equal to all real numbers.

- A. $g(x) = f(x^4 + x^2 + 1)$
- B. $g(x) = f(x^2 - 4x + 3)$
- C. $g(x) = f(|1 - x|)$
- D. $g(x) = f(1 - x)$
- E. $g(x) = f(x^2 + x + 1)$

44. Two community activists plan to contact local residents to urge them to vote for their preferred candidate for mayor.

Part A Albert plans to contact 10 residents per day. Write a function that models the number of residents he contacts after x days.

$f(x) = \boxed{}x$

Nakeeda uses a different strategy. She contacts 2 people on the first day. Those people will then contact 2 people the next day. This pattern continues each day. Write a function that models the number of people contacted by both Albert and Nakeeda after x days.

$g(x) = \boxed{}x + \boxed{}^x$

Part B Past experience shows that only 30% of people contacted will actually vote for their preferred candidate. Write a function that models the number of votes Albert and Nakeeda can expect to gain for their candidate after x days.

$h(x) = \boxed{}(\boxed{}x + \boxed{}^x)$

If Albert and Nakeeda start contacting people 10 days before the election, how many additional votes does the model predict they will gain for their candidate? Round to the nearest whole number.

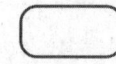

$\boxed{}$

45. A lunar explorer vehicle lifts off from the surface of the moon at a constant rate of 1,000 m/s. The radius of the Moon is about 1.737×10^6 m.

Part A

Write a function that models the distance of the lunar explorer from the center of the Moon x seconds after it takes off from the surface.

$f(x) = \boxed{} \times 10^{\boxed{}} + \boxed{}$

As the lunar explorer rises, the effect of the Moon's gravity weakens. In order to maintain a constant speed, the lunar explorer must adjust the force of its thrust to account for this.

The acceleration on an object due to the Moon's gravity is 4.904×10^{12} m³/s² divided by the square of its distance from the center of the Moon. Write a function that models the acceleration due to the Moon's gravity experienced by the lunar explorer in terms of the number of seconds after it takes off from the surface.

$g(x) = \dfrac{\boxed{} \times 10^{\boxed{}}}{(\boxed{} \times 10^{\boxed{}} + \boxed{}x)^2}$

Part B

Complete the sentence.

$\boxed{\tfrac{1}{2}}$ $\boxed{\tfrac{1}{4}}$ $\boxed{\tfrac{2}{5}}$ $\boxed{\tfrac{4}{5}}$

After 12 minutes, the acceleration due to gravity is about $\boxed{}$ of what it is on the surface.

46. What are the solutions of $x^3 - 64 = 0$?

Ⓐ $4, 2 + 2i\sqrt{3}, 2 - 2i\sqrt{3}$
Ⓑ $4, -2 + 2i\sqrt{3}, -2 - 2i\sqrt{3}$
Ⓒ $-4, 2 + 2i\sqrt{3}, 2 - 2i\sqrt{3}$
Ⓓ $-4, -2 + 2i\sqrt{3}, -2 - 2i\sqrt{3}$

47. Subtract and simplify.

$\dfrac{5x}{3x^2} - \dfrac{7}{6x}$

Ⓐ $\dfrac{1}{2x}$
Ⓑ $\dfrac{-1}{3x}$
Ⓒ $\dfrac{1}{6x^2}$
Ⓓ $\dfrac{5x - 7}{6x^2}$

48. At a lake, 210 fish are caught, tagged, and released. Of that number, 38 were bass. If there are approximately 2,500 fish in the lake, estimate how many are bass.

Ⓐ 68
Ⓑ 121
Ⓒ 414
Ⓓ 452

49. Kyle challenges you to a game. Each player rolls a standard number cube. If the sum of the results is divisible by 3 you win. If it is not, Kyle wins. What is your probability of winning? Is this a fair game?

Ⓐ $\tfrac{1}{3}$; No, the game is not fair.
Ⓑ $\tfrac{4}{11}$; No, the game is not fair.
Ⓒ $\tfrac{1}{2}$; Yes, the game is fair.
Ⓓ $\tfrac{2}{3}$; No, the game is not fair.

Progress Monitoring Assessment Form B

1. The graph below is translated 2 units left, and 4 units up. What is the equation of the new graph?

   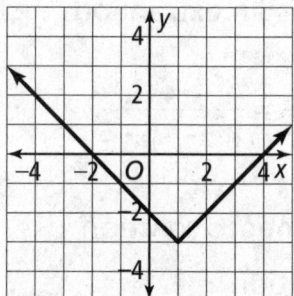

   Ⓐ $y = |x + 1| - 1$
   Ⓑ $y = |x + 1| + 1$
   Ⓒ $y = |x - 1| + 1$
   Ⓓ $y = |x - 3| - 1$

2. Select all solutions to the system of equations.

   $y = -(x + 2)^2 + 4$
   $2x + y = -3$

   ☐ A. no solution
   ☐ B. $(-4, 0)$
   ☐ C. $(0, -3)$
   ☐ D. $(-3, 3)$
   ☐ E. $(1, -5)$
   ☐ F. $(1, -1)$

3. Which of the following is equivalent to the expression $(4i + 3)(6 - i)$?

   Ⓐ $27i + 14$
   Ⓑ $21i + 22$
   Ⓒ $27i + 22$
   Ⓓ $21i + 14$

4. The graph of a quadratic function $f(x)$ has a vertex at $(3, -5)$. What is the vertex of $g(x)$ if $g(x) = f(x + 2) + 1$?

   ( ,)

5. The height above sea level of a flying fish is modeled by the function $f(x) = -x^4 + 3x^3 + x^2 - 3x$. Select all the x-values where the fish enters or exits the water.

   ☐ A. -2 ☐ D. 1
   ☐ B. -1 ☐ E. 3
   ☐ C. 0 ☐ F. 4

6. Solve $x^2 + 3x = 5$ over the set of complex numbers.

   Ⓐ $\frac{3 + i\sqrt{11}}{2}, \frac{3 - i\sqrt{11}}{2}$
   Ⓑ $\frac{-3 + i\sqrt{11}}{2}, \frac{-3 - i\sqrt{11}}{2}$
   Ⓒ $\frac{3 + \sqrt{29}}{2}, \frac{3 - \sqrt{29}}{2}$
   Ⓓ $\frac{-3 + \sqrt{29}}{2}, \frac{-3 - \sqrt{29}}{2}$

7. Tuning standard A has a frequency of 440 cycles per second, or Hertz. The frequency of a musical note, in Hertz, can be given by $f = 440(2^x)$, where x is the number of octaves above the tuning standard A. How many octaves above the tuning standard A is a note that has a frequency of 2,637 Hertz? Round the solution to the nearest tenth.

   x is approximately ____ octaves.

8. Divide $x^3 + 2x^2 - 5x + 1$ by $x + 3$. Complete the quotient using the choices provided.

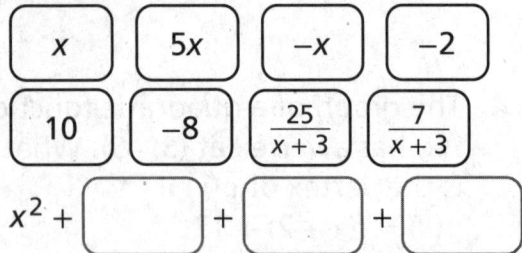

$x^2 + \boxed{} + \boxed{} + \boxed{}$

9. **Part A** Solve. Check for extraneous solutions.
   $\sqrt{44 - 5x} + 4 = x$

   Ⓐ $x = -4$ or $x = 7$
   Ⓑ $x = 4$ or $x = -7$
   Ⓒ $x = -4$ only
   Ⓓ $x = 7$ only

   Part B Which step could lead to finding extraneous solutions?

   Ⓐ Using the distributive property
   Ⓑ Factoring the trinomial
   Ⓒ Subtracting 4 from both sides
   Ⓓ Squaring both sides

10. The function $f(x) = \frac{1}{3}\pi x^3$ represents the volume of a cone with both height and radius of x. Which function represents the radius of the cone as a function of the volume?

    Ⓐ $f^{-1}(x) = \left(\frac{3}{\pi}\right)\sqrt[3]{x}$, for $x \geq 0$
    Ⓑ $f^{-1}(x) = \left(\frac{3}{\pi}\right)\sqrt[3]{x}$, for $x \leq 0$
    Ⓒ $f^{-1}(x) = \sqrt[3]{\frac{3x}{\pi}}$, for $x \leq 0$
    Ⓓ $f^{-1}(x) = \sqrt[3]{\frac{3x}{\pi}}$, for $x \geq 0$

11. What is the average rate of change for the function $f(x) = 8x^2 - 1$ over the interval $-\frac{3}{2} \leq x \leq 0$?

    Ⓐ 11
    Ⓑ 12
    Ⓒ -12
    Ⓓ -11

12. Simplify.
    $2\sqrt{12} + \sqrt{75} - 3^{\frac{3}{2}}$

    Ⓐ $9\sqrt{3} - \sqrt[3]{9}$
    Ⓑ $6\sqrt{3}$
    Ⓒ $10\sqrt{3}$
    Ⓓ $9\sqrt{3} - 3$

13. **Part A** Solve the equation for x and check the solution to determine whether it is an extraneous solution.
    $\frac{6}{x+1} + \frac{2}{x-5} = \frac{4}{x^2 - 4x - 5}$

    Ⓐ 4; solution
    Ⓑ 4; extraneous solution
    Ⓒ -4; solution
    Ⓓ -4; extraneous solution

    Part B If the value 5 was a solution, why would it be an extraneous solution?

    Ⓐ Both sides of the equation would be equal to 0.
    Ⓑ The left side of the equation would be equal to 0.
    Ⓒ At least one denominator would be equal to 0.
    Ⓓ The right side of the equation would be equal to 0.

14. Solve the equation $-5 \ln(3x) = 4$.

    Ⓐ 1.348
    Ⓑ 0.742
    Ⓒ 0.150
    Ⓓ 0.450

15. The augmented matrix $\begin{bmatrix} 1 & 1 & | & 7 \\ -5 & -1 & | & -27 \end{bmatrix}$ represents a system of equations. Find the solution to this system of equations.

    Ⓐ (2, 5)
    Ⓑ (2, -5)
    Ⓒ (5, 2)
    Ⓓ (-5, 2)

16. Where will the discontinuities occur in the graph of the rational function?

$f(x) = \dfrac{x^2 - 4x}{x^2 - x - 12}$

Ⓐ at $x = 4$

Ⓑ at $x = -3$

Ⓒ at $x = 4$ and $x = -3$

Ⓓ at $x = 0$, $x = 4$ and $x = -3$

---

17. An auditorium has 20 seats in the first row and 30 seats in the sixth row. The number of seats in each row forms an arithmetic sequence. Which describes the sequence where n is the row number?

Ⓐ $a_n = 30 + 2(n - 1)$

Ⓑ $a_n = 20 + 2n$

Ⓒ $a_n = 20 + 2(n + 1)$

Ⓓ $a_n = 20 + 2(n - 1)$

---

18. A ball is dropped from 16 feet. The heights of each successive bounce form a geometric series. What is the total height of the bounces shown, including the starting height?

$16 + 6.4 + 2.56 + \ldots + 0.16384$

Ⓐ 25.53344 ft

Ⓑ 26.14784 ft

Ⓒ 26.55744 ft

Ⓓ 25.12384 ft

---

19. Which of the following is true for the graph of $y = -\dfrac{1}{12}x^2$?

Ⓐ A The equation of the directrix is $y = -3$.

Ⓑ The focus is at $(0, -3)$.

Ⓒ The parabola opens to the left.

Ⓓ The vertex is at $(0, -3)$.

---

20. You are conducting a survey to compare the popularity of different types of music. You survey the first 25 students who arrive at band practice. Is the sample likely to be biased? Why or why not?

Ⓐ Yes; all the students surveyed are more likely to enjoy band or orchestral music than other students.

Ⓑ Yes; all the students surveyed do not play music.

Ⓒ No; the sample is representative of the whole student body.

Ⓓ No; the students being surveyed know more about music than the other students.

---

21. The scores for the final test in an English class are displayed in the box. The teacher tells the class that everyone who scores above the 70th percentile will receive a grade of B. Which of the given scores is the lowest to receive a B on the test?

53	95	67	50	70
85	63	83	55	72
87	62	59	74	68
95	91	75	88	68

Ⓐ 72   Ⓑ 85   Ⓒ 83   Ⓓ 70

---

22. Joan has a bag of 20 tiles, numbered 1 through 20. Her friend draws a tile from the bag at random. What is the probability the tile shows a number that is a multiple of 3 or is a number less than 10?

Ⓐ $\dfrac{3}{20}$ Ⓒ $\dfrac{3}{5}$

Ⓑ $\dfrac{9}{20}$ Ⓓ $\dfrac{3}{4}$

23. The number of people attending a local fair has been increasing over the last several days. On Monday, 300 people attended. On Tuesday, 340 people attended. And on Thursday, 420 people attended.

    Part A Is the sequence that represents the fair attendance arithmetic? If it is, choose the recursive formula for the sequence.

    Ⓐ No; the fair attendance cannot be represented by an arithmetic sequence.

    Ⓑ Yes; $a(n) = 340 + n$

    Ⓒ Yes; $a_1 = 300$, $a_n = a_{n-1} + 40$

    Ⓓ Yes; $a_1 = 300$, $a_n = a_{n+1} + 40$

    Part B If the trend continues, how many people will attend on Saturday?

    ☐ people

24. Use a graph to solve $|x + 2| - 4 = -(x + 2)^2 + 2$.

    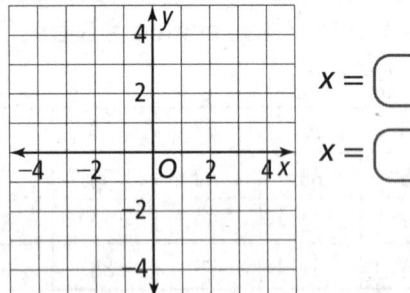

    $x =$ ☐
    $x =$ ☐

25. The enrollment at a local community college can be modeled by the function $P(t) = 825(1 + 0.01)^t$, where t is time in years since 2017. Rounded to the nearest student, what will be the college's expected enrollment in 2023?

    ☐ students

26. Select the solutions of the equation $x^2 = -100$.

    ☐ A. 10   ☐ E. −10
    ☐ B. 10i ☐ F. −10i
    ☐ C. 50   ☐ G. −50
    ☐ D. 50i ☐ H. −50i

27. Simplify $(x^2 + 3x)(x^2 + x + 4)$.

    Ⓐ $x^4 + x^3 + 4x^2 + 3x(x^2 + x + 4)$
    Ⓑ $x^4 + 4x^3 + 4x^2 + 12x$
    Ⓒ $4x^7 + 2x^5 + 16x^3$
    Ⓓ $x^4 + 4x^3 + 7x^2 + 12x$

28. Use a graph of the polynomial function $f(x) = -x^3 + 4x$ to complete the following:

    The zeros of f are ☐, ☐, and ☐.

    As x decreases, $f(x)$ ☐ increases.
                        ☐ decreases.

    As x increases, $f(x)$ ☐ increases.
                        ☐ decreases.

29. A town has a population of 20,000. The population is increasing at a rate of 2% per year. How can you write an exponential growth function to find the monthly growth rate?

    Ⓐ $y = 20{,}000(0.00165)^{12t}$
    Ⓑ $y = 20{,}000(1.02^{\frac{1}{12}})\, t$
    Ⓒ $y = 20{,}000(1.00165)^{12t}$
    Ⓓ $y = 20{,}000(1.02)^{12t}$

30. Nine percent of the students at the local high school play soccer, 4% are in the band, and 2% are in both. If a student is selected at random, what is the probability that the student plays soccer or is in the band?

    Ⓐ 15%
    Ⓑ 11%
    Ⓒ 9%
    Ⓓ 6%

31. For the triangle below, what are the values of $\cos\theta$ and $\tan\theta$?

    [2] [$2\sqrt{2}$] [6]
    [$\sqrt{2}$] [3] [4]

    Triangle with legs 2 and 6, hypotenuse opposite, angle θ.

    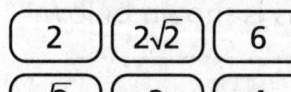,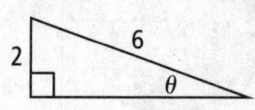

32. A bicycle tire has an outer diameter of about 26 inches. To the nearest inch, how far does a point on the outside of the tire travel as it rotates through $\frac{2\pi}{3}$ radians?

    [   ] inches

33. The median age of the residents in a town is 36. In a random sample of residents, the median age was 24. Which word best describes the figure 36?

    Ⓐ parameter
    Ⓑ statistic
    Ⓒ variable
    Ⓓ sample

34. Solve $x^2 - 6x + 4 = 0$ by completing the square. Use the choices provided to complete the solution.

    [3] [−3] [6] [−6]
    [$\sqrt{4}$] [$\sqrt{7}$] [$\sqrt{5}$]

    $x = [\quad] \pm [\quad]$

35. Select the properties of logarithms used in each step to rewrite the expression shown below as the sum of three logarithmic expressions.

    $\log \frac{x^4}{2y}$

    (1) $= \log x^4 - \log 2y$
    (2) $= 4\log x - \log 2y$
    (3) $= 4\log x - \log 2 + \log y$

    1. ☐ Quotient Property
       ☐ Power Property
       ☐ Product Property

    2. ☐ Quotient Property
       ☐ Power Property
       ☐ Product Property

    3. ☐ Quotient Property
       ☐ Power Property
       ☐ Product Property

36. James has $240 to give to charity. He has ranked his favorite charities in a list. He gives 15% of his money to the first charity, then 15% of what is left to the second, and so on. How much money does he have left after giving to ten charities? Round to the nearest dollar.

    $[   ]

37. What constant do you add to each side of the equation to solve by completing the square?

$4x^2 - 6x = 1$

Ⓐ $\frac{9}{4}$ Ⓒ $\frac{2}{9}$

Ⓑ $\frac{4}{9}$ Ⓓ 4

38. A phone app simulates a fair coin flip. Which result is most likely to make you question whether the app is providing a good simulation?

Ⓐ Heads: 52, Tails: 48

Ⓑ Heads: 42, Tails: 58

Ⓒ Heads: 41, Tails: 59

Ⓓ Heads: 19, Tails: 81

39. A ball bearing manufacturer requires that the radii of the bearings be within 0.5 mm of the target size. They tested five lots of cases and reported the mean, $\bar{x}$, and standard deviation, s, of their radii. A lot is rejected if more than 5% of bearings are greater than 0.5 mm above or below the target radius.

Which of the following lots would be rejected?

☐ A. target radius = 9 mm
  $\bar{x}$ = 9.1 mm; s = 0.3 mm

☐ B. target radius = 10 mm
  $\bar{x}$ = 10.2 mm; s = 0.1 mm

☐ C. target radius = 8 mm
  $\bar{x}$ = 8.3 mm; s = 0.2 mm

☐ D. target radius = 10 mm
  $\bar{x}$ = 10.1 mm; s = 0.5 mm

☐ E. target radius = 12 mm
  $\bar{x}$ = 11.9 mm; s = 0.2 mm

40. A company tests a new type of laptop battery that they have designed to last longer than older versions. The table shows the battery life for the old batteries (Group A) and the new batteries (Group B).

| A | 8.3 | 8.1 | 8.4 | 8.0 | 8.3 |
| B | 8.5 | 8.2 | 8.6 | 8.1 | 8.1 |

What is the difference of the means of Group A and Group B?

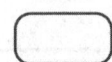

The data are resampled 200 times and a histogram of the difference of the means is shown below.

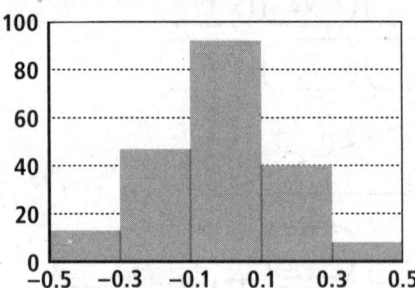

What can you conclude from the histogram? Choose from the phrases below to complete the sentences.

| less than | greater than |
| support | do not support |

A significant portion of data in the histogram is ☐ the difference of the means of the original samples. The data ☐ the hypothesis that there is a meaningful difference between Group A and Group B.

41. Select all functions whose graph has a vertical asymptote at $x = -3$.
    - A. $f(x) = \ln(x + 3)$
    - B. $f(x) = \log_2 x + 3$
    - C. $f(x) = 3 \ln x + 3$
    - D. $f(x) = \log(x + 3) - 3$
    - E. $f(x) = \log 3x$

42. A point $P(a, b)$ lies on the unit circle. It corresponds to angle θ. Select all of the statements that are true.
    - A. As θ increases, the value of b increases.
    - B. The radian measure of θ is equivalent to the distance around the circle from $(a, 0)$ to point P.
    - C. As θ increases, the value of a increases.
    - D. $\sin \theta = b$
    - E. As θ increases, the absolute value of a decreases then increases in a cycle.

43. The function f has domain $[0, \infty)$. Select the functions that have domains equal to all real numbers.
    - A. $g(x) = f(-x^4 - x^2 + 1)$
    - B. $g(x) = f(x^2 + 3x + 15)$
    - C. $g(x) = f(3 - x)$
    - D. $g(x) = f(|3 - x|)$
    - E. $g(x) = f(x^2 + x + 1)$

44. Two neighbors plan to contact other neighborhood residents to urge them to vote for their preferred school committee candidates.

    Part A Ania plans to contact 15 residents per day. Write a function that models the number of residents she contacts after x days.

    $f(x) = \boxed{} x$

    Izabela uses a different strategy. She contacts 3 people on the first day. Those people will then contact 3 people the next day. This pattern continues each day. Write a function that models the number of people contacted by both Ania and Izabela after x days.

    $g(x) = \boxed{} x + \boxed{}^x$

    Part B Ania and Izabela expect only half the people they contact to actually vote in the election. Write a function that models the number of people that Ania and Izabela contact who will vote in the election.

    $h(x) = \boxed{}(\boxed{} x + \boxed{}^x)$

    If Ania and Izabela start contacting people 5 days before the election, how many people that they contact does the model predict will vote in the election?

    $\boxed{}$

45. Part A

A submersible drone is equipped with a camera to take underwater videos.

The drone travels at a constant rate of 2 ft/s. Write a function that models the number of feet it has traveled in t seconds.

$f(t) = \boxed{}$

The drone starts at the surface of the ocean and moves in a straight line that makes a 60° angle with the surface of the ocean. Write a function that models the depth of the drone below the surface after t seconds.

$g(t) = \boxed{}$

As the drone descends, the pressure due to the water above it increases. The atmospheric pressure at the surface is 14.7 psi. The pressure from the water increases 0.445 psi with each additional foot below the surface. Write a function that models the total pressure on the drone after t seconds.

$h(t) = \boxed{} + \boxed{}\boxed{}$

Part B

The drone can withstand pressures of up to 200 psi. How long does it take for the drone to descend to its maximum depth if it continues in a straight line that makes a 60° angle with the surface? Round to the nearest second.

$\boxed{}$ s

46. What are the solutions of $x^3 - 125 = 0$?

Ⓐ $5, \dfrac{-5 + 5\sqrt{3}}{2}, \dfrac{-5 - 5\sqrt{3}}{2}$

Ⓑ $5, \dfrac{5 + 5i\sqrt{3}}{2}, \dfrac{5 - 5i\sqrt{3}}{2}$

Ⓒ $5, \dfrac{-5 + 5i\sqrt{3}}{2}, \dfrac{-5 - 5i\sqrt{3}}{2}$

Ⓓ $5, \dfrac{5 + 5\sqrt{3}}{2}, \dfrac{5 - 5\sqrt{3}}{2}$

47. Add and simplify.

$\dfrac{8}{7x} + \dfrac{4x}{9}$

Ⓐ $\dfrac{8 + 4x}{7x + 9}$

Ⓑ $\dfrac{72 + 28x^2}{63x}$

Ⓒ $\dfrac{72 + 28x}{63x}$

Ⓓ $\dfrac{72 + 28x^2}{126x}$

48. During a single hour, a traffic camera showed that 12 out of 74 drivers were speeding in a school zone. If approximately 435 drivers pass through the school zone during the day, estimate how many were likely to be speeding.

Ⓐ 12
Ⓑ 71
Ⓒ 74
Ⓓ 96

49. Kelly challenges you to a game. Each player rolls a standard number cube. If the sum of the results is a prime number, you win. If it is not, Kelly wins. What is your probability of winning? Is this a fair game?

Ⓐ $\dfrac{7}{18}$; No, the game is not fair.

Ⓑ $\dfrac{13}{36}$; No, the game is not fair.

Ⓒ $\dfrac{1}{2}$; Yes, the game is fair.

Ⓓ $\dfrac{5}{12}$; No, the game is not fair.

Name _____

Progress Monitoring Assessment Form C

1. The graph below is translated 3 units right, and 5 units down. What is the equation of the new graph?

   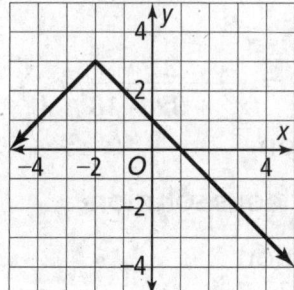

   Ⓐ $y = -|x + 1| - 2$
   Ⓑ $y = -|x + 1| + 2$
   Ⓒ $y = -|x - 1| - 2$
   Ⓓ $y = -|x - 1| + 2$

2. Select all solutions to the system of equations.

   $y = -(x - 2)^2 + 4$
   $x + y = 4$

   ☐ A. no solution
   ☐ B. (0, 4)
   ☐ C. (2, 3)
   ☐ D. (−2, −4)
   ☐ E. (4, 0)
   ☐ F. (1, 3)

3. Which of the following is equivalent to the expression $(i - 5)(3 + 2i)$?

   Ⓐ $-7i - 13$
   Ⓑ $13i - 17$
   Ⓒ $-7i - 17$
   Ⓓ $-13i - 17$

4. The graph of a quadratic function $f(x)$ has a vertex at $(2, -4)$. What is the vertex of $g(x)$ if $g(x) = f(x - 3) - 2$?

   (⬚ , ⬚)

5. The height above sea level of a pelican diving for fish is modeled by $f(x) = x^4 - 2x^3 - 29x^2 + 30x$. Select all the x-values where the pelican enters or exits the water.

   ☐ A. −6   ☐ D. 1
   ☐ B. −5   ☐ E. 4
   ☐ C. 0   ☐ F. 6

6. Solve $-x^2 + 5x = 7$ over the set of complex numbers.

   Ⓐ $\frac{5 + i\sqrt{3}}{2}, \frac{5 - i\sqrt{3}}{2}$
   Ⓑ $\frac{5 + i\sqrt{53}}{2}, \frac{5 - i\sqrt{53}}{2}$
   Ⓒ $\frac{-5 + i\sqrt{53}}{2}, \frac{-5 - i\sqrt{53}}{2}$
   Ⓓ $\frac{-5 + i\sqrt{3}}{2}, \frac{-5 - i\sqrt{3}}{2}$

7. Tuning standard A has a frequency of 440 cycles per second, or Hertz. The frequency of a musical note, in Hertz, can be given by $f = 440(2^x)$, where x is the number of octaves above the tuning standard A. How many octaves above the tuning standard A is a note that has a frequency of 4,186 Hertz? Round the solution to the nearest tenth. x is approximately ⬚ octaves.

8. Divide $x^3 - 4x^2 + 6x - 2$ by $x - 1$. Complete the quotient using the choices provided.

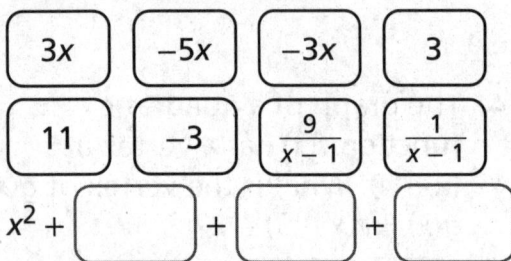

9. **Part A** Solve. Check for extraneous solutions.

   $\sqrt{4x + 24} - 3 = x$

   Ⓐ $x = 3$ only
   Ⓑ $x = -5$ only
   Ⓒ $x = 3$ or $x = -5$
   Ⓓ $x = -3$ or $x = 5$

   Part B Which step could lead to finding extraneous solutions?

   Ⓐ Adding 3 to both sides
   Ⓑ Squaring both sides
   Ⓒ Using the distributive property
   Ⓓ Factoring the trinomial

10. The function $f(x) = \sqrt{x - 10}$ represents the profits of a company after x years in business. Which function represents the number of years as a function of the profits?

    Ⓐ $f^{-1}(x) = (x - 10)^2$, for $x \geq 0$
    Ⓑ $f^{-1}(x) = (x - 10)^2$, for $x \geq -10$
    Ⓒ $f^{-1}(x) = x^2 + 10$, for $x \geq 0$
    Ⓓ $f^{-1}(x) = x^2 + 10$, for $x \geq -10$

11. What is the average rate of change for the function $f(x) = -2x^2 + 5$ over the interval $-3.5 \leq x \leq 0$?

    Ⓐ 19.5
    Ⓑ 7
    Ⓒ −7
    Ⓓ −19.5

12. Simplify.

    $\sqrt{8} + \sqrt{32} - 2^{\frac{3}{2}}$

    Ⓐ $-2\sqrt{2} - \sqrt[3]{2}$
    Ⓑ $8\sqrt{2}$
    Ⓒ $4\sqrt{2}$
    Ⓓ 0

13. **Part A** Solve the equation for x and check the solution to determine whether it is an extraneous solution.

    $\dfrac{1}{x - 3} + \dfrac{5}{x + 6} = \dfrac{3}{x^2 + 3x - 18}$

    Ⓐ 2; solution
    Ⓑ 2; extraneous solution
    Ⓒ −1; solution
    Ⓓ −1; extraneous solution

    Part B If the value 3 was a solution, why would it be an extraneous solution?

    Ⓐ At least one denominator would be equal to 0.
    Ⓑ The right side of the equation would be equal to 0.
    Ⓒ Both sides of the equation would be equal to 0.
    Ⓓ The left side of the equation would be equal to 0.

14. Solve the equation $-2 \ln(3x) = 5$.

    Ⓐ 0.082
    Ⓑ 0.027
    Ⓒ 4.061
    Ⓓ 36.547

15. The augmented matrix $\begin{bmatrix} 4 & 2 & | & -2 \\ 2 & -1 & | & 9 \end{bmatrix}$ represents a system of equations. Find the solution to this system of equations.

    Ⓐ (2, 5)
    Ⓑ (2, −5)
    Ⓒ (5, 2)
    Ⓓ (−5, 2)

16. Where will the discontinuities occur in the graph of the rational function?
$$f(x) = \frac{x^2 + 5x}{x^2 - 2x - 35}$$
   (A) at $x = -5$
   (B) at $x = 7$
   (C) at $x = 0$, $x = -5$ and $x = 7$
   (D) at $x = -5$ and $x = 7$

17. Sally records her car's total mileage at the end of each month. After 2 months the mileage is 2,500 miles; after 5 months the mileage is 7,000 miles. The values follow an arithmetic sequence. Which describes the sequence, where n is the month?
   (A) $a_n = 1500 + 1000(n - 1)$
   (B) $a_n = 1000 + 1500(n - 1)$
   (C) $a_n = 1000 + 1500(n + 1)$
   (D) $a_n = 1500 + 1000(n + 1)$

18. The values of the following finite geometric series represent the annual rainfall amounts in a certain region in inches. What is the total rainfall for the values shown?
   $48 + 36 + 27 + \ldots + 11.390625$
   (A) 166.37109375 in.
   (B) 157.828125 in.
   (C) 146.4375 in.
   (D) 122.390625 in.

19. Which of the following is true for the graph of $y = -\frac{1}{20}x^2$?
   (A) The equation of the directrix is $y = -5$.
   (B) The focus is at $(0, -5)$.
   (C) The parabola opens to the left.
   (D) The vertex is at $(0, -5)$.

20. You are conducting a survey about the quality of the food in your school cafeteria. You put out forms and a box near the entrance, and ask students to rate the food quality on a scale from 1 to 5. Is the sample likely to be biased? Why or why not?
   (A) No; the sample is representative of the whole student body.
   (B) Yes; the sample is self-selected.
   (C) Yes; all the students surveyed are likely to enjoy the cafeteria food.
   (D) No; the students who respond will be the ones with the strongest opinions.

21. The scores for the midterm test in a math class are displayed in the box. The teacher tells the class that everyone who scores above the 70th percentile will receive a grade of B. Which of the given scores is the lowest to receive a B on the test?

35	95	67	48	70
81	63	83	55	72
78	62	59	74	68
68	91	75	88	65

   (A) 72   (B) 74   (C) 75   (D) 78

22. Jared has a bag of 24 tiles, numbered 1 through 24. His friend draws a tile from the bag at random. What is the probability the tile shows a number that is a multiple of 2 or a multiple 3?
   (A) $\frac{1}{6}$
   (B) $\frac{2}{3}$
   (C) $\frac{5}{6}$
   (D) $\frac{1}{2}$

23. The number of people attending a music festival has been increasing over the last several days. On Monday, 240 people attended. On Tuesday, 290 people attended. And on Friday, 440 people attended.

   Part A Is the sequence that represents the festival attendance arithmetic? If it is, choose the recursive formula for the sequence.

   Ⓐ No; the music festival attendance cannot be represented by an arithmetic sequence.

   Ⓑ Yes; $a(n) = 290 + n$

   Ⓒ Yes; $a_1 = 240$, $a_n = a_{n-1} + 50$

   Ⓓ Yes; $a_1 = 240$, $a_n = a_{n+1} + 50$

   Part B If the trend continues, how many people will attend on Saturday?

   ☐ people

24. Use a graph to solve $(x - 2)^2 - 1 = (x - 2)^3 + 1$.

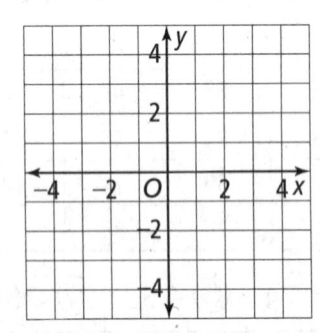

    $x = $ ☐

25. The enrollment at a local tutoring center can be modeled by the function $P(t) = 45(1 + 0.03)t$, where t is time in years since 2019. Rounded to the nearest student, what will be the center's expected enrollment in 2025?

    ☐ students

26. Select the solutions of the equation $x^2 = -64$.

    ☐ A. 8 ☐ D. $32i$
    ☐ B. $-8i$ ☐ E. $8i$
    ☐ C. -8 ☐ F. $-32i$

27. Simplify $(x^2 + 4x)(x^2 + x + 2)$.

    Ⓐ $8x^2 + 5x^3 + 8x$
    Ⓑ $x^4 + 5x^3 + 6x^2 + 8x + 2$
    Ⓒ $x^4 + 5x^3 + 6x^2 + 8x$
    Ⓓ $4x^5 + 4x^4 + 8x^3$

28. Use a graph of the polynomial function $f(x) = x^3 + 3x^2$ to complete the following:

    The zeros of f are ☐ and ☐.

    As x decreases, $f(x)$ ☐ increases.
    ☐ decreases.

    As x increases, $f(x)$ ☐ increases.
    ☐ decreases.

29. A city has a population of 120,000. The population is increasing at a rate of 3% per year. How can you write an exponential growth function to find the monthly growth rate?

    Ⓐ $y = 120{,}000(1.002466)^{12t}$
    Ⓑ $y = 120{,}000(1.03^{\frac{1}{12}})^t$
    Ⓒ $y = 120{,}000(0.0025)^{12t}$
    Ⓓ $y = 120{,}000(1.03)^{12t}$

30. Ten percent of the vehicles in a parking lot are silver, 5% are pickup trucks, and 3% are both. If a vehicle is selected at random, what is the probability that it is silver or a pickup truck?

   Ⓐ 9%
   Ⓑ 10%
   Ⓒ 12%
   Ⓓ 15%

31. For the triangle below, what are the values of $\cos\theta$ and $\tan\theta$?

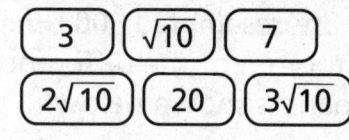

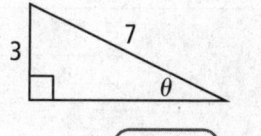

   $\boxed{3}$ $\boxed{\sqrt{10}}$ $\boxed{7}$
   $\boxed{2\sqrt{10}}$ $\boxed{20}$ $\boxed{3\sqrt{10}}$

   $\cos\theta = \dfrac{\boxed{}}{\boxed{}}$, $\tan\theta = \dfrac{\boxed{}}{\boxed{}}$

32. A Ferris wheel has a diameter of about 175 feet. To the nearest foot, how far does a rider travel as the wheel rotates through $\frac{\pi}{3}$ radians?

   $\boxed{}$ feet

33. A high school basketball team had a season average of 42 points per game. For the first 3 games of the season, they averaged 45 points per game. Which word best describes the figure 45?

   Ⓐ variable
   Ⓑ sample
   Ⓒ parameter
   Ⓓ statistic

34. Solve $x^2 + 10x + 6 = 0$ by completing the square. Use the choices provided to complete the solution.

   $\boxed{10}$ $\boxed{-10}$ $\boxed{5}$ $\boxed{-5}$
   $\boxed{\sqrt{19}}$ $\boxed{\sqrt{6}}$ $\boxed{\sqrt{10}}$

   $x = \boxed{} \pm \boxed{}$

35. Select the properties of logarithms used in each step to rewrite the expression shown below as the sum of three logarithmic expressions.

   $\log\left(\dfrac{5y}{x}\right)^4$

   (1) $= 4\log\left(\dfrac{5y}{x}\right)$
   (2) $= 4\log 5y - 4\log x$
   (3) $= 4\log 5 + 4\log y - 4\log x$

   1. ☐ Quotient Property
      ☐ Power Property
      ☐ Product Property

   2. ☐ Quotient Property
      ☐ Power Property
      ☐ Product Property

   3. ☐ Quotient Property
      ☐ Power Property
      ☐ Product Property

36. Noah deposits $350 in an account that earns 4% annual interest. He earns $14 interest after the first year. The following year he earns 4% interest on the initial deposit and the first year's interest, and so on. How much interest will he earn if he leaves the money in the account for 10 years? Round to the nearest dollar.

   $ $\boxed{}$

37. What constant do you add to each side of the equation to solve by completing the square?

$3x^2 + 4x = 5$

Ⓐ $\frac{9}{16}$ Ⓒ $\frac{3}{2}$

Ⓑ $\frac{4}{3}$ Ⓓ 6

38. A computer program simulates a spinner with 4 equal-sized sections. After several groups of 100 spins, which result is most likely to make you question whether the program is providing a good simulation?

Ⓐ R: 25%; B: 28%; G: 25%, Y: 22%

Ⓑ R: 21%; B: 27%; G: 31%, Y: 21%

Ⓒ R: 24%; B: 73%; G: 3%

Ⓓ R: 23%; B: 22%; G: 28%, Y: 27%

39. A jewelry company requires that its rings be within 0.4 grams of a target weight. They tested five lots of cases and reported the mean, $\bar{x}$, and standard deviation, s, of their weights. A lot is rejected if more than 5% of rings are greater than 0.4 grams above or below the target weight.

Which of the following lots would be rejected?

☐ A. target weight = 13 g
$\bar{x} = 13.1$ g; $s = 0.08$ g

☐ B. target weight = 11 g
$\bar{x} = 11.3$ g; $s = 0.3$ g

☐ C. target weight = 12 g
$\bar{x} = 12.1$ g; $s = 0.4$ g

☐ D. target weight = 10 g
$\bar{x} = 9.9$ g; $s = 0.1$ g

☐ E. target weight = 13 g
$\bar{x} = 12.9$ g; $s = 0.15$ g

40. A class is testing a fertilizer on bean plants for a science project. There are six bean plants in Group A, which receives the fertilizer, and six bean plants in Group B, which does not. The height in centimeters of each bean plant is shown in the table.

| A | 12.6 | 12.3 | 12.0 | 12.9 | 12.8 | 12.8 |
| B | 12.0 | 11.9 | 11.8 | 12.2 | 11.6 | 12.0 |

What is the difference of the means of Group A and Group B?

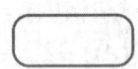

☐

The data are resampled 300 times and a histogram of the difference of the means is shown below.

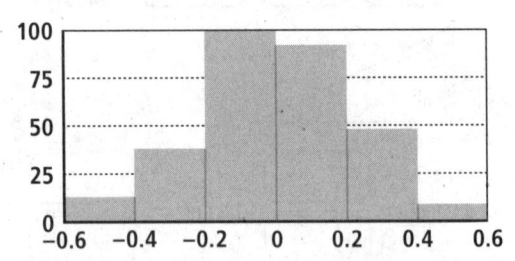

What can you conclude from the histogram? Choose from the phrases below to complete the sentences.

| less than | greater than |
| support | do not support |

A large majority of data in the histogram is ☐ the difference of the means of the original samples. The data ☐ the hypothesis that there is a meaningful difference between Group A and Group B.

41. Select all functions whose graph has a vertical asymptote at $x = 4$.
    - ☐ A. $f(x) = \log_4 x - 4$
    - ☐ B. $f(x) = \ln(x - 4)$
    - ☐ C. $f(x) = \log(x - 4) + 4$
    - ☐ D. $f(x) = 4 \ln x - 4$
    - ☐ E. $f(x) = \log(x - 4)$

42. A point $P(a, b)$ lies on the unit circle. It corresponds to angle θ. Select all of the statements that are true.
    - ☐ A. $\cos \theta = a$
    - ☐ B. As θ increases, the value of a decreases.
    - ☐ C. The values of a and b are never equal.
    - ☐ D. The radian measure of θ is equivalent to the distance around the circle from $(a, 0)$ to point P.
    - ☐ E. As θ increases, the absolute value of b increases then decreases in a cycle.

43. The function f has domain $(-\infty, 0]$. Select the functions that have domains equal to all real numbers.
    - ☐ A. $g(x) = f(-x^4 - x^2 - 5)$
    - ☐ B. $g(x) = f(x^2 + 3x - 8)$
    - ☐ C. $g(x) = f(3 + x)$
    - ☐ D. $g(x) = f(-|3 - x|)$
    - ☐ E. $g(x) = f(x^2 + x + 1)$

44. Two community activists plan to contact local residents to urge them to vote for their preferred candidate for county sheriff.

    Part A Lucía plans to contact 12 residents per day. Write a function that models the number of residents she contacts after x days.

    $f(x) = \boxed{} x$

    Caleb uses a different strategy. He contacts 4 people on the first day. Those people will then contact 4 people the next day. This pattern continues each day. Write a function that models the number of people contacted by both Lucía and Caleb after x days.

    $g(x) = \boxed{} x + \boxed{}^x$

    Part B Past experience shows that only 35% of people contacted will actually vote for their preferred candidate. Write a function that models the number of votes Lucía and Caleb can expect to gain for their candidate after x days.

    $h(x) = \boxed{}(\boxed{} x + \boxed{}^x)$

    If Lucía and Caleb start contacting people 7 days before the election, how many additional votes does the model predict they will gain for their candidate? Round to the nearest whole number.

    $\boxed{}$

45. Part A

A car travels on a straight road at 35 ft/s, approaching a green traffic light. Write a function that models the distance of the car from the traffic light after t seconds, if the car is 400 feet from the traffic light at $t = 0$.

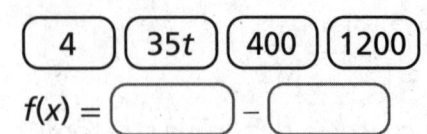

[4] [35t] [400] [1200]

$f(x) = \boxed{} - \boxed{}$

The light emitted by the traffic light is measured in *lumens*. The green traffic light emits 1200 lumens. The *brightness* of the light depends on how far you are away from it. In particular, the brightness of a light is equal to the number of lumens the light emits times $\frac{1}{4\pi}$, divided by the square of the distance from the light.

Write a function that models the brightness of the traffic light as seen by the driver of the car after t seconds.

$g(x) = \dfrac{\boxed{}}{\boxed{} \pi (\boxed{} - \boxed{})^2}$

Part B

When is the brightness of the traffic light as seen by the driver twice the brightness at $t = 0$? Round to the nearest tenth of a second.

$\boxed{}$ s

46. What are the solutions of $x^3 - 27 = 0$?

Ⓐ $3, \dfrac{-3 + 3\sqrt{3}}{2}, \dfrac{-3 - 3\sqrt{3}}{2}$

Ⓑ $3, \dfrac{3 + 3\sqrt{3}}{2}, \dfrac{3 - 3\sqrt{3}}{2}$

Ⓒ $3, \dfrac{3 + 3i\sqrt{3}}{2}, \dfrac{3 - 3i\sqrt{3}}{2}$

Ⓓ $3, \dfrac{-3 + 3i\sqrt{3}}{2}, \dfrac{-3 - 3i\sqrt{3}}{2}$

47. Subtract and simplify.

$\dfrac{8}{5x} - \dfrac{7x}{4x^2}$

Ⓐ $\dfrac{1}{x}$ Ⓒ $\dfrac{33}{10x}$

Ⓑ $\dfrac{1}{20x}$ Ⓓ $-\dfrac{3}{20x}$

48. At a lake, 320 fish are caught, tagged, and released. Of that number, 42 were perch. If there are approximately 2,700 fish in the lake, estimate how many are perch.

Ⓐ 42

Ⓑ 420

Ⓒ 354

Ⓓ 320

49. Stephanie challenges you to a game. Each player rolls a standard number cube. If the product of the results is odd you win. If it is not, Stephanie wins. What is your probability of winning? Is this a fair game?

Ⓐ $\frac{1}{3}$; No, the game is not fair.

Ⓑ $\frac{1}{4}$; No, the game is not fair.

Ⓒ $\frac{1}{2}$; Yes, the game is fair.

Ⓓ $\frac{3}{4}$; No, the game is not fair.

1 Readiness Assessment

1. Graph the linear inequality $6x - 3y > 12$.

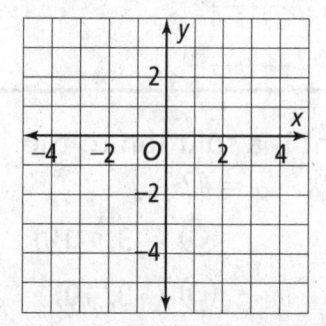

2. Select all the expressions that describe the pattern 6, 9, 12, 15, ...
   - ☐ A. $3 + 3x$, where $x = 1, 2, 3, 4,...$
   - ☐ B. $x + 3$, where $x = 3, 4, 5, 6,...$
   - ☐ C. $6 + x$, where $x = 0, 1, 2, 3,...$
   - ☐ D. $x - 6$, where $x = 12, 13, 14, 15,...$
   - ☐ E. $3x$, where $x = 2, 3, 4, 5,...$

3. Find $f(-3)$ for $f(x) = -2x + 5$.
   - Ⓐ -1 Ⓑ 10 Ⓒ -10 Ⓓ 11

4. Evaluate the expression $g(-2)$ for $g(x) = |3x - 1|$.
   - Ⓐ -7 Ⓑ 7 Ⓒ 5 Ⓓ -5

5. The table represents the observed number of leaves y on x branches of a tree. Calculate the rate of change between 3 and 4 branches.

x	y
2	42
3	75
4	100
5	119

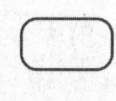

6. The graph represents the recent and expected decline in Paulo's profit from smartphone sales. Estimate the average rate of change from 0 to 2 months.

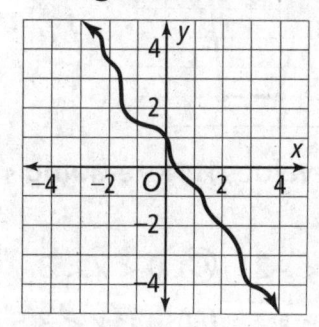

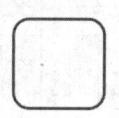

7. Where does the graph of the line $y = x - 2$ intersect the x-axis?
   - Ⓐ (0, 2)   Ⓒ (0, −2)
   - Ⓑ (2, 0)   Ⓓ (−2, 0)

8. Where does the graph of the function $f(x) = \frac{3}{4}x - 3$ intersect the y-axis?
   - Ⓐ (4, 0)   Ⓒ (0, 3)
   - Ⓑ (−4, 0) Ⓓ (0, −3)

9. Identify the domain and range of the graph below.

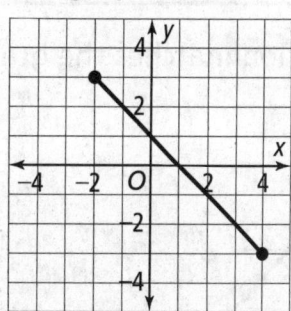

   Domain: ☐ $\leq x \leq$ ☐

   Range: ☐ $\leq y \leq$ ☐

For Items 10 and 11, use the graph. The graph shows Nate's height, y, relative to ground level at the start of a dirt bike course. x represents his distance from his friend as he rides past.

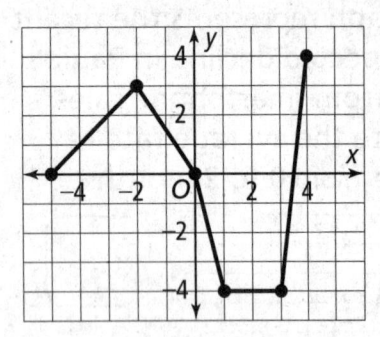

10. For what x-values is Nate going downhill?
    Ⓐ $-5 < x < -2$ Ⓒ $0 < x < 3$
    Ⓑ $-2 < x < 1$ Ⓓ $0 < x < 3.5$

11. Select all the x-values where Nate is above ground level.
    ☐ A. $-5 < x < 0$ ☐ D. $3 < x < 4$
    ☐ B. $0 < x < 3$ ☐ E. $3.5 < x < 4$
    ☐ C. $-2 < x < 1$

12. Graph $f(x) = x^2 - 3$.

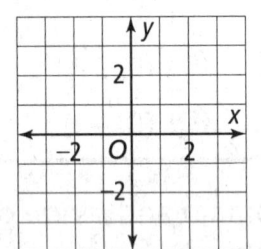

13. Which function matches the graph below?

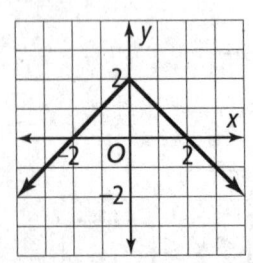

    Ⓐ $f(x) = -|x| + 2$ Ⓒ $f(x) = |x| - 2$
    Ⓑ $f(x) = -|x| - 2$ Ⓓ $f(x) = |x| + 2$

14. Graph the line $y = -\frac{3}{4}x + 1$.

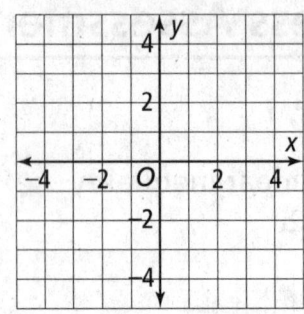

15. Which point is a solution to the equation $2x - y = 4$?
    Ⓐ $(0, 4)$ Ⓒ $(-3, -10)$
    Ⓑ $(1, 2)$ Ⓓ $(-3, 10)$

16. Which point is a solution to the equation $y = (x - 2)^2$?
    Ⓐ $(3, 1)$ Ⓒ $(1, -1)$
    Ⓑ $(4, 0)$ Ⓓ $(-3, 1)$

17. What is the solution to the system shown in the graph?

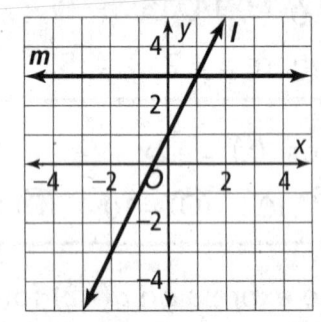

    (☐ , ☐)

18. Select all the points that are solutions to the inequality $-x - 2y > 3$.
    ☐ A. $(-1, -2)$
    ☐ B. $(1, -2)$
    ☐ C. $(-2, -1)$
    ☐ D. $(2, -4)$
    ☐ E. $(0, -1.5)$

Name _____

1-1 Lesson Quiz

Key Features of Functions

1. Benito embroiders and sells T-shirts. The graph shows his profit as a function of the number of shirts sold. After selling a certain number of shirts, Benito uses some earnings to buy more materials and then increases the price of the shirts. Which of the following is true?

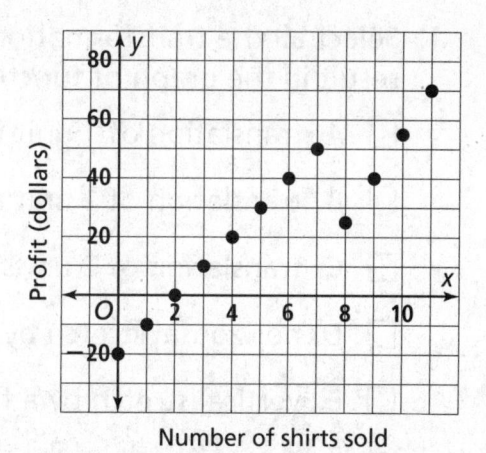

   Ⓐ Benito increases the price after selling 50 shirts.

   Ⓑ The y-intercept represents the cost of one T-shirt.

   Ⓒ The x-intercept represents the shirts he has to sell before making a profit.

   Ⓓ The domain of the function is {x | x is a real number greater than or equal to 0}.

2. The graph of the function $f(x) = -16x^2 + 10$ shown at the right represents the distance, in feet, between a diver and th surface of the water, where x is the number of seconds after the diver leaves the diving board. What is the height of the diving board?

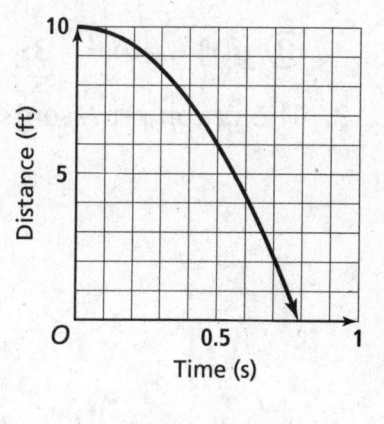

   ( ) feet

3. Which of the following correctly compares the two parts of the function in Item 1, over the intervals [0, 7] and [8, 11]?

   Ⓐ Benito made an extra $25 after selling 7 shirts.

   Ⓑ Benito spent $1 after selling 50 shirts.

   Ⓒ Benito's profit per shirt decreases from $50 to $25.

   Ⓓ Benito's profit per shirt increases from $10 to $15.

Use the graph shown.

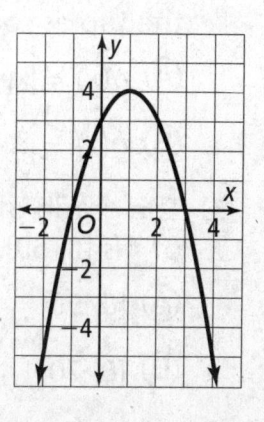

4. Identify the intervals on which the function is increasing and on which the function is decreasing.

   Intervals on which the function increases: (−∞, ( ))

   Intervals on which the function decreases: (( ), ∞)

5. At what point does the function switch from increasing to decreasing? (( ), ( ))

enVision® Algebra 2 • Assessment Sourcebook

Name _____

1-2 Lesson Quiz

Transformations of Functions

1. Select all the transformations of $f(x) = x^2$ that combine to result in the graph of function g at the right.

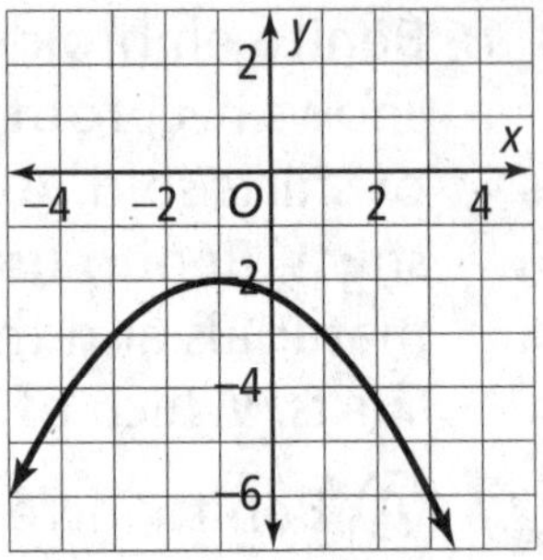

   ☐ A. translation of 1 unit left

   ☐ B. translation of 1 unit right

   ☐ C. translation of 2 units down

   ☐ D. horizontal stretch by a factor of 2

   ☐ E. vertical stretch by a factor of 2

   ☐ F. reflection across the x-axis

2. What is the equation for g, which is $f(x) = 2x^2 + 3x - 1$ reflected across the y-axis?

   Ⓐ $g(x) = 2x^2 + 3x - 1$ Ⓒ $g(x) = 2x^2 - 3x - 1$

   Ⓑ $g(x) = -2x^2 - 3x + 1$ Ⓓ $g(x) = -2x^2 - 3x - 1$

3. The graph represents f. Graph $g(x) = 2f(x - 1)$.

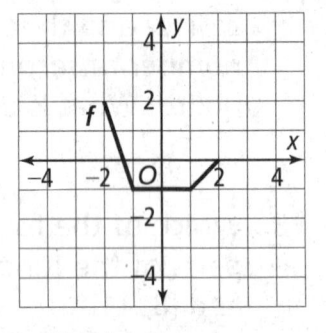

4. A bucket has a leak that started 6 hours ago. At time 0, when the bucket just emptied, a tap was turned on for 3 hours. The amount of water in the bucket can be modeled by the function $f(x) = |x|$ over the interval $[-6, 3]$, where x is the time, in hours, and y is the amount of water in the bucket, in gallons. A similarly full bucket started to leak only 3 hours ago. Which translation of the graph represents the amount of water in the second bucket if it is moved under the tap as soon as it empties?

   Ⓐ $g(x) = |x| + 3$ Ⓒ $g(x) = |x| - 3$

   Ⓑ $g(x) = |x + 3|$ Ⓓ $g(x) = |x - 3|$

5. The graph of the function f is shown. The domain of f is $[0, 50]$. What is the range of $g(x) = 4f(x)$?

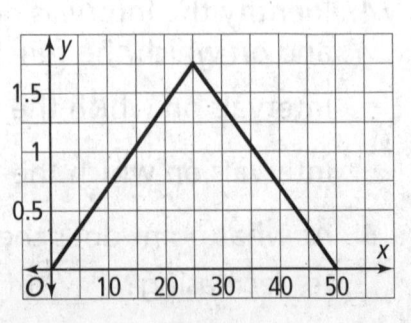

   Ⓐ $[0, 50]$ Ⓒ $[0, 1.75]$

   Ⓑ $[0, 70]$ Ⓓ $[0, 7]$

enVision® Algebra 2 • Assessment Sourcebook

1-3 Lesson Quiz
Piecewise-Defined Functions

1. Which rule defines the function in the graph?

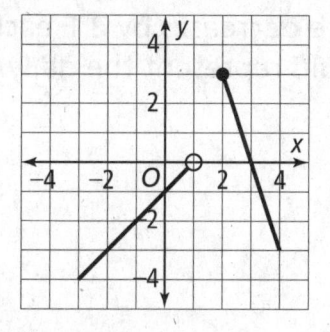

   Ⓐ $f(x) = \begin{cases} x - 1, & \text{if } -3 < x \leq 1 \\ -3x + 9, & \text{if } 2 < x < 4 \end{cases}$

   Ⓑ $f(x) = \begin{cases} x - 1, & \text{if } -3 \leq x < 1 \\ -3x + 9, & \text{if } 2 \leq x \leq 4 \end{cases}$

   Ⓒ $f(x) = \begin{cases} x - 1, & \text{if } -3 \leq x < 1 \\ x - 3, & \text{if } 2 \leq x \leq 4 \end{cases}$

   Ⓓ $f(x) = \begin{cases} x - 1, & \text{if } -3 < x \leq 1 \\ x - 3, & \text{if } 2 < x < 4 \end{cases}$

2. A scuba diver returning to the surface swims to move up quickly, then waits a few meters below the surface to avoid pressure issues. They complete the ascent more slowly. The function f represents the diver's height above sea level over time, in seconds. Which of the following is true for f?

   $f(x) = \begin{cases} 3x + 1, & -9 < x \leq -2 \\ -5, & -2 < x \leq 1 \\ x - 6, & 1 < x < 7 \end{cases}$

   Ⓐ The domain is the set of times $-9 < x < -2$, $-2 < x < 1$, and $1 < x < 7$.

   Ⓑ The domain is the depth interval $(-26, 1)$.

   Ⓒ The domain is the time interval $(-9, 7)$.

   Ⓓ The domain is the depth interval $(-9, 1]$.

3. Write the piecewise-defined function shown in the graph.

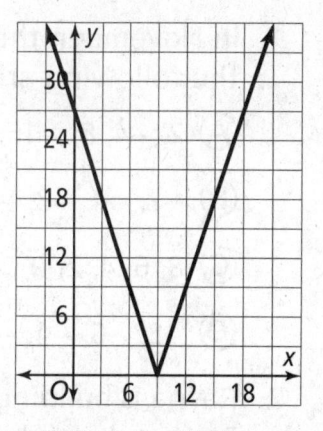

   $f(x) = \begin{cases} \square(x + \square), & x \leq \square \\ \square(x + \square), & x > \square \end{cases}$

4. The table shows the admission prices for an amusement park. Graph the function.

Age	Admission Price
under 5	free
5–17	$25
18–64	$40
65 and over	$35

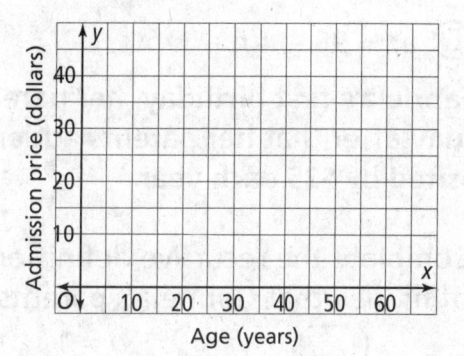

5. Identify the domain and range of the function in Item 4. Write the range values in ascending order.

   domain: $x > \square$

   range: $\{\square, \square, \square, \square\}$

Name _____

1-4 Lesson Quiz

Arithmetic Sequences and Series

1. In November, the daily low temperature decreases by 2°F each day. Which of the following arithmetic sequences could represent the daily low temperature?

   Ⓐ 2, −4, 8, −16, 32, …

   Ⓑ −2, −4, −8, −16, −32, …

   Ⓒ 8, 6, 4, 2, 0, …

   Ⓓ −8, −6, −4, −2, 0, …

2. Rayna is building a tapered staircase using wooden boards. The bottom stair is $3\frac{1}{2}$ ft wide, and the top stair is $2\frac{1}{6}$ ft wide. Each stair is 4 in. shorter than the one below. What is the total length of wooden boards Rayna needs for the stair tops, in feet? Give your answer as an improper fraction.

   $\frac{\Box}{\Box}$

3. A bucket holds 100 potatoes. Hal removes and cleans 4 potatoes per minute. Which explicit definition matches the sequence that represents the potatoes left in the bucket after n minutes?

   Ⓐ $a_n = 4 − 100(n − 1)$

   Ⓑ $a_n = 100 − 4(n − 1)$

   Ⓒ $a_n = 96 + 4(n − 1)$

   Ⓓ $a_n = 96 − 4(n − 1)$

On Gabriela's first birthday, her parents gave her a $50 savings account. On every birthday after that her parents added to the account, increasing the amount they deposited by $25 each year.

4. Complete the recursive definition for the sequence that represents the amount of money that Gabriela's parents deposit into the account on her nth birthday.

   $f(n) = \begin{cases} \Box, & n = 1 \\ f_{(n-1)} + \Box, & n > 1 \end{cases}$

5. Calculate the total amount Gabriela's parents will have deposited into the account on her birthdays by her 18th birthday.

   $\$\Box$

enVision® Algebra 2 • Assessment Sourcebook

Name _____

enVision Algebra 2
SavvasRealize.com

1-5 Lesson Quiz

Solving Equations and Inequalities by Graphing

1. Sketch a graph that you could use to solve the equation.
   $-2|x - 1| + 3 = \frac{2}{5}x - \frac{11}{5}$

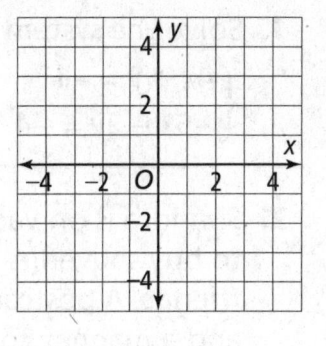

2. What is the solution to the equation in Item 1?
   Ⓐ $x = 1$
   Ⓑ $x = -2$
   Ⓒ $x = -2, x = 3$
   Ⓓ $x = -2, x = 1, x = 3$

3. Each time Henry visits the art museum, he pays $15 for parking and $25 for admission. If he buys a membership for $110, parking will cost $10 and admission will be free. Graph two equations that represent the situation.

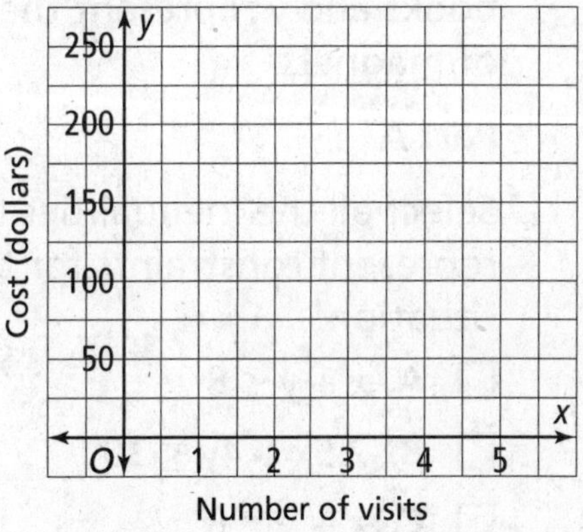

4. Use the equations you graphed in Item 3 to write an inequality that represents the numbers of museum visits for which the total member cost is less than the nonmember cost. What is the fewest number of visits that satisfies the inequality?

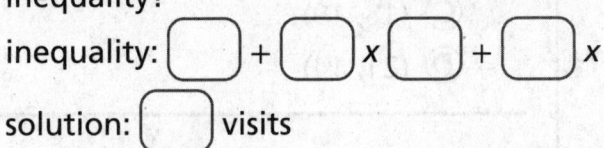

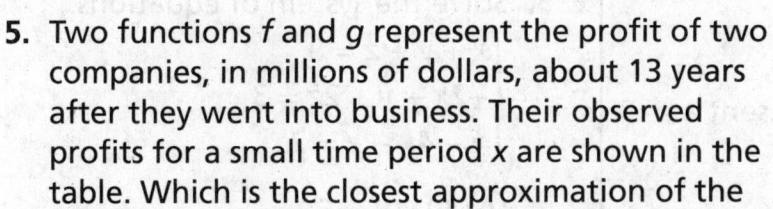

   inequality: ☐ + ☐ x ☐ + ☐ x

   solution: ☐ visits

5. Two functions f and g represent the profit of two companies, in millions of dollars, about 13 years after they went into business. Their observed profits for a small time period x are shown in the table. Which is the closest approximation of the time where the two companies have equal profit or loss?

x	f(x)	g(x)
13.252	0.9406	−0.6205
13.253	0.1203	0.1212
13.254	−0.7000	0.8629
13.255	−1.5203	1.6046
13.256	−2.3406	2.3463
13.257	−3.1609	3.0880

   Ⓐ 0.1207 years
   Ⓑ 2.3435 years
   Ⓒ 13.253 years
   Ⓓ 13.256 years

enVision® Algebra 2 • Assessment Sourcebook

1-6 Lesson Quiz

Linear Systems

1. Solve the system of equations.
$$\begin{cases} 4x + y = -1 \\ -5x - 2y = -4 \end{cases}$$ (☐ , ☐)

2. Shandra is on vacation and wants to buy souvenirs for at least 8 friends. A postcard book costs $2.50 and a magnet costs $4.00. She can spend up to $30 altogether. Let x represent the number of postcard books and y represent the number of magnets.

   Part A

   Select all the inequalities that represent constraints for the situation.
   - ☐ A. $x + y \leq 8$
   - ☐ B. $2.5x + 4y \leq 30$
   - ☐ C. $x + y \geq 8$
   - ☐ D. $2.5x + 4y \geq 8$
   - ☐ E. $x \geq 0$
   - ☐ F. $y \geq 0$
   - ☐ G. $x + y \geq 0$

   Part B

   Select all points that represent a viable solution.
   - ☐ A. (2, 6)
   - ☐ B. $\left(1\frac{1}{3}, 6\frac{2}{3}\right)$
   - ☐ C. (0, 8)
   - ☐ D. (7, 2)
   - ☐ E. (12, 0)
   - ☐ F. (10, 3)

3. Solve the system of equations.
$$\begin{cases} -2x + y = 3 \\ 4y = -2 + x \end{cases}$$
   - Ⓐ (−2, −1)
   - Ⓑ (−1, −2)
   - Ⓒ (−1, 1)
   - Ⓓ (1, −1)

4. Jamie wants to build a rectangular fence around a new chicken pen. He can afford at most 70 ft of fencing, and must fit the pen in a space that is 20 ft by 20 ft. Which of the following is a solution to the system of inequalities that represents this situation?
   - Ⓐ (9, 22)
   - Ⓑ (16, 17)
   - Ⓒ (18, 19)
   - Ⓓ (21, 14)

5. Solve the system of equations.
$$\begin{cases} x + y + z = 9 \\ -2x + y + 2z = 3 \\ x - 4y - z = 2 \end{cases}$$
   - Ⓐ (0, 15, −6)
   - Ⓑ (3, 3, 3)
   - Ⓒ (4, −1, 6)
   - Ⓓ (7, 1, 1)

enVision® Algebra 2 • Assessment Sourcebook

Name _____

1 Topic Assessment Form A

Use this graph for Items 1–3.

The graph represents Quinten's distance from the start line as he runs a cross country race. The x-axis represents the time, in hours, and the y-axis represents distance, in miles.

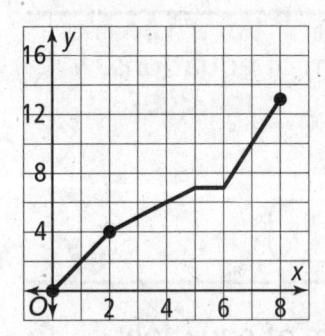

1. What is the range of the function?

   [☐ , ☐]

2. What does the domain of the function tell you about the race?
   - Ⓐ The race is 13 miles long.
   - Ⓑ Quinten takes 8 hours to finish the race.
   - Ⓒ Quinten takes a break at the 7-mile mark.
   - Ⓓ Quinten runs fastest in the last 2 hours.

3. What is the average rate of change over the interval [0, 2]?

   ☐ mi/h

4. Over what interval is the graph of $y = -|x - 2|$ increasing?
   - Ⓐ $(2, \infty)$
   - Ⓑ $(-\infty, 2)$
   - Ⓒ $(-\infty, -2)$
   - Ⓓ $(-2, \infty)$

5. Identify the translations of the parent function $f(x) = x^2$ that give $g(x) = (x - 5)^2 - 4$.
   - Ⓐ up 4 units, left 5 units
   - Ⓑ up 4 units, right 5 units
   - Ⓒ down 4 units, left 5 units
   - Ⓓ down 4 units, right 5 units

6. Graph the function.

   $y = \begin{cases} 3, & \text{if } -2 \leq x < -1 \\ 2 - x, & \text{if } -1 < x \leq 0 \\ 2, & \text{if } 0 \leq x \leq 4 \end{cases}$

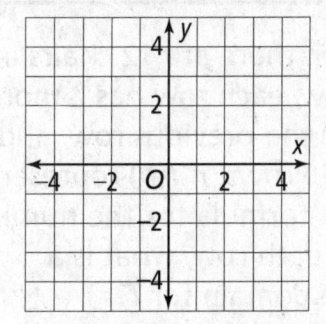

7. Enzo's profit over the last few months has been falling. In December he made $900, in January his profit was $500, and in March, he lost $300. Write the recursive formula for the arithmetic sequence that represents Enzo's profit.

   $a_1 = $ ☐

   $a_n = a_{n-1} + $ ☐

8. The following recursive formula represents the number of prizes offered in each round of a game show.

$$a_n = \begin{cases} 2, & \text{if } n = 1 \\ a_{n-1} + 7, & \text{if } n > 1 \end{cases}$$

Write the explicit formula for the number of prizes and use it to calculate the number of prizes in round 7.

$a_n = \boxed{} + \boxed{}(n-1)$

$\boxed{}$ prizes

9. Mya is testing out her new drone. She flies it 11 m and lands, then flies 22 m, then 33 m, and so on. The last test flight is 77 m. What is the total distance that Mya's drone travels during the tests?

Ⓐ 275 m Ⓒ 143 m
Ⓑ 308 m Ⓓ 385 m

10. In a theater, there are 12 chairs in the first row, each row has 2 more chairs than the previous row, and there are 10 rows. If $f(n)$ represents the explicit formula for the number of seats in each row, what is a reasonable domain for f?

Ⓐ All positive integers
Ⓑ Multiples of 2, 12 through 30
Ⓒ Integers 1 through 10
Ⓓ Integers 0 through 10

11. Use the graph to solve $|x + 3| - 1 = (x + 2)^2$.

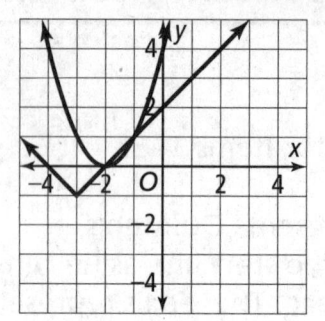

$x = \boxed{}, x = \boxed{}$

12. Solve the system of equations.
$$\begin{cases} x + 4y = 15 \\ 2x - y = -15 \end{cases}$$

$x = \boxed{}, y = \boxed{}$

13. Solve the system of equations.
$$\begin{cases} 3x + 2y + z = 16 \\ 4x - y = -5 \\ y + z = 11 \end{cases}$$

Ⓐ (0, 5, 6) Ⓒ (16, −5, 11)
Ⓑ (0, $\frac{5}{3}$, 2) Ⓓ (−2, 11, 6)

14. Dwayne buys 1 loaf of bread and 6 eggs for $4.45. Sheila buys 1 loaf of bread and 1 dozen eggs for $5.65. Write and solve a system of equations to find how much the store charges for bread and for eggs. Then calculate how much Mina pays for 3 loaves of bread and 2 dozen eggs.

Bread costs $\boxed{}$ per loaf.

Eggs cost $\boxed{}$ per egg.

Mina pays $\boxed{}$.

1 Topic Assessment Form B

Use this graph for Items 1–3.

The graph shows the distance of a remote control drone above the ground as it flies west to east. The x-axis represents the distance from a central point and the y-axis represents the distance above the ground, in m.

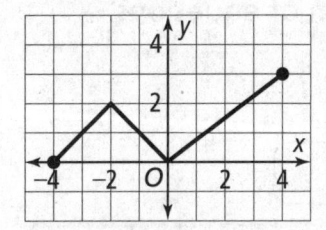

1. What is the range of the function?

   [☐ , ☐]

2. What does the domain of the function tell you about the drone's flight?

   Ⓐ The drone landed once along its flight.
   Ⓑ The drone flew up to 3 m high.
   Ⓒ The drone traveled 8 m horizontally.
   Ⓓ The drone flew for 8 minutes.

3. What is the average rate of change over the interval [−4, 4]?

   ☐ m/min

4. Over what interval is the graph of $y = -2 + |x - 2|$ increasing?

   Ⓐ $(2, \infty)$
   Ⓑ $(-\infty, 2)$
   Ⓒ $(-\infty, -2)$
   Ⓓ $(-2, \infty)$

5. Identify the translations of the parent function $f(x) = |x|$ that give $g(x) = 2 + |x + 3|$.

   Ⓐ down 3 units, left 2 units
   Ⓑ down 3 units, right 2 units
   Ⓒ up 2 units, left 3 units
   Ⓓ up 2 units, right 3 units

6. Graph the function.

   $$y = \begin{cases} -2, & \text{if } 0 \leq x < 1 \\ 3 - x, & \text{if } 1 \leq x \leq 2 \\ 1, & \text{if } 2 \leq x \leq 4 \end{cases}$$

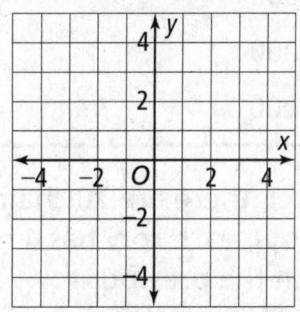

7. The wait time at the DMV increases for each new person who arrives. Jane arrived first and waited 1 minute. Pete arrived next and waited 1.2 minutes. Kal arrives fourth and waits 1.6 minutes. Write the recursive formula for the arithmetic sequence that represents the wait time.

   $a_1 = $ ☐

   $a_n = a_{n-1} + $ ☐

8. The following recursive formula represents the number of players left after week n of a reality show.

$$a_n = \begin{cases} 15, \text{ if } n = 1 \\ a_{n-1} - 2, \text{ if } n > 1 \end{cases}$$

Write the explicit formula for the number of players left and use it to calculate how many players are left after 6 weeks.

$a_n = \boxed{} + \boxed{} (n-1)$

$\boxed{}$ players

9. Manny's Pizza shows declining sales over the last few months. Their monthly net profit in hundreds of dollars follows the arithmetic sequence 4, 1, −2, −5, ..., −56. What is their total profit over this time period?

Ⓐ −$77,700
Ⓑ −$54,600
Ⓒ −$54,200
Ⓓ −$49,000

10. In a theater, there are 20 chairs in the first row, each row has 4 more chairs than the previous row, and there are 15 rows. If $f(n)$ represents the explicit formula for the number of seats in each row, what is a reasonable domain for f?

Ⓐ All positive integers
Ⓑ Multiples of 4, 20–76
Ⓒ Integers 1–15
Ⓓ Integers 0–15

11. Use the graph to solve $\frac{1}{2}|x+1| + 1 = |x|$.

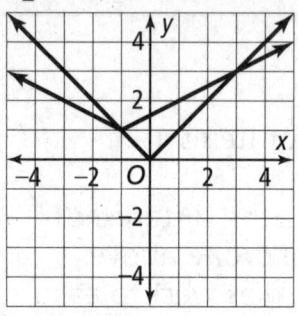

$x = \boxed{}$, $x = \boxed{}$

12. Solve the system of equations.

$$\begin{cases} 2x - y = 7 \\ x - y = 10 \end{cases}$$

$x = \boxed{}$, $y = \boxed{}$

13. Solve the system of equations.

$$\begin{cases} x + 3y + 2z = 1 \\ x - z = 4 \\ -4x + 3y = -12 \end{cases}$$

Ⓐ (6, −1, −1)
Ⓑ (29, 5, −11)
Ⓒ (3, 0, −1)
Ⓓ (1, 4, −12)

14. Emery makes 8 necklaces and 3 bracelets, using a total of 172 beads. Then she makes 1 more necklace and 5 more bracelets, using 77 beads. Write and solve a system of equations to find how many beads Emery uses in each necklace and bracelet. Then calculate how many beads Emery uses to make 4 necklaces and 7 bracelets.

Emery uses $\boxed{}$ beads for each necklace and $\boxed{}$ beads for each bracelet.

Emery uses $\boxed{}$ beads.

1 Performance Assessment Form A

enVision Algebra 2
SavvasRealize.com

Past voyages of space rockets and shuttles can be represented by many different types of functions, depending on the aspects of the expeditions to be analyzed.

1. The piecewise-defined function in the graph shows three stages of a rocket's flight starting at liftoff. The y-axis represents the distance travelled from the ground in miles and the x-axis represents the time in minutes from liftoff. The intervals are described as follows:

   - First stage: 0 min to 2 min
   - Second stage: 2 min to 3 min
   - Third stage: 3 min to 4 min

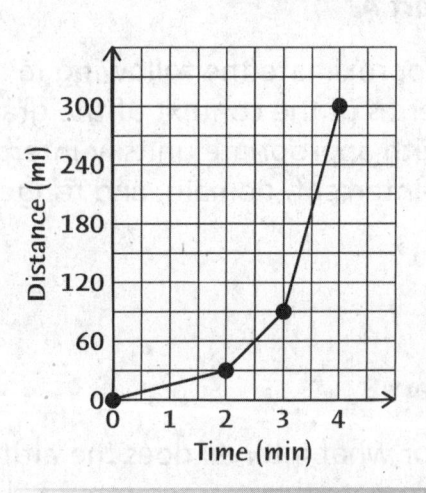

Part A

What is the average rate of change over each interval? How would you interpret the rate of change in the context of the trip?

Part B

What is a function that represents the distance f at time x for the first interval of the trip?

Part C

The approximate distances and times of a model used by engineers to show a flight pattern are represented by the piecewise-defined function below, where f represents the altitude of the model in meters and x represents the time in seconds. Graph the function.

$$f(x) = \begin{cases} 3x, & \text{if } 0 \leq x < 2 \\ 5x - 4, & \text{if } 2 \leq x < 4 \\ 16, & \text{if } 4 \leq x < 10 \end{cases}$$

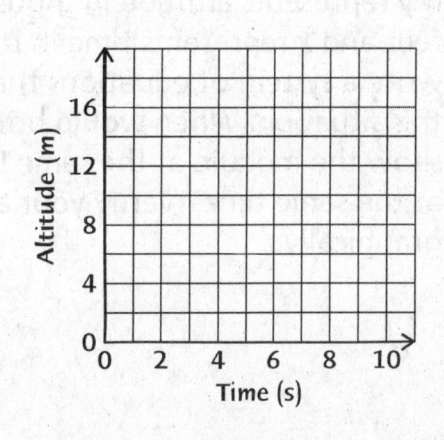

2. Scientists tested whether potential astronauts could adapt to a variety of gravitational conditions by having them fly in a C-9 jet at high speeds. The graph at the right shows part of a typical flight pattern of the jet with altitude, y, in meters and time, x, in seconds.

Part A

Approximate the following in terms of the context of the graph with appropriate units: y-intercept, x-intercept, domain, and range.

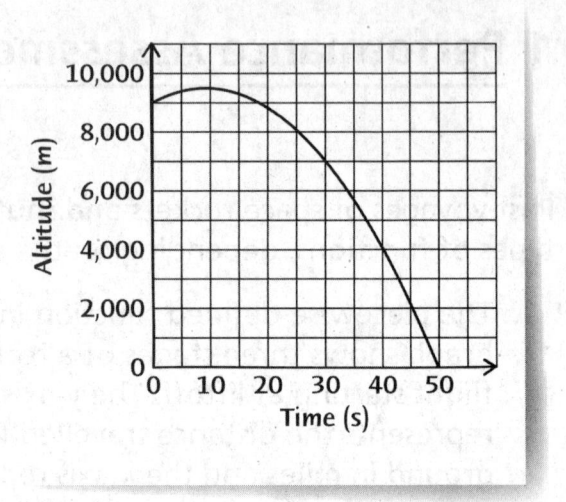

Part B

For what interval does the altitude appear to be increasing? decreasing? Estimate the average rate of change for the entire flight.

3. When rockets approached the moon, engineers needed to plan how the lunar modules would land on the moon. They developed two plans:

- Plan 1: At 100 thousand feet, the module drops at a steady rate of about 0.5 thousand feet per minute.

- Plan 2: At 150 thousand feet, the module drops at a steady rate of about one thousand feet per minute.

If y represents altitude in thousands of feet and x represents time in minutes, write a system of equations that models this situation. When would both plans show the module at the same height and at the same time? Verify your answer graphically.

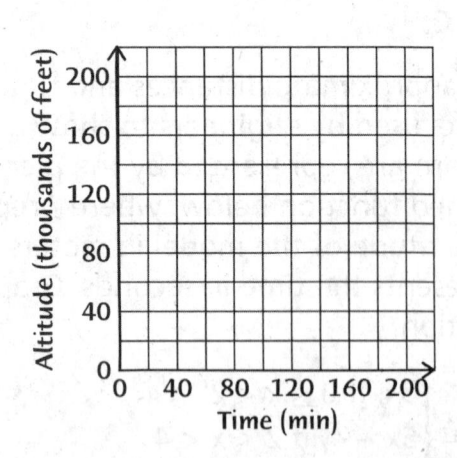

Name _____

1 Performance Assessment Form B

Modern factories depend on assembly lines that use specialized machines, specific production rates, and schedules.

1. A juice-bottling machine fills bottles at a certain rate until a manager slows down production in order to stop it to check the machinery. The equation $y = 1{,}200 - 30x$ represents the number, y, of bottles filled per minute at time, x, in minutes. Graph the equation. Then find the x- and y-intercepts of the graph and interpret them in context.

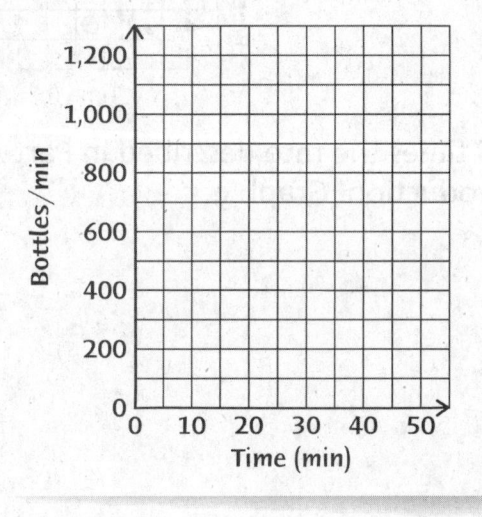

2. A controller at the factory calls in employees on a flexible work schedule during increased production cycles according to the sequence below.

    10, 14, 18, 22, 26...

    Part A

    What type of sequence is shown? Find the common difference d of the sequence. Then write a recursive definition for the sequence.

Part B

Given the recursive definition in Part A, write an explicit definition of the sequence. What is the value of the twelfth term?

3. During an eight-hour day, cellphone assembly at an adjacent facility is split into two phases. The graph shows the cellphone assembly rates for each phase.

Part A

Write an absolute-value function f to model the cellphone production throughout the day.

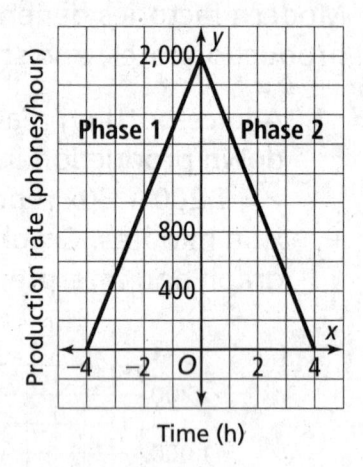

Part B

Suppose the cellphone assembly rate is 1.5 times the rate described in Part A. Write a function g that models the new production. Graph g.

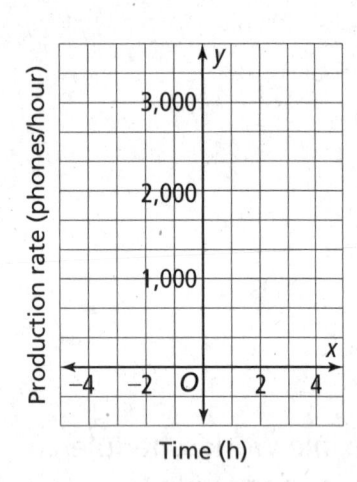

Name _____

2 Readiness Assessment

1. Which of the following situations could be represented by a graph with a y-intercept of −8?

   Ⓐ Hal bought $8 worth of supplies, then sold x buttons for $3 each. His profit is y dollars.

   Ⓑ Mr. May has 3 sticks left, and each student needs 8 sticks to make their craft project. There are x students, and they need y sticks in all.

   Ⓒ Kim ran 3 laps clockwise and 8 laps counterclockwise, for a total of 5 miles of the track. The track is x miles long and she ran a total of y laps.

   Ⓓ Jian bought 8 packs of paper and sold 3 origami swans. His current profit is −$5. A pack of paper costs x dollars and he sells the swans for y dollars.

2. The drama club buys $24 of supplies for a one-act play. They sell tickets for $3 each. Write an equation to represent their profit y in terms of number of tickets sold, x.

   y = ☐ x + ☐

3. Solve $(6x - 1)^2 = 289$. Select all the values of x, if any, that make the equation true.

   ☐ A. $x = -\frac{8}{3}$
   ☐ B. $x = \frac{8}{3}$
   ☐ C. $x = 0$
   ☐ D. $x = -3$
   ☐ E. $x = 3$
   ☐ F. no real solutions

4. Moshe lives 4 miles from school. If he walks home, it takes $2\frac{2}{3}$ hours. What is an equation for the line that represents his walk, where x is the amount of time Moshe walks, and y is his distance from home?

   Ⓐ $y = \frac{3}{2}x - 14$
   Ⓑ $y = -\frac{3}{2}x - 1$
   Ⓒ $y = \frac{3}{2}x + 28$
   Ⓓ $y = -\frac{3}{2}x + 4$

5. Carl is sledding down a hill at a rate of 2 m/s. After 3 seconds, he is 3 m from the bottom of the hill. Which of the following equations represents Carl's distance from the bottom of the hill y, in meters, over time x, in seconds?

   Ⓐ $y = (-2x - 3) + 3$
   Ⓑ $y = (-2x + 3) - 3$
   Ⓒ $y - 3 = -2(x - 3)$
   Ⓓ $y + 3 = -2(x + 3)$

6. Solve $(-4x+9)^2 = 121$

   $x = \boxed{}$, $x = \boxed{}$

7. Solve $-\frac{1}{4}x^2 + 15 = y$ when $x = 2$.

   Ⓐ $y = \frac{29}{2}$ Ⓑ $y = 18\frac{3}{4}$
   Ⓒ $y = 14$ Ⓓ $y = 16$

8. Simplify $\sqrt{54}$.

   Ⓐ $2\sqrt{27}$ Ⓑ $6\sqrt{3}$
   Ⓒ $3\sqrt{6}$ Ⓓ $9\sqrt{6}$

9. Select all the expressions that are equivalent to $\sqrt{48}$.

   ☐ A. $2\sqrt{6}$
   ☐ B. $2\sqrt{12}$
   ☐ C. $4\sqrt{3}$
   ☐ D. $4\sqrt{12}$
   ☐ E. $3\sqrt{2}$

10. Multiply $(x-4)^2$.

    Ⓐ $x^2 - 4x - 16$
    Ⓑ $x^2 - 4x + 16$
    Ⓒ $x^2 - 8x - 16$
    Ⓓ $x^2 - 8x + 16$

11. Multiply $(2x - 6)(x + 7)$.

    $\boxed{}x^2 + \boxed{}x + \boxed{}$

12. Multiply $(x + 5)(x - 5)$.

    Ⓐ $x^2 + 10x - 25$
    Ⓑ $x^2 - 10x - 25$
    Ⓒ $x^2 + 25$
    Ⓓ $x^2 - 25$

13. Solve the system $\begin{cases} y = 2x + 7 \\ 3x + 2y = 7 \end{cases}$ using substitution.

    Ⓐ $(-2, 3)$
    Ⓑ $\left(-\frac{35}{3}, \frac{28}{3}\right)$
    Ⓒ $(-1, 5)$
    Ⓓ $(0, 7)$

14. Solve the system $\begin{cases} 4x + 3y = -2 \\ 2x - 5y = -40 \end{cases}$.

    $(\boxed{}, \boxed{})$

15. How many solutions does the system of linear equations have?

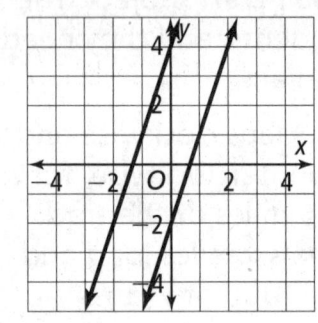

    Ⓐ 0
    Ⓑ 1
    Ⓒ 2
    Ⓓ infinitely many

16. Graph the solution to the system of inequalities $\begin{cases} x + y \geq -3 \\ y < \frac{1}{2}x - 1 \end{cases}$.

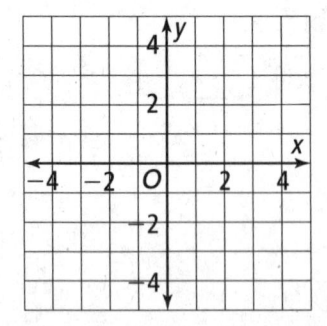

2-1 Lesson Quiz

Vertex Form of a Quadratic Function

1. The function $g(x) = (x + 2)^2 + 4$ is a transformation of the parent function $f(x) = x^2$. Select all the statements that are true about the transformation.

   ☐ A. Function g is the result of f being translated right 2 units and down 4 units.

   ☐ B. Function g is the result of f being translated left 2 units and up 4 units.

   ☐ C. The graph of function f opens upward.

   ☐ D. The graph of function g opens downward.

   ☐ E. The graph of function f is compressed by a factor of 2.

2. The function $h(x) = -\frac{1}{2}(x - 4)^2 + 3$ represents the height of a bird y over time x, as it flies past the school. What point on the graph represents the greatest height of the bird above the ground?

   Ⓐ (4, 3) 　　　Ⓒ $\left(\frac{1}{2}, 4\right)$

   Ⓑ (3, 4) 　　　Ⓓ $\left(3, \frac{1}{2}\right)$

3. What is the equation written in vertex form of a parabola with a vertex of (9, −1) that passes through (7, 7)?

   Ⓐ $y = 2(x - 9)^2 - 1$

   Ⓑ $y = 2(x + 1)^2 - 9$

   Ⓒ $y = 2(x - 7)^2 + 7$

   Ⓓ $y = 7(x - 9)^2 - 1$

4. Which of the following is an equation in the form $y = ax^2 + bx + c$ of the parabola shown in the graph?

   Ⓐ $y = -5x^2 - 20x - 65$

   Ⓑ $y = -5x^2 - 20x - 20$

   Ⓒ $y = -x^2 - 27x - 90$

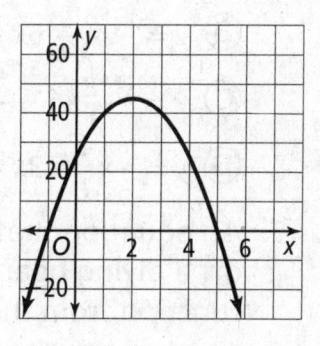

   Ⓓ $y = -5x^2 + 20x + 25$

5. Function g is a transformation of the parent function $f(x) = x^2$. The graph of g is a translation right 3 units and down 5 units of the graph of f. What is the equation of function g written in the form $y = ax^2 + bx + c$?

   Ⓐ $y = x^2 + 6x + 4$

   Ⓑ $y = x^2 - 6x + 4$

   Ⓒ $y = x^2 + 10x + 22$

   Ⓓ $y = x^2 - 6x + 14$

Name _____

2-2 Lesson Quiz

Standard Form of a Quadratic Function

1. What is the minimum point of the graph of the function $f(x) = x^2 - 4x$?

   Ⓐ (2, 4)

   Ⓑ (0, 0)

   Ⓒ (4, 0)

   Ⓓ (2, –4)

2. The amount of profit Bill makes per toy when he increases or decreases the price of his handmade toys can be modeled by the function $f(x) = -x^2 - 2x + 3$. What price change gives him the highest profit? What is highest profit per toy?

   Price change: $ ☐

   Maximum profit per toy: $ ☐

3. A pebble is tossed into the air from the top of a cliff. The height, in feet, of the pebble over time is modeled by the equation $y = -16x^2 + 32x + 80$. What is the maximum height, in feet, reached by the pebble?

   ☐

4. What is the equation of a parabola that passes through the points (–5, –10), (–1, 6), and (2, –3)?

   Ⓐ $y = -x^2 - 2x + 5$

   Ⓑ $y = -x^2 + 6x - 7$

   Ⓒ $y = -\frac{18}{9}x^2 - \frac{28}{9}x + \frac{35}{3}$

   Ⓓ $y = -x^2 - 3x + 2$

5. An equation that represents the path of a diver jumping off a diving board is $y = -7x^2 + 5x + 16$. Graph this function from the point where the diver jumped to the point where they reach the water.

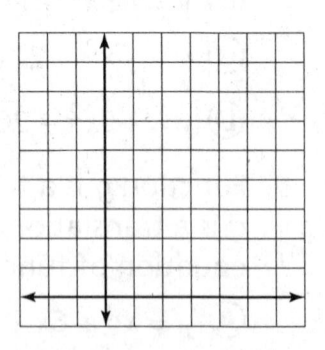

2-3 Lesson Quiz

Factored Form of a Quadratic Function

1. Factor the expression $3x^2 - 11x - 4$.

    (☐ $x +$ ☐) $(x -$ ☐ $)$

2. Solve the equation $x^2 + 7x = 30$.

    Ⓐ $x = 15$ and $x = -2$

    Ⓑ $x = -6$ and $x = 5$

    Ⓒ $x = -10$ and $x = 3$

    Ⓓ $x = 10$ and $x = -3$

3. A projectile is launched into the air. The function $h(t) = -16t^2 + 32t + 128$ gives the height, h, in feet, of the projectile t seconds after it is launched. After how many seconds will the projectile land back on the ground?

    ☐

4. Identify the intervals on which the function $f(x) = x^2 + 12x + 27$ is positive.

    $(-\infty,$ ☐ $)$ and $($ ☐ $, \infty)$

5. A long-jumper lifts off 3 m after starting his run, and lands 6 m from where he lifted off. When he is 8 m from the start line, he is 5 cm above the ground. Write the equation of a parabola that models his path through the air, where x is his horizontal distance from the start line in m and y is his height, in cm.

    Ⓐ $y = -x^2 + 12x - 27$

    Ⓑ $y = -3x^2 + 4x - 9$

    Ⓒ $y = 3x^2 - 4x + 9$

    Ⓓ $y = x^2 - 12x + 27$

2-4 Lesson Quiz

Complex Numbers and Operations

1. Use square roots to solve the equation $x^2 = -64$ over the complex numbers. Select all solutions that apply.
   - ☐ A. $8i$
   - ☐ B. -8
   - ☐ C. $-8i^2$
   - ☐ D. $-8i$
   - ☐ E. $8i^2$

2. What is the difference of $(5 + 3i)$ and $(2 + 9i)$?
   - Ⓐ $7 + 12i$
   - Ⓑ $3 + 6i$
   - Ⓒ $3 - 6i$
   - Ⓓ $7 + 6i$

3. Write the product $(2 + 7i)(2 - 7i)$ in the form $a + bi$.
   - Ⓐ $4 - 49i$
   - Ⓑ 53
   - Ⓒ $4 - 14i^2$
   - Ⓓ $53 + 14i$

4. Write the expression $3i(2 - 5i)(4 + i)$ in the form $a + bi$.

   ( ) + ( )i

5. Match each product with its factors.

	$9x^2 + 1$	$18x^2 + 2$	$3x^2 + 12$	$36x^2 + 25$
2, $(3x - i)$, and $(3x + i)$	☐	☐	☐	☐
3, $(x - 2i)$, and $(x + 2i)$	☐	☐	☐	☐
$(6x - 5i)$ and $(6x + 5i)$	☐	☐	☐	☐
$(3x - i)$ and $(3x + i)$	☐	☐	☐	☐

Name _____

2-5 Lesson Quiz

Completing the Square

1. Solve $x^2 - 18x + 81 = 4$ by completing the square. Select all solutions that apply.
   - ☐ A. $x = -11$
   - ☐ B. $x = -7$
   - ☐ C. $x = 7$
   - ☐ D. $x = 11$
   - ☐ E. $x = 0$

2. Write the equation $x^2 + 24x + 60 = 0$ in the form $(x + p)^2 = q$.
   - Ⓐ $(x + 12)^2 = -60$
   - Ⓑ $(x + 12)^2 = 84$
   - Ⓒ $(x + 12)^2 = 204$
   - Ⓓ $(x + 6)^2 = -24$

3. Solve $0 = x^2 + 6x + 13$ by completing the square.
   - Ⓐ $x = 5$ and $x = 1$
   - Ⓑ $x = 3 + i\sqrt{22}$ and $x = 3 - i\sqrt{22}$
   - Ⓒ $x = -1$ and $x = 1$
   - Ⓓ $x = -3 + 2i$ and $x = -3 - 2i$

4. The perimeter of a rectangular baking sheet is 58 inches and its area is 201.25 in.². What are the length and width of the baking sheet?
   - Ⓐ length 17.5 in., width 11.5 in.
   - Ⓑ length 83.3 in., width 17.3 in.
   - Ⓒ length 14.2 in., width 14.2 in.
   - Ⓓ length 50.3 in., width 50.3 in.

5. Find the zeros of the function $f(x) = -5x^2 + 4x - 1$ by completing the square.

   $x = \boxed{} + \boxed{} i$ and $x = \boxed{} - \boxed{} i$

enVision® Algebra 2 • Assessment Sourcebook

Name _____

enVision Algebra 2
SavvasRealize.com

2-6 Lesson Quiz

The Quadratic Formula

1. Solve $x^2 + 8x - 6 = 0$ using the Quadratic Formula.

   Ⓐ $x = 32 + 2\sqrt{2}$ and $x = 32 - 2\sqrt{2}$

   Ⓑ $x = -4 + \sqrt{22}$ and $x = -4 - \sqrt{22}$

   Ⓒ $x = 12$ and $x = -\frac{1}{2}$

   Ⓓ $x = 4 + 2\sqrt{22}$ and $x = 4 - 2\sqrt{22}$

2. Solve $x^2 + 2x + 7 = 0$ using the Quadratic Formula.
   Select all solutions that apply.

   ☐ A. $x = -1 + i\sqrt{6}$

   ☐ B. $x = -1 + \sqrt{6}$

   ☐ C. $x = -1 - i\sqrt{6}$

   ☐ D. $x = -1 - \sqrt{6}$

   ☐ E. $x = 1 - \sqrt{6}$

3. Describe the nature of the roots for the equation $49x^2 - 28x + 4 = 0$.

   Ⓐ two real roots

   Ⓑ one real root

   Ⓒ two complex roots

   Ⓓ one complex root

4. Richard tosses a ball into the air. The function $h(t) = -5t^2 + 10t + 6$ gives the approximate height h, in meters, of the ball t seconds after he tosses it. After how many seconds does the ball reach a height of 12 meters?

   Ⓐ 0.5 seconds

   Ⓑ 1 second

   Ⓒ 1.5 seconds

   Ⓓ The ball does not reach a height of 12 meters.

5. What value(s) of b will cause $27x^2 + bx + 3 = 0$ to have one real solution?
   Select all that apply.

   ☐ A. $b = -18$ ☐ D. $b = 3$

   ☐ B. $b = -9$ ☐ E. $b = 9$

   ☐ C. $b = -3$ ☐ F. $b = 18$

enVision® Algebra 2 • Assessment Sourcebook

Name _____

2-7 Lesson Quiz

Linear-Quadratic Systems

enVision Algebra 2
SavvasRealize.com

1. Determine the number of real solutions of the system $\begin{cases} y = x^2 - 3 \\ y = -2x + 4 \end{cases}$.

   Ⓐ 2

   Ⓑ 1

   Ⓒ 3

   Ⓓ 0

2. Use substitution to solve the system $\begin{cases} y = -\frac{1}{2}x^2 \\ y = x - 4 \end{cases}$.

   Ⓐ −4 and 2

   Ⓑ (4, −8) and (−2, −2)

   Ⓒ (−4, −8) and (2, −2)

   Ⓓ (0, 0) and (0, −4)

3. Nate tosses a ball up a hill for his dog to chase. The path of the ball is modeled by the function $y = -\frac{1}{4}x^2 + \frac{33}{5}x$, where x is the ball's horizontal distance from Nate in feet and y is the ball's height in feet. The hill is modeled by the line $y = \frac{1}{5}x$. How far does the ball travel horizontally before it hits the ground?

   ⬚ ft

4. Solve the system of inequalities $\begin{cases} y \geq 2x^2 + 2x - 3 \\ y \leq \frac{1}{3}x + 6 \end{cases}$ using shading.

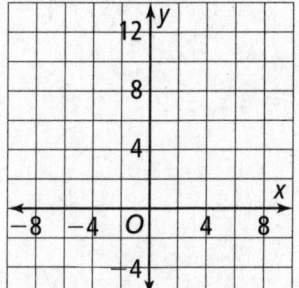

5. Solve the equation $2x^2 + 5x - 8 = \frac{5}{2}x + 20$ by writing a linear-quadratic system and solving using the intersection feature of a graphing calculator. Round to the nearest tenth.

   The graphing calculator shows the curve and line intersect at

   $x \approx$ ⬚ and $x \approx$ ⬚.

enVision® Algebra 2 • Assessment Sourcebook

Name _____

2 Topic Assessment Form A

1. The distance of a golf ball from the hole can be represented by the right side of a parabola with vertex (−1, 8). The ball reaches the hole 1 second after it is hit, at time 0. What is the equation of the parabola, in vertex form, that represents the ball's distance from the hole, y, at time x?

   $y = \boxed{}(x + \boxed{})^2 + \boxed{}$

2. Function g is a transformation of the parent function $f(x) = x^2$. The graph of f is reflected across the x-axis, and then translated left 4 units and down 2 units to form the graph of g. Write the equation for g in the form $y = ax^2 + bx + c$.

   Ⓐ $y = -x^2 + 8x + 14$
   Ⓑ $y = -x^2 - 8x - 18$
   Ⓒ $y = x^2 - 8x + 18$
   Ⓓ $y = -x^2 - 8x + 14$

3. The shape of the inside of a glass follows a parabola with the function $f(x) = x^2 + 6x + 9$. What point represents the bottom of the inside of the glass?

   Ⓐ (−3, 0)   Ⓒ (0, 3)
   Ⓑ (0, −3)   Ⓓ (3, 0)

4. A rectangular painting has length 1 ft longer than its width. What is the width of the painting if its area is 12 ft²?

   Ⓐ 4 feet   Ⓒ 6 feet
   Ⓑ 2 feet   Ⓓ 3 feet

5. The equation $y = -4.9x^2 + 14$ represents the height y in meters of a rock dropped off a bridge over time x in seconds. Graph this equation from the time the rock dropped to when it reached the water.

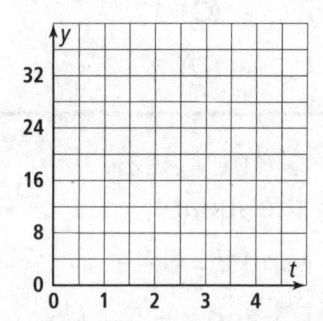

6. The height of a projectile launched from a 16-ft-tall tower is modeled by the equation $y = -16t^2 + 64t + 16$. Graph the equation. What is the maximum height, in feet, reached by the projectile?

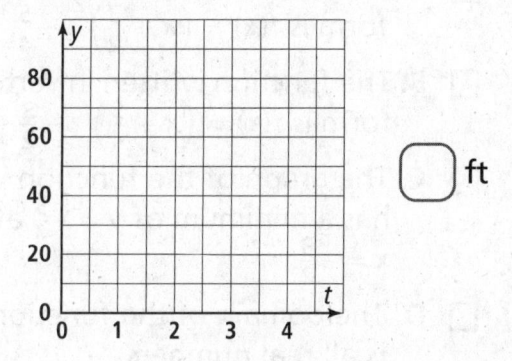

   $\boxed{}$ ft

7. A ball is thrown from the top row of seats in a stadium. The function $h(t) = -16t^2 + 64t + 80$ gives the height, in feet, of the ball t seconds after it is thrown. How long will it be before the ball hits the ground?

   $\boxed{}$ s

8. Use square roots to solve the equation $x^2 = -25$ over the complex numbers. Select all solutions for the equation.
   - ☐ A. $-5i$
   - ☐ B. -5
   - ☐ C. $-i$
   - ☐ D. i
   - ☐ E. 5
   - ☐ F. $5i$

9. Write the product $(4 + i)(4 - i)$ in the form $a + bi$.
   - Ⓐ $16 - i$
   - Ⓑ $16 - i^2$
   - Ⓒ 17
   - Ⓓ 8

10. Solve $5 = x^2 - 10x + 35$ by completing the square.
    - Ⓐ $x = 5 + i$ and $x = 5 - i$
    - Ⓑ $x = 5 + i\sqrt{5}$ and $x = 5 - i\sqrt{5}$
    - Ⓒ $x = -6 - i\sqrt{6}$ and $x = -5 + i\sqrt{6}$
    - Ⓓ $x = -5 - i\sqrt{5}$ and $x = -5 + i\sqrt{5}$

11. A function is given by $f(x) = x^2 + 3x + 1$. Select all the statements that are true about this function.
    - ☐ A. The function written in vertex form is $f(x) = \left(x + \frac{3}{2}\right)^2 - \frac{5}{4}$.
    - ☐ B. The function written in vertex form is $f(x) = \left(x + \frac{5}{4}\right)^2 - \frac{3}{2}$.
    - ☐ C. The graph of the function has a minimum of $y = -\frac{5}{4}$ at $x = -\frac{3}{2}$.
    - ☐ D. The domain of the function is all real numbers.
    - ☐ E. The range of the function is all real numbers.

12. Solve $x^2 + 3x = -4$ using the Quadratic Formula.

    $x = \dfrac{\boxed{} \pm i\sqrt{\boxed{}}}{\boxed{}}$

13. What is an equation for the quadratic function through the origin, (4, 2), and (−4, 2)?

    $y = \dfrac{\boxed{}}{\boxed{}} x^2$

14. A toy cannon ball is launched from a cannon on top of a platform. The function $h(t) = -5t^2 + 20t + 4$ gives the height, in meters, of the ball t seconds after it is launched. Write and solve an inequality to find the times where the ball is more than 12 meters above the ground. Round to the nearest hundredth.

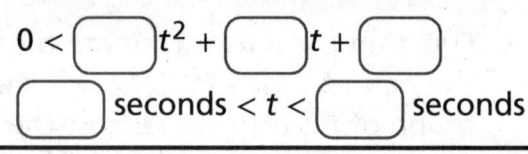

    $0 < \boxed{} t^2 + \boxed{} t + \boxed{}$

    $\boxed{}$ seconds $< t <$ $\boxed{}$ seconds

15. What value(s) of b will cause $4x^2 + bx + 25 = 0$ to have one real solution?
    - ☐ A. -200
    - ☐ B. -20
    - ☐ C. -2
    - ☐ D. 2
    - ☐ E. 20
    - ☐ F. 200

16. Determine the number of real solutions of the system $\begin{cases} y = x^2 + 8 \\ y = x + 15 \end{cases}$.
    - Ⓐ 0
    - Ⓑ 1
    - Ⓒ 2
    - Ⓓ 3

17. Solve $-3x^2 + 2x + 4 = -x - 3$ by writing a linear-quadratic system and using the intersection feature of a graphing calculator. Round to the nearest hundredth.

    The graphing calculator shows the curve and line intersect at

    $x \approx \boxed{}$ and $x \approx \boxed{}$.

enVision® Algebra 2

Name _____

2 Topic Assessment Form B

1. The graph of a toy car's speed y over time x is a parabola that shows a minimum speed of 2 m/s after 3 seconds. After 5 seconds, the car's speed is 3 m/s. What is the equation in vertex form of the parabola?

    $y = \boxed{}(x + \boxed{})^2 + \boxed{}$

2. Function g is a transformation of the parent function $f(x) = x^2$. The graph of f is translated right 2 units and up 3 units, and then reflected across the y-axis to form the graph of g. Write the equation for g in the form $y = ax^2 + bx + c$.

    Ⓐ $y = x^2 + 2x + 3$
    Ⓑ $y = x^2 + 6x + 7$
    Ⓒ $y = x^2 - 4x + 1$
    Ⓓ $y = x^2 + 4x + 7$

3. The shape of an underground pool follows a parabola with the function $f(x) = x^2 + 8x$. What point represents the bottom of the pool?

    Ⓐ (−4, 16)   Ⓒ (−4, −16)
    Ⓑ (0, 8)   Ⓓ (0, −8)

4. A rectangular frame has length 7 in. longer than its width. What is the length of the painting if its area is 18 in²?

    Ⓐ 9 inches   Ⓒ 2 inches
    Ⓑ 3 inches   Ⓓ 6 inches

5. An equation that represents the height y, in meters, of a bird over time x, in seconds, as it lands is $y = \frac{1}{2}(x - 4)^2$. Graph this function from time 0 to when the bird lands.

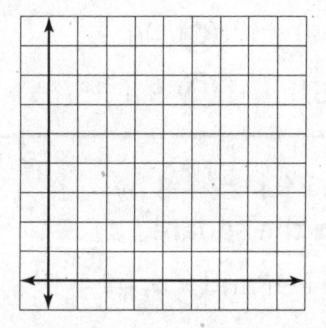

6. The height of a projectile launched from a 20-ft-tall tower is modeled by the equation $y = -16t^2 + 32t + 20$. Graph the equation. What is the maximum height, in feet, reached by the projectile?

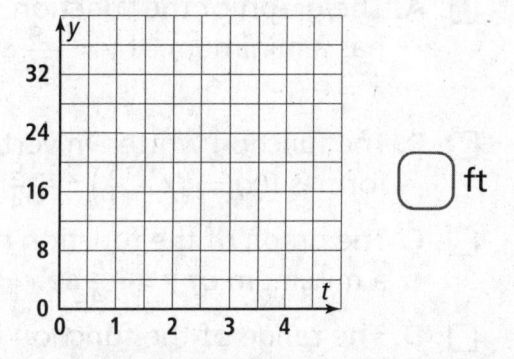

    $\boxed{}$ ft

7. A ball is thrown from the top row of seats in a stadium. The function $h(t) = -16t^2 + 80t + 96$ gives the height, in feet, of the ball t seconds after it is thrown. How long will it be before the ball hits the ground?

    $\boxed{}$ s

8. Use square roots to solve the equation $x^2 = -121$ over the complex numbers. Select all solutions for the equation.

   ☐ A. i
   ☐ B. 11
   ☐ C. $11i$
   ☐ D. $-11i$
   ☐ E. -11
   ☐ F. $-i$

9. Write the product $3i(5 - 3i)$ in the form $a + bi$.

   Ⓐ $6 + 8i$
   Ⓑ $-9 + 15i$
   Ⓒ -6
   Ⓓ $9 + 15i$

10. Solve $-2 = x^2 + 2x + 8$ by completing the square.

    Ⓐ $x = -1 - 9i$ and $x = -1 + 9i$
    Ⓑ $x = -1 + 3i$ and $x = -1 - 3i$
    Ⓒ $x = 4$ and $x = 2$
    Ⓓ $x = \sqrt{10} - 1$ and $x = -\sqrt{10} - 1$

11. A function is given by $f(x) = x^2 + 5x + 4$. Select all the statements that are true about this function.

    ☐ A. The graph of the function has a minimum of $y = -\frac{9}{4}$ at $x = -\frac{5}{2}$.
    ☐ B. The function written in vertex form is $f(x) = \left(x + \frac{5}{2}\right)^2 - \frac{9}{4}$.
    ☐ C. The graph of the function has a minimum of $y = -\frac{9}{4}$ at $x = \frac{5}{4}$.
    ☐ D. The range of the function is all real numbers.
    ☐ E. The domain of the function is all real numbers.

12. Solve $x^2 + 5x = -8$ using the Quadratic Formula.

    $x = \dfrac{\boxed{} \pm i\sqrt{\boxed{}}}{\boxed{}}$

13. What is an equation for the quadratic function through the origin, (10, 2.5), and (–10, 2.5)?

    $y = \dfrac{\boxed{}}{\boxed{}} x^2$

14. A toy cannon ball is launched from a cannon on top of a platform. The function $h(t) = -5t^2 + 15t + 10$ gives the height, in meters, of the ball t seconds after it is launched. Write and solve an inequality to find the times where the ball is more than 21 meters above the ground. Round to the nearest hundredth.

    $0 < \boxed{} t^2 + \boxed{} t + \boxed{}$

    $\boxed{}$ seconds $< t < \boxed{}$ seconds

15. What value(s) of b will cause $8x^2 + bx + 2 = 0$ to have one real solution?

    ☐ A. -16
    ☐ B. -8
    ☐ C. -4
    ☐ D. 4
    ☐ E. 8
    ☐ F. 16

16. Determine the number of real solutions of the system $\begin{cases} y = x^2 + 1 \\ y = 1 \end{cases}$

    Ⓐ 0
    Ⓑ 1
    Ⓒ 2
    Ⓓ 3

17. Solve $-3x^2 - 6x + 21 = 6x + 8$ by writing a linear-quadratic system and using the intersection feature of a graphing calculator. Round to the nearest hundredth.

    The graphing calculator shows the curve and line intersect at

    $x \approx \boxed{}$ and $x \approx \boxed{}$.

Name _____

2 Performance Assessment Form A

Felix wants to make a graphic design as decoration for a new website. His initial idea for the design involves using the shapes of three parabolas graphed on a coordinate plane, as shown.

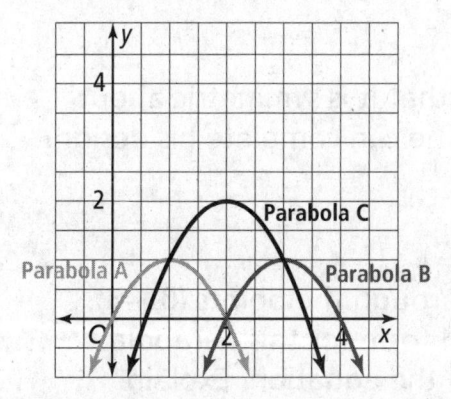

1. Felix first graphs parabola A. Describe how he can use translations of parabola A to graph parabolas B and C. Then write an equation in vertex form for each parabola.

2. What are the exact x-intercepts of parabola C? Explain.

3. Felix adds to his design by graphing the line $y = x + \frac{1}{4}$ on the same coordinate grid as the parabolas. Graph the line using the grid shown. Then describe the geometric relationship between the line and the graphs of parabolas A and C. Explain.

4. Felix wants to complete his design by making sure that it is symmetric about the axis of symmetry for parabola C. Describe how he can complete his design.

5. Felix starts a new design by graphing a parabola through the points (0, −5), (1, −4), and (4, −13). Write an equation in standard form for this parabola. Then find the zeros of the function represented by the equation. Explain.

Name _____

2 Performance Assessment Form B

A group of students want to build three identical rectangular gardens, each of which has a width of x ft. The gardens will be arranged in one of two ways, as shown by the plans below. The students have 480 ft of fencing and plan to build a fence around each of the three gardens. They will also install lighting for the gardens.

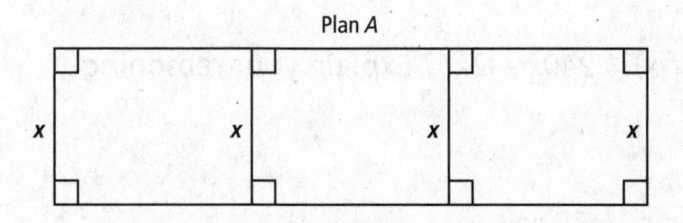

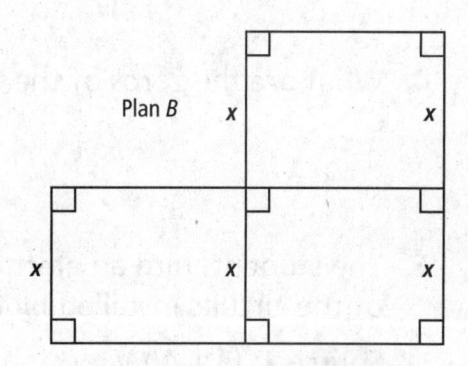

Plan A

Plan B

1. Suppose that the students use all of the fencing. Given that the width of a small rectangular garden is x ft, write an expression in terms of x for the length of one of the small rectangular gardens in Plan A. Then write an expression in terms of x for the length of one of the small rectangular gardens in Plan B. Explain.

2. Write an expression for the combined area of the three gardens in Plan A and of the three gardens in Plan B. Show two different ways to write each expression. Explain.

   Area for Plan A:

   Area for Plan B:

3. The students want to choose the plan that will give the maximum combined area for the 3 gardens. Use a graphing calculator to identify the plan they should choose. Explain your reasoning.

4. What are the zeros of the function $f(x) = 240x - 2x^2$? Explain your reasoning.

5. The students hire an electrician to set up the lighting for their garden. For one of the circuits installed by the electrician, there are three source voltages:

   Source 1: $(9 + 4i)$ V
   Source 2: $(5 - 3i)$ V
   Source 3: $(2 + 6i)$ V

   Find the total voltage for the circuit. Explain.

Name _____

Benchmark Assessment 1

1. The graph represents the profit of a company, y in thousands of dollars, in the time, x in months, before and after it changed management at x = 0. What was the average rate of change in profits over the 8 months since the company changed management?

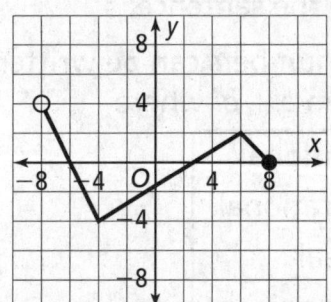

   Ⓐ $2,000 per month
   Ⓑ −$1,600 per month
   Ⓒ $8,000 per month
   Ⓓ $200 per month

2. Which of the following is an intermediate step in solving $ax^2 + bx + c = 0$ for x?

   Ⓐ $\left(x + \frac{b}{2a}\right)^2 = \frac{\pm\sqrt{b^2 - 4ac}}{2a}$
   Ⓑ $\left(x + \frac{b}{2a}\right)^2 = \frac{b^2 - 4ac}{2a}$
   Ⓒ $\left(x + \frac{b}{2a}\right)^2 = \frac{b^2 - 4ac}{(2a)^2}$
   Ⓓ $\left(x + \frac{b}{2a}\right)^2 = \frac{(b^2 - 4ac)^2}{(2a)^2}$

3. The graph of $y = |x − 3| + 2$ is reflected across the y-axis and then translated down 2 units. What is an equation of the transformed graph?

   Ⓐ $y = |−x + 3| − 2$
   Ⓑ $y = |x + 3|$
   Ⓒ $y = |−x − 3|$
   Ⓓ $y = −|x + 3| + 4$

4. Paige is filling a 3.5-L bucket at a rate of 0.25 L per minute. What is the domain of the function that represents the volume of water in the bucket after x minutes if the bucket was empty when Paige arrived?

   Ⓐ [0, 0.875]
   Ⓑ [0, 7]
   Ⓒ [0, 14]
   Ⓓ [0, 3.75]

5. Identify the translations of the graph of the parent function $f(x) = x^2$ that result in the graph of $g(x) = (x + 2)^2 + 6$.

   Ⓐ down 2 units, right 6 units
   Ⓑ up 2 units, right 2 units
   Ⓒ up 6 units, left 2 units
   Ⓓ up 2 units, left 6 units

6. Graph the function.
$$f(x) = \begin{cases} -x - 3 & \text{if } -5 \leq x < 0 \\ -3 & \text{if } 0 < x < 4 \\ -x + 1 & \text{if } 4 < x \leq 8 \end{cases}$$

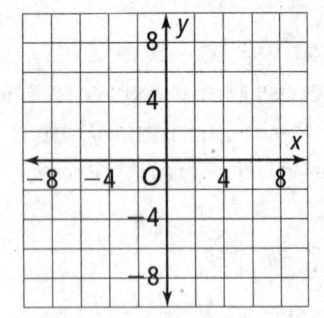

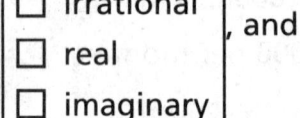

7. Chris' Cafe is increasing its customer base by advertising. On the first day of the campaign, they had 3 customers. On the second, they had 11, and on the third, they had 19. Write the recursive formula for the arithmetic sequence.

$a_1 = \boxed{}$, $a_n = a_{n-1} + \boxed{}$

8. The following recursive formula represents the value of the jackpot in a game show after each round, in hundreds of dollars.

$$a_n = \begin{cases} 1, & \text{if } n = 1 \\ a_{n-1} + 5, & \text{if } n > 1 \end{cases}$$

Write the explicit formula for the prize value and use it to calculate the value of the prize in round 8.

$a_n = \boxed{} + \boxed{}(n-1)$

Value of jackpot in round 8:

$\$\boxed{}$

9. Which equation has the same solutions as $9x^2 - 18x - 16 = 0$?
   Ⓐ $9(x-1)^2 = 16$
   Ⓑ $(3x-4)^2 = 0$
   Ⓒ $3(x-1)^2 = 16$
   Ⓓ $9(x-1)^2 = 25$

10. In a concert hall, there are 16 chairs in the first row, and each row has 4 more chairs than the previous row. There are 14 rows altogether. How many chairs are there in the concert hall?
    Ⓐ 68
    Ⓑ 588
    Ⓒ 616
    Ⓓ 1,176

11. Complete the sentence.

Complex numbers can be written in the form $a + bi$ where

a is ☐ rational ☐ irrational ☐ real ☐ imaginary ,

b is ☐ rational ☐ irrational ☐ real ☐ imaginary , and

i is ☐ rational ☐ irrational ☐ real ☐ imaginary .

12. Which equation has the same solutions as $ax^2 + bx + c = 0$?

Ⓐ $\left(x + \dfrac{b}{2a}\right)^2 = \left(\dfrac{b}{2a}\right)^2 - c$

Ⓑ $a\left(x + \dfrac{b}{2a}\right)^2 = a\left(\dfrac{b}{2a}\right)^2 - c$

Ⓒ $\left(x + \dfrac{b}{2a}\right)^2 + \left(\dfrac{b}{2a}\right)^2 = -c$

Ⓓ $a\left(x + \dfrac{b}{2a}\right)^2 + a\left(\dfrac{b}{2a}\right)^2 = -c$

enVision® Algebra 2

13. Solve the system of equations.
$$\begin{cases} 8x + 16y = -42 \\ -2x + 3y = 7 \end{cases}$$

Ⓐ (−4, 1)
Ⓑ (0.5, −2.69)
Ⓒ (4.3, 0.5)
Ⓓ (−4.25, −0.5)

14. Brenda has at most 4 hours to make food for a picnic. She must make at least 6 sandwiches and at least 3 dozen cookies. It takes her 4 minutes to make a sandwich, x, and 45 minutes to make a dozen cookies, y. Select all the inequalities that represent constraints for the situation.

☐ A. $4x + 45y \leq 240$
☐ B. $x \geq 6$
☐ C. $y \geq 3$
☐ D. $4x + 45y \leq 4$
☐ E. $x \leq 6$
☐ F. $y \leq 3$
☐ G. $x + y \geq 9$

15. What is the equation in vertex form of a parabola with a vertex of (4, −2) that passes through (2, −14)?

Ⓐ $y = -3(x - 4)^2 - 2$
Ⓑ $y = -3(x - 4)^2 + 2$
Ⓒ $y = 3(x - 4)^2 - 2$
Ⓓ $y = 3(x + 4)^2 + 2$

16. Solve the system of equations.
$$\begin{cases} 2x + y = 18 \\ x + 2y = -6 \end{cases}$$

$x =$ ☐, $y =$ ☐

17. Function g is a transformation of parent function $f(x) = x^2$. The graph of f is reflected across the x-axis and then translated left 6 and up 5 units to form the graph of g. What is the function rule for g?

Ⓐ $g(x) = -x^2 + 10x + 19$
Ⓑ $g(x) = -x^2 - 10x - 19$
Ⓒ $g(x) = -x^2 - 12x - 31$
Ⓓ $g(x) = x^2 - 12x + 31$

18. The path of a projectile launched from a 26-ft-tall tower is modeled by the equation $y = -16x^2 + 64x + 26$. What is the maximum height, in ft, reached by the projectile?

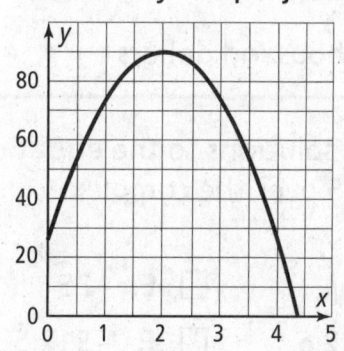

The maximum height is ☐ feet.

19. The function $f(x) = -5x^2 + 5x + 49$ represents the height, in m, of a ball thrown off a ledge as it moves away from the ledge with distance x, in m. What is the appropriate domain for $f(x)$?

Ⓐ [0, 3.7]   Ⓒ [0, 50.25]
Ⓑ [0, 49]   Ⓓ [0, ∞)

20. Solve the equation $-x^2 + 10x = -24$.

Ⓐ $x = 4$ and $x = 6$
Ⓑ $x = -4$ and $x = -6$
Ⓒ $x = 2$ and $x = -12$
Ⓓ $x = -2$ and $x = 12$

21. A small business recorded its revenue in thousands of dollars over a 6-month period, as shown in the table.

Month, x	1	2	3	4	5	6
Revenue (y)	5.2	5.8	6	5.8	5.2	4.2

Part A

Write the quadratic function in vertex form that models the data. Use decimals when necessary.

$y = \boxed{}(x + \boxed{})^2 + \boxed{}$

Part B

If this trend continues, what will be the revenue of the company during the 8th month?

$\boxed{}$ thousand dollars

22. Select all solutions to the equation $x^2 = -625$ over the complex numbers.

☐ A. $25i$ ☐ E. -25
☐ B. 312.5 ☐ F. -312.5
☐ C. 25 ☐ G. $-25i$
☐ D. $312.5i$ ☐ H. $-312.5i$

23. Write the product $(6 - i)(6 + i)$ in the form $a + bi$.

Ⓐ 37 Ⓒ 35
Ⓑ $36 - i^2$ Ⓓ $12 - i^2$

24. Simplify the expression $2i(4.5 - 20i) + 3i$. Write your answer in the form $a + bi$.

$\boxed{} + \boxed{}i$

25. Divide $\frac{1 + 5i}{1 - 3i}$. Round answers to the nearest tenth, if necessary.

$\boxed{} + \boxed{}i$

26. Consider the quadratic equation $0 = 0.5x^2 + 2x - 2$.

Part A

Rewrite the equation in vertex form by completing the square.

$0 = \boxed{}(x + \boxed{})^2 + \boxed{}$

Part B

Select all solutions to the equation.

☐ A. $-2 + \sqrt{2}$ ☐ D. $-2 - 2\sqrt{2}$
☐ B. $-2 + 2\sqrt{2}$ ☐ E. 0
☐ C. $-2 - \sqrt{2}$ ☐ F. 2

27. Solve $x^2 + 8x = -5$ using the Quadratic Formula.

$x = \boxed{} + \sqrt{\boxed{}}$

28. What value(s) of b will cause $2x^2 + bx + 128 = 0$ to have one real solution?

$b = \boxed{}$ and $b = \boxed{}$

29. Solve $6x^2 - 8x + 1 = x + 4$ to the nearest hundredth by writing a linear-quadratic system and using the intersection feature of a graphing calculator. The curve and line intersect at

$x \approx \boxed{}$

and $x \approx \boxed{}$.

30. Select all solutions, if any, to the system $\begin{cases} y = (x - 1)^2 + 1 \\ 2x - y = 1 \end{cases}$.

☐ A. no solution ☐ D. $(-3, -5)$
☐ B. $(-1, 1)$ ☐ E. $(3, 5)$
☐ C. $(1, 1)$ ☐ F. $(5, 3)$

3 Readiness Assessment

1. Which equation could be the one shown in the graph?

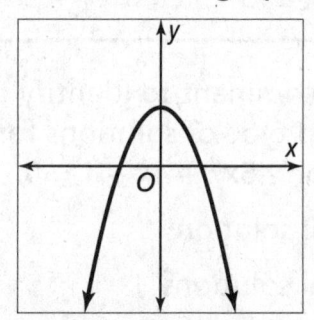

   Ⓐ $y = x^2 + 2$
   Ⓑ $y = -x^2 + 2$
   Ⓒ $y = -x^2 - 2$
   Ⓓ $y = -(x^2 + 2)$

2. Which of the following describes how the graph of $f(x) = x^2$ is translated to the graph of $g(x) = (x + 8)^2 - 1$?

   Ⓐ up 8 units and left 1 unit
   Ⓑ down 8 units and right 1 unit
   Ⓒ left 8 units and down 1 unit
   Ⓓ right 8 units and up 1 unit

3. The shape of a hill is represented by the graph of $f(x) = -(x - 7)^2 + 4$. What point represents the peak?

   Ⓐ (−7, 4)
   Ⓑ (9, 0)
   Ⓒ (4, 7)
   Ⓓ (7, 4)

4. A football is thrown toward the end zone. The function $h(x) = -0.1x^2 + 2.2x + 1.4$ gives the height, in yards, of the football when it is x yards from the quarterback. If the receiver misses the pass, how many yards does the ball travel before it hits the ground? Round to the nearest tenth of a yard.

   ☐ yards

5. Simplify $-4x + 2x^2 - x^2 + 5 - 3x$.

   Ⓐ $x^2 + 7x + 5$
   Ⓑ $3x^2 - x + 5$
   Ⓒ $x^2 - 7x + 5$
   Ⓓ $x^2 - x + 5$

6. Simplify $-3x(7x + 4y - 10)$.

   Ⓐ $-21x^2 - 12xy + 30x$
   Ⓑ $-21x^2 + 12xy - 30x$
   Ⓒ $-21x^2 + 12xy - 10$
   Ⓓ $-21x^2 - 12xy - 10$

7. Multiply $(2x - 5)(x + 1)$.

   Ⓐ $x^2 - 3x - 5$ Ⓒ $2x^2 - 3x - 5$
   Ⓑ $x^2 - 4x - 5$ Ⓓ $2x^2 - 4x - 5$

8. Multiply $(5x - 7)(4x - 3)$.

   Ⓐ $20x^2 - 43x - 21$
   Ⓑ $20x^2 + 21$
   Ⓒ $20x^2 + 13x + 21$
   Ⓓ $20x^2 - 43x + 21$

9. Multiply $-2(x + 6)(3x - 5)$.
   - Ⓐ $3x^2 + 13x - 30$
   - Ⓑ $6x^2 + 26x - 60$
   - Ⓒ $-6x^2 - 26x + 60$
   - Ⓓ $-6x^2 + 60$

10. Factor $3x^2 + 5x - 12$.
    - Ⓐ $3(x + 1)(x - 4)$
    - Ⓑ $3(x - 1)(x + 4)$
    - Ⓒ $(x + 3)(3x - 4)$
    - Ⓓ $(x - 3)(3x + 4)$

11. A ball thrown off a cliff follows an arc with height $h(t) = -16t^2 + 40t + 8$. Complete the sentence.

    The maximum height of the ball is ⬚ feet, and it takes ⬚ seconds for the ball to reach this height.

12. Simplify $(3 + 5i)^2$.

    ⬚ + ⬚ i

13. What are the solutions to $2x^2 + 100 = 0$?
    - Ⓐ $x = \pm 5\sqrt{2}$
    - Ⓑ $x = \pm 5i\sqrt{2}$
    - Ⓒ $x = \pm 10$
    - Ⓓ $x = \pm 10i$

14. What are the solutions to $x^2 + 2x - 5 = 0$?
    - Ⓐ $x = 1, x = -5$
    - Ⓑ $x = -1, x = 5$
    - Ⓒ $x = -1 \pm \sqrt{6}$
    - Ⓓ $x = -1 \pm 2\sqrt{5}$

15. Use the discriminant to identify the number and type of solutions for the equation $-5x^2 + 4x + 1 = 0$.
    - Ⓐ one real solution
    - Ⓑ two real solutions
    - Ⓒ one non-real solution
    - Ⓓ two non-real solutions

16. Select all the equations that have two x-intercepts.
    - ☐ A. $y = x^2 - 30$
    - ☐ B. $y = x^2 + 2x + 6$
    - ☐ C. $y = x^2 + 3x - 4$
    - ☐ D. $y = x^2 - 10x + 25$
    - ☐ E. $y = -x^2 + x - 1$

17. Which of the following expressions is equal to 25?
    - Ⓐ $(5i)^2$
    - Ⓑ $(3 + 2i)^2$
    - Ⓒ $(3 + 2i)(3 - 2i)$
    - Ⓓ $(3 + 4i)(3 - 4i)$

3-1 Lesson Quiz

Graphing Polynomial Functions

1. Which statement is true of the function $f(x) = x^2 + 6x^3 - 4 + 2x^5$?

   Ⓐ The function is positive for all values of x.

   Ⓑ The end behavior of the graph of $f(x)$ is similar to that of $g(x) = -x$.

   Ⓒ The graph has exactly one x-intercept.

   Ⓓ The function is increasing for all real numbers.

2. Use the leading coefficient and degree of the polynomial function $f(x) = x^3 - 7x^2 + 10x$ to determine the end behavior of its graph. Select all the true statements.

   ☐ A. As $x \to \infty$, $y \to \infty$.
   ☐ B. As $x \to \infty$, $y \to -\infty$.
   ☐ C. As $x \to \infty$, $y \to 0$.
   ☐ D. As $x \to -\infty$, $y \to \infty$.
   ☐ E. As $x \to -\infty$, $y \to -\infty$.

3. The graph of a function f is shown. Use the graph to estimate all turning points. Select all x-values that are turning points of f.

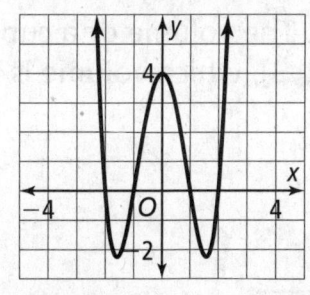

   ☐ A. −3   ☐ E. 1
   ☐ B. 0   ☐ F. −1
   ☐ C. 4   ☐ G. 1.5
   ☐ D. −1.5

4. Use the graph of the polynomial function $f(x) = -x^3 + 5x^2 - 2x - 8$ to complete the sentences.

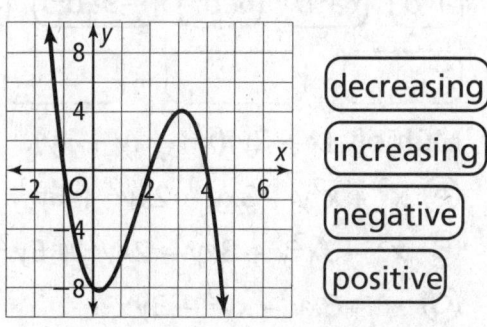

   Options: decreasing, increasing, negative, positive

   f is _____ on the intervals $(-\infty, \frac{1}{3})$ and $(3, \infty)$.

   f is _____ on the intervals $(-1, 2)$ and $(4, \infty)$.

   f is _____ on the interval $(\frac{1}{3}, 3)$.

   f is _____ on the intervals $(-\infty, -1)$ and $(2, 4)$.

5. The volume of water in a tank is modeled by $y = 1.15x^3 - 0.1x^2 + 2$, where x is the number of minutes after the faucet is turned on. What is the y-intercept of the graph, and what does it represent in this context?

   Complete the sentence.

   The y-intercept is _____ and represents the

   ☐ volume of water
   ☐ number of minutes

   before the faucet is
   ☐ turned off.
   ☐ turned on.

enVision® Algebra 2 • Assessment Sourcebook

3-2 Lesson Quiz

Adding, Subtracting, and Multiplying Polynomials

1. Add $(4a^2b - 3ab^2 + 2ab + 5)$ and $(2a^2b + 3ab^2 - 7ab)$. Complete the expression in standard form.

   $\boxed{a^2b}$ $\boxed{6a^2b}$ $\boxed{6ab^2}$ $\boxed{-9ab^2}$ $\boxed{-5ab}$ $\boxed{9ab}$ $\boxed{5ab}$ $\boxed{5}$

   $\boxed{} + \boxed{} + \boxed{}$

2. Multiply $(x + 2y)(x^2 - xy + 3y)$.
   - Ⓐ $x^3 + x^2y + 3xy - 2xy^2 + 6y^2$
   - Ⓑ $x^3 - 3x^2y + 3xy - 2xy^2 + 6y^2$
   - Ⓒ $x^3 + 3xy - xy^2 + 3y^2$
   - Ⓓ $x^3 - xy + 6y^2$

3. Is the set of monomials closed under multiplication? Which of the following gives a correct answer and an explanation?
   - Ⓐ Yes; the sum of any two monomials is a monomial.
   - Ⓑ No; the product of two monomials could be a polynomial.
   - Ⓒ Yes; the product of any two monomials is a monomial.
   - Ⓓ No; the product of two monomials could be a rational number.

4. Jae is constructing an open box from a piece of cardboard that is 9 in. wide and 12 in. long. Jae cuts squares of equal size from each corner of the cardboard, and then folds up the sides of the box. Write and simplify a polynomial function V in standard form for the volume of the box in terms of x.

   $V(x) = \boxed{}x^3 - \boxed{}x^2 + \boxed{}x$

5. The volume of a hemisphere with radius x is $V(x) = \frac{2}{3}\pi x^3$. The volume of a cube with height x is shown in the graph. Over the interval [2, 3], which volume is increasing faster? Complete the sentence.

   The volume of the ☐ hemisphere ☐ cube is increasing faster.

enVision® Algebra 2 • Assessment Sourcebook

Name _____

3-3 Lesson Quiz

Polynomial Identities

1. Prove the identity $x^3 - y^6 = (x - y^2)(x^2 + xy^2 + y^4)$.

Distributive	Associative	Commutative	Reflexive
Add	Subtract	Multiply	Divide	1	−1
x	y	variables	coefficients	like terms	constants

   $(x - y^2)(x^2 + xy^2 + y^4)$

   $= x(x^2 + xy^2 + y^4) - y^2(x^2 + xy^2 + y^4)$ Use the [ ] Property.

   $= x^3 + x^2y^2 + xy^4 - (x^2y^2 + xy^4 + y^6)$ [ ].

   $= x^3 + x^2y^2 + xy^4 - x^2y^2 - xy^4 - y^6$ Distribute the factor of [ ].

   $= x^3 - y^6$ Combine [ ].

2. **Part A** Use polynomial identities to multiply $(5 - 4x^3)(5 + 4x^3)$.

   Ⓐ $25 - 4x^9$ Ⓑ $25 - 40x^3 + 16x^6$ Ⓒ $25 - 4x^6$ Ⓓ $25 - 16x^6$

   Part B What identity did you use?
   Ⓐ Difference of squares   Ⓒ Sum of cubes
   Ⓑ Difference of cubes   Ⓓ Square of a sum

3. **Part A** Use polynomial identities to factor $1 - 125n^3$. Select all factors.

   ☐ A. $1 - 5n$ ☐ C. $1 + 5n + 5n^2$ ☐ E. $1 + 5n + 25n^2$
   ☐ B. $1 + 5n$ ☐ D. $1 - 5n + 5n^2$ ☐ F. $1 - 5n + 25n^2$

   Part B What identity did you use?
   Ⓐ Difference of squares   Ⓒ Sum of cubes
   Ⓑ Difference of cubes   Ⓓ Square of a sum

4. Use Pascal's Triangle to expand the expression $(x + 2)^8$.

   Ⓐ $x^8 + 256$

   Ⓑ $256 + x + 16x^2 + 112x^3 + 448x^4 + 1120x^5 + 1792x^6 + 1792x^7 + 1024x^8$

   Ⓒ $x^8 + 16x^7 + 112x^6 + 448x^5 + 1120x^4 + 1792x^3 + 1792x^2 + 1024x + 256$

   Ⓓ $x^7 + 14x^6 + 84x^5 + 280x^4 + 560x^3 + 672x^2 + 448x + 128$

5. Expand $(a + 4)^5$: $a^5 +$ [ ] $a^4 +$ [ ] $a^3 +$ [ ] $a^2 +$ [ ] $a +$ [ ]

enVision® Algebra 2 • Assessment Sourcebook

Name _____

3-4 Lesson Quiz

Dividing Polynomials

1. Use long division to divide $x^3 + x^2 - 2x + 14$ by $x + 3$.

   $\boxed{x^2}$ $\boxed{2x}$ $\boxed{(-2x)}$ $\boxed{4x}$ $\boxed{(-8)}$ $\boxed{4}$ $\boxed{10}$ $\boxed{\left(-\dfrac{10}{x+3}\right)}$ $\boxed{\dfrac{2}{x+3}}$ $\boxed{\dfrac{38}{x+3}}$ $\boxed{\dfrac{44}{x+3}}$

   $\boxed{}$ + $\boxed{}$ + $\boxed{}$ + $\boxed{}$

2. Morgan begins to use synthetic division to divide $x^4 + x^3 - 6x^2 - 4x + 8$ by $x - 2$, as shown at the right. Which of the following shows the correct values to replace the question marks, and also gives the quotient?

   $\begin{array}{r|rrrrr} 2 & 1 & 1 & -6 & -4 & 8 \\ & & ? & ? & ? & ? \\ \hline \end{array}$

   Ⓐ 2, 6, 0, −8; $x^3 - 3x^2 + 4$
   Ⓑ 2, 6, 0, −8; $x^3 + 3x^2 - 4$
   Ⓒ 1, 3, 0, −4; $x^2 + 3x - 4$
   Ⓓ 1, 1, −6, −4; $x^3 + 3x^2 - 4$

3. Verify the Remainder Theorem if $P(x) = 2x^3 - x^2 + 4x + 5$ is divided by $x + 2$. Complete the sentences.

   When $P(x)$ is divided by $x + 2$, the remainder is $\begin{array}{l} \square \ -23. \\ \square \ -7. \\ \square \ 1. \\ \square \ 33. \end{array}$

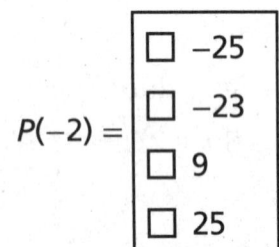

   $P(-2) = \begin{array}{l} \square \ -25 \\ \square \ -23 \\ \square \ 9 \\ \square \ 25 \end{array}$

   Does this example verify the Remainder Theorem? $\begin{array}{l} \square \ \text{Yes} \\ \square \ \text{No} \end{array}$

4. Find $f(3)$ if $f(x) = x^4 - 5x^2 - 6x - 10$

   Ⓐ −46   Ⓑ 8   Ⓒ 44   Ⓓ 224

5. If $x + 2$ is a factor of $P(x) = 2x^3 + 5x^2 + 5x + 6$, select the two factors that express $P(x)$ as a product.

   ☐ A. $(x + 2)$
   ☐ B. $(2x^2 - x - 3)$
   ☐ C. $(2x^2 - x + 3)$
   ☐ D. $(2x^2 + x - 3)$
   ☐ E. $(2x^2 + x + 3)$
   ☐ F. not a factor

enVision® Algebra 2 • Assessment Sourcebook

3-5 Lesson Quiz

Zeros of Polynomial Functions

1. Part A

What are all the zeros of $f(x) = x^3 + 2x^2 - 3x$?

Zeros: ☐ , ☐ , ☐

Part B

Use the zeroes to sketch the graph of f.

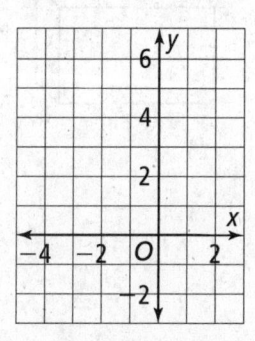

2. What x-values are solutions of $x^3 + 5x^2 - x - 7 = x^2 + 6x + 3$? Simplify the polynomial and find the zeros. Complete the sentence.

The zeros are at $x = $ ☐ , $x = $ ☐ , and $x = $ ☐ .

3. What values of x are solutions of the inequality $x^3 - 4x > 0$?

The inequality is true for

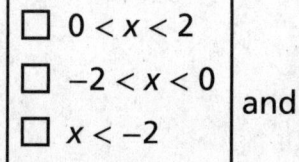

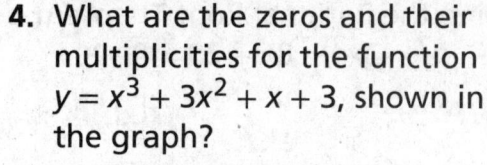

☐ $0 < x < 2$		☐ $0 < x < 2$.
☐ $-2 < x < 0$	and	☐ $x > 0$.
☐ $x < -2$		☐ $x > 2$.
☐ $x < 2$		☐ $x > 4$.

4. What are the zeros and their multiplicities for the function $y = x^3 + 3x^2 + x + 3$, shown in the graph?

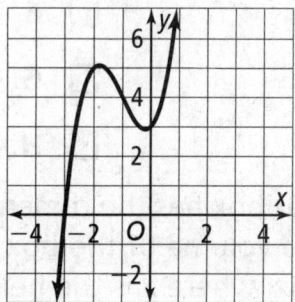

Ⓐ $-3, -1$, and 1, each multiplicity 1

Ⓑ -3, multiplicity 1

Ⓒ 3, multiplicity 2

Ⓓ -3, multiplicity 3

5. Find the zeros of $f(x) = -x^3 - 2x^2 + 7x - 4$. Then describe the behavior of the graph of f at each zero.

Ⓐ $4, -1$; As $x \to -\infty$, $f \to -\infty$. When $-1 < x < 4$, $f < 0$. At $x = 4$, f is tangent to the x-axis, so when $x > 1$, $f \to \infty$.

Ⓑ $-4, 1$; As $x \to -\infty$, $f \to -\infty$. When $-4 < x < 1$, $f > 0$. At $x = 1$, f is tangent to the x-axis, so when $x > 1$, $f \to -\infty$.

Ⓒ $4, -1$; As $x \to -\infty$, $f \to \infty$. When $-1 < x < 4$, $f > 0$. At $x = 4$, f is tangent to the x-axis, so when $x > 1$, $\to \infty$.

Ⓓ $-4, 1$; As $x \to -\infty$, $f \to \infty$. When $-4 < x < 1$, $f < 0$. At $x = 1$, f is tangent to the x-axis, so when $x > 1$, $f \to -\infty$.

enVision® Algebra 2 • Assessment Sourcebook

Name _____

3-6 Lesson Quiz

Theorems About Roots of Polynomial Equations

1. Using the Rational Root Theorem, select all the possible rational solutions of $x^4 - x^3 - 3x^2 - 8x + 20 = 0$.

   ☐ A. $\pm\frac{1}{2}$ ☐ E. $\pm\frac{1}{20}$ ☐ I. ± 5

   ☐ B. $\pm\frac{1}{4}$ ☐ F. ± 1 ☐ J. ± 10

   ☐ C. $\pm\frac{1}{5}$ ☐ G. ± 2 ☐ K. ± 20

   ☐ D. $\pm\frac{1}{10}$ ☐ H. ± 4

2. A rectangular box has the dimensions shown in the diagram. The volume of the box is given by the function $V(x) = x^3 - 4x$, where x is the height in inches. What is the height of the box if the volume is 15 in.^{3}?

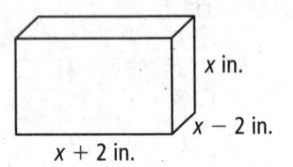

   x in.
   $x - 2$ in.
   $x + 2$ in.

   Part A
   Select the equation for the volume:

   Ⓐ $x^2 - 4 = 15$ Ⓒ $x^3 - 4x = 15$

   Ⓑ $x^3 - 4 = 15$ Ⓓ $x^3 + 4x = 15$

   Part B
   Complete each sentence.

   The solution to the equation is $x = \boxed{}$.

   The height of the box is $\boxed{}$ inches.

3. What are all the real and complex solutions of $x^3 + 2x^2 + 3x + 6 = 0$? If necessary, round to the nearest tenth.

   Ⓐ $-1.5, 0.3 + 1.9i, 0.3 - 1.9i$ Ⓒ $-2, i\sqrt{3}, -i\sqrt{3}$

   Ⓑ $-2, \sqrt{3}, -\sqrt{3}, i\sqrt{3}$ Ⓓ $-1.5, 0.3 + i\sqrt{1.9}, 0.3 - \sqrt{1.9}$

4. Select all real and complex solutions of $x^3 - x^2 - x - 15 = 0$.

   ☐ A. -3 ☐ D. $1 - 2i$
   ☐ B. 3 ☐ E. $-1 - 2i$
   ☐ C. $-1 + 2i$ ☐ F. $1 + 2i$

5. Select all real and complex solutions of $x^4 - 2x^2 - 24 = 0$.

   ☐ A. $\sqrt{6}$ ☐ E. $i\sqrt{3}$
   ☐ B. $2\sqrt{2}$ ☐ F. $2i$
   ☐ C. $-i\sqrt{3}$ ☐ G. $-\sqrt{6}$
   ☐ D. $-2i$ ☐ H. $-2\sqrt{2}$

enVision® Algebra 2 • Assessment Sourcebook

Name _____

3-7 Lesson Quiz

Transformations of Polynomial Functions

1. Use the graph to classify the polynomial function as *even*, *odd*, or *neither*.

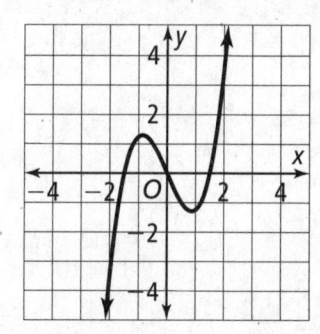

   The function is ☐ even.
                   ☐ odd.
                   ☐ neither.

2. Identify the parent function of the function $f(x) = -x^4 - 1$, and list the transformations from the parent function to create $f(x)$.

   Ⓐ x^4; translate down 1 unit, reflect over the *x*-axis

   Ⓑ x^4; reflect over the *x*-axis, translate down 1 unit

   Ⓒ x^3; reflect over the *x*-axis, translate down 1 unit

   Ⓓ x^3; compress the graph by a factor of *x*, translate down 1 unit

3. How does the graph of $g(x) = 3x^3 + 6$ differ from the graph of its parent function $f(x) = x^3$? Select all the transformations.

   ☐ A. The leading coefficient, 3, translates the graph up 3 units.

   ☐ B. The leading coefficient, 6, compresses the graph vertically.

   ☐ C. The leading coefficient, 3, stretches the graph vertically.

   ☐ D. Adding 6 translates the graph up 6 units.

   ☐ E. Adding 6 translates the graph right 6 units.

4. Determine the equation of the graph as it relates to either its parent cubic function or quartic function.

   Ⓐ $f(x) = (x - 2)^3 - 3$

   Ⓑ $f(x) = (x - 3)^4 - 2$

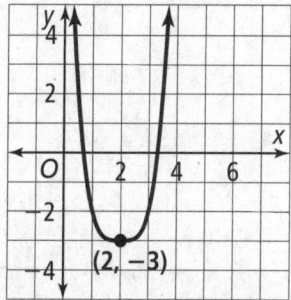

   Ⓒ $f(x) = (x + 3)^4 + 2$

   Ⓓ $f(x) = (x - 2)^4 - 3$

5. The volume of a cube, in cubic centimeters, is given by the function $V(x) = x^3$, where *x* is the side length of the cube in centimeters. Write a new function for the volume of the cube in cubic millimeters.

   $V(x) =$ ☐ x^3

enVision® Algebra 2 • Assessment Sourcebook

Name _____

3 Topic Assessment Form A

1. What is the remainder when $f(x) = 2x^4 + x^3 - 8x - 1$ is divided by $x - 2$?
   - Ⓐ −23
   - Ⓑ 23
   - Ⓒ −3
   - Ⓓ 3

2. Describe the coefficients of a cubic polynomial function f that has one rational zero, a, and two irrational zeros, $\sqrt{b}$ and $-\sqrt{b}$, where b is rational.
   - Ⓐ Some are irrational numbers.
   - Ⓑ They are all complex numbers.
   - Ⓒ They are all rational numbers.
   - Ⓓ They are all irrational numbers.

3. Use the Binomial Theorem to expand $(x - 2)^6$.
   - Ⓐ $x^6 - 2x^5 + 4x^4 - 8x^3 + 16x^2 - 32x + 64$
   - Ⓑ $x^6 - 12x^5 + 24x^4 - 36x^3 + 48x^2 - 60x + 12$
   - Ⓒ $x^6 - 12x^5 + 60x^4 - 160x^3 + 240x^2 - 192x + 64$
   - Ⓓ $x^6 - 32x^5 + 16x^4 - 8x^3 + 4x^2 - 2x + 64$

4. Simplify $(x^2 + 2x)(x^2 + x + 5)$. Write the simplified polynomial in standard form.

   [x^4] [$2x^3$] [$3x^3$] [$5x^2$] [$7x^2$]

   [$10x$] [10]

   [ ] + [ ] + [ ] + [ ]

5. If $x - 3$ is a factor of $P(x) = x^3 + x^2 - 17x + 15$, select the two factors that express $P(x)$ as a product.
   - ☐ A. $(x - 3)$
   - ☐ B. $(x^2 - 4x - 5)$
   - ☐ C. $(x^2 + 4x + 5)$
   - ☐ D. $(x^2 + 4x - 5)$
   - ☐ E. not a factor

6. Sketch a graph of the polynomial function $f(x) = x^3 - 2x^2$.

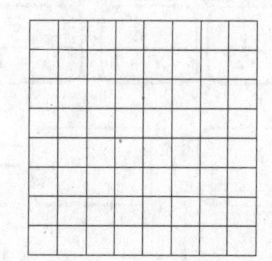

7. Lucy cuts 4 squares with side length x in. from the corners of a 6-by-9-in. piece of paper. She folds the paper to make a tray that is x in. high. Complete the function for the tray's volume V in terms of x.

   $V(x) = $ [ ] $x^3 - $ [ ] $x^2 + $ [ ] x

8. Use polynomial identities to factor $64 + 27a^3$. Select all factors.
   - ☐ A. $(4 - 3a)$
   - ☐ B. $(4 + 3a)$
   - ☐ C. $(16 + 12a + 9a^2)$
   - ☐ D. $(16 - 12a + 9a^2)$
   - ☐ E. $(16 - 12a + 3a^2)$

9. The volume of a cube with length x is $V(x) = x^3$. The volume of a sphere with radius x is shown in the graph. 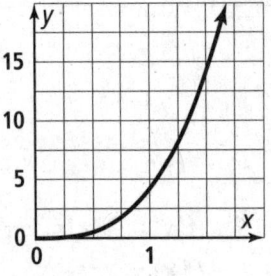
Over the interval [0.5, 1], which volume is increasing faster?

The volume of the ☐ sphere / ☐ cube is increasing faster.

10. Use synthetic division to divide $2x^4 - 3x^3 + 2x^2 - 8x - 1$ by $x - 1$. Complete the quotient.

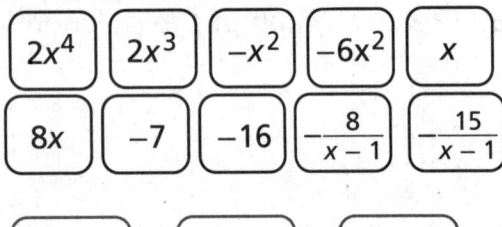

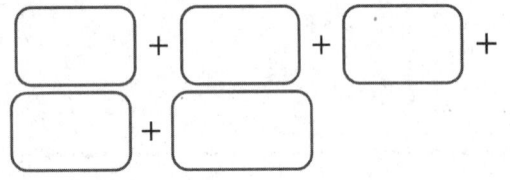

$\boxed{2x^4}$ $\boxed{2x^3}$ $\boxed{-x^2}$ $\boxed{-6x^2}$ $\boxed{x}$

$\boxed{8x}$ $\boxed{-7}$ $\boxed{-16}$ $\boxed{-\dfrac{8}{x-1}}$ $\boxed{-\dfrac{15}{x-1}}$

☐ + ☐ + ☐ + ☐

☐ + ☐

11. Describe the behavior at each zero of $f(x) = (x - 5)(x - 1)(x + 4)$.

Ⓐ The graph touches the x-axis at 4 and crosses the x-axis at −1 and −5.

Ⓑ The graph touches the x-axis at 4, −5, and −1.

Ⓒ The graph crosses the x-axis at 5, 1, and −4.

Ⓓ The graph touches the x-axis at −4 and crosses the x-axis at 1 and 5.

12. Identify the zeros of the function $f(x) = x(x - 3)(x + 1)$.

☐ , ☐ , ☐

13. Use the binomial theorem to expand $(2a + 2b)^5$. Select all of the terms below that are in the standard form of the expansion. (Not all terms are given.)

☐ A. $5a^4b$

☐ B. $384a^3b^3$

☐ C. $160ab^4$

☐ D. $16a^2b^2$

☐ E. $32a^5$

☐ F. $20a^2b^3$

14. How does the graph of the function $f(x) = 2x^4 - 3$ differ from the graph of its parent function? Select all the transformations.

☐ A. The graphs are the same.

☐ B. Subtracting 3 translates the graph down 3 units.

☐ C. The leading coefficient, 2, stretches the graph vertically.

☐ D. Subtracting 3 translates the graph up 3 units.

☐ E. Subtracting 3 translates the graph right 3 units.

Name _____

3 Topic Assessment Form B

1. What is the remainder when $f(x) = x^4 - 8x^2 + 10x + 22$ is divided by $x + 3$?

   Ⓐ −107 　Ⓒ 61
   Ⓑ −17   　Ⓓ 1

2. Describe the coefficients of a cubic polynomial function f that has one rational zero, a, and two complex numbers $i\sqrt{b}$ and $-i\sqrt{b}$, where b is rational.

   Ⓐ None are real numbers.
   Ⓑ They are all real numbers.
   Ⓒ Only one is a real number.
   Ⓓ Only two are real numbers.

3. Use the binomial theorem to expand $(2x - 2)^6$.

   Ⓐ $2x^6 - 12x^5 + 30x^4 - 20x^3 + 30x^2 - 12x + 2$
   Ⓑ $2x^6 - 24x^5 + 120x^4 - 320x^3 + 480x^2 - 384x + 128$
   Ⓒ $64x^6 - 192x^5 + 240x^4 - 160x^3 + 60x^2 - 12x + 1$
   Ⓓ $64x^6 - 384x^5 + 960x^4 - 1280x^3 + 960x^2 - 384x + 64$

4. Simplify $(m + 3)(m^2 - 2m + 2)$. Write the simplified polynomial in standard form.

   ⬚ 5 　⬚ 6 　⬚ m^3 　⬚ m^2 　⬚ $-m^2$
   ⬚ $2m$ 　⬚ $-4m$ 　⬚ $10m$

   ⬚ + ⬚ + ⬚ + ⬚

5. If $x + 5$ is a factor of $P(x) = x^3 + 4x^2 + 2x + 35$, select the two factors that express $P(x)$ as a product.

   ☐ A. $(x + 5)$
   ☐ B. $(x^2 + x + 7)$
   ☐ C. $(x^2 + x - 3)$
   ☐ D. $(x^2 - x + 7)$
   ☐ E. not a factor

6. Sketch a graph of the polynomial function $f(x) = x^3 + \frac{1}{2}x^2 - x - \frac{1}{2}$.

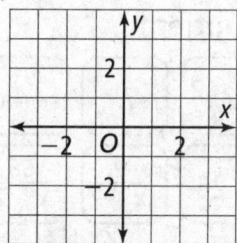

7. Teo cuts 4 squares with side length x in. from the corners of a 10-by-15-in. piece of paper. He folds the paper to make a tray that is x in. high. Complete the function for the tray's volume V.

   $V(x) = \boxed{} x^3 - \boxed{} x^2 + \boxed{} x$

8. Use polynomial identities to factor $64x^3 - 1$. Select all factors.

   ☐ A. $(4x + 1)$
   ☐ B. $(4x - 1)$
   ☐ C. $(16x^2 - 4x + 1)$
   ☐ D. $(16x^2 + 4x + 1)$
   ☐ E. $(4x^2 + 4x + 1)$

9. The volume of a cube with length x is $V(x) = x^3$. The volume of a sphere with radius $\frac{1}{2}x$ is shown in the graph. 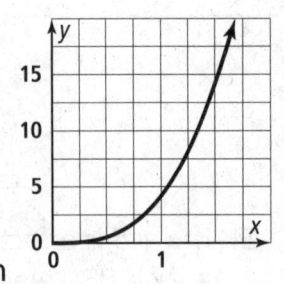
Over the interval [1, 2], which volume is increasing faster?

The volume of the ☐ sphere ☐ cube is increasing faster.

10. Use synthetic division to divide $x^4 - 5x^3 + 2x^2 + 6x + 6$ by $x - 2$. Complete the quotient.

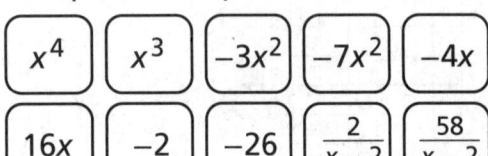

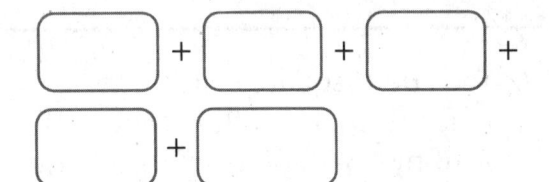

| x^4 | x^3 | $-3x^2$ | $-7x^2$ | $-4x$ |

| $16x$ | -2 | -26 | $\frac{2}{x-2}$ | $\frac{58}{x-2}$ |

☐ + ☐ + ☐ +

☐ + ☐

11. Describe the behavior at each zero of the function $f(x) = (x - 5)(x - 1)^2$.

Ⓐ The graph touches the x-axis at 1 and crosses the x-axis at 5.

Ⓑ The graph touches the x-axis at −5 and 1.

Ⓒ The graph touches the x-axis at −1 and crosses the x-axis at −5.

Ⓓ The graph crosses the x-axis at −1 and 11.

12. Identify the zeros of the function $f(x) = x(x - 1)(x + 2)$.

☐ , ☐ , ☐

13. Use the binomial theorem to expand $(3a + 3b)^4$. Select all of the terms below that are in the standard form of the expansion. (Not all terms are given.)

☐ A. $486a^2$

☐ B. $486a^2b^2$

☐ C. $81ab^3$

☐ D. $324a^3b$

☐ E. $324ab^3$

☐ F. $729a^2b^3$

14. How does the graph of the function $f(x) = 2x^3 - 1$ differ from the graph of its parent function? Select all the transformations.

☐ A. The graphs are the same.

☐ B. Subtracting 1 translates the graph right 3 units.

☐ C. The leading coefficient, 2, stretches the graph vertically.

☐ D. Subtracting 3 translates the graph left 3 units.

☐ E. Subtracting 1 translates the graph down 1 unit.

3 Performance Assessment Form A

Arthur wants to make a raised rectangular frame, shown below, to grow basil plants. The basil plants are transplanted, with their soil, from 2-in.-wide pots into the frame. The diagram at the right below shows a top-down view of the frame. Each circle represents a transplanted basil plant with its soil. Arthur will add more soil to the frame until the soil is $3x$ in. deep.

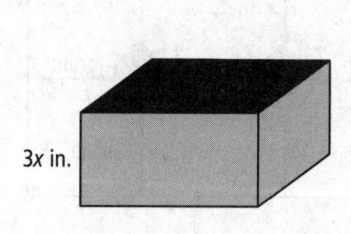

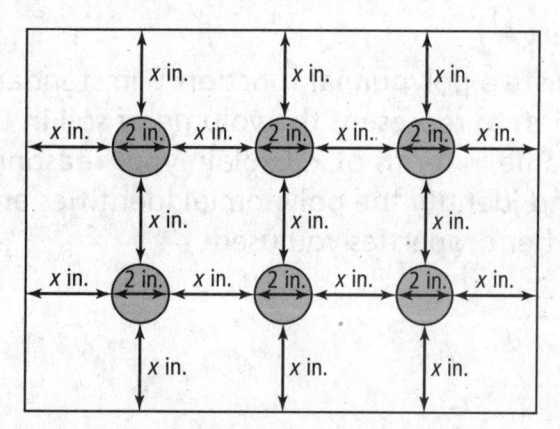

1. Write a polynomial function V to represent the volume of soil in the frame in terms of x. Explain.

2. Predict the end behavior of the graph of function V. Explain.

3. Graph function V on a graphing calculator. Identify the x-intercepts, and tell which, if any, of these intercepts has meaning in the context of the problem. Explain.

4. Assume that each basil plant needs 1300 cubic inches of soil. In that case, about how far apart should each basil plant be from the plants next to it? Explain.

5. Arthur plants 4 basil plants in a square frame like the one shown. The soil in this frame will be 2x in. deep.

   Part A
   Write a polynomial function V in standard form to represent the volume of soil in the frame in terms of x. Explain your reasoning, and identify the polynomial identities and other properties you used.

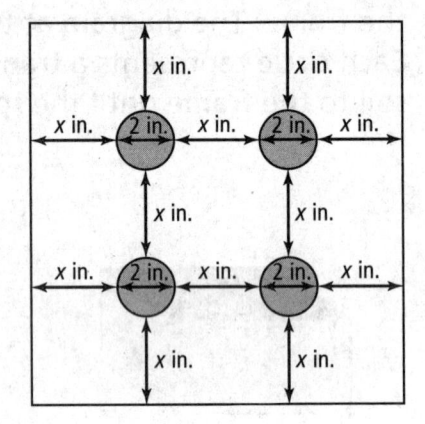

   Part B
   Given that each basil plant needs 1300 ft³ of soil, will neighboring plants in the square frame be closer to each other or farther apart than neighboring plants in the rectangular frame? Explain.

3 Performance Assessment Form B

Jamie is constructing shipping containers for a sporting goods store. The containers are to be rectangular prisms.

1. The first container Jamie constructs will be used to ship baseballs. It will have a width of x ft, a length of $(x + 8)$ ft and a height of $(x - 4)$ ft. Its volume will be 135 ft^3.

   Part A

   Write a function V for the volume of the container. Write an equation to find one possible width for the container.

   Part B

   Find the possible rational solutions of the equation from Part A. Are the solutions viable? Explain.

   Part C

   Are there viable irrational dimensions possible for width of the container? If so give the approximate dimensions for the container. Explain.

2. Jamie decides that the container described in the previous section will not be practical to handle because of its shape. He plans to build containers with sides which increase by 1 foot. Let x be the smallest dimension of the container.

Part A
Write and graph a function V for the volume of the new containers.

Part B
The volume of the container will be 150 ft³. Transform the graph of the function V from Part A, so that the x-intercept is the width of the container. Write a function f to represent this graph. How does the graph of this f relate to the graph of function V in Part A?

Part C
What are the dimensions of the container to the nearest tenth?

3. Jamie builds a second, larger container to ship basketballs. The volume V (in cubic feet) of the container is a function of some unknown value x, where $V(x) = x^3 + 11x^2 + 4x + 44$.

Jamie needs to ship boxes of basketballs in this larger container. These boxes haven't been constructed yet, but he knows that their volume in terms of x will be $(x - 2)$ ft³. How many basketball boxes, in terms of x, can Jamie fit in the new container? Explain your reasoning.

4 Readiness Assessment

1. What are the coordinates of the vertex of $y = (x-5)^2 - 2$?
   - Ⓐ (5, 2)
   - Ⓒ (5, −2)
   - Ⓑ (−5, 2)
   - Ⓓ (−5, −2)

2. What are the coordinates of the vertex of $y = -x^2 + 7$?
   - Ⓐ (0, 7)
   - Ⓒ (0, −7)
   - Ⓑ (7, 0)
   - Ⓓ (−7, 0)

3. What are the coordinates of the vertex of $y = -(x+1)^2$?

   (⬚ , ⬚)

4. How does the graph of $g(x) = -(x^3 - 4) + 6$ differ from the graph of $f(x) = x^3$?
   - Ⓐ g is a reflection of f.
   - Ⓑ g is stretched vertically.
   - Ⓒ g is translated left 4 units.
   - Ⓓ g is translated up 10 units.

5. Select all the statements that describe how the graph of $g(x) = 2x^3 + 8$ differs from the graph of $f(x) = x^3$?
   - ☐ A. g is a reflection of f.
   - ☐ B. g is stretched vertically.
   - ☐ C. g is translated right 8 units.
   - ☐ D. g is translated left 8 units.
   - ☐ E. g is translated up 8 units.
   - ☐ F. g is translated down 8 units.

6. What is the domain of the function?

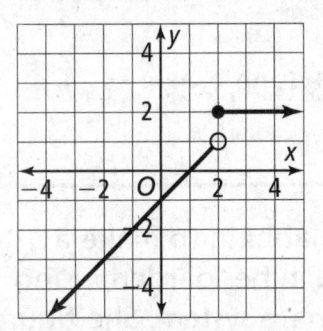

   - Ⓐ $(-\infty, 2), (2, \infty)$
   - Ⓑ $(-\infty, \infty)$
   - Ⓒ $(-\infty, 1), 2$
   - Ⓓ $(-\infty, 1), [2, \infty)$

7. Ashley has an after school job at the local library. She makes $8.50 an hour. She never works more than 15 hours in a week. The equation $y = 8.5x$ can be used to model this situation, where x represents the number of hours Ashley works in a week. What is the domain?
   - Ⓐ [0, 127.50]
   - Ⓑ $(-\infty, 15)$
   - Ⓒ $(-\infty, 8.5), (8.5, 15), (15, \infty)$
   - Ⓓ [0, 15]

8. What is the domain of $y = \frac{1}{5}\left|\frac{1}{2}x + 5\right| - 1$ if x represents the distance in miles and y represents gas mileage, in liters, of a 200-mile trip?

   Ⓐ $[0, \infty)$
   Ⓑ $[0, 200]$
   Ⓒ $(-\infty, 0], [200, \infty)$
   Ⓓ $(-\infty, \infty)$

9. Fatima is planning to make a flower bed in her garden, using the coordinate system. She figured out that the equation of the circumference of the flower bed is $y = -\sqrt{(x^2 - 9)}$. What is the domain of this function?

   Ⓐ $(-3, 3)$
   Ⓑ $[-3, 3]$
   Ⓒ $(-\infty, \infty)$
   Ⓓ $(-\infty, 3), (3, \infty)$

10. Add $(4x^5 - 3x^4 - 7x^3 + 7x^2) + (5x^4 + x^3 - 2x + 1)$.

11. Subtract $(2x^4 + x^3 - 3x + 8) - (x^4 - x^3 - 6x^2 + 7x)$.

12. Solve $3(x - 4) - 2(x - 7) = \frac{4(x + 2)}{5}$.

    Ⓐ $x = -2$
    Ⓑ $x = 138$
    Ⓒ $x = 6$
    Ⓓ $x = -1$

13. Solve $a(bx + 1) = b(x + a)$ for x.

    Ⓐ $x = \frac{ab}{ab - b}$
    Ⓑ $x = \frac{a}{b}$
    Ⓒ $x = \frac{ab - a}{ab - b}$
    Ⓓ $x = \frac{a}{a - 1}$

14. Solve $\frac{2}{3}\left(\frac{3}{5}x + 9\right) = \frac{1}{4}(2x + 40)$.

    $x = \boxed{}$

15. Factor $2x^2 + 13x - 24$.

    Ⓐ $2(x + 6)(x - 2)$
    Ⓑ $2(x - 3)(x + 4)$
    Ⓒ $(x + 8)(2x - 3)$
    Ⓓ $(x - 8)(2x + 3)$

16. Find the common zero between the functions $y = 3x^2 + 7x - 6$ and $y = 5x^2 + 14x - 3$.

    $x = \boxed{}$

17. Factor completely $4x^2 - 36$.

    Ⓐ $4(x - 3)(x + 3)$
    Ⓑ $(2x - 6)(2x - 6)$
    Ⓒ $2(x - 3)(x + 3)$
    Ⓓ $(2x - 6)(2x + 6)$

18. What are the solution(s) of $x^2 + 3x = -5(x + 3) - 1$?

    Ⓐ $x = 3, x = -3$
    Ⓑ $x = 4, x = -4$
    Ⓒ $x = 3$
    Ⓓ $x = -4$

4-1 Lesson Quiz

Inverse Variation and the Reciprocal Function

1. The chart represents an inverse variation. Find the value of p.

x	3	10	15	30
y	5	p	1	0.5

   p = ☐

2. Write an equation for the inverse variation represented by the table.

x	−3	−1	$\frac{1}{2}$	$\frac{2}{3}$
y	4	12	−24	−18

   Ⓐ $y = \frac{x}{-12}$ Ⓒ $y = \frac{12}{x}$

   Ⓑ $y = \frac{-x}{12}$ Ⓓ $y = \frac{-12}{x}$

3. Three students can wash a car in 16 minutes. If the time varies inversely with the number of students washing the car, how many minutes will it take two students to complete that same job?

   Ⓐ 20
   Ⓑ 22
   Ⓒ 24
   Ⓓ 26

4. What is the equation of the horizontal asymptote of the graph of $y = \frac{1}{x+5} - 4$?

   y = ☐

5. The graph of $y = \frac{1}{x}$ is translated 3 units up and 2 units to the left. What is an equation of the translated graph?

   Ⓐ $y = \frac{1}{x+2} + 3$
   Ⓑ $y = \frac{1}{x-2} + 3$
   Ⓒ $y = \frac{1}{x-3} + 2$
   Ⓓ $y = \frac{1}{x+3} - 2$

Name _____

4-2 Lesson Quiz

Graphing Rational Functions

1. Which equation is shown in the graph?

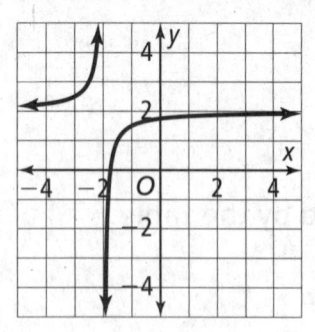

   Ⓐ $p(x) = 2 - \dfrac{1}{2x - 4}$

   Ⓑ $p(x) = 2 + \dfrac{1}{2x + 4}$

   Ⓒ $p(x) = 2 - \dfrac{1}{2x + 4}$

   Ⓓ $p(x) = 2 + \dfrac{1}{2x - 4}$

2. Identify any vertical asymptotes of the graph of $y = \dfrac{(x + 1)^2}{x^2 - 3x - 4}$.

   Ⓐ $x = -4$ and $x = -1$ Ⓒ $x = -1$ and $x = 4$

   Ⓑ $x = -1$ Ⓓ $x = 4$

3. What are the vertical and horizontal asymptotes of the graph of $f(x) = \dfrac{3 - 2x}{4 - 3x}$?

   Ⓐ $x = \dfrac{4}{3}$ and $y = \dfrac{2}{3}$ Ⓒ $x = \dfrac{3}{4}$ and $y = \dfrac{2}{3}$

   Ⓑ $x = \dfrac{2}{3}$ and $y = \dfrac{4}{3}$ Ⓓ $x = \dfrac{3}{2}$ and $y = \dfrac{4}{3}$

4. A scientist mixes x liters of water into a container that has 10 liters of a mixture that is 12% salt and 88% water. The function $f(x) = \dfrac{1.2}{x + 10}$ represents the percent of salt in the new mixture. How many liters of water must be added to make a 1% salt mixture?

   Water = ⬚ liters

5. The graph of which equation below has a horizontal asymptote at $y = -3$?

   Ⓐ $y = \dfrac{x - 3}{x + 1}$

   Ⓑ $y = \dfrac{x}{2 - 3x}$

   Ⓒ $y = \dfrac{1 - 3x}{2 + x}$

   Ⓓ $y = \dfrac{1 + 3x}{2 - 3x}$

enVision® Algebra 2 • Assessment Sourcebook

Name _____

4-3 Lesson Quiz
Multiplying and Dividing Rational Expressions

1. Simplify $\dfrac{x^2 - 2x}{(x-2)(x+3)}$.

   Ⓐ $\dfrac{1}{(x-2)(x+3)}$ Ⓒ $\dfrac{x}{x+3}$

   Ⓑ $\dfrac{2x}{x+3}$ Ⓓ $\dfrac{x-2}{x+3}$

2. Simplify $\dfrac{(x+5)(x^2-25)}{(x+5)^2(x-5)^2}$. What is the domain?

   Ⓐ $\dfrac{x+5}{x-5}$; all real numbers except -5 and 5

   Ⓑ $\dfrac{1}{x-5}$; all real numbers except -5 and 5

   Ⓒ $\dfrac{1}{x+5}$; all real numbers except 0

   Ⓓ $\dfrac{x-5}{x+5}$; all real numbers except -5

3. Simplify $\dfrac{ab^2 - a^2b}{ab} \cdot \dfrac{a^2b^2}{a-b}$.

   Ⓐ $-a^2b^2$; $a \neq 0$; $b \neq 0$

   Ⓑ $\dfrac{a^2b^2}{a-b}$; all real numbers except 0

   Ⓒ $\dfrac{b-a}{ab}$; $a \neq 0$ or b; $b \neq 0$ or a

   Ⓓ $ab^2 - a^2b$; $a \neq 0$ or b; $b \neq 0$ or a

4. What is the quotient of $\dfrac{9 - x^2}{3x}$ and $\dfrac{x^2 + 6x + 9}{3x}$?

   Ⓐ $\dfrac{x-3}{3-x}$ Ⓒ $\dfrac{3-x}{x+3}$

   Ⓑ $\dfrac{x-3}{x+3}$ Ⓓ $\dfrac{x+3}{x-3}$

5. The area of a rectangle is $\dfrac{x^2 - 4}{2x}$ in.² and its length is $\dfrac{(x+2)^2}{2}$ in. What is the width in inches?

   Ⓐ $\dfrac{x(x+2)}{x-2}$

   Ⓑ $\dfrac{x+2}{x(x+2)}$

   Ⓒ $\dfrac{x-2}{x(x-2)}$

   Ⓓ $\dfrac{x-2}{x(x+2)}$

enVision® Algebra 2 • Assessment Sourcebook

4-4 Lesson Quiz

Adding and Subtracting Rational Expressions

1. Add $\dfrac{5}{2x+1} + \dfrac{8}{4x+2}$, with $x \neq -\dfrac{1}{2}$.

   Ⓐ $\dfrac{9}{2x+1}$ 　　　Ⓒ $\dfrac{5x+8}{4x+2}$

   Ⓑ $\dfrac{13}{4x+2}$ 　　Ⓓ $\dfrac{18}{2x+1}$

2. What is the LCM for $(x+3)^2(x-2)$ and $(x+3)(x^2-16)$?

   Ⓐ $x+3$ 　　　Ⓒ $(x+3)^3(x-2)(x^2+16)$

   Ⓑ $(x+3)(x-2)(x-16)$ 　　Ⓓ $(x+3)^2(x-2)(x^2-16)$

3. Subtract $\dfrac{3}{x-1} - \dfrac{4}{x+3}$.

   Ⓐ $\dfrac{-x+13}{(x-1)(x+3)}$; $x \neq -3$ or 1 　　Ⓒ $\dfrac{7x+5}{(x-1)(x+3)}$; $x \neq -3$ or 1

   Ⓑ $\dfrac{-x+5}{(x-1)(x+3)}$; $x \neq -3$ or 1 　　Ⓓ $\dfrac{7x+13}{(x-1)(x+3)}$; $x \neq -3$ or 1

4. Simplify $\dfrac{\dfrac{1}{x} - \dfrac{1}{x+2}}{2}$.

   Ⓐ $\dfrac{1}{x+2}$; $x \neq -2$ 　　Ⓒ $\dfrac{1}{x(x+2)}$; $x \neq -2$ or 0

   Ⓑ $\dfrac{1}{x}$; $x \neq 0$ 　　Ⓓ $\dfrac{1}{x(x-2)}$; $x \neq 2$ or 0

5. The equation $r = \dfrac{1}{\dfrac{1}{r_1} + \dfrac{1}{r_2}}$ represents the total resistance, r, when two resistors whose resistances are r_1 and r_2 are connected in parallel. Find the total resistance when r_1 is x and r_2 is $x+1$.

   Ⓐ $\dfrac{1}{2x+1}$; $x \neq -1, -\dfrac{1}{2}$, or 0 　　Ⓒ $\dfrac{x(x+1)}{2x+1}$; $x \neq -1, -\dfrac{1}{2}$, or 0

   Ⓑ $2x+1$; $x \neq -1$ or 0 　　Ⓓ $\dfrac{2x+1}{x(x+1)}$; $x \neq -1$ or 0

Name _____

4-5 Lesson Quiz

Solving Rational Equations

1. Solve the equation $\frac{1}{2x-3} = 4$.

    Ⓐ $\frac{1}{2}$

    Ⓑ $\frac{8}{13}$

    Ⓒ $\frac{11}{8}$

    Ⓓ $\frac{13}{8}$

2. Aaron can paint a door in 6 hours, and Anna can do the same job in 3 hours. Working together, how many hours will it take them to paint a door?

    $h = \boxed{}$

3. Solve the equation $\frac{3}{x-1} = \frac{4}{2x+3}$.

    $x = \boxed{}$

4. Solve the equation $\frac{-3}{x+3} = \frac{x}{x+3} - \frac{x}{5}$; identify any extraneous solutions.

    solution: $x = \boxed{}$

    extraneous solution: $x = \boxed{}$

5. In still water, the speed of a boat is 10 mi/h. Camilla drives the boat 5 miles upstream and 5 miles back to her starting point in an hour and 20 minutes. What is the speed of the stream?

    Ⓐ 2 mi/h

    Ⓑ 3 mi/h

    Ⓒ 4 mi/h

    Ⓓ 5 mi/h

Name _____

4 Topic Assessment Form A

1. The width, y, of a rectangle with a fixed area varies inversely with its length, x. The width is 3 inches when the length is 14 inches. Find the width when the length is 30 inches.
   - Ⓐ 0.71 inches
   - Ⓒ 6.43 inches
   - Ⓑ 4.48 inches
   - Ⓓ 1.4 inches

2. What is the domain of the function $f(x) = \frac{x^2 - x - 2}{x^2 - 5x + 6}$?
   - Ⓐ All real numbers except 3
   - Ⓑ All real numbers except 2 and 3
   - Ⓒ All real numbers except −1 and 3
   - Ⓓ All real numbers except −1, 2, and 3

3. What are the horizontal and vertical asymptotes of the graph of $y = \frac{x^2 - 3x - 4}{1 - 3x - 4x^2}$?
   - Ⓐ $y = -\frac{1}{4}$ and $x = -\frac{1}{4}$
   - Ⓑ $y = -\frac{1}{4}$ and $x = \frac{1}{4}$
   - Ⓒ $y = \frac{1}{4}$, $x = 1$, and $x = \frac{1}{4}$
   - Ⓓ $y = -\frac{1}{4}$, $x = -1$, and $x = \frac{1}{4}$

4. Simplify $\frac{2x}{x-3} - \frac{-6}{3-x}$. What are the restrictions on the domain of the expression?

   ◯

   The domain is $\{x | x \neq \bigcirc \}$.

5. Describe the transformations needed to translate the graph of $y = \frac{1}{x}$ to the graph of $y = \frac{1}{x+3} - 4$.
   - Ⓐ to the right 3 and up 4
   - Ⓑ to the left 3 and up 4
   - Ⓒ to the right 3 and down 4
   - Ⓓ to the left 3 and down 4

6. Solve $\frac{10}{x^2 - 2x} = \frac{5}{x-2} - \frac{3}{x}$.
   - Ⓐ $x = 0$
   - Ⓒ $x = 2$
   - Ⓑ $x = 0$ and 2
   - Ⓓ no solution

7. Luke and Nora can peel 20 carrots in 6 min, working together. Luke can peel 5 carrots in 2 min, working alone. How many minutes would it take Nora to peel 10 carrots, working alone?
   - Ⓐ 15
   - Ⓑ 12
   - Ⓒ 8
   - Ⓓ 4

8. What is the remainder when $5x^3 - 11x^2 + 5x + 2$ is divided by $5x - 4$?
   - Ⓐ $-\frac{3}{5}$
   - Ⓑ $\frac{38}{25}$
   - Ⓒ $\frac{2}{5}$
   - Ⓓ $-\frac{22}{5}$

9. Solve $\frac{3(1+x)}{4x} = 1 - \frac{1}{x}$. $x = \bigcirc$

10. What is the sum $\frac{1}{x+3} + \frac{-6}{x^2 - 9}$?
    - Ⓐ $\frac{-6}{x^2 + x - 12}$
    - Ⓑ $\frac{1}{x^2 + x + 2}$
    - Ⓒ $\frac{x-9}{x^2-9}$
    - Ⓓ $\frac{-5}{x+3}$

11. Solve $\frac{1}{3} = \frac{x^2 + 2x - 3}{3x^2 - 2x - 1}$.
   - Ⓐ $\frac{8}{3}$
   - Ⓑ $-\frac{1}{3}$
   - Ⓒ 1
   - Ⓓ no solution

12. What are the horizontal and vertical asymptotes of the graph of $y = \frac{x+3}{x^4 - 81}$?
   - Ⓐ $y = 0; x = 3$
   - Ⓑ $y = 0; x = -3$ and $x = 3$
   - Ⓒ $y = 1; x = 9$
   - Ⓓ $y = 1; x = -9$

13. It takes 2 h for Faucet A to fill a tank, and it takes Faucet B 3 h. How many hours will it take the two faucets to fill the tank together?
   - Ⓐ 0.2
   - Ⓑ 1.2
   - Ⓒ 0.8
   - Ⓓ 1.8

14. The graph of $xy = 6$ is translated up 3 units and to the right 2 units. Select all the possible equations for the translated graph.
   - ☐ A. $y = 3 + \frac{6}{x-2}$
   - ☐ B. $y = \frac{3x}{x-2}$
   - ☐ C. $(x-2)(y-3) = 6$
   - ☐ D. $y = \frac{3}{x-2}$
   - ☐ E. $(y-2)(x-3) = 6$

15. If $a = \frac{1}{x} + \frac{1}{y}$, what is the value of $\frac{1}{a}$?
   - Ⓐ $x + y$
   - Ⓑ $\frac{x+y}{xy}$
   - Ⓒ $\frac{xy}{x+y}$
   - Ⓓ $x^2 + y^2$

16. What are the horizontal and vertical asymptotes of the graph of $y = \frac{5x+1}{2x-5}$?
   - Ⓐ $y = 2.5; x = 2.5$
   - Ⓑ $y = 2.5; x = -2.5$
   - Ⓒ $y = 0; x = 2.5$
   - Ⓓ $y = 0; x = -2.5$

17. Solve $\frac{1}{x(x-3)} = \frac{2}{x-3} + \frac{3}{x}$.
   - Ⓐ -2
   - Ⓑ 2
   - Ⓒ 1
   - Ⓓ -3

18. Select all the functions whose graphs have a horizontal asymptote at $y = 7$.
   - ☐ A. $y = \frac{7}{x-2}$
   - ☐ B. $y = \frac{7x^2 + 1}{x^2 + 7}$
   - ☐ C. $y = 7 + \frac{1}{x}$
   - ☐ D. $y = \frac{7x+3}{x^2+1}$
   - ☐ E. $y = \frac{2x-1}{x^2-49}$

19. A rectangle has area $x^3 + 3x^2 - 18x$ in.² and width $x + 6$ in. What is the length in inches?
   - Ⓐ $x^2 + 3x$
   - Ⓑ $x^2 + 6x$
   - Ⓒ $x^2 - 3x$
   - Ⓓ $x^2 - 6x$

Name _____

4 Topic Assessment Form B

1. The width, y, of a rectangle with a fixed area varies inversely with its length, x. The width is 4 inches when the length is 18 inches. Find the width when the length is 40 inches.
   - Ⓐ 0.56 inches
   - Ⓒ 10.08 inches
   - Ⓑ 8.9 inches
   - Ⓓ 1.8 inches

2. What is the domain of the function $f(x) = \frac{x^2 - x - 2}{x^4 - 81}$?
   - Ⓐ All real numbers except 3
   - Ⓑ All real numbers except −1 and 3
   - Ⓒ All real numbers except −3 and 3
   - Ⓓ All real numbers except −3, 1, and 3

3. What are the horizontal and vertical asymptotes of the graph of $y = \frac{x^2 - 3x - 4}{3 - x^2}$?
   - Ⓐ $y = -1; x = \pm\sqrt{3}$
   - Ⓑ $y = 1; x = \pm\sqrt{3}$
   - Ⓒ $y = -1; x = 1$ and $x = \sqrt{3}$
   - Ⓓ $y = -1; x = 1$ and $x = -\sqrt{3}$

4. Simplify $\frac{1}{x-y} - \frac{-6}{y-x}$. What are the any restrictions on the domain of the expression?

   ▢

   The domain is $\{x | x \neq$ ▢ $\}$.

5. Describe the transformations needed to translate the graph of $y = \frac{1}{x}$ to the graph of $y = 2 + \frac{1}{x-5}$.
   - Ⓐ to the left 5 and up 2
   - Ⓑ to the left 2 and down 5
   - Ⓒ to the right 2 and down 5
   - Ⓓ to the right 5 and up 2

6. Solve $\frac{2x+4}{x^2+4x+3} = \frac{1}{x+1} + \frac{1}{x+3}$.
   - Ⓐ no solution
   - Ⓑ $x = 2$
   - Ⓒ $x = 1$ and 2
   - Ⓓ all values of x, $x \neq -1$ and $x \neq -3$

7. Two robots can do a task in 5 min, working together. The first robot, working alone, can do the task in 15 min. How many minutes will it take the second robot, working alone, to do the task?
   - Ⓐ 10   Ⓑ 7.5   Ⓒ 5   Ⓓ 2

8. What is the remainder when $4x^4 - 10x^2 + 2x + 1$ is divided by $4x - 1$?
   - Ⓐ $-\frac{1}{2}$ Ⓑ 4   Ⓒ $\frac{57}{64}$ Ⓓ $-\frac{18}{37}$

9. Solve $\frac{2(1-x)}{3x} = 1 - \frac{3}{x}$.

   $x =$ ▢

enVision® Algebra 2   Assessment Sourcebook

10. What is the sum $\frac{1}{x-4} + \frac{-8}{x^2-16}$?

  (A) $\frac{-8}{x^2+x-20}$

  (B) $\frac{-7}{x+4}$

  (C) $\frac{1}{x^2+x+2}$

  (D) $\frac{1}{x+4}$

11. Solve $x = \frac{2x^2+x-7}{2x+8}$.

  (A) 1
  (B) $\frac{1}{2}$
  (C) -1
  (D) no solution

12. What are the horizontal and vertical asymptotes of the graph of $y = \frac{x^4+3}{x^4+2x^2-3}$?

  (A) $y = 1; x = \pm 1$
  (B) $y = 1; x = \pm 3$
  (C) $y = 0; x = 1$
  (D) $y = 0; x = -1$

13. It takes 4 h for Faucet A to fill a tank, and it takes Faucet B 6 h. How many hours will it take the two faucets to fill the tank together?

  (A) 1.4 (B) 2.4 (C) 2.0 (D) 5.0

14. The graph of $xy = 6$ is translated up 2 units and to the left 2 units. Select all the possible equations for the translated graph.

  ☐ A. $y = 2 + \frac{6}{x+2}$
  ☐ B. $\frac{y}{2} = \frac{x+5}{x+2}$
  ☐ C. $y = \frac{2x+10}{x+2}$
  ☐ D. $y = \frac{6x+10}{x-2}$
  ☐ E. $y = 4 + \frac{4}{x-2}$

15. If $a = \frac{2}{x} + \frac{1}{y}$, what is the value of $\frac{1}{a}$?

  (A) $\frac{2y+x}{xy}$
  (B) $\frac{x+2y}{2xy}$
  (C) $\frac{xy}{x+2y}$
  (D) $x + 2y$

16. What are the horizontal and vertical asymptotes of the graph of $y = \frac{-x+3}{x-8}$?

  (A) $y = -1; x = 8$
  (B) $y = -1; x = -8$
  (C) $y = 1; x = 8$
  (D) $y = 1; x = -8$

17. Solve $\frac{x^2+x-4}{x-2} = x - \frac{1}{x-2}$.

  (A) -2
  (B) 1
  (C) -1
  (D) 3

18. Select all the functions whose graphs have a horizontal asymptote at $y = \frac{2}{3}$.

  ☐ A. $y = \frac{2}{3x-1}$
  ☐ B. $y = \frac{2x^2+1}{3x^2-2}$
  ☐ C. $y = \frac{2}{3} + \frac{1}{x}$
  ☐ D. $y = \frac{2x-3}{3x^2+1}$
  ☐ E. $y = 3 + \frac{3}{2x}$

19. A rectangle has area $x^3 - 15x - 4$ cm^2 and width $x - 4$ cm. What is the length in centimeters?

  (A) $x^2 + 4x$
  (B) $x^2 - 4x + 2$
  (C) $x^2 + 4x + 1$
  (D) $x^2 + 1$

Name _____

4 Performance Assessment Form A

enVision Algebra 2
SavvasRealize.com

Modern scuba-diving equipment allows divers to stay underwater for long periods of time. Underwater instructors use mathematics to explore safety issues related to scuba diving. An instructor gives scuba-diving students the handout shown at the right.

Divers' Information

- At the water's surface, the air around a diver exerts 1 atmosphere (atm) of pressure.
- Underwater, the pressure P (atm) around the diver increases. It varies with the diver's depth d, in feet, according to the equation $P = \frac{d}{33} + 1$.
- The volume V of a given amount of air varies inversely with the pressure P around it, so the volume of air in the diver's lungs increases as she ascends.

1. Use the information in the handout.

   Part A

   Suppose that a certain amount of air takes up a volume of 4 qt in a diver's lungs at a depth of 66 ft, where the pressure is 3 atm. As the diver changes depth, the volume taken up by this fixed amount of air changes. Write an equation that defines the volume V, in quarts, taken up by that amount of air at a given depth d, in feet. Explain.

   Part B

   Complete the table and graph below to show how the volume of the given amount of air in the diver's lungs varies with depth. What are the asymptote(s) of your graph, and how do they apply to the real-world situation?

Depth (ft)	Volume (qt)
0	
33	
66	
99	
132	
165	

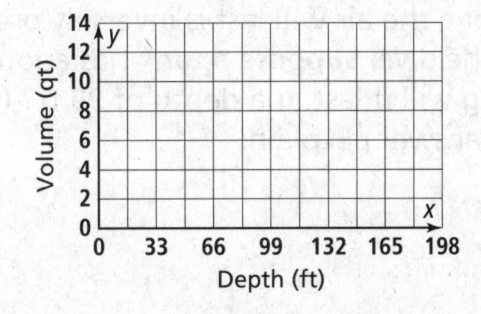

2. The volume of air in a diver's lungs increases as the diver resurfaces. This expansion can cause damage to the membranes of the lungs.

   Part A

   A diver fills her lungs with 4 qt of air at a depth of 66 ft. How many quarts of air will she need to exhale during her ascent to still have 4 qt of air in her lungs when she reaches the surface? Explain.

   Part B

   Suppose the situation in Item 1 changes. The air that occupied a certain volume, V, when the diver was at a certain depth, d, now occupies that volume when she is 5 ft deeper. How does this affect the graph and the values for V in Part B of Item 1? Explain.

   Part C

   Use the information from the graph and table in Item 1 to write an explanation for the reason that beginning divers are told, "Don't hold your breath!"

3. At greater depths, a diver uses the air in the tank more quickly. Assume that the amount of time the air will last is inversely proportional to the pressure at the depth of the dive. Suppose a tank has enough air to last 60 min at the surface. How long will it last at a depth of 99 ft? (*Hint*: Determine P in terms of t to find your answer.) Explain.

4 Performance Assessment Form B

Engineers study different shapes for storage tanks for liquid hydrogen, an important component of rocket fuel. One engineer is testing both the spherical and cylindrical designs below. Both shapes have the same radius, x. The height of the cylinder is $2x^2$.

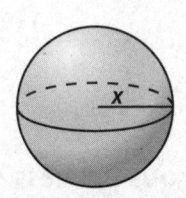

Surface area: $4\pi x^2$
Volume: $\frac{4}{3}\pi x^3$

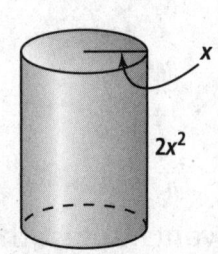

Surface area: $2\pi x^2 + 4\pi x^3$
Volume: $2\pi x^4$

1. The engineer wants to choose the tank that has the least ratio of surface area to volume.

   Part A

   Write a function f to represent the ratio of surface area to volume for the sphere. Then write a function g to represent the ratio of surface area to volume for the cylinder. Simplify the expression for each function. Explain.

   Part B

   Use technology to graph the functions f and g you found in Part A. Use the graph to find the x-value where the two designs have the same surface area to volume ratio.

Part C

Use algebra to confirm the x-value you found in Part B. For which value(s) of x would the engineer choose the spherical design? The cylindrical design? Explain.

2. An engineer wants to test the complex and dangerous process of filling and emptying a tank of liquid hydrogen. The tank has a volume of 400,000 cm³. The tank can be filled 5,000 cm³ per hour faster than it can be emptied.

Part A

Suppose r is the rate at which this tank is filled in thousands of cubic centimeters per hour. Write an equation for t, the total number of hours it takes to fill and empty this tank, in terms of r. Simplify the expression and explain.

Part B

Use technology to graph the equation from Part A to find the fill rate that would allow you to fill and empty the tank in 100 hours. Check for extraneous solutions, and explain your work. Round to the nearest tenth.

Benchmark Assessment 2

Name _____

1. A preschool has 100 feet of fencing to enclose 3 sides of a rectangular playground. The fourth side is formed by a wall of the school. The function $A(x) = 100x - 2x^2$ represents the possible area of the playground with side length x feet. Which range is appropriate for this situation?

   Ⓐ $0 < A < 1250$
   Ⓑ $0 < A \leq 25$
   Ⓒ $0 < A \leq 1250$
   Ⓓ $0 < A < 25$

2. Over what interval is the graph of $y = |x + 6|$ decreasing?

   Ⓐ $(-\infty, -6)$ Ⓒ $(-6, \infty)$
   Ⓑ $(-\infty, 6)$ Ⓓ $(6, \infty)$

3. How many terms are in this finite arithmetic sequence?

   6, 14, 22, 30, … 62

   Ⓐ 6   Ⓒ 8
   Ⓑ 7   Ⓓ 9

4. A teacher uses a strong slingshot to release an object from the roof of the school. The function $a(t) = -16t^2 + 128t + 50$ gives the approximate altitude, in feet, of the object t seconds after it is released. How long will it be before the object hits the ground? Round to the nearest second.

   ☐ seconds

5. Solve the system.

   $y = -x + 9$
   $y = x^2 + 3$

   Select all points that are a solution to the system.

   ☐ A. $(-3, 12)$
   ☐ B. $(-3, 0)$
   ☐ C. $(2, 7)$
   ☐ D. $(2, 0)$
   ☐ E. $(-2, 7)$
   ☐ F. $(3, 6)$

6. Emaan simplified a system of equations and obtained the following result.

   $x - 2y = 7$
   $5x - 10y = 35$

   How many solutions does Emaan's system of equations have?

   Ⓐ 0
   Ⓑ 1
   Ⓒ 2
   Ⓓ infinitely many

7. Simplify $(2 - 3i)(1 + 5i) - 3(-2 + i)$.

   ☐ + ☐ i

8. Solve $0 = x^2 + 16x + 128$ by completing the square.
   - Ⓐ $x = 8 + 8i$ and $x = 8 - 8i$
   - Ⓑ $x = -8 + 8i$ and $x = -8 - 8i$
   - Ⓒ $x = -8 + i\sqrt{2}$ and $x = -8 - i\sqrt{2}$
   - Ⓓ $x = -16 + i\sqrt{2}$ and $x = -16 - i\sqrt{2}$

9. A soccer ball is kicked into the air from a 22-m-high hill. The equation $h(t) = -5t^2 + 10t + 22$ gives the height h, in m, of the ball t seconds after it is kicked.

   Part A

   Complete the equation that can be used to tell if the ball reaches a height of 35 m.

   $\boxed{}t^2 + \boxed{}t + \boxed{} = \boxed{}$

   Part B

   Does the ball reach a height of 35 m? Complete the sentence.

   The ball ☐ does / ☐ does not reach a height of 35 m because the equation from Part A ☐ does / ☐ does not have a solution.

10. Determine the number of real solutions of the system
    $\begin{cases} y = 2x^2 + 1 \\ y = -x \end{cases}$
    - Ⓐ more than 2
    - Ⓑ 2
    - Ⓒ 1
    - Ⓓ 0

11. Consider the polynomial function $f(x) = x^3 + 2x^2 + x^4 - 8 + 4x$. Select all the statements that are true about the function.
    - ☐ A. The degree of the polynomial is 3.
    - ☐ B. Written in standard form the function is $f(x) = x^4 + x^3 + 2x^2 + 4x - 8$.
    - ☐ C. As x increases or decreases, $f(x)$ increases.
    - ☐ D. The polynomial function has a maximum.
    - ☐ E. The x-intercepts are at $x = -1$ and $x = 2$.
    - ☐ F. The function is negative over the interval $(-2, 1)$.

12. Use the choices provided to simplify $(24x^3 - 16x^2) - (6x^3 + 18x^2 - 14)$.

    $\boxed{18x^3}$ $\boxed{30x^3}$ $\boxed{34x^2}$ $\boxed{2x^2}$
    $\boxed{-34x^2}$ $\boxed{-14}$ $\boxed{14}$

    $\boxed{} + \boxed{} + \boxed{}$

13. Use a graph of the polynomial function $f(x) = x^3 - 6x^2 + 3x + 10$ to complete the sentences.

    $\boxed{\text{increasing}}$ $\boxed{\text{decreasing}}$
    $\boxed{\text{positive}}$ $\boxed{\text{negative}}$

    f is $\boxed{}$ on the intervals $(-\infty, 0.27)$ and $(3.73, \infty)$.

    f is $\boxed{}$ on the intervals $(-1, 2)$ and $(5, \infty)$.

    f is $\boxed{}$ on the intervals $(-\infty, -1)$ and $(2, 5)$.

14. An artist cuts 4 squares with side length x ft from the corners of a 12 ft-by-18 ft piece of sheet metal. She bends up the sides and welds the corners to form a rectangular garden fountain that is x ft high. Write and simplify a function V for the volume of the fountain in terms of x.

    $V(x) = \boxed{}x^3 + \boxed{}x^2 + \boxed{}x$

15. Use polynomial identities to factor $64x^9 - 125y^6$.

    Ⓐ $(4x^2 + 5y)(16x^4 + 20x^2y + 25y^2)$
    Ⓑ $(4x^2 - 5y)(16x^4 - 20x^2y + 25y^2)$
    Ⓒ $(4x^3 + 5y^2)(16x^6 - 20x^3y^2 + 25y^4)$
    Ⓓ $(4x^3 - 5y^2)(16x^6 + 20x^3y^2 + 25y^4)$

16. Use the Binomial Theorem to expand $(2a + 2b)^6$. What is the third term of the expansion?

    $\boxed{}a^{\boxed{}}b^{\boxed{}}$

17. The volume of a cube with side length x is $V(x) = x^3$. The volume of a cylinder with radius x and height 0.5x is shown in the graph. Over the interval [1, 1.25], which volume is increasing faster?

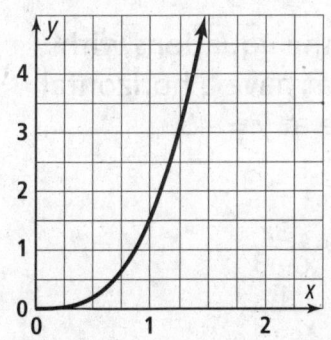

    The volume of the ☐ cylinder ☐ cube is increasing faster.

18. Use synthetic division to divide $6x^3 - 10x^2 + 20$ by $x + 1$.

    quotient:

    $\boxed{}x^2 + \boxed{}x + \boxed{}$

    remainder: $\boxed{}$

19. Find the zeros of the function $f(x) = x^3 - 8x^2 + 9x + 18$, and describe the behavior of the graph at each zero.

    Ⓐ The graph crosses the x-axis at −1, 3, and 6.
    Ⓑ The graph touches the x-axis at −1 and crosses the x-axis at −3 and 6.
    Ⓒ The graph crosses the x-axis at −1, 3, and 9.
    Ⓓ The graph touches the x-axis at −3 and −1 and crosses the x-axis at 6.

20. P varies inversely with x. If P = 14 when x = 16, find the value of P when x = 21.

    Ⓐ 224
    Ⓑ $\frac{21}{16}$
    Ⓒ $\frac{32}{3}$
    Ⓓ 4704

21. Select the domain of the function $f(x) = \frac{2x^2 - 2x - 4}{x^2 + 2x - 24}$.

    Ⓐ $x \neq -6, 4$
    Ⓑ $x \neq -4, 6$
    Ⓒ $x \neq -2, 1$
    Ⓓ $x \neq -1, 2$

22. Let $f(x) = \frac{x-1}{x+2}$ and $g(x) = \frac{x+2}{x-2}$.

    Part A

    What is $(fg)(x)$ in simplest form?

    - $x - 1$
    - $x - 2$
    - $x^2 + x - 2$
    - $x^2 - 2$
    - $x^2 - 4$

    ☐
    ───
    ☐

    Part B

    What is $(f + g)(x)$ in simplest form?

    - $2x + 1$
    - $x + 1$
    - $2x^2 + x + 6$
    - $2x^2 + 4$
    - $x^2 - 4$

    ☐
    ───
    ☐

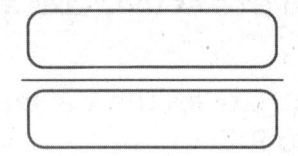

23. It takes 24 h to fill a large basin with two hoses. The water flows 4 times as fast in one hose as in the other. How long will it take the slower hose to fill the basin if the faster hose is not functioning?

    Ⓐ 60 h   Ⓒ 72 h
    Ⓑ 96 h   Ⓓ 120 h

24. What is the remainder when $6x + 12$ is divided by $2x - 8$?

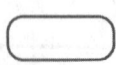

    ☐

25. Solve $2x + \frac{12}{x-3} = \frac{4x}{x-3}$.

    Ⓐ 2
    Ⓑ 2, 3
    Ⓒ 2, −3
    Ⓓ $\frac{1}{2}$

26. Is $x - 2$ a factor of the polynomial $P(x) = x^5 - 5x^3 + 5x^2 - x - 10$? Explain.

    Ⓐ Yes, because $P(-2) = 0$.
    Ⓑ Yes, because $P(2) = 0$.
    Ⓒ No, because $P(-2) \neq 0$.
    Ⓓ No, because $P(2) \neq 0$.

27. What are the horizontal and vertical asymptotes of the graph of $y = \frac{x - 10}{x^3 - 125}$?

    Ⓐ $y = 10; x = 125$ Ⓒ $y = 0; x = 5$
    Ⓑ $y = 10; x = 5$ Ⓓ $y = 0; x = 10$

28. The graph of $xy = 12$ is translated down 6 units and left 4 units. Which equation could represent the translated graph?

    Ⓐ $y = 6 + \frac{12}{x - 4}$ Ⓒ $y = \frac{-6 - 12x}{x + 4}$
    Ⓑ $y = -6 + \frac{12}{x + 4}$ Ⓓ $y = \frac{12}{x} + 10$

29. If $b = \frac{3}{x} + \frac{3}{y}$, what is the value of $\frac{1}{b}$?

    Ⓐ $\frac{x + y}{3y + 3x}$ Ⓒ $\frac{xy}{3y + 3x}$
    Ⓑ $\frac{3xy}{y + x}$ Ⓓ $\frac{xy}{3y + x}$

30. Select all the equations with graphs that have a horizontal asymptote at $y = -3$.

    ☐ A. $y = \frac{1}{x} - 3$
    ☐ B. $y = \frac{-3x}{x - 3}$
    ☐ C. $y = \frac{1}{x - 3}$
    ☐ D. $y = \frac{3}{x + 3}$
    ☐ E. $y = \frac{3x}{x + 3}$

5 Readiness Assessment

1. Select all the expressions that are equivalent to 9.
   - ☐ A. 3^2
   - ☐ B. $4 - \sqrt[3]{-125}$
   - ☐ C. $\sqrt{-81}$
   - ☐ D. $\sqrt{81}$
   - ☐ E. $-3(-27)^{\frac{1}{3}}$

2. If the area of a square is represented by $A = x^2 - 144$, which of the following would also represent this area?
   - Ⓐ $(x - 12)^2$
   - Ⓑ $(x + 12)^2$
   - Ⓒ $(x + \sqrt{144})(x - \sqrt{144})$
   - Ⓓ $(x + \sqrt{144})(x + \sqrt{-144})$

3. What are all the real and complex solutions of the equation $x^3 - x^2 - 6x = 0$?
   - Ⓐ $\{0\}$
   - Ⓑ $\{0, 6i, -6i\}$
   - Ⓒ $\{0, \frac{-1 \pm i\sqrt{23}}{2}\}$
   - Ⓓ $\{-2, 0, 3\}$

4. What is the greatest number of real and complex solutions that the equation $81x^4 - 16 = 0$ can have?
   - Ⓐ 1
   - Ⓑ 2
   - Ⓒ 3
   - Ⓓ 4

5. Multiply and simplify $\sqrt{8}(\sqrt{2} + 2)$.
   - Ⓐ 6
   - Ⓑ $\sqrt{32}$
   - Ⓒ $4\sqrt{2}$
   - Ⓓ $4 + 4\sqrt{2}$

6. Which of the following is equivalent to 2^5?
   - Ⓐ 64
   - Ⓑ $(2^2)^3$
   - Ⓒ $2^3 + 2^2$
   - Ⓓ $(2^7)(2^{-2})$

7. Which of the following is equivalent to 3^2?
   - Ⓐ $\frac{3}{3^{-1}}$
   - Ⓑ $\frac{3^5}{3^{-3}}$
   - Ⓒ 27
   - Ⓓ $3^5 - 3^3$

8. Use an exponent to complete the equation: $(3^2)(4^2) = (3 \cdot 4)^{\square}$

9. Which of the following is equivalent to $\frac{4^{-4} \cdot (2^3)^2}{4^{-2} \cdot 2^2}$?
   - Ⓐ 256
   - Ⓑ 2^5
   - Ⓒ 2^{-1}
   - Ⓓ 2^0

10. Sketch the graph of $g(x) = (x - 2)^2 + 4$.

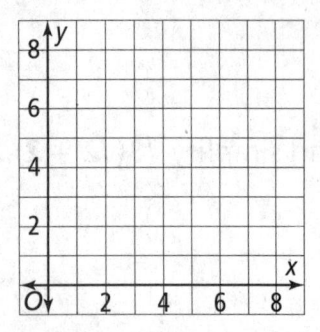

11. How does the graph of $g(x) = (x - 3)^3 - 2$ differ from the graph of $f(x) = x^3$?

Ⓐ g is shifted 3 units right and 2 units up.

Ⓑ g is shifted 3 units right and 2 units down.

Ⓒ g is reflected across the y-axis.

Ⓓ g is rotated 90° clockwise.

12. Which function represents the quadratic function $f(x) = x^2$ after a shift of 2 units to the right and a vertical stretch by a factor of 2?

Ⓐ $g(x) = (2x - 2)^2$

Ⓑ $g(x) = 2x^2 + 2$

Ⓒ $g(x) = 2(x - 2)^2$

Ⓓ $g(x) = (\frac{1}{2}x - 2)^2$

13. Sketch and label the graph of $y = (x - 3)^2$ and the graph of its reflection across the x-axis.

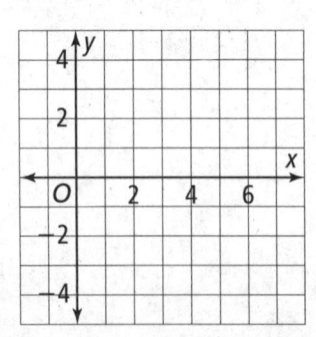

14. Solve the system by graphing.

$y + 2 = \frac{1}{2}(x - 1)^2$

$y = -x + 3$

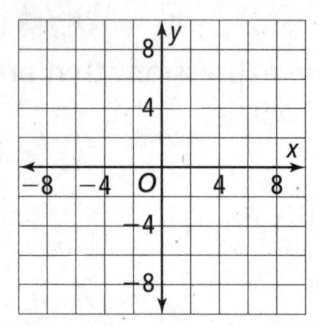

(☐ , ☐) and (☐ , ☐)

15. Find the product $(x^2 + 4)(x^4 - 4x^2 + 16)$.

Ⓐ $x^6 - 6x - 9$

Ⓑ $x^8 + 4x - 1$

Ⓒ $x^6 + 64$

Ⓓ $x^6 - 64$

16. Find $(2 + 5x)^2$.

☐ + ☐ x + ☐ x^2

17. Identify the function with the range $\{y \mid y \leq -2\}$.

Ⓐ $f(x) = -(x - 2)^2 + 2$

Ⓑ $f(x) = -x^2 + 2$

Ⓒ $f(x) = x^2 - 4x + 2$

Ⓓ $f(x) = -x^2 + 4x - 6$

18. The function $f(x) = x^2 - 3x - 10$ represents the area of a rectangle with length x. Identify the domain and range of f.

Ⓐ Domain: All real numbers
Range: $\{y \mid y \geq -12.25\}$

Ⓑ Domain: $\{x \mid x > 0\}$
Range: $\{y \mid y > -12.25\}$

Ⓒ Domain: $\{x \mid x > 5\}$
Range: $\{y \mid y > 0\}$

Ⓓ Domain: Positive real numbers
Range: Positive real numbers

5-1 Lesson Quiz

nth Roots, Radicals, and Rational Exponents

1. What are the real fourth roots of 256?

   Real fourth roots ☐ and ☐

2. Select all expressions that are equivalent to $x^{\frac{3}{4}}$.

   ☐ A. $(x^3)^{\frac{1}{4}}$
   ☐ B. $x^{\frac{8}{6}}$
   ☐ C. $(x^{\frac{1}{4}})^{\frac{2}{4}}$
   ☐ D. $(x^{\frac{1}{4}})^3$
   ☐ E. $\sqrt[3]{x^4}$
   ☐ F. $\sqrt[4]{x^3}$

3. Explain what $243^{\frac{3}{5}}$ means, then evaluate it.

   $243^{\frac{3}{5}}$ is the
   ☐ square
   ☐ cube
   ☐ fourth
   ☐ fifth
   root of 243
   ☐ squared
   ☐ cubed
   ☐ to the fourth power
   ☐ to the fifth power
   .

   Its value is
   ☐ 3
   ☐ 9
   ☐ 27
   ☐ 81
   .

4. Simplify the expression $\sqrt[4]{81m^{12}n^4}$. Assume all variables are positive.

   Ⓐ $9m^3n$
   Ⓑ $9m^6n^2$
   Ⓒ $3m^3n$
   Ⓓ $3m^8$

5. Solve the equation $-4x^3 = 32$.

   $x = $ ☐

Name _____

5-2 Lesson Quiz

Properties of Exponents and Radicals

1. Rewrite the expression $\sqrt[3]{81y^7}$ using the properties of exponents.

    Ⓐ $9y^3\sqrt{y}$

    Ⓑ $3y^2$

    Ⓒ $3y^2\sqrt[3]{3y}$

    Ⓓ The expression cannot be simplified.

2. What is $\sqrt[4]{\dfrac{3a^2}{8b^7}}$ in reduced radical form?

    Ⓐ $\dfrac{\sqrt[4]{6a^2b}}{2b^2}$

    Ⓑ $\dfrac{\sqrt[4]{24a^2b^7}}{8b^7}$

    Ⓒ $\dfrac{a\sqrt[4]{24ab^7}}{8b^7}$

    Ⓓ $\dfrac{a\sqrt[4]{9b}}{2b^2\sqrt[4]{4}}$

3. What is the reduced radical form of $\sqrt[3]{250} + \sqrt[3]{54} + \sqrt{72}$?

    Ⓐ $\sqrt[3]{250} + \sqrt[3]{54} + \sqrt{72}$

    Ⓑ $8\sqrt[3]{2} + 6\sqrt{2}$

    Ⓒ $14\sqrt[3]{2}$

    Ⓓ $5\sqrt{10} + 3\sqrt{6} + 6\sqrt{2}$

4. Multiply $(2\sqrt{x} + 3)(2\sqrt{x} - 3)$.

    ☐ $x +$ ☐

5. What is $\dfrac{7 - \sqrt{98}}{3 - \sqrt{2}}$ in reduced radical form?

    Ⓐ $-\sqrt{2}$

    Ⓑ $7\sqrt{2}$

    Ⓒ $1 - 2\sqrt{2}$

    Ⓓ $9\dfrac{1}{3}$

Name _____

5-3 Lesson Quiz

Graphing Radical Functions

1. Complete the sentence to describe the function $f(x) = \sqrt{x+2}$. Consider graphing the function first.

   The domain of $f(x) = \sqrt{x+2}$ is
   - ☐ $\{x \mid x \geq -2\}$
   - ☐ $\{x \mid x \geq 0\}$
   - ☐ $\{x \mid x \geq \sqrt{2}\}$
   - ☐ $\{x \mid x \geq 2\}$

   and the range is
   - ☐ $\{y \mid y \geq -2\}$.
   - ☐ $\{y \mid y \geq 0\}$.
   - ☐ $\{y \mid y \geq \sqrt{2}\}$.
   - ☐ $\{y \mid y \geq 2\}$.

2. The function $g(x) = \sqrt{x-5}$ is a transformation of the parent function $f(x) = \sqrt{x}$. Which of the following is true?

   Ⓐ The graph of g is a translation of the graph of f left 5 units.

   Ⓑ The graph of g is a translation of the graph of f down 5 units.

   Ⓒ The domain of f is $\{x \mid x \geq 0\}$, and the domain of g is $\{x \mid x \geq 5\}$.

   Ⓓ The range of f is $\{x \mid x \geq 0\}$, and the range of g is $\{x \mid x \geq 5\}$.

3. Select all the statements that describe the relationship between the graph of $k(x) = \sqrt{4x+12} - 1$ and the graph of the parent function $f(x) = \sqrt{x}$.

   ☐ A. Adding 12 to 4x translates the graph left 12 units.

   ☐ B. Adding 12 to 4x translates the graph left 3 units.

   ☐ C. Multiplying x by 4 stretches the graph vertically by a factor of 4.

   ☐ D. Multiplying x by 4 stretches the graph vertically by a factor of 2.

   ☐ E. Multiplying x by 4 compresses the graph horizontally by a factor of 2.

4. What radical function is represented by the graph?

   Ⓐ $f(x) = \sqrt[3]{x-1} + 3$

   Ⓑ $f(x) = \sqrt[3]{x+1} + 3$

   Ⓒ $f(x) = \sqrt{x+1} + 3$

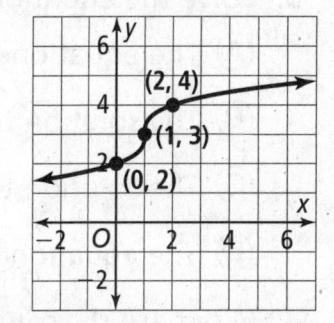

   Ⓓ $f(x) = \sqrt[3]{3x}$

5. The length of one side, s, of a shipping box is $s(x) = \sqrt[3]{2x}$, where x is the volume of the box in cubic inches. A manufacturer needs the volume of the box to be between 108 in.³ and 256 in.³. What are the minimum and maximum possible lengths of s?

   minimum: ☐ in.; maximum: ☐ in.

Name _____

5-4 Lesson Quiz
Solving Radical Equations

1. Solve the radical equation $\sqrt{x-1} + 5 = 9$.

   $x = \boxed{}$

2. **Part A**

   Leo solved the equation $b = \frac{1}{2}\sqrt[3]{a-1}$ for a, but made an error. His work is shown. Complete the sentences that follow.

   (i) $b = \frac{1}{2}\sqrt[3]{a-1}$

   (ii) $2b = \sqrt[3]{a-1}$

   (iii) $4b^2 = a - 1$

   (iv) $4b^2 + 1 = a$

   The error is in line
   - ☐ (i)
   - ☐ (ii)
   - ☐ (iii)
   - ☐ (iv)

   Part B

   What is the correct solution to the equation?

   Ⓐ $a = 8b^3 + 1$ Ⓒ $a = 8b^3$

   Ⓑ $a = 8b^3 - 1$ Ⓓ $a = b^3 + 1$

3. Solve the equation $x + 3 = \sqrt{x + 33}$.

   Ⓐ The equation has two solutions, −8 and 3.

   Ⓑ The solution to the equation is 3, and −8 is an extraneous solution.

   Ⓒ The solution to the equation is −8, and 3 is an extraneous solution.

   Ⓓ The equation has no real solutions.

4. What are the solutions to the equation $2(x^2 + x - 11)^{\frac{3}{2}} = 54$?

   $x = \boxed{}$ and $x = \boxed{}$

5. Solve the radical equation $\sqrt{2x} - \sqrt{36 - 2x} = 6$. Check for extraneous solutions.

   The solution is $\boxed{}$. The extraneous solution is $\boxed{}$.

enVision® Algebra 2 • Assessment Sourcebook

Name _____

5-5 Lesson Quiz
Function Operations

1. Let $f(x) = 3x^2 - 2x + 6$ and $g(x) = 7x - 4$. Identify the rule for $g(f(x)) + g(x)$.

   Ⓐ $21x^2 - 7x + 34$

   Ⓑ $21x^2 - 21x + 50$

   Ⓒ $147x^2 - 182x + 62$

   Ⓓ $21x^3 - 26x^2 + 57x - 28$

2. The demand d for a company's product at cost x is predicted by the function $d(x) = 500 - 2x$. The price p in dollars that the company can charge for the product is given by $p(x) = x + 5$. Use the formula Revenue = price × demand to find the revenue function for the product.

   $R(x) = \boxed{} + \boxed{}x - \boxed{}x^2$

3. **Part A**

   Identify the rule for $\frac{f}{g}$ when $f(x) = -3x - 6$ and $g(x) = x^2 - x - 6$.

   Ⓐ $\frac{f(x)}{g(x)} = \frac{-2}{(x+2)}$ Ⓒ $\frac{f(x)}{g(x)} = \frac{3}{(x+2)}$

   Ⓑ $\frac{f(x)}{g(x)} = \frac{-3(x-2)}{(x-6)(x+1)}$ Ⓓ $\frac{f(x)}{g(x)} = \frac{-3}{x-3}$

   Part B

   Select all values that are NOT in the domain of $\frac{f}{g}$.

   ☐ A. -1 ☐ D. 6

   ☐ B. 3 ☐ E. -2

   ☐ C. -3

4. Let $h(x) = \sqrt{x+3}$ and $k(x) = 2x + 7$. Find the value $\frac{h(k(3)) - k(h(1))}{k(h(-2)) - h(k(-3))}$.

   Ⓐ $\frac{2\sqrt{6} - 2\sqrt{3}}{\sqrt{6} - 7}$ Ⓒ $2\sqrt{6} - \sqrt{12} + 7$

   Ⓑ 4 Ⓓ -1

5. Let $f(x) = 3x^2 + 2$ and $g(x) = \sqrt{x - 4}$. What is the rule for the composition $f \circ g$?

   Ⓐ $(f \circ g)(x) = \sqrt{3x^2 - 2}$, domain is all real numbers

   Ⓑ $(f \circ g)(x) = \sqrt{3x^2 - 2}$, domain is $x \geq 4$

   Ⓒ $(f \circ g)(x) = 3x - 10$, domain is all real numbers

   Ⓓ $(f \circ g)(x) = 3x - 10$, domain is $x \geq 4$

Name _____

5-6 Lesson Quiz

Inverse Relations and Functions

1. The bottom table of values represents the inverse of the top table of values. Find the missing numbers represented by letters in the bottom table.

x	−2	−1	0	1	2	3
y	5	3	1	−1	−3	−5

x	−5	−3	a	b	c	5
y	c	2	1	0	a	d

a = ☐
b = ☐
c = ☐
d = ☐

2. Sketch the graph of f and the inverse of f, if $f(x) = \frac{1}{2}x + 3$.

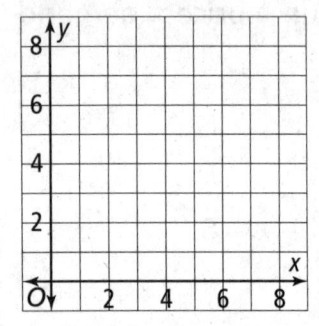

3. Let $f(x) = x^2 − 2x + 1$. Find the inverse function of f by identifying an appropriate restriction of its domain.

   Ⓐ The inverse is $f^{-1}(x) = \sqrt{x + 1}$ if the domain of f is restricted to $x \geq -1$.

   Ⓑ The inverse is $f^{-1}(x) = \sqrt{x} + 1$ if the domain of f is restricted to $x \geq 1$.

   Ⓒ The inverse is $f^{-1}(x) = \sqrt{x} - 1$ if the domain of f is restricted to $x \geq 0$.

   Ⓓ The function does not have an inverse.

4. Write an equation of the inverse function of $f(x) = \frac{1}{2}\sqrt[3]{x - 3} + 5$.

   $f^{-1}(x) = \boxed{} + \boxed{}(x - \boxed{})^3$

5. Let $f(x) = 2x + 4$ and $g(x) = \frac{1}{2}x - 2$. Complete the sentence.

   The function $g(x) = \frac{1}{2}x - 2$
   ☐ is the inverse of
   ☐ is equivalent to
   ☐ is the opposite of
   ☐ has the same intercepts as
   $f(x) = 2x + 4$.

5 Topic Assessment Form A

1. Simplify $\sqrt[3]{27x^9y^3}$.
   $\boxed{} x^3 y$

2. Multiply $(\sqrt{a+4} - 2)(\sqrt{a+4} + 2)$.
   Ⓐ $a - 8$ Ⓒ a
   Ⓑ a^2 Ⓓ $a^2 + 4a$

3. $121^{\frac{1}{11}}$ is equivalent to
   ☐ 2
   ☐ 11
   ☐ $\sqrt[11]{121}$
   ☐ $\sqrt{121^{11}}$

   because
   ☐ $11^2 = 121$.
   ☐ $(\sqrt[11]{121})^{11} = 121$.
   ☐ $11 = \sqrt{121}$.
   ☐ $\sqrt{121^{11}} = 1$.

4. The graph of $y = \sqrt{x}$ has been translated to the right 3 units and down 9 units. What is the equation of the translated graph?
   Ⓐ $y = 3 + \sqrt{x+9}$
   Ⓑ $y = 9 - \sqrt{x+3}$
   Ⓒ $y = 3 - \sqrt{9-x}$
   Ⓓ $y = -9 + \sqrt{x-3}$

5. Which expression is equivalent to $(\sqrt[3]{17})^4$?
   Ⓐ $17^{\frac{4}{3}}$ Ⓒ 17^{12}
   Ⓑ $17^{\frac{3}{4}}$ Ⓓ $\frac{4^{17}}{3}$

6. Let $f(x) = 64x^3 - 1$.
   The inverse relation
   ☐ is an inverse function.
   ☐ is not an inverse function.

7. Graph the function $f(x) = 3 + \sqrt{x}$.

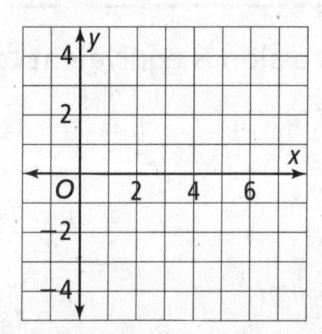

8. Multiply $\sqrt{2}(2\sqrt{x} + \sqrt{x})$.
   Ⓐ $2\sqrt{3x}$ Ⓒ $3\sqrt{2x}$
   Ⓑ $2\sqrt{2x} + 2x$ Ⓓ $6\sqrt{x}$

9. Which pair of function values proves that $g(x)$ is not the inverse of $f(x)$?

x	2	4	6	8	10
f(x)	6	3	2	8	4

x	2	4	6	8	10
g(x)	6	3	2	8	5

   $f\boxed{}$ and $g\boxed{}$

10. Which expression is equivalent to $\sqrt[3]{-x}$?
    Ⓐ $(-x)^3$ Ⓒ x^{-3}
    Ⓑ $(-x)^{\frac{1}{3}}$ Ⓓ $x^{-\frac{1}{3}}$

11. Let $f(x) = \sqrt{x}$ and $g(x) = 3 - x$. What is the domain of $f \circ g$?

$x \leq \boxed{}$

12. If $a(x) = 2 + \sqrt{2 - 8x}$, what is an equation for $a^{-1}(x)$?

   Ⓐ $a^{-1}(x) = \dfrac{(x+2)^2 - 2}{8}$

   Ⓑ $a^{-1}(x) = \dfrac{2 - (x-2)^2}{8}$

   Ⓒ $a^{-1}(x) = \dfrac{x^2 - 4x - 8}{2}$

   Ⓓ $a^{-1}(x) = 8x^2 - 4$

13. Which expression is equivalent to $\dfrac{\sqrt{x}}{2\sqrt{x} - 3}$?

   Ⓐ $\dfrac{5\sqrt{x}}{2x - 9}$

   Ⓑ $\dfrac{5\sqrt{x}}{2x - 9}$

   Ⓒ $\dfrac{2x + 3\sqrt{x}}{2x - 9}$

   Ⓓ $\dfrac{2x + 3\sqrt{x}}{4x - 9}$

14. Some values of $f(x)$ are given in the table. Find the value of $f^{-1}f(10)$.

x	−6	6	10
f(x)	−6	3	6

   $f^{-1}(f(10)) = \boxed{}$

15. A cylindrical pipe is 9 ft long and has a volume of 100 ft³. Find its approximate diameter to the nearest hundredth of a foot.

   $\boxed{}$ ft

16. Solve $(x + 5)^{\frac{3}{2}} = (x - 1)^3$.

   $x = \boxed{}$

17. Let $f(x) = 1 + \sqrt{x}$. Select all the true statements.

   ☐ A. $f^{-1}(-1) = 0$
   ☐ B. $f^{-1}(1) = 0$
   ☐ C. $f^{-1}(2) = 1$
   ☐ D. $(f \circ f^{-1})(4) = 4$
   ☐ E. $f^{-1}(1) \cdot f(1) = 1$

18. What property provides for the definition of $x^{\frac{a}{b}}$ as $\sqrt[b]{x^a}$?

   Ⓐ Power of a Power Property
   Ⓑ Product of Powers Property
   Ⓒ Quotient of Powers Property
   Ⓓ Square Root Property

19. A store is having a 10% sale on all items. There is an additional $30 discount to the the sale price of any bicycle. Let x represent the price in dollars, and let $f(x) = x - 30$ and $g(x) = x - 0.10x = 0.90x$ represent the discounts. Which function can the store manager use to find the final price of a bicycle?

   Ⓐ $f + g$ Ⓒ $g - f$
   Ⓑ $g \circ f$ Ⓓ $f \circ g$

20. Solve $\sqrt{4x - 16} = 3 - \sqrt{x - 4}$.

   $x = \boxed{}$

21. The volume of a sphere is $V(r) = \frac{4}{3}\pi r^3$ and the radius is increasing 2 mm per second. The function $r(t) = 2t$ gives the radius at time t seconds. Which function gives the volume at time t?

   Ⓐ $(V \circ r)(t)$ Ⓒ $(r + V)(t)$
   Ⓑ $(r \circ V)(t)$ Ⓓ $(V \cdot r)(t)$

Name _____

5 Topic Assessment Form B

1. Simplify $\sqrt{\dfrac{a^8}{b^{12}}}$. $\dfrac{a^{\boxed{}}}{b^{\boxed{}}}$

2. Multiply $(\sqrt{x+9} - 3)(\sqrt{x+9} + 3)$.
   - Ⓐ x
   - Ⓑ $x + 9x$
   - Ⓒ x^2
   - Ⓓ $x - 18$

3. $343^{\frac{1}{7}}$ is equivalent to
   - ☐ 3
   - ☐ $\dfrac{1}{49}$
   - ☐ $\sqrt[2]{343}$
   - ☐ $\sqrt[7]{343}$

   because
   - ☐ $7^3 = 343$.
   - ☐ $\dfrac{1}{7} + \dfrac{2}{7} = 1$.
   - ☐ $\sqrt[7]{7^3} = \dfrac{1}{7^2}$.
   - ☐ $(\sqrt[7]{343})^7 = 343$.

4. The graph of $y = 2 + \sqrt{x}$ has been translated to the left 2 units and up 1 unit. What is the equation of the translated graph?
   - Ⓐ $y = 3 + \sqrt{x+2}$
   - Ⓑ $y = 1 + \sqrt{x-2}$
   - Ⓒ $y = 3 - \sqrt{x+2}$
   - Ⓓ $y = 1 + \sqrt{x+2}$

5. Which expression is equivalent to $(\sqrt[3]{13})^5$?
   - Ⓐ $13^{\frac{5}{3}}$
   - Ⓑ $13^{\frac{3}{5}}$
   - Ⓒ 13^{15}
   - Ⓓ $\dfrac{5^{13}}{3}$

6. Let $a(x) = -x^2 + 6x - 10$.
   The inverse relation
   - ☐ is an inverse function.
   - ☐ is not an inverse function.

7. Graph the function $f(x) = \sqrt[3]{x} - 5$.

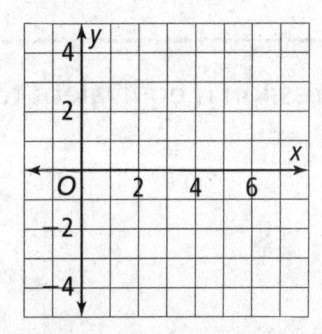

8. Multiply $12\sqrt{x} \cdot \sqrt{8x}$.
   - Ⓐ $4x\sqrt{x}$
   - Ⓑ $4\sqrt{6x}$
   - Ⓒ $24\sqrt{2x}$
   - Ⓓ $24x\sqrt{2}$

9. Which pair of function values proves that $g(x)$ is not the inverse of $f(x)$?

x	3	6	10	12	13
f(x)	6	3	13	14	15

x	3	6	10	12	13
g(x)	6	3	13	11	10

   $f \boxed{}$ and $g \boxed{}$

10. Which expression is equivalent to $\sqrt[5]{-x}$?
    - Ⓐ $(-x)^{\frac{1}{5}}$
    - Ⓑ $(-x)^5$
    - Ⓒ $x^{-\frac{1}{5}}$
    - Ⓓ x^{-5}

11. Let $f(x) = \sqrt{x}$ and $g(x) = \frac{1}{x-5}$. What is the domain of $f \circ g$?

   $x \leq \boxed{}$

12. If $a(x) = 1 + \sqrt{2x - 7}$, what is an equation for $a^{-1}(x)$?

   Ⓐ $a^{-1}(x) = \frac{(x+1)^2 + 7}{14}$

   Ⓑ $a^{-1}(x) = \frac{(x-1)^2 + 7}{2}$

   Ⓒ $a^{-1}(x) = 2(x-1)^2 + 7$

   Ⓓ $a^{-1}(x) = x^2 + 2x + 8$

13. Which expression is equivalent to $\frac{2\sqrt{x}}{\sqrt{x} - 3}$?

   Ⓐ $\frac{2 + 6\sqrt{x}}{x - 9}$

   Ⓑ $\frac{2x + 3\sqrt{x}}{2x - 9}$

   Ⓒ $\frac{2x + 6\sqrt{x}}{x - 9}$

   Ⓓ $\frac{8\sqrt{x}}{2x - 9}$

14. Some values of $f(x)$ are given in the table. Find the value of $f^{-1}f(2)$.

x	2	3	5
f(x)	3	1	5

   $f^{-1}(f(2)) = \boxed{}$

15. A cylindrical pipe is 25 ft long and has a volume of 900 ft³. What is its approximate diameter?

   Ⓐ 3.39 ft
   Ⓑ 6 ft
   Ⓒ 6.77 ft
   Ⓓ 12 ft

16. Solve $x - 7 = \sqrt{x - 5}$.

   $x = \boxed{}$

17. Let $f(x) = 1 + \sqrt{x}$. Select all the true statements.

   ☐ A. $f^{-1}(x) = (x - 1)^2$
   ☐ B. $f^{-1}(0) = 1$
   ☐ C. $f^{-1}(1) = 4$
   ☐ D. $(f^{-1} \circ f)(x) = x$
   ☐ E. $f^{-1}(0) = -4$

18. What property provides for the definition of $a^{\frac{m}{n}}$ as $\sqrt[n]{a^m}$?

   Ⓐ Product of Powers Property
   Ⓑ Quotient of Powers Property
   Ⓒ Power of a Power Property
   Ⓓ Square Root Property

19. A store increases all its prices by 20% and then offers a $50 discount on all purchase prices. Let x represent the price in dollars. Let $f(x) = 1.20x$ represent the increase and $g(x) = x - 50$ represent the discount. Which function can the store manager use to find the final purchase prices?

   Ⓐ $f + g$
   Ⓑ $f \times g$
   Ⓒ $g \circ f$
   Ⓓ $f \circ g$

20. Solve $\sqrt{x + 1} + \sqrt{x - 1} = 2$.

   $x = \boxed{}$

21. The volume of a sphere is $V(r) = \frac{4}{3}\pi r^3$ and the radius is increasing at 5 mm per second. The function $r(t) = 5t$ gives the radius at time t seconds. Which function gives the volume at time t?

   Ⓐ $(V \circ r)(t)$
   Ⓑ $(r \circ V)(t)$
   Ⓒ $(r + V)(t)$
   Ⓓ $(V \cdot r)(t)$

Name _____

5 Performance Assessment Form A

enVision Algebra 2
SavvasRealize.com

After observing a swinging lantern, Italian scientist Galileo Galilei made an important discovery about the timing of a pendulum's swing. Christiaan Huygens, from Holland, discovered the relationship between the length of a pendulum and the time it takes to make a complete swing. These discoveries led to the use of pendulums in clocks.

1. The *period* of a pendulum is the time it takes for the pendulum to swing from one extreme to the other and back. The function $t(L) = 2\pi\sqrt{\dfrac{L}{980}}$ represents the period t, in seconds, for a pendulum of length L, in centimeters.

   ### Part A

   Use the function to complete the table below for L and t. Then graph the function. Round values of t to the nearest tenth.

Length (cm)	Period (s)
0	
50	
100	
200	
400	

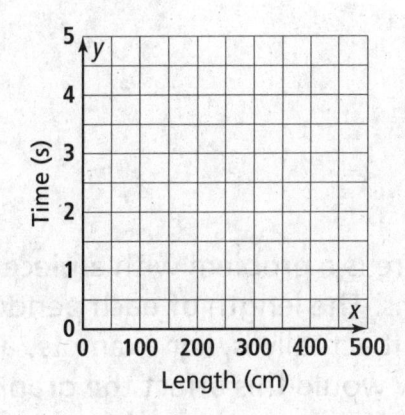

   ### Part B

   Find a function L in terms of t. Describe each step in your solution. What is the domain of your function? Is the function increasing or decreasing over the domain? Explain.

2. Return to the original pendulum function $t(L) = 2\pi\sqrt{\frac{L}{980}}$. How can you represent the inverse relation of function t algebraically? Is the inverse relation a function? If so, what is its domain? Verify that t and t^{-1} are inverses using function composition.

3. Suppose there is a problem with a piece of equipment that reads the period t of pendulums. The length of each pendulum is incorrectly read as being 100 cm longer than it actually is. For example, a pendulum that is 50 cm long is read as 150 cm. How would this affect the graph of function t? What is the equation of the resulting incorrect graph of function t?

4. The frequency f of a pendulum is defined by $f(t) = \frac{1}{t}$. Use the function $t(L) = 2\pi\sqrt{\frac{L}{980}}$ for the period of a pendulum to find the composite function $f \circ t$. Write this function in simplest form by rationalizing denominators where necessary. Show your work.

Name _____

5 Performance Assessment Form B

According to a popular, but untrue, urban legend, oceanographers have discovered images of giant pyramids made of crystal-like substances deep in the ocean. Suppose one of these imaginary pyramids has the dimensions shown at the right.

1. The volume V of a pyramid is $\frac{1}{3}Bh$ where B is the area of the base and h is the height of the pyramid.

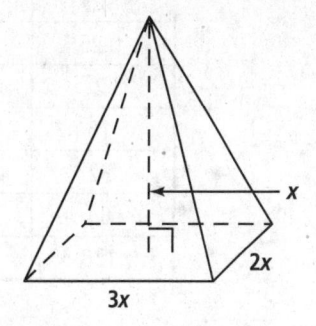

   Part A

   Find an equation that represents V in terms of x. Then find x in terms of V. Write your equation for x in rational exponent form, and rationalize denominators where necessary. Explain.

   Part B

   Suppose the urban legend were true, and a contractor could be hired to raise one of these pyramids and bring it to the surface of the ocean. The estimated cost of the operation $c(x)$ is $200,000 per meter of pyramid height, with an additional cost $a(V)$ of $300 per cubic meter of pyramid volume. Suppose a pyramid has a volume of 2,000,000 m³. What is the height x of the pyramid? What is an equation that represents the total retrieval cost t for a pyramid of any volume with these proportions in terms of x? How much would it cost to excavate this pyramid? Explain.

2. Complete the table that relates the pyramid's height to its volume. Then graph the equation $x = \frac{(4V)^{\frac{1}{3}}}{2}$. Where necessary, round values to the nearest tenth.

Volume (V)	Height (x)
0	
0.25	
2	
16	
32	
64	
128	

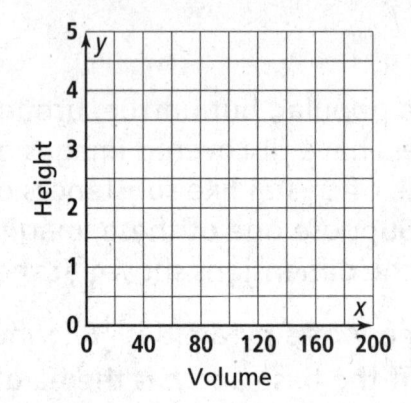

3. What is the inverse of the relation represented in the table in Item 2? Complete the table of values.

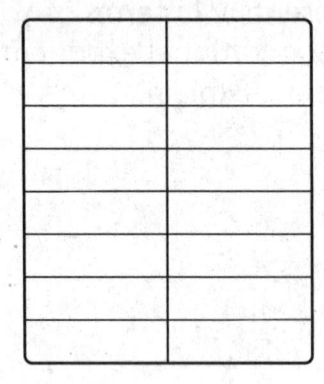

Name _____

6 Readiness Assessment

1. Evaluate the expression $8^{\frac{x}{3}}$ for $x = 2$.
   - Ⓐ 2
   - Ⓒ 4
   - Ⓑ $2\sqrt{2}$
   - Ⓓ $16\sqrt{2}$

2. What is the domain of the function $d(x)$ that gives the number of diagonals of a polygon with x vertices?
   - Ⓐ all real numbers
   - Ⓑ all real numbers at least 3
   - Ⓒ all integers
   - Ⓓ all integers at least 3

3. For the function $g(x) = (-2)^{0.5x}$, select all the equations that are true.
   - ☐ A. $g(-4) = -\frac{1}{4}$
   - ☐ D. $g(4) = 4$
   - ☐ B. $g(-2) = \frac{1}{2}$
   - ☐ E. $g(2) = -2$
   - ☐ C. $g(0) = -1$

4. The number of muffins, y, The Cozy Cafe bakes each day, x, increases as their advertising campaign brings in more customers. They recorded how many muffins they baked every second day. What is the line of best fit for these data?
   (0, 5), (2, 12), (4, 21), (6, 28), (8, 38), (10, 45)
   - Ⓐ $y = 0.12x - 0.54$
   - Ⓑ $y = 0.24x - 1.09$
   - Ⓒ $y = 4.07x + 4.48$
   - Ⓓ $y = 8.14x + 4.47$

5. Ina recorded the wait time y, in days, for popular books at the library based on how many people were on the waiting list, x. Draw a scatterplot and find the line of best fit for these data: (0, 3), (1, 5), (2, 9), (3, 13), (4, 15), (5, 18)
   $y = \boxed{}x + \boxed{}$

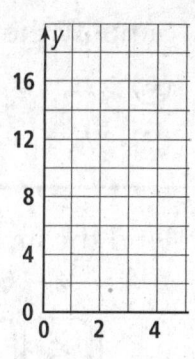

6. How does the graph of $y = (x + 2)^2 - 5$ relate to the graph of its parent function, $y = x^2$?
   - Ⓐ It is a translation 2 units left and reflection across the y-axis.
   - Ⓑ It is a translation 5 units down, and a strech vertically by a factor of 2.
   - Ⓒ It is a translation 2 units left and 5 units down.
   - Ⓓ It is a translation 2 units right and 5 units up.

7. Identify the parent function of the function $y = -\frac{1}{2}(x - 3)^3$. Then graph the function and its parent function.

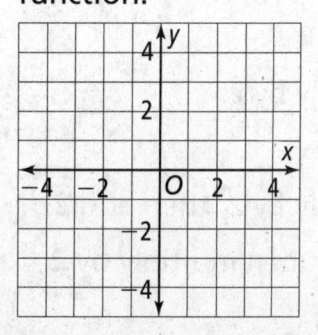

8. Simplify the expression $\left(x^{\frac{1}{3}} \cdot x^{\frac{1}{3}}\right)^6$.
   - Ⓐ x^4
   - Ⓑ x^3
   - Ⓒ x^6
   - Ⓓ x^2

9. Simplify the expression $(9x^4)^{\frac{3}{2}}$.
   - Ⓐ $27x^4$
   - Ⓑ $27x^6$
   - Ⓒ $81x^6$
   - Ⓓ $81x^{12}$

10. Find the inverse of the function $f(x) = \frac{3}{2}x - 6$.

    $\boxed{\frac{3}{2}}$ $\boxed{\frac{2}{3}}$ $\boxed{-\frac{2}{3}}$ $\boxed{6}$ $\boxed{4}$ $\boxed{9}$

    $f^{-1}(x) = \boxed{} x + \boxed{}$

11. What is the inverse of the function $f(x) = (x-1)^3 + 8$?
    - Ⓐ $f^{-1}(x) = \sqrt[3]{x-7}$
    - Ⓑ $f^{-1}(x) = -1 + \sqrt[3]{x}$
    - Ⓒ $f^{-1}(x) = 1 + \sqrt[3]{x-2}$
    - Ⓓ $f^{-1}(x) = 1 + \sqrt[3]{x-8}$

12. The table shows the function f. Complete the table for the inverse of function f.

x	0	1	2	3	4
f(x)	4	2	0	3	1
$f^{-1}(x)$					

13. What describes the pattern between sequential terms in the following sequence?

    2, 4, 6, 8, 10 ...
    - Ⓐ Multiply by 2.
    - Ⓑ Add 2.
    - Ⓒ Multiply by 2, then add 2.
    - Ⓓ Add 2, then multiply by 2.

14. For the function $f(x) = -3x + 1$, what is the value of $f^{-1}(x)$ for $x = 4$?

    $f^{-1}(4) = \boxed{}$

15. The table shows a function f. What is the domain of f^{-1}, the inverse of function f?

x	1	2	3	4	5
f(x)	1	4	9	16	25

    - Ⓐ {1, 2, 3, 4, 5}
    - Ⓑ {1, 4, 9, 16, 25}
    - Ⓒ {1, 2, 3, 4, 5, 9, 16, 25}
    - Ⓓ {−5, −4, −3, −2, −1, 1, 2, 3, 4, 5}

16. The function $f(x) = 2x^2 - 5x + 3$ represents the height in meters, y, of a marble on a marble run after x seconds. What is the average rate of change of the function from $x = 0$ to $x = 3$?
    - Ⓐ −2
    - Ⓑ −1
    - Ⓒ 1
    - Ⓓ 4

17. The graph represents the population of a bacterium, y, after x seconds. Find the average rate of change of the function, from $x = -1$ to $x = 2$.

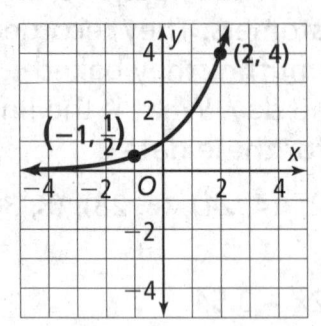

    - Ⓐ $\frac{9}{2}$
    - Ⓑ $\frac{7}{6}$
    - Ⓒ $\frac{3}{2}$
    - Ⓓ $\frac{19}{5}$

Name _____

6-1 Lesson Quiz

Key Features of Exponential Functions

1. Which function represents the exponential function $f(x) = 3^x$ after a vertical stretch by a factor of 8 and a reflection across the x-axis?

   Ⓐ $g(x) = 3^{-8x}$　　Ⓒ $g(x) = 8 \cdot 3^{-x}$

   Ⓑ $g(x) = -3^{8x}$　　Ⓓ $g(x) = -8 \cdot 3^x$

2. 15,000 blue trout were released into the Meherrin River for a scientific study. The function $f(x) = 15,000\left(\frac{9}{8}\right)^x$ represents the number of blue trout after x years. After 5 years, what happens to the population?

   Ⓐ It decreases by about 2,000.

   Ⓑ It decreases by about 12,000.

   Ⓒ It increases by about 2,000.

   Ⓓ It increases by about 12,000.

3. For the function $f(x) = \left(\frac{1}{2}\right) \cdot 6^x$, identify the domain, range, y-intercept, and asymptote. Write one of the given phrases or values in each blank.

   (linear)　　(quadratic)　　(exponential)

   (all real numbers)　　(0.5)　　(0)　　(0)

   Domain: (⬚)　　y-Intercept: (⬚)

   Range: {y | y > (⬚)}　　Asymptote: y = (⬚)

   Function type: (⬚)

4. The rabbit population of Springfield, Ohio, was 144,000 in 2016. It is expected to decrease by about 7.2% per year. Write and graph the exponential decay function of the rabbit population, P(t).

   P(t) = (⬚)(⬚)^t

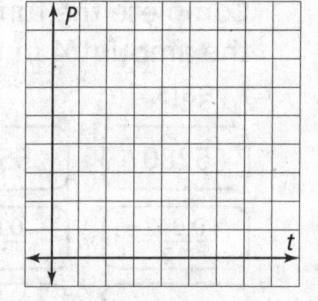

5. Which of the following functions has a greater growth factor than the function shown in the graph?

   Ⓐ $f(x) = \left(\frac{3}{2}\right) \cdot 3^x$

   Ⓑ $f(x) = 8\left(\frac{3}{2}\right)^x$

   Ⓒ $f(x) = 20(1.4)^x$

   Ⓓ $f(x) = 12(0.8)^x$

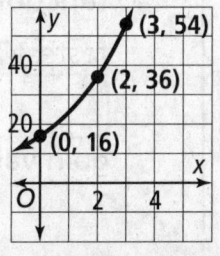

enVision® Algebra 2 • Assessment Sourcebook

Name _____

6-2 Lesson Quiz

Exponential Models

1. In 1970, the population of a small town was 4,200. The population is decreasing at a rate of 2.4% per year.

   Complete the function that models the population y in the town, t years after 1970.

   $y = ()()^t$

   To the nearest thousandth of a percent, the population is decreasing about $\boxed{}$% per quarter.

2. The graph of an exponential model in the form $y = a \cdot b^x$ passes through the points (3, 5) and (4, 10). Which point is also on the graph?

   Ⓐ (2, 0)   Ⓒ (5, 15)
   Ⓑ (2, 1)   Ⓓ (5, 20)

3. Micah invests $5,280 in an account that earns 4.2% interest, compounded monthly.

   Complete the function that models the amount A in the account after t years.

5280	5501	5298.48
$\frac{0.042}{12}$	$\frac{0.042}{6}$	0.042
12t	t	$\frac{t}{12}$

   $A(t) = \boxed{} (1 + \boxed{})^{\boxed{}}$

4. Steve invests $1,800 in an account that earns 3.7% annual interest, compounded continuously. What is the approximate value of the account after 10 years?

   Ⓐ $2,466   Ⓒ $2,601
   Ⓑ $2,589   Ⓓ $2,606

5. Paul considers investing $8,000 in three different accounts for 6 years.

   Option A: 5% simple interest

   Option B: 4.5% interest compounded continuously

   Option C: 4.75% interest compounded yearly

   After 6 years, Option B, to the nearest dollar, will be worth
   $ $\boxed{}$ more than Option A and
   $ $\boxed{}$ less than Option C.

   [linear] [exponential]
   [quadratic] [constant]

   Option A is a $\boxed{}$ function while Options B and C are $\boxed{}$ functions.

   While the $\boxed{}$ function gains value the fastest initially, over time the $\boxed{}$ functions will gain value faster.

Name _____

6-3 Lesson Quiz

Logarithms

1. Which function is the inverse of the exponential function $y = 3^x$?
   - Ⓐ $y = x^3$
   - Ⓑ $y = 3^x$
   - Ⓒ $y = \log_3 x$
   - Ⓓ $y = \log_x 3$

2. Which is the best estimate of the value of ln 16?
   - Ⓐ 1.20
   - Ⓑ 2.77
   - Ⓒ 3.23
   - Ⓓ 4.00

3. Which is the logarithmic equation $\log_8 64 = a$, written in exponential form?
   - Ⓐ $64^a = 8$
   - Ⓑ $a^8 = 64$
   - Ⓒ $a^{64} = 8$
   - Ⓓ $8^a = 64$

4. Select all the logarithmic expressions that have been evaluated correctly.
   - ☐ A. $\ln 1 = 0$
   - ☐ B. $\log_2 9 = 3$
   - ☐ C. $\log \frac{1}{100} = \frac{1}{2}$
   - ☐ D. $\log_3 (-1) = \frac{1}{3}$
   - ☐ E. $\log_5 \frac{1}{125} = -3$

5. What is the solution to the equation $\log(2x + 4) = 2$? Round to the nearest thousandth, if necessary.

   $x = $ ☐

enVision® Algebra 2 • Assessment Sourcebook

6-4 Lesson Quiz

Logarithmic Functions

1. The graph shows the function $f(x) = 3^x$.

   What is the value of $f^{-1}(x)$ at $x = 3$?

   $f^{-1}(3) = \boxed{}$

2. The logarithmic function $f(x) = \log x$ is transformed to $g(x) = \log(x + 1) + 3$. Which statement is true?

   Ⓐ The graph of $f(x)$ is translated 1 unit upward.

   Ⓑ The graph of $f(x)$ is translated 3 units downward.

   Ⓒ The vertical asymptote shifts from $x = 0$ to $x = -1$.

   Ⓓ The vertical asymptote shifts from $x = -1$ to $x = 3$.

3. Complete the equation of the inverse of the function $f(x) = \log_2(9x)$.

   Ⓐ $f^{-1}(x) = \frac{1}{9}(2^x)$

   Ⓑ $f^{-1}(x) = \frac{1}{2}(9^x)$

   Ⓒ $f^{-1}(x) = 9(2^x)$

   Ⓓ $f^{-1}(x) = \log_9(2x)$

4. An internet service provider uses the function $R = 3\log(a + 2) + 15$ to relate R, its sales revenue from hosting websites, to a, the cost of advertising. Solve for a in terms of R.

   Ⓐ $a = \frac{R - 15}{3} - 2$

   Ⓑ $a = \frac{1}{10}\left(\frac{R - 15}{3} - 2\right)$

   Ⓒ $a = 10^{\frac{R-15}{3}} - 2$

   Ⓓ $a = 10^{\frac{R-15}{3}} + 2$

5. Consider $f(x) = 3x - 1$ and the graph of $g(x)$ shown.

   Select the function that makes the statement true.

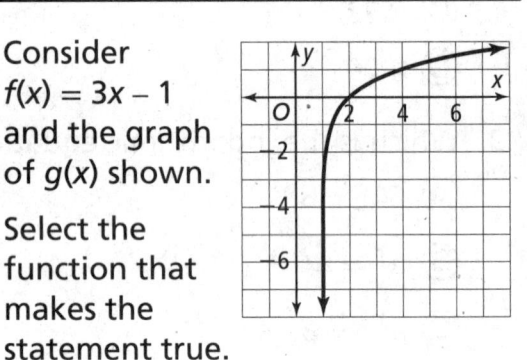

	$f(x)$	$g(x)$	Both
Has the greater x-intercept	☐	☐	☐
Has an asymptote of $y = -1$	☐	☐	☐
Is always increasing	☐	☐	☐
Is positive over the interval $(2, \infty)$	☐	☐	☐

Name _____

6-5 Lesson Quiz

Properties of Logarithms

1. Select the steps to write the expression $5\log_3 a + \log_3 b - 2\log_3 c$ as a single logarithm using the properties of logarithms.

   [Power Property]   [Quotient Property]   [Product Property]

   $5\log_3 a + \log_3 b - 2\log_3 c = \log_3 a^5 + \log_3 b - \log_3 c^2$ [   ]

   $= \log_3 a^5 b - \log_3 c^2$ [   ]

   $= \log_3\left(\dfrac{a^5 b}{c^2}\right)$ [   ]

2. The pH of a solution is a measure of its concentration of hydrogen ions. This concentration, written [H⁺] and measured in moles per liter, is given by the formula $pH = \log\dfrac{1}{[H^+]}$. What is the concentration of hydrogen ions in a liter of vinegar that has a pH level of 2.5?

   Ⓐ $10^{2.5}$ Ⓑ $10^{-2.5}$ Ⓒ $\log(2.5)$ Ⓓ $\log(-2.5)$

3. Use the properties of logarithms to write the expression $\tfrac{1}{2}\ln 4 + 2\ln x$ as a single logarithm.

   Ⓐ $4\ln(2x)$ Ⓑ $\ln(2x^2)$ Ⓒ $\ln(4x)$ Ⓓ $\ln(4x^2)$

4. Select all the logarithmic expressions that have been evaluated correctly.
   - ☐ A. $\log_3 8 = 0.43$
   - ☐ B. $\log_3 6 = 1.63$
   - ☐ C. $\log_4 5 = 1.16$
   - ☐ D. $\log_2 32 = 1.51$
   - ☐ E. $\log_4 7 = 2.21$

5. Solve the equation $5^x = 7$ for x. Select the exact solution as a logarithm and use the change of base formula to find an approximate solution.
   - ☐ A. $x = \log_7 5$
   - ☐ B. $x = \log_5 7$
   - ☐ C. $x = 0.827$
   - ☐ D. $x = 1.209$
   - ☐ E. $x = \log 5$
   - ☐ F. $x = \log 7$
   - ☐ G. $x = 0.699$
   - ☐ H. $x = 1.845$

enVision® Algebra 2 • Assessment Sourcebook

Name _____

6-6 Lesson Quiz

Exponential and Logarithmic Equations

1. What is the solution to the equation $7^{x-1} = 3$?

   Ⓐ $x = \dfrac{\log 3}{\log 7} + 1$ Ⓑ $x = \dfrac{\log 7}{\log 3} - 1$ Ⓒ $x = \log\left(1\tfrac{3}{7}\right)$ Ⓓ $x = \log\left(\tfrac{7}{3}\right) + 1$

2. The volume of one cloud, in cubic kilometers, grows according to the expression 4^{3x-1}, where x is time in hours. Another cloud grows according to the expression 8^x. After how many hours will the two clouds have the same volume? What is their volume, in cubic kilometers?

   Ⓐ 0 hours; 1   Ⓑ $\tfrac{1}{2}$ hour; 2.83   Ⓒ $\tfrac{2}{3}$ hour; 4   Ⓓ 2 hours; 64

3. Max solved the equation, $5^{x+3} = 25^{x-2}$, but made an error. His work is shown.

   Part A Select each step that Max completed.

Property of Equality for Exponential Equations		Power of a Power Property
		Rewrite with a common base

   $25^{x-2} = 5^{x+3}$
   $(5^2)^{x-2} = 5^{x+3}$ .... ▢

   $5^{2x-2} = 5^{x+3}$ .... ▢

   $2x - 2 = x + 3$ .... ▢
   $x = 5$

   Part B Identify and fix Max's mistake.

   Max made an error in line ▢. The correct solution is $x = $ ▢.

4. Select all solutions of the equation $2\log x = \log(5x - 4)$.

   ☐ A. $x = 1$
   ☐ B. $x = 4$
   ☐ C. $x = 5$
   ☐ D. $x = 0$
   ☐ E. $x = -1$

5. Solve the equation $\ln(3x) = 2x - 5$. If there is more than one solution, solve for the larger x-value. Round to the nearest hundredth.

   $x = $ ▢

6-7 Lesson Quiz

Geometric Sequences and Series

1. Tim is playing a game. His score in round 1 is 1.7 points, in round 2 is 5.1 points, in round 3 is 15.3 points, and it continues to increase in the same way. Is his score a geometric sequence? If so, write a recursive definition for the sequence.

   Ⓐ No; the sequence does not have a common ratio.

   Ⓑ Yes; $a_n = \begin{cases} 1.7, n = 1 \\ 3a_{n-1}, n > 1 \end{cases}$

   Ⓒ Yes; $a_n = \begin{cases} 0.6, n = 1 \\ 3a_{n-1}, n > 1 \end{cases}$

   Ⓓ Yes; $a_n = \begin{cases} 3, n = 1 \\ 1.7a_{n-1}, n > 1 \end{cases}$

2. The recursive definition for a sequence is $a_n = \begin{cases} 32, \text{ if } n = 1 \\ \frac{1}{4}a_{n-1}, \text{ if } n > 1 \end{cases}$. What is the explicit definition of the sequence?

   Ⓐ $a_n = 16\left(\frac{1}{2}\right)^n$

   Ⓑ $32, 8, 2, \frac{1}{2}, \frac{1}{8}, \ldots$

   Ⓒ $a_n = 32\left(\frac{1}{2}\right)^n$

   Ⓓ $a_n = 32\left(\frac{1}{4}\right)^{n-1}$

3. **Part A**

   Use the formula for the sum of a finite geometric series to find $\sum_{n=1}^{6} 3(2)^{n-1}$.

   sum = ☐

   Part B

   Which finite series could you use to check your result in **Part A**?

   Ⓐ $3 + 9 + 27 + 81 + 243 + 729$

   Ⓑ $2 + 6 + 18 + 54 + 162 + 486$

   Ⓒ $3 + 6 + 12 + 24 + 48 + 96$

   Ⓓ $1 + 3 + 6 + 12 + 24 + 48$

4. How many terms are in the geometric series $2.1 + 10.5 + \ldots + 820{,}312.5$?

   Ⓐ 3

   Ⓑ 7

   Ⓒ 9

   Ⓓ 180

5. What is the monthly payment rate for a $20,000 loan for 4 years with an annual interest rate of 4.8%?

   $ ☐

Name _____

6 Topic Assessment Form A

1. Which function g represents the exponential function $f(x) = 5^x$ after a vertical stretch by a factor of 2 and a reflection across the x-axis?
   - Ⓐ $g(x) = (2 \cdot 5)^{-x}$
   - Ⓑ $g(x) = -(2 \cdot 5)^x$
   - Ⓒ $g(x) = 2 \cdot (5)^{-x}$
   - Ⓓ $g(x) = -2 \cdot (5)^x$

2. A population of butterflies increases from 2000 to 2800 over 7 years. Which function best models the population x years from the first measurement?
   - Ⓐ $f(x) = 2000(1 + 0.4)^{\frac{1}{7}x}$
   - Ⓑ $f(x) = 2000(1 + 0.4^7)^x$
   - Ⓒ $f(x) = 2000\left(1 + \frac{0.4}{7}\right)^x$
   - Ⓓ $f(x) = 2000\left(1 + \frac{0.4}{7}\right)^{7x}$

3. In the expression shown $t \neq s$.
   $$\frac{(s - t) + (2s - 2t)^2}{t - s}$$
   When x replaces $(s - t)$ which expression is equivalent to the expression shown. Select all that apply.
   - ☐ A. $\frac{x + 4x^2}{-x}$
   - ☐ B. $\frac{x - 2x^2}{x}$
   - ☐ C. $\frac{x + (4x)^2}{x}$
   - ☐ D. $\frac{-x - 4x^2}{x}$
   - ☐ E. $\frac{x + (2x)^2}{x}$

4. Which of the following functions has a faster decay factor than the function shown in the graph?

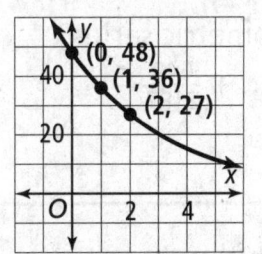

   (graph showing points (0, 48), (1, 36), (2, 27))

   - Ⓐ $f(x) = 48(0.6)^x$
   - Ⓑ $f(x) = 48(0.75)^x$
   - Ⓒ $f(x) = 48(0.772)^x$
   - Ⓓ $f(x) = 48(0.8)^x$

5. The number of views y on a viral video after x days can be represented by an exponential model, $y = a \cdot b^x$. After 1 day, a cat video has 10 views, and after 2 days it has 20 views. Which represents another point on the graph of this model?
   - Ⓐ (3, 25)
   - Ⓑ (3, 30)
   - Ⓒ (3, 40)
   - Ⓓ (3, 60)

6. A warren of rabbits has a population of 25. The population is increasing at a rate of 20% per year. Select the model of the population after t years that reveals the monthly growth rate.
   - Ⓐ $y = 25(1.2)^t$
   - Ⓑ $y = 25(1.0167)^{12t}$
   - Ⓒ $y = 25(1.0167)^t$
   - Ⓓ $y = 25(1.0153)^{12t}$

7. What function is the inverse of the exponential function $y = 4^x$?
   - Ⓐ $y = x^{\frac{1}{4}}$
   - Ⓑ $y = \left(\frac{1}{4}\right)^x$
   - Ⓒ $y = \log_x 4$
   - Ⓓ $y = \log_4 x$

8. What is the value of n in the formula $S = \frac{a_1(1 - r^n)}{(1 - r)}$ for the sum of the geometric series $5 + 3\frac{1}{3} + 2\frac{2}{9} + \ldots + \frac{640}{2187}$?

   $n = \boxed{}$

9. What is the solution to the equation $\log_4(5x + 9) = 3$?

   $x = \boxed{}$

10. The graph shows the function $f(x) = 6(3)^x$. What is the value of the inverse function, f^{-1}, at $x = 2$?

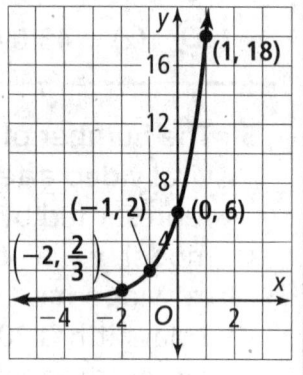

    $f^{-1}(2) = \boxed{}$

11. What is the asymptote of the graph of $g(x) = \ln x + 5$?
    - Ⓐ vertical at $x = e$
    - Ⓑ vertical at $x = 5$
    - Ⓒ horizontal at $y = e$
    - Ⓓ horizontal at $y = 5$

12. Complete the equation of the inverse of the function $f(x) = \log(2x)$.

    $\boxed{\frac{1}{2}}$ $\boxed{2}$ $\boxed{10}$ $\boxed{\frac{1}{10}}$

    $f^{-1}(x) = \boxed{}(\boxed{})^x$

13. Use the properties of logarithms to choose the expression $2\log 5 + 5\log x$ as a single logarithm.
    - Ⓐ $\log(10 + 5x)$
    - Ⓑ $\log(10x^5)$
    - Ⓒ $\log(25x^5)$
    - Ⓓ $\log(25 + x^5)$

14. A new kind of rocket takes off with exponential acceleration with height in miles represented by 3^x, where x is time in minutes. Find the time when the rocket's height is 8 miles. Select the exact solution as a logarithm, and select an approximate solution.
    - ☐ A. $x = \log_8 3$
    - ☐ B. $x = \log_3 8$
    - ☐ C. $x = \log 8$
    - ☐ D. $x = 1.893$
    - ☐ E. $x = 0.528$
    - ☐ F. $x = 0.903$

15. What is the sum of the geometric series $S = \frac{27}{64} + \frac{81}{128} + \frac{54}{256} + \ldots + \frac{19{,}683}{4096}$? Round to the nearest thousandth.

    $S = \boxed{}$

16. Complete the steps to write the expression $\log a + 3\log b - 2\log c$ as a single logarithm using the properties of logarithms.

    $\boxed{\text{Product}}$ $\boxed{\text{Quotient}}$ $\boxed{\text{Power}}$

    $\log a + 3\log b - 2\log c$
    $= \log a + \log b^3 - \log c^2$ $\boxed{}$
    $= \log ab^3 - \log c^2$ $\boxed{}$
    $= \log\left(\frac{ab^3}{c^2}\right)$ $\boxed{}$

17. For the function $f(x) = -4 \cdot (0.3)^x + 1$, identify the y-intercept and asymptote.

    y-Intercept: $\boxed{}$

    Asymptote: $y = \boxed{}$

Name _____

6 Topic Assessment Form B

1. Which function g represents the exponential function $f(x) = 3^x$ after a horizontal stretch by a factor of 4 and a reflection across the y-axis?

   Ⓐ $g(x) = (3)^{-\frac{x}{4}}$
   Ⓑ $g(x) = (3)^{-4x}$
   Ⓒ $g(x) = -(3)^{\frac{x}{4}}$
   Ⓓ $g(x) = -(3)^{4x}$

2. A population of mice increases from 400 to 1400 over 7 years. Which function best models the population x years from the first measurement?

   Ⓐ $f(x) = 400\left(1 + 2.5^{\frac{1}{7}}\right)^x$
   Ⓑ $f(x) = 400(1 + 2.5)^{\frac{1}{7}x}$
   Ⓒ $f(x) = 400\left(1 + \frac{2.5}{7}\right)^x$
   Ⓓ $f(x) = 400\left(1 + \frac{2.5}{7}\right)^{7x}$

3. In the expression shown $t \neq s$.
   $$\frac{(s - t) + (2s - 2t)^2}{t - s}$$

   When x replaces $(s - t)$ which expression is equivalent to the expression shown. Select all that apply.

   ☐ A. $\frac{x + 4x^2}{-x}$
   ☐ B. $\frac{x - 2x^2}{x}$
   ☐ C. $\frac{x + (4x)^2}{x}$
   ☐ D. $\frac{-x - 4x^2}{x}$
   ☐ E. $\frac{x + (2x)^2}{x}$

4. Which of the following functions has a slower growth rate than the function shown in the graph?

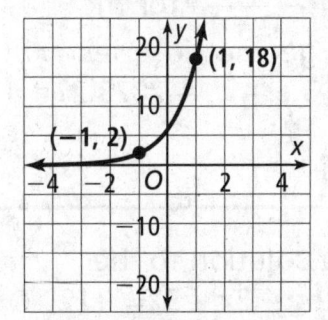

   Ⓐ $f(x) = 4(4.5)^x$
   Ⓑ $f(x) = 6(3.5)^x$
   Ⓒ $f(x) = 8(3.1)^x$
   Ⓓ $f(x) = 10(2)^x$

5. The height of a launched weather balloon can be represented by an exponential model, $y = a \cdot b^x$, where y is the height in km after x min. After 2 min, the height is 3 km, and after 3 min it is 9 km. Which represents another point on the graph of this model?

   Ⓐ (1, –3)   Ⓒ (4, 15)
   Ⓑ (1, 1)   Ⓓ (4, 16)

6. A school of fish has a population of 200. The population is decreasing at a rate of 5% per year. Select the model of the population after t years that reveals the quarterly decay factor.

   Ⓐ $y = 200(0.95)^t$
   Ⓑ $y = 200(0.9875)^{4t}$
   Ⓒ $y = 200(0.9875)^t$
   Ⓓ $y = 200(0.9873)^{4t}$

7. What function is the inverse of the exponential function $y = \left(\frac{1}{3}\right)^x$?
   - Ⓐ $y = x^{\frac{1}{3}}$
   - Ⓑ $y = \left(\frac{1}{3}\right)^x$
   - Ⓒ $y = \log_{\frac{1}{3}} x$
   - Ⓓ $y = \log_x \left(\frac{1}{3}\right)$

8. What is the value of n in the formula $S = \frac{a_1(1 - r^n)}{(1 - r)}$ for the sum of the geometric series $0.4 + 1.2 + 3.6 + \ldots + 7873.2$?

   $n = \boxed{}$

9. What is the solution to the equation $\log_3(2x - 3) = -1$? Round to the nearest thousandth.

   $x = \boxed{}$

10. The graph shows the function $f(x) = 32\left(\frac{1}{2}\right)^x - 2$. What is the value of the inverse function f^{-1} at $x = 2$?

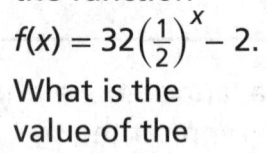

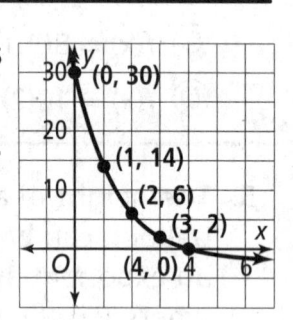

    $f^{-1}(2) = \boxed{}$

    (Graph points: (0, 30), (1, 14), (2, 6), (3, 2), (4, 0))

11. What is the asymptote of the graph of $g(x) = \log_2(x + 4)$?
    - Ⓐ vertical at $x = 0$
    - Ⓑ vertical at $x = -4$
    - Ⓒ horizontal at $y = 0$
    - Ⓓ horizontal at $y = -4$

12. Complete the equation of the inverse of the function $f(x) = \log_4(3x)$.

    $\boxed{\frac{1}{3}} \quad \boxed{3} \quad \boxed{4} \quad \boxed{\frac{1}{4}}$

    $f^{-1}(x) = \boxed{} \left(\boxed{}\right)^x$

13. Use the properties of logarithms to choose the expression $x \log 2 - \log \frac{1}{3}$ as a single logarithm.
    - Ⓐ $\log\left(2x - \frac{1}{3}\right)$
    - Ⓑ $\log\left(\frac{2}{3x}\right)$
    - Ⓒ $\log\left(2^x - \frac{1}{3}\right)$
    - Ⓓ $\log(3(2)^x)$

14. The profit for a new website, in thousands of dollars, can be represented by 5^x, where x is time in months. Find the time when the company's profit is $15,000. Select the exact solution as a logarithm, and select an approximate solution.
    - ☐ A. $x = \log_{15} 5$
    - ☐ B. $x = \log_5 15$
    - ☐ C. $x = \log 15$
    - ☐ D. $x = 1.689$
    - ☐ E. $x = 0.594$
    - ☐ F. $x = 0.176$

15. What is the sum of the geometric series $S = 1.375 + 1.1 + 0.88 + \ldots + 0.031$? Round to the nearest thousandth.

    $S = \boxed{}$

16. Complete the steps to write the expression $2\log a + 2\log b - 3\log c$ as a single logarithm using the properties of logarithms.

    $\boxed{\text{Product}} \quad \boxed{\text{Quotient}} \quad \boxed{\text{Power}}$

    $2\log a + 2\log b - 3\log c$
    $= \log a^2 + \log b^2 - \log c^3 \quad \boxed{}$
    $= \log a^2 b^2 - \log c^3 \quad \boxed{}$
    $= \log\left(\frac{a^2 b^2}{c^3}\right) \quad \boxed{}$

17. For the function $f(x) = 2 \cdot (3)^{-x}$, identify the y-intercept and asymptote.

    y-Intercept: $\boxed{}$

    Asymptote: $y = \boxed{}$

6 Performance Assessment Form A

Olivia's power went out at midnight. She knows that during a power outage, it is important to leave the freezer and refrigerator doors closed. This keeps the food inside at a safe temperature for as long as possible.

The temperature inside Olivia's freezer t hours after midnight can be modeled by the equation $T = 70 - 70e^{-0.035t}$, where T is the temperature in degrees Fahrenheit.

1. What was the initial temperature inside the freezer when the power failed at midnight? Explain how you know.

2. What would the temperature inside the freezer be at 4 A.M.?

According to the U.S. Food and Drug Administration, food in your freezer that has partially or completely thawed may be safely refrozen if it still contains ice crystals or is 40°F or below.

3. For how many hours will Olivia's freezer maintain a cold enough temperature? Round your answer to the nearest hour. Show your work.

4. Olivia also wants to know how long the food in her refrigerator will remain safe to eat. She knows the temperature inside the refrigerator can be modeled by an equation of the form $T = 70 - Ce^{-rt}$ for an unknown constant, C, and growth rate, r.

Part A

The temperature inside the refrigerator was 35°F when the power went out. Use this information to find the value of C. Show your work.

Part B

After 1 hour, the temperature inside the refrigerator had risen to 36°F. Use this information, and the value of C from Part A, to find the value of the growth rate, r. Explain how you know.

5. For how many hours will Olivia's refrigerator maintain an inside temperature less than 40°F? Round your answer to the nearest hour. Show your work.

Name _____

6 Performance Assessment Form B

Leah has just inherited $12,000. She wants to invest the money so that she can increase the value of her inheritance. What are some of the ways she can do this?

1. Leah wants to invest the $12,000 in an account that pays 4.5% annual interest.

   Part A

   Write equations for the amount $A(t)$ that will be in the account after t years, if the interest is compounded continuously, daily, and monthly. Then, find the amount after 10 years, rounded to the nearest cent, for each method of compounding. Complete the table.

Compounding	Equation	Amount After 10 Years
Continuously	$A(t) =$	
Daily	$A(t) =$	
Monthly	$A(t) =$	

   Part B

   Which method of compounding has the highest yield? Why?

2. Leah would like to double her $12,000 investment in 10 years. Assuming the interest is compounded daily, what interest rate, r, would she need to earn? Show your work.

3. At Leah's current interest rate of 4.5%, how long will it take to double her $12,000 investment? Assume the interest is compounded daily, and round your answer to the nearest tenth of a year. Show your work.

4. Leah is also planning to make annual contributions to an investment account that pays 4.5% annual interest, compounded monthly.

   Part A

   Complete the tables to find the amount in the account if she deposits either $600 or $1200 per year.

Year	Amount with Interest	Deposit	Total Amount
0		600	600
1		600	
2		600	
3		600	
4		600	
5		600	

Year	Amount with Interest	Deposit	Total Amount
0		1200	1200
1		1200	
2		1200	
3		1200	
4		1200	
5		1200	

   Part B

   Use a graphing calculator to make a scatter plot of the amounts Leah will accumulate for years 1 through 5.

   Part C

   Use a calculator to find an exponential regression model, of the form $A(t) = a \cdot b^t$, that best fits each set of data.

   Part D

   Compare the graphs of the two models. What is the range of each function? How does the value of a affect the graphs? Which function has a greater rate of change?

Benchmark Assessment 3

1. **Part A**

    Graph the function.

    $$y = \begin{cases} -4, & x < 1 \\ 5x - 9, & 1 < x \leq 2 \\ 1, & x > 2 \end{cases}$$

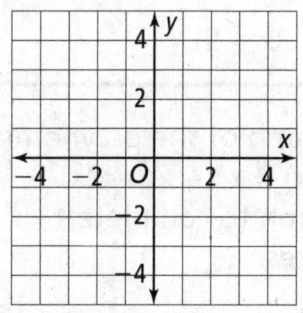

    Part B

    What is the domain of the function?

    Ⓐ $(-\infty, \infty)$

    Ⓑ $[-4, 1]$

    Ⓒ $(-\infty, 1), (1, \infty)$

    Ⓓ $(-\infty, 1), (1, 2), (2, \infty)$

2. Write the explicit formula of the sequence defined by

    $$a_n = \begin{cases} 5, & n = 1 \\ a_{n-1} + 3, & n > 1 \end{cases}$$

    Ⓐ $a_n = 5 + 3n$

    Ⓑ $a_n = 3 + 5n$

    Ⓒ $a_n = 2 + 3n$

    Ⓓ $a_n = -2 + 5n$

3. Write the product $(7 + 3i)(7 - 3i)$ in the form $a + bi$.

    Ⓐ $49 - 9i$ Ⓒ 40

    Ⓑ $49 - 9i^2$ Ⓓ 58

4. Select all solutions to the system:

    $2x - y = 4$

    $y = -(x - 2)^2$

    ☐ A. $(0, -4)$ ☐ D. $(2, -4)$
    ☐ B. $(2, 0)$ ☐ E. $(6, -16)$
    ☐ C. $(6, -4)$ ☐ F. $(4, -4)$

5. Ping's walking route to school goes over a hill. He represents the changing elevation with a graph, where x is the distance from home and y is the elevation. The peak of the hill is at $(-3, 4)$, and the route takes him past city hall at $(-5, 2)$. What is the equation in vertex form of a parabola that represents Ping's elevation?

    Ⓐ $y = \frac{1}{2}(x + 3)^2 - 4$

    Ⓑ $y = -\frac{1}{2}(x - 3)^2 - 4$

    Ⓒ $y = -\frac{1}{2}(x + 3)^2 + 4$

    Ⓓ $y = -2(x + 3)^2 - 4$

6. Solve the equation $4x^2 - 4x = 24$.

    Ⓐ $x = 4, -6$ Ⓒ $x = 2, -3$

    Ⓑ $x = -2, 3$ Ⓓ $x = -3, -4$

7. A stone is tossed from the top of a cliff. The function $h(t) = -16t^2 - 48t + 160$ gives the height, in feet, of the stone t seconds after it is tossed. How long will it be before the stone hits the ground?

    ☐ seconds

8. Solve $x^2 - 2x + 9 = 0$ using the Quadratic Formula.
   - Ⓐ $x = 1 + 2i\sqrt{2}$ and $x = 1 - 2i\sqrt{2}$
   - Ⓑ $x = 1 + 2\sqrt{10}$ and $x = 1 - 2\sqrt{10}$
   - Ⓒ $x = 1$ and $x = 9$
   - Ⓓ $x = \frac{1}{2} + 2i$ and $x = \frac{1}{2} - 2i$

9. For the polynomial function $f(x) = x^5 - 2x^6 + 3$, select all the statements that are true.
   - ☐ A. As x increases, $f(x)$ always decreases.
   - ☐ B. The degree of the polynomial is 6.
   - ☐ C. The graph of the polynomial has five zeros.
   - ☐ D. $f(x) = -2x^6 + x^5 + 3$ is the polynomial written in standard form.
   - ☐ E. $f(x)$ is increasing over the interval $(-\infty, 1)$.

10. The graph of function f is shown. Use the zeros to find a possible rule for f. 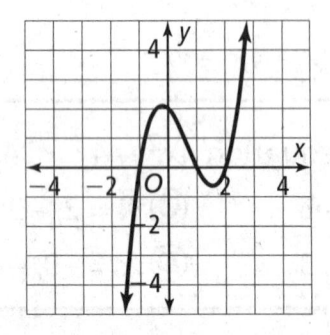
    - Ⓐ $f(x) = x^3 - 2x^2 - x + 2$
    - Ⓑ $f(x) = x^3 + 2x^2 - x - 2$
    - Ⓒ $f(x) = -x^3 + 2x^2 + x - 2$
    - Ⓓ $f(x) = x^3 - 2$

11. If $x + 2$ is a factor of $P(x) = x^3 + 5x^2 + 11x + 10$, select all factors that express $P(x)$ as a product.
    - ☐ A. not a factor
    - ☐ B. $(x + 2)$
    - ☐ C. $(x^2 - 3x + 5)$
    - ☐ D. $(x^2 + 3x - 5)$
    - ☐ E. $(x^2 - 3x - 5)$
    - ☐ F. $(x^2 + 3x + 5)$

12. Sketch a graph of the polynomial function $f(x) = x^3 - x^2 - 2x$. Use the graph to complete the sentences.

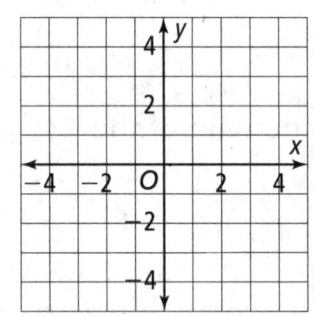

    (increasing) (decreasing)
    (positive) (negative)

    f is [ ] on the intervals $(-\infty, -1)$ and $(0, 2)$.

    f is [ ] on the intervals $(-1, 0)$ and $(2, \infty)$.

    f is [ ] on the intervals $(-\infty, -0.5)$ and $(1.2, \infty)$.

    f is [ ] on the interval $(-0.5, 1.2)$.

13. What are all the real and complex solutions of $x^3 - 2x^2 + 9x - 8 = 10$?

    Ⓐ $3i, -3i, 2$
    Ⓑ $3i, -2, 2$
    Ⓒ $3i, -3i, -2$
    Ⓓ $3, -3, 2i$

14. Simplify $\frac{12}{a-4} + \frac{3a}{4-a}$. What are the restrictions on the variable?

    $\boxed{\dfrac{12 - 3a}{a - 4}}$

    restrictions: $a \neq \boxed{}$

15. R varies inversely with x. If $R = -2$ when $x = 6$, what is the value of R when $x = -3$?

    Ⓐ -4
    Ⓑ -1
    Ⓒ 1
    Ⓓ 4

16. Select all the horizontal and vertical asymptotes for the graph of
    $y = \dfrac{x^2 - x - 6}{14 - 9x + x^2}$.

    ☐ A. $y = 1$
    ☐ B. $y = 0$
    ☐ C. $y = -6$
    ☐ D. $x = -2$
    ☐ E. $x = 7$
    ☐ F. $x = 2$

17. Describe the transformations needed to translate the graph of $y = \frac{1}{x}$ to the graph of $y = \frac{1}{x+1} - 3$.

    Ⓐ to the right 1 and down 3
    Ⓑ to the right 1 and up 3
    Ⓒ to the left 1 and down 3
    Ⓓ to the left 1 and up 3

18. If $a = \frac{1}{x} - \frac{1}{y}$, what is the value of $\frac{1}{a}$?

    Ⓐ $\dfrac{xy}{y-x}$
    Ⓑ $\dfrac{1}{x-y}$
    Ⓒ $\dfrac{xy}{x-y}$
    Ⓓ $x - y$

19. Simplify $\sqrt[4]{16a^8 b^{24}}$.

    Ⓐ $4a^4 b^{12}$
    Ⓑ $4a^4 b^6$
    Ⓒ $2b^{16}$
    Ⓓ $2a^2 b^6$

20. Consider the equation
    $(x - 3)^2 = |x - 1|$.

    Part A

    Graph the system of equations that reveals the solutions to the equation.

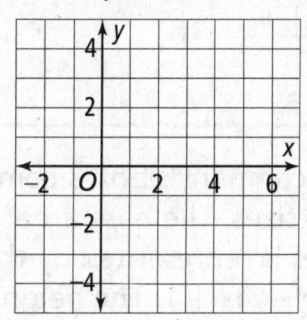

    Part B

    What are the solutions?

    $x = \boxed{}$ and $x = \boxed{}$

21. The graph of $y = \sqrt{x}$ has been translated to the right 1 unit and up 4 units. What is the equation of the translated graph?

Ⓐ $y = 1 + \sqrt{x+4}$
Ⓑ $y = 4 - \sqrt{x-1}$
Ⓒ $y = 4 + \sqrt{x-1}$
Ⓓ $y = 3 + \sqrt{x}$

22. If $f(x) = 3 - x$ and $g(x) = \sqrt{2x}$, what is the domain of $(g \circ f)(x)$? Use the choices provided.

$\boxed{>}$ $\boxed{<}$ $\boxed{\geq}$ $\boxed{\leq}$ $\boxed{0}$ $\boxed{3}$
$\boxed{-3}$ $\boxed{-2}$ $\boxed{2}$ $\boxed{6}$ $\boxed{-6}$

Domain: x ▢ ▢
Range: y ▢ ▢

23. Graph the function $f(x) = -2 + \sqrt{x}$.

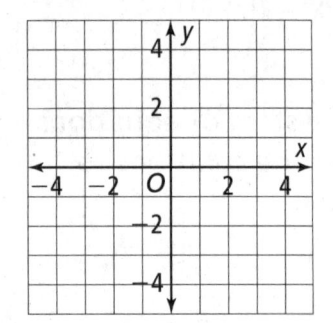

24. A shipping company's boxes come in different sizes. The base area of the boxes is represented by the function $4x^2 - 4x + 1$. The height of the boxes is $2x - 1$. Select all the expressions that represent the volume of the boxes.

☐ A. $6x^3 + 6x^2 - 6x + 1$
☐ B. $(2x - 1)^3$
☐ C. $8x^3 - 12x^2 + 6x - 1$
☐ D. $4x^2 - 2x$
☐ E. $(2x + 1)(2x - 1)^2$

25. Let $f(x) = \sqrt{x-2}$ and $g(x) = 3x$. What is the domain of $f \circ g$?

Ⓐ $x > \frac{3}{2}$
Ⓑ $x < \frac{1}{3}$
Ⓒ $x \geq \frac{2}{4}$
Ⓓ $x \geq \frac{2}{3}$

26. If $h(x) = 4x - 3$, what is an equation for $h^{-1}(x)$?

Ⓐ $h^{-1}(x) = 3x + 4$
Ⓑ $h^{-1}(x) = 3x - 4$
Ⓒ $h^{-1}(x) = \frac{x+3}{4}$
Ⓓ $h^{-1}(x) = \frac{x-3}{4}$

27. If $f(x) = \sqrt{x-3}$, select all the statements that are true.

☐ A. $f^{-1}(0) = 3$
☐ B. $f^{-1}(-1) = 4$
☐ C. $f \circ f^{-1}(7) = 7$
☐ D. $f^{-1}(12) = 3$
☐ E. $f^{-1}(-2) = 1$

28. Solve $\sqrt{x+7} - 1 = \sqrt{3x+10}$.

Ⓐ -3
Ⓑ 0
Ⓒ 2
Ⓓ $-3, 2$

29. Which function represents the exponential function $f(x) = 5^x$ after a horizontal stretch by a factor of 2 and a reflection across the x-axis?

   Ⓐ $g(x) = \left(-\frac{1}{2}\right) 5^x$
   Ⓑ $g(x) = -5^{\frac{x}{2}}$
   Ⓒ $g(x) = -2 \cdot 5^x$
   Ⓓ $g(x) = -5^{2x}$

30. For the function $f(x) = \frac{1}{4} \cdot 6^x$, identify the y-intercept and the asymptote. Write answers as decimals when necessary.

   y-intercept: (☐, ☐)
   asymptote: $y =$ ☐

31. Which of the following functions has a greater growth factor than the function shown in the graph?

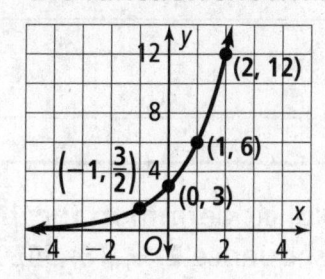

   [Graph showing points $(-1, \frac{3}{2})$, $(0, 3)$, $(1, 6)$, $(2, 12)$]

   Ⓐ $f(x) = 5 \cdot 3^x$
   Ⓑ $f(x) = 1.2^x$
   Ⓒ $f(x) = \left(\frac{1}{2}\right)^x$
   Ⓓ $f(x) = \frac{1}{3} \cdot 0.2^x$

32. A colony of spiders has a population of 350. The population is decreasing at a rate of 3% per year.

   Part A

   Complete the exponential decay function for the quarterly decay rate.

   $y =$ ☐(☐)^☐^{t}

   Part B

   Select the correct phrase and number to complete the sentence.

   The y-intercept is the

   ☐ number of spiders
   ☐ number of quarters   at time
   ☐ number of years

   ☐ 0.
   ☐ 1.
   ☐ 350.

33. Which function is the inverse of the exponential function $y = \left(\frac{3}{2}\right)^x$?

   Ⓐ $y = \left(\frac{2}{3}\right)^x$
   Ⓑ $y = x^{\frac{3}{2}}$
   Ⓒ $y = \log_{\frac{3}{2}} x$
   Ⓓ $y = \log_x \left(\frac{2}{3}\right)$

34. What is the solution to the equation $\log_2(5x - 2) = -2$?

   (2)(3)(5)(9)(10)(20)
   $\dfrac{\boxed{}}{\boxed{}}$

35. The graph shows the function $f(x) = \frac{1}{2} \cdot 4^x + 3$. What is the value of the inverse function f^{-1} at $x = 5$?

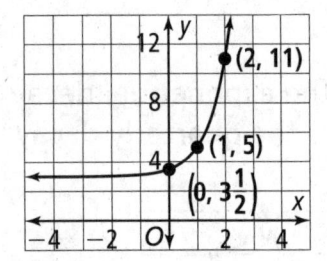

[Graph showing points $(2, 11)$, $(1, 5)$, $(0, 3\frac{1}{2})$]

Ⓐ 5
Ⓑ $3\frac{1}{2}$
Ⓒ 1
Ⓓ 2

---

36. Complete the equation of the inverse of the function $f(x) = \log_5(2x)$. Write values as decimals when necessary.

$y = \boxed{}(\boxed{})^x$

---

37. Is $g(x) = 2|x| + 5$ odd, even, or neither?

Ⓐ odd
Ⓑ even
Ⓒ neither
Ⓓ either

---

38. The formula for the area of a sphere is $2\pi r^2 + 2\pi rh$ where r and h represent the radius and height respectively. Which term of this formula is not dependent on the height?

Ⓐ π
Ⓑ $2\pi r^2$
Ⓒ $2\pi rh$
Ⓓ $2\pi r$

---

39. Select the steps to write the expression $2 \log m - \log n - 4 \log p$ as a single logarithm using the properties of logarithms.

| Product Property of Logarithms |
| Quotient Property of Logarithms |
| Power Property of Logarithms |

$2 \log m - \log n - 4 \log p$
$= \log m^2 - \log n - \log p^4$

$\boxed{}$

$= \log m^2 - \log np^4$

$\boxed{}$

$= \log\left(\dfrac{m^2}{np^4}\right)$

$\boxed{}$

---

40. Write an explicit definition for the geometric sequence 2, 6, 18, 54,.... What is the value of the 8th term of the sequence?

$a_n = \boxed{}(\boxed{})^{n-1}$

8th term: $\boxed{}$

7 Readiness Assessment

In $\triangle ABC$, $m\angle A = 90$, $m\angle C = 20$, $BC \approx 12$ cm, and $AB \approx 4.1$ cm. Also, $\triangle ABC \sim \triangle DEF$ and $EF = 6$ cm. Use this information for Items 1–2. Round to the nearest tenth of a unit if necessary.

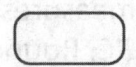

1. What is $m\angle E$?
   ☐

2. What is DF?
   ☐ cm

Use the figure for Items 3–4.

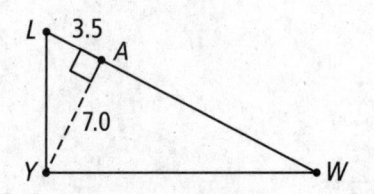

3. What is LW?
   ☐ units

4. What is the area of $\triangle YWL$?
   ☐ units^2

For Items 5–7, describe each function as a transformation of the parent function $f(x) = x^2$.

5. $g(x) = x^2 - 2x + 4$
   Ⓐ translation 1 unit to the left and 2 units up
   Ⓑ translation 1 unit down and 2 units to the right
   Ⓒ translation 1 unit to the right and 3 units up
   Ⓓ translation 1 unit up and 3 units to the right

6. $h(x) = 2x^2 + 4x + 2$
   Ⓐ vertical stretch and translation 1 unit to the left
   Ⓑ vertical compression and translation 1 unit to the right
   Ⓒ vertical stretch and translation 2 units up
   Ⓓ horizontal compression and translation 2 units to the right

7. $j(x) = x^2 - 4x$
   Ⓐ translation 2 units down and 4 units to the right
   Ⓑ translation 2 units to the left and 4 units down
   Ⓒ translation 2 units to the right and 4 units down
   Ⓓ translation 4 units to the left and horizontal stretch

8. Graph $f(x) = (x - 1)(x - 5)$.

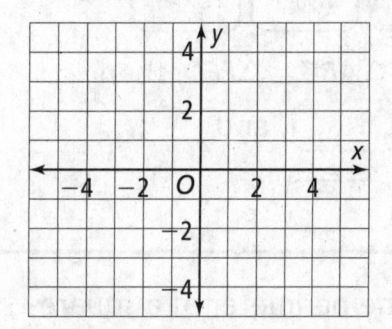

9. Graph $g(x) = \dfrac{1}{x - 2}$.

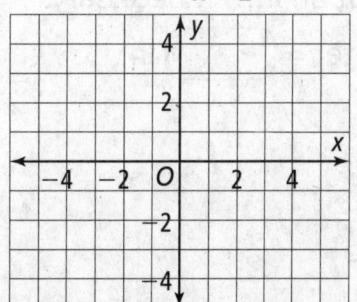

10. Find the distance between the points (−1, 5) and (3, 2).
    (A) $\sqrt{5}$
    (B) $\sqrt{58}$
    (C) 5
    (D) $\frac{1}{2}$

11. Use the Pythagorean Theorem to find the missing side length of the triangular table.

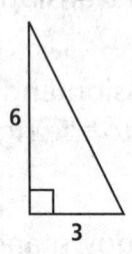

    (A) $3\sqrt{5}$
    (B) 7
    (C) 9
    (D) $6\sqrt{3}$

12. Complete:

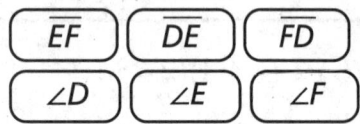

    | EF | DE | FD |
    | ∠D | ∠E | ∠F |

    Given $\triangle ABC \cong \triangle FED$, then
    $\angle C \cong$ ☐, and
    $\overline{AC} \cong$ ☐.

13. Find the perimeter of a square tile knowing that its diagonal is 5 inches long. Round to the nearest tenth of an inch if necessary.
    Perimeter = ☐ in.

14. An acute angle of a right triangle has a measure of 30, and the length of the triangle's hypotenuse is 10 ft. Find the missing angle measure and side lengths.
    (A) 60, 5 ft, $5\sqrt{3}$ ft
    (B) 30, 5 ft, $5\sqrt{3}$ ft
    (C) 60, 2 ft, $2\sqrt{3}$ ft
    (D) 30, 2 ft, $2\sqrt{3}$ ft

15. Find the missing angle measures and side lengths of $\triangle ABC$. Round to the nearest tenth.

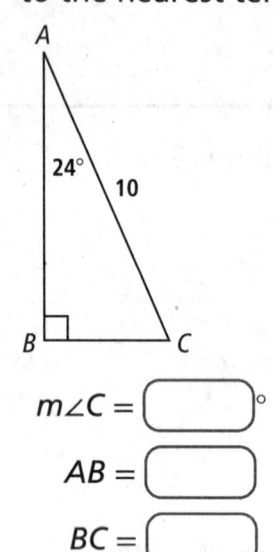

    $m\angle C =$ ☐°
    $AB =$ ☐
    $BC =$ ☐

16. Complete:

    | BD | CD | FG |
    | ∠E | ∠F | ∠G |

    Given $\triangle BCD \sim \triangle EFG$, then $\frac{BC}{EF} = \frac{☐}{EG}$
    and $\angle C \cong$ ☐.

Name _____

7-1 Lesson Quiz
The Unit Circle

1. Select all the possible measures for the angle shown.

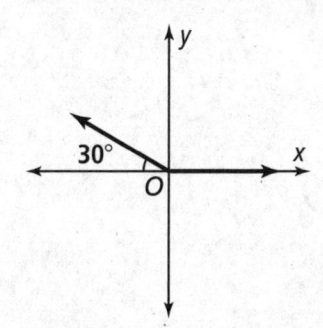

    ☐ A. $-\frac{4\pi}{3}$ ☐ B. −210°   ☐ C. $\frac{5\pi}{6}$ ☐ D. 210°   ☐ E. 510°

2. An angle has a reference angle measuring 35° and its terminal side lies in Quadrant IV. What are possible positive and negative measures for the angle?

    Ⓐ 325°, −35°
    Ⓑ 35°, −145°
    Ⓒ 35°, −325°
    Ⓓ 145°, −35°

3. Find the measure of an angle that is positive and less than 360° in standard position for each reference angle.

    68° in quadrant II: ◯ °

    75° in quadrant IV: ◯ °

    22° in quadrant III: ◯ °

4. Convert the angle measures $\frac{\pi}{6}$ radians and $\frac{5\pi}{3}$ radians to degrees.

    $\frac{\pi}{6}$ radians = ◯ °

    $\frac{5\pi}{3}$ radians = ◯ °

5. A carousel horse travels on a circular path with a radius of 15 feet. How many feet does the horse travel over an angle of $\frac{2\pi}{3}$ radians? Round to the nearest foot.

    $\frac{2\pi}{3}$ radians = ◯ ft

enVision® Algebra 2 • Assessment Sourcebook

7-2 Lesson Quiz

Evaluating Trigonometric Functions

1. What are the sine and cosine of $\frac{2\pi}{3}$?

   $\boxed{\frac{\sqrt{3}}{2}}$ $\boxed{-\frac{1}{2}}$ $\boxed{\frac{1}{2}}$ $\boxed{-\frac{\sqrt{3}}{2}}$ $\boxed{\sqrt{3}}$ $\boxed{4}$

   $\sin \frac{2\pi}{3} = \boxed{}$ $\cos \frac{2\pi}{3} = \boxed{}$

2. What is $\sin \theta$ if $\cos \theta = \frac{12}{13}$ and θ is in Quadrant IV?

   Ⓐ $\sin \theta = \frac{12}{13}$ Ⓒ $\sin \theta = \frac{5}{13}$

   Ⓑ $\sin \theta = -\frac{5}{13}$ Ⓓ $\sin \theta = -\frac{12}{13}$

3. Select all the correct statements.

   ☐ A. $\tan\left(-\frac{4\pi}{3}\right) = -\sqrt{3}$

   ☐ B. $\cos\left(-\frac{7\pi}{4}\right) = \frac{-\sqrt{2}}{2}$

   ☐ C. $\cot\left(-\frac{11\pi}{3}\right) = \frac{-\sqrt{3}}{3}$

   ☐ D. $\sec\left(\frac{7\pi}{6}\right) = \frac{-2\sqrt{3}}{3}$

   ☐ E. $\sin\left(\frac{13\pi}{6}\right) = \frac{1}{2}$

4. Which of the following are true? Select all that apply.

   ☐ A. $\csc 225° = -\sqrt{2}$ ☐ D. $\sec 225° = 1$

   ☐ B. $\cot 225° = \sqrt{2}$ ☐ E. $\sec 225° = -\sqrt{2}$

   ☐ C. $\cot 225° = 1$ ☐ F. $\csc 225° = \sqrt{2}$

5. Using a two-way radio, Melissa can talk to anyone within an 8-mile radius of her location. Oscar is 30° west of south of Melissa's location. What is Oscar's exact location, relative to Melissa's location, at the greatest distance where they can talk using two-way radios?

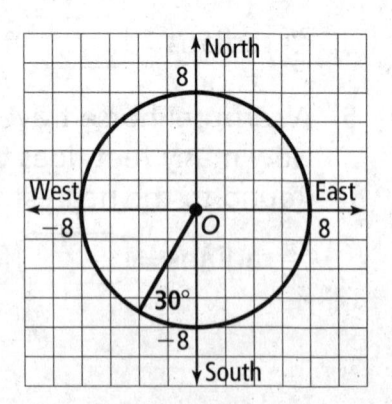

   $\boxed{-4}$ $\boxed{-4\sqrt{3}}$ $\boxed{2\sqrt{3}}$ $\boxed{-3\sqrt{4}}$ $\boxed{3}$ $\boxed{-2}$

   $(\boxed{}, \boxed{})$

7-3 Lesson Quiz

Graphing Sine and Cosine Functions

1. Select all the correct statements.
   - ☐ A. The amplitude of $y = 2\cos\left(\frac{1}{2}x\right)$ is $\frac{1}{2}$.
   - ☐ B. The period of $y = 2\cos\left(\frac{1}{2}x\right)$ is π.
   - ☐ C. The amplitude of $y = \frac{\pi}{2}\sin\left(\frac{\pi}{2}x\right)$ is $\frac{\pi}{2}$.
   - ☐ D. The period of $y = 4\pi\sin\left(\frac{1}{2}x\right)$ is 4π.
   - ☐ E. The period of $y = \cos(2\pi x)$ is 1.
   - ☐ F. The amplitude of $y = 2\sin\left(\frac{1}{2}x\right)$ is 2.

2. What is the average rate of change of the function $y = 3\sin(2x)$ on the interval $\left[0, \frac{\pi}{4}\right]$?

   Ⓐ $-\frac{12}{\pi}$ Ⓑ $-\frac{6}{\pi}$ Ⓒ $\frac{6}{\pi}$ Ⓓ $\frac{12}{\pi}$

3. The equation for f and the graph of g are given. How do the period and the amplitude of the functions compare? $f(x) = 2\cos\left(\frac{\pi}{2}x\right)$

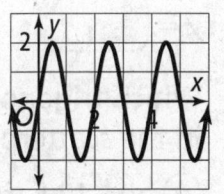

   Ⓐ The amplitudes are the same, but the period of f is half as long as the period of g.

   Ⓑ The amplitudes are the same, but the period of f is twice as long as the period of g.

   Ⓒ The periods are the same, but the amplitude of f is half as great as the amplitude of g.

   Ⓓ The periods are the same, but the amplitude of f is twice as great as the amplitude of g.

4. The graph of the function $f(x) = 5\cos(2x)$ is a reflection over the x-axis of the graph of $g(x) = $ ☐ ☐ (☐).

   [−5] [cos] [2x] [sin] [−2x] [5]

5. High tides at a beach occur at intervals of 12 hours 25 minutes. Yesterday, high tide was measured at 5 feet above sea level and low tide was measured at 1 foot above sea level. What is the amplitude of a cosine function modeling the depth of the water in feet as a function of time in hours?

   amplitude = ☐ ft

7-4 Lesson Quiz

Translating Trigonometric Functions

1. Select all the correct statements about the graphs of $y = \frac{1}{2}\sin x$ and $y = \frac{1}{2}\sin\left(x - \frac{\pi}{2}\right)$.
   - ☐ A. The graph of $y = \frac{1}{2}\sin\left(x - \frac{\pi}{2}\right)$ is shifted $\frac{\pi}{2}$ units left from the graph of $y = \frac{1}{2}\sin x$.
   - ☐ B. The graph of $y = \frac{1}{2}\sin\left(x - \frac{\pi}{2}\right)$ is shifted $\frac{\pi}{2}$ units right from the graph of $y = \frac{1}{2}\sin x$.
   - ☐ C. The period of $y = \frac{1}{2}\sin\left(x - \frac{\pi}{2}\right)$ is $\frac{\pi}{2}$, and the period of $y = \frac{1}{2}\sin x$ is 2π.
   - ☐ D. The amplitude of $y = \frac{1}{2}\sin\left(x - \frac{\pi}{2}\right)$ is half the amplitude of $y = \frac{1}{2}\sin x$.
   - ☐ E. The amplitude of $y = \frac{1}{2}\sin\left(x - \frac{\pi}{2}\right)$ is the same as the amplitude of $y = \frac{1}{2}\sin x$.

2. Function f is a cosine function with period 8π, amplitude 3, and a local maximum at $f(0) = -3$. What is the equation of the midline of the graph of f?

   $y = \boxed{}$

3. Which trigonometric function best models the average low temperatures shown in the scatterplot?
   - Ⓐ $y = 12.5 \sin\left[\frac{\pi}{6}(x + 4)\right] + 17.5$
   - Ⓑ $y = 17.5 \sin\left(\frac{\pi}{6}x\right) + 12.5$
   - Ⓒ $y = 12.5 \sin\left(\frac{\pi}{6}x\right) + 17.5$
   - Ⓓ $y = 12.5 \sin\left[\frac{\pi}{6}(x - 4)\right] + 17.5$

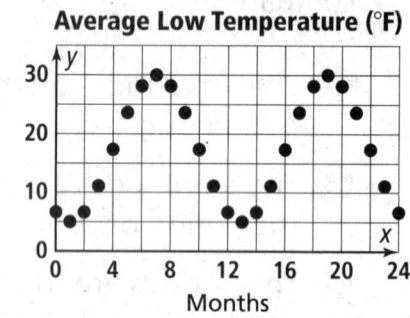

4. What is the phase shift of the graph of $y = -2 \sin\left(\frac{3}{2}x - \frac{\pi}{2}\right) - 4$?
   - Ⓐ $\frac{\pi}{2}$ units right
   - Ⓑ $\frac{\pi}{3}$ units right
   - Ⓒ 4 units left
   - Ⓓ $\frac{3\pi}{4}$ units right

5. Select all the statements that describe the key features of the graph of $y = 2 \cos\left[\frac{1}{2}\left(x + \frac{\pi}{4}\right)\right] + 5$.
   - ☐ A. amplitude = 5
   - ☐ B. period = 4π
   - ☐ C. phase shift is $\frac{\pi}{4}$ units left
   - ☐ D. phase shift is 5 units left
   - ☐ E. vertical shift is $\frac{\pi}{4}$ units up
   - ☐ F. vertical shift is 5 units up

7-5 Lesson Quiz

Graphing Other Trigonometric Functions

1. Select all the correct statements about the graph of $y = \tan x$.

   ☐ A. The period of the function is π.

   ☐ B. The range of the function is $\left(-\frac{\pi}{2}, \frac{\pi}{2}\right)$.

   ☐ C. The function has vertical asymptotes whenever $\sin x = 0$.

   ☐ D. The function has zeros whenever $\cos x = 0$.

   ☐ E. The function is increasing everywhere in its domain.

2. The graph of $y = \tan x$ is stretched vertically by a factor of 4 and compressed horizontally to have a period of $\frac{\pi}{3}$. What is the equation of the new graph?

   $y = \boxed{} \tan \boxed{}$

3. Choose from $\cot x$, $\sec x$, and $\csc x$ to complete the sentences below.

   $\boxed{\sin x}$ $\boxed{\cos x}$ $\boxed{\tan x}$ $\boxed{\csc x}$ $\boxed{\sec x}$ $\boxed{\cot x}$

   The graph of $y = \frac{1}{\sin x}$ is the same as the graph of $y = \boxed{}$.

   The graph of $y = \frac{1}{\cos x}$ is the same as the graph of $y = \boxed{}$.

   The graph of $y = \frac{\cos x}{\sin x}$ is the same as the graph of $y = \boxed{}$.

4. The function $y = f(x)$ is a tangent or cotangent function and its graph is as shown.

   What is the equation of this function? Use decimals rounded to one decimal place.

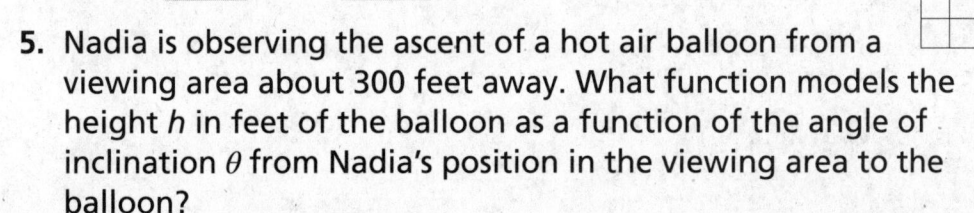

   $f(x) = \boxed{} \cot (\boxed{} x)$

5. Nadia is observing the ascent of a hot air balloon from a viewing area about 300 feet away. What function models the height h in feet of the balloon as a function of the angle of inclination θ from Nadia's position in the viewing area to the balloon?

   Ⓐ $h = \tan(150\,\theta)$ Ⓑ $h = 150 \tan \theta$ Ⓒ $h = \tan(300\,\theta)$ Ⓓ $h = 300 \tan \theta$

Name _____

7 Topic Assessment Form A

1. Given $\sin \theta = \frac{12}{13}$, what is $\sec \theta$?
   $\boxed{} \over \boxed{}$

2. The graph of f is given. How are f and $g(x) = 2\cos(\pi x)$ different?

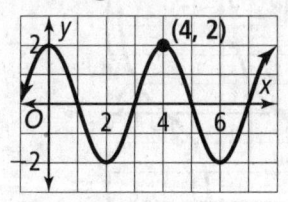

   [graph showing sinusoidal curve with point (4, 2)]

   Ⓐ The period of f is half as long as the period of g.

   Ⓑ The period of f is twice as long as the period of g.

   Ⓒ The amplitude of f is half as great as the amplitude of g.

   Ⓓ The amplitude of f is twice as great as the amplitude of g.

3. If $\cot \theta = 3$, what is $\sin \theta$? Round to the nearest hundredth. $\boxed{}$

4. What are the sine and cosine of $\frac{4\pi}{3}$?

   $\boxed{-\frac{\sqrt{3}}{2}}$ $\boxed{\sqrt{3}}$ $\boxed{\frac{\sqrt{3}}{2}}$

   $\boxed{-\frac{1}{2}}$ $\boxed{2}$ $\boxed{\frac{1}{2}}$

   $\sin \frac{4\pi}{3} = \boxed{}$

   $\cos \frac{4\pi}{3} = \boxed{}$

5. Tyler is observing the ascent of a steel beam being lifted by a crane from a position about 250 feet away. What function models the height h in feet of the beam as a function of the angle of inclination θ from Tyler's position to the steel beam?

   $h = \boxed{} \boxed{} \theta$

6. Today, high tide measured 7.5 ft and low tide measured 3 ft. What is the amplitude of a cosine function modeling the depth of the water in feet as a function of time in hours? $\boxed{}$ ft

7. Write a trigonometric function that models the average high temperatures shown in the graph.

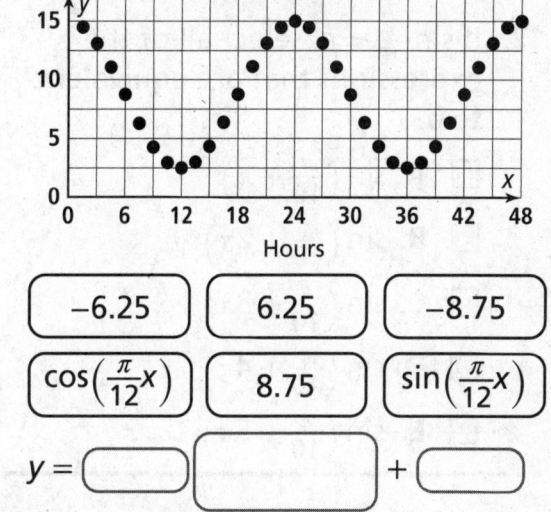

   Average High Temperature (°F)

   [scatter plot with x-axis Hours from 0 to 48, y-axis from 0 to 15]

   $\boxed{-6.25}$ $\boxed{6.25}$ $\boxed{-8.75}$

   $\boxed{\cos\left(\frac{\pi}{12}x\right)}$ $\boxed{8.75}$ $\boxed{\sin\left(\frac{\pi}{12}x\right)}$

   $y = \boxed{} \boxed{} + \boxed{}$

8. Function f is a cosine function with period 8π, amplitude 2, and a local maximum at $f(0) = -1$. What is the equation of the midline of the graph of f? $y = \boxed{}$

9. Select all the possible measures for the angle shown.
   - A. $-\frac{17\pi}{6}$
   - B. $-210°$
   - C. $-\frac{2\pi}{3}$
   - D. $\frac{5\pi}{6}$
   - E. $210°$

10. What is the phase shift of the graph of $y = -\sin(x + \frac{\pi}{4}) + 2$?
    - A. $\frac{\pi}{4}$ units left
    - B. 2 units left
    - C. $\frac{\pi}{4}$ units right
    - D. 2 units right

11. What is the average rate of change for the function in Item 12, over the interval $[0, 2\pi]$?
    - A. -1
    - B. 0
    - C. 2
    - D. 2π

12. If $\sin\frac{\pi}{10} = a$, select all of the expressions that are equivalent to a.
    - A. $\sin\left(\frac{\pi}{10} + \pi\right)$
    - B. $\sin\left(\frac{\pi}{10} + 2\pi\right)$
    - C. $\sin\left(\frac{\pi}{10} + 3\pi\right)$
    - D. $\sin\left(\frac{\pi}{10} + 4\pi\right)$
    - E. $\sin\left(\frac{\pi}{10} + 5\pi\right)$

13. A car is on a Ferris wheel with a radius of 20 feet. To the nearest foot, how far does the car travel over an angle of $\frac{\pi}{3}$ radians?

    ☐ ft

14. An angle intercepts an arc of length $\frac{31\pi}{36}$ radians on the unit circle. What are a possible positive measure and negative measure for the angle?
    - A. $335°, -25°$
    - B. $25°, -335°$
    - C. $205°, -155°$
    - D. $155°, -205°$

15. What equation is represented by the graph?
    - A. $y = \frac{1}{2}\tan x$
    - B. $y = \frac{1}{2}\cot x$
    - C. $y = \tan\frac{1}{2}x$
    - D. $y = \cot\frac{1}{2}x$

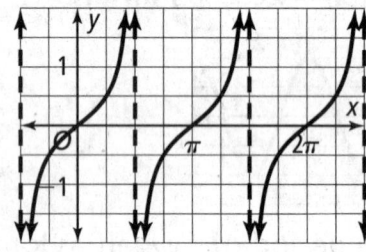

16. What is $\cos\theta$ if $\sin\theta = -\frac{8}{10}$ and θ is in Quadrant III?
    - A. $\cos\theta = -\frac{6}{10}$
    - B. $\cos\theta = \frac{6}{10}$
    - C. $\cos\theta = -\frac{6}{8}$
    - D. $\cos\theta = \frac{6}{8}$

17. What is the frequency of the graph of $y = 2\sin\left(\frac{1}{2}x + 2\pi\right) - 3$?

    | $\frac{1}{2\pi}$ | $\frac{1}{4\pi}$ | π |
    | 2π | 4π | $\frac{1}{\pi}$ |

18. What is the average rate of change of the function $y = 2\sin\left(\frac{1}{2}x\right)$ on the interval $[0, \pi]$?
    - A. 2
    - B. $\frac{\pi}{2}$
    - C. 1
    - D. $\frac{2}{\pi}$

Name _____

7 Topic Assessment Form B

enVision Algebra 2
SavvasRealize.com

1. Given $\sin\theta = \frac{24}{25}$, what is $\cos\theta$?

   ▢/▢

   _____

2. The graph of f is given. How are f and $g(x) = 2\sin(\pi x)$ different?

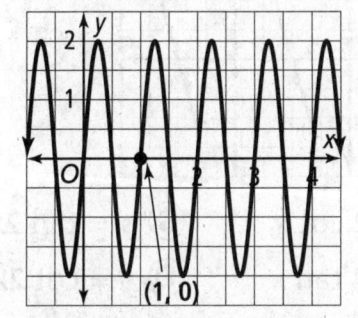

   (1, 0)

   Ⓐ The period of f is half as long as the period of g.

   Ⓑ The period of f is twice as long as the period of g.

   Ⓒ The amplitude of f is half as great as the amplitude of g.

   Ⓓ The amplitude of f is twice as great as the amplitude of g.

3. If $\tan\theta = 2$, what is $\cos\theta$? Round to the nearest hundredth. ▢

4. What are the sine and cosine of $\frac{5\pi}{3}$?

   | $-\frac{\sqrt{3}}{2}$ | $\sqrt{3}$ | $\frac{\sqrt{3}}{2}$ |
   | $-\frac{1}{2}$ | 2 | $\frac{1}{2}$ |

   $\sin\frac{5\pi}{3} =$ ▢

   $\cos\frac{5\pi}{3} =$ ▢

5. Nicholas observes a box being hoisted onto a ship. Nicholas stands on a dock about 150 feet away. Which function models the height, h, in feet, of the cargo as a function of the angle of inclination, θ, from Nicholas to the box?

   $h =$ ▢ ▢ θ

6. Today, high tide is measured at 6 ft and low tide is measured at 2.5 ft. What is the amplitude of a cosine function modeling the depth of the water in feet as a function of time in hours? ▢ ft

7. Write a trigonometric function that models the average rainfall shown in the graph?

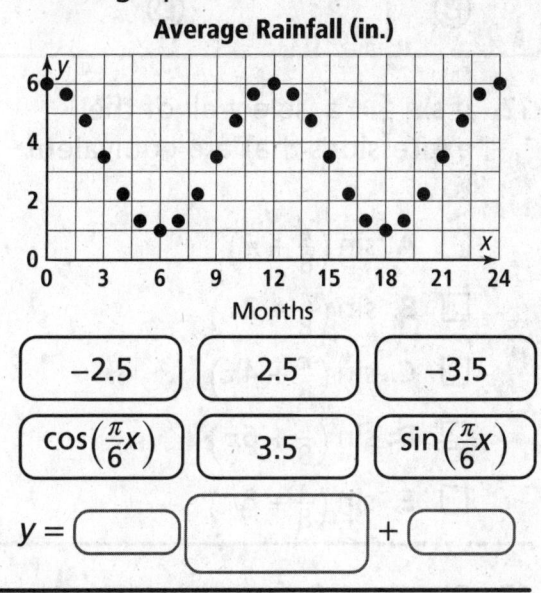

   Average Rainfall (in.)

   Months

   | -2.5 | 2.5 | -3.5 |
   | $\cos(\frac{\pi}{6}x)$ | 3.5 | $\sin(\frac{\pi}{6}x)$ |

   $y =$ ▢ ▢ $+$ ▢

8. Function f is a cosine function with period 8π, amplitude 2.5, and a local maximum at $f(0) = 6$. What is the equation of the midline of the graph of f? $y =$ ▢

enVision® Algebra 2 — Assessment Sourcebook

9. Select all the possible measures for the angle shown. 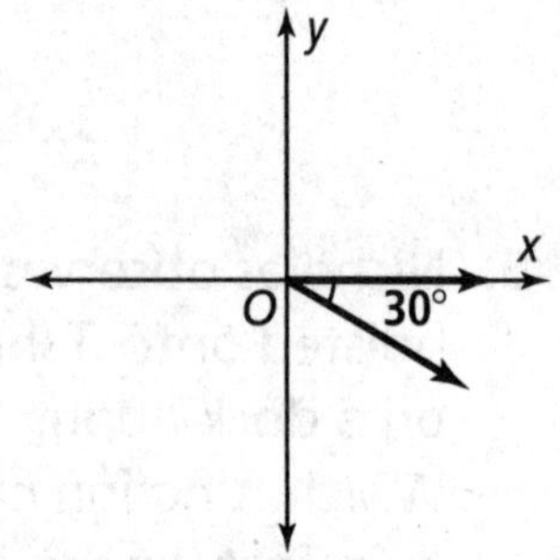
   - A. $-\frac{23\pi}{6}$
   - B. $-\frac{13\pi}{6}$
   - C. $-\frac{7\pi}{6}$
   - D. $-330°$
   - E. $330°$

10. What is the phase shift of the graph of $y = -\sin(x - \pi) - 3$?
    - Ⓐ π units left
    - Ⓑ 3 units left
    - Ⓒ π units right
    - Ⓓ 3 units right

11. What is the average rate of change for the function in Item 12, over the interval $[0, \pi]$?
    - Ⓐ $-\pi$
    - Ⓑ -1
    - Ⓒ 0
    - Ⓓ π

12. If $\sin \frac{\pi}{8} = a$, select all of the expressions that are equivalent to a.
    - A. $\sin\left(\frac{\pi}{8} + \pi\right)$
    - B. $\sin\left(\frac{\pi}{8} + 2\pi\right)$
    - C. $\sin\left(\frac{\pi}{8} + 4\pi\right)$
    - D. $\sin\left(\frac{\pi}{8} + 6\pi\right)$
    - E. $\sin\left(\frac{\pi}{8} + 8\pi\right)$

13. Reagan rides on a playground roundabout with a radius of 2.5 feet. To the nearest foot, how far does Reagan travel over an angle of $\frac{4\pi}{3}$ radians? ☐ ft

14. An intercepts an arc of length $\frac{29\pi}{36}$ radians on the unit circle. What are a possible positive measure and negative measure for the angle?
    - Ⓐ $325°, -35°$
    - Ⓑ $35°, -325°$
    - Ⓒ $215°, -145°$
    - Ⓓ $145°, -215°$

15. What equation is represented by the graph? 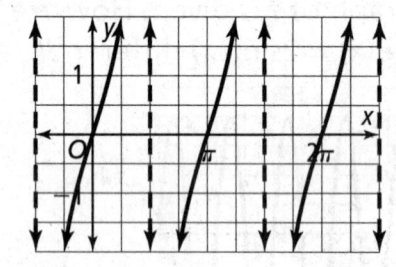
    - Ⓐ $y = 2\cot x$
    - Ⓑ $y = 2\tan x$
    - Ⓒ $y = \tan 2x$
    - Ⓓ $y = \cot 2x$

16. What is $\cos\theta$ if $\sin\theta = -\frac{8}{10}$ and θ is in Quadrant IV?
    - Ⓐ $\cos\theta = -\frac{6}{10}$
    - Ⓑ $\cos\theta = \frac{6}{10}$
    - Ⓒ $\cos\theta = -\frac{6}{8}$
    - Ⓓ $\cos\theta = \frac{6}{8}$

17. What is the frequency of the graph of $y = 4\sin(x + \pi) - 2$?

    | $\frac{1}{2\pi}$ | $\frac{1}{4\pi}$ | π |
    | 2π | 4π | $\frac{1}{\pi}$ |

18. What is the average rate of change of the function $y = 4\sin(x)$ on the interval $\left[0, \frac{3\pi}{2}\right]$?
    - Ⓐ $-\frac{16}{\pi}$
    - Ⓑ $-\frac{8}{3\pi}$
    - Ⓒ $-\frac{4}{\pi}$
    - Ⓓ $-\frac{2}{\pi}$

7 Performance Assessment Form A

The first Ferris wheel was designed and built by an American engineer named George W. G. Ferris in 1893. The radius of the wheel was 125 feet. A Ferris wheel modeled on the original design takes 20 seconds to complete one revolution counterclockwise.

1. Suppose a Ferris wheel with the above characteristics is tested for functionality. Two engineers are in non-adjacent cars where the central angle between the cars is $\frac{\pi}{6}$ radians. Find the arc length between the cars of the engineers. Show your work.

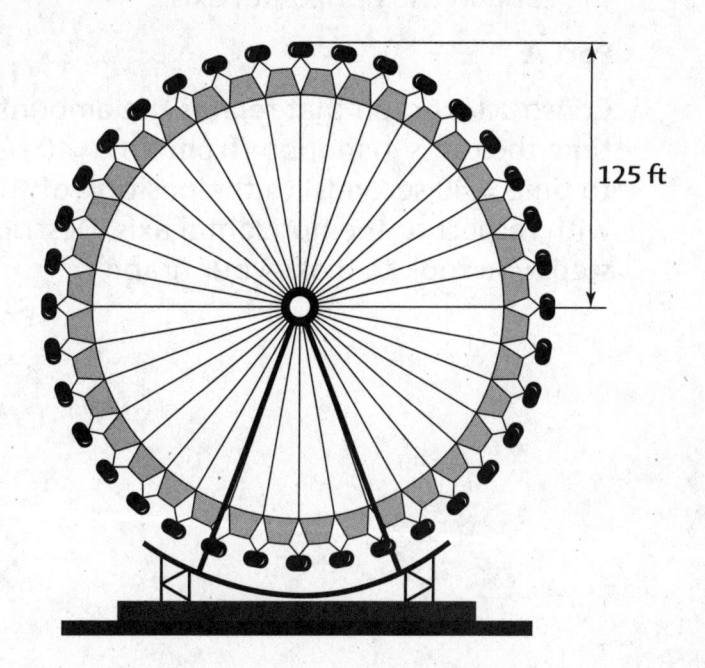

2. An architect transposes a unit circle over a Ferris wheel drawing where the center of the circle is the center of the Ferris wheel. The start position for a car is when $\theta = 0°$.

   ### Part A

   He sketches the motion of the car to a position where $\cos \theta \approx \frac{9}{41}$. Use trigonometric identities to find the other trigonometric ratios for θ.

   ### Part B

   The architect draws the 30°-60°-90° right triangle at the right to show the location of a car on the Ferris wheel with respect to its center O. What are the sine and cosine ratios for $\angle O$? What is the length of $\overline{AB}$? $\overline{AO}$? Show your work. If necessary, round to the nearest tenth.

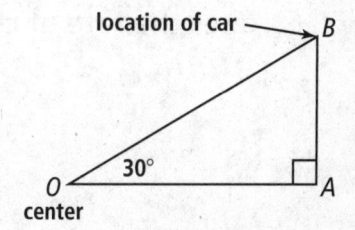

3. A teacher places a sketch of the original Ferris wheel on a coordinate plane. The center of the Ferris wheel is at the origin, and one car lies on the x-axis at (125, 0). The teacher wants to demonstrate the relationship between the number of seconds a car has been moving and the distance in feet between the car and the horizontal axis.

   Part A

   Construct a graph that relates the amount of time the car is in motion (from time = 0 seconds to time = 40 seconds) to the position of the car with respect to the horizontal axis. Describe the steps you took to make your graph.

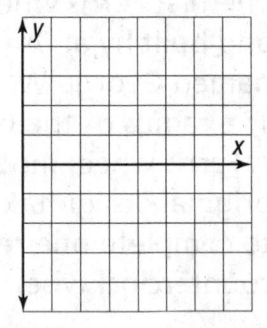

   Part B

   From the graph in Part A, what are the amplitude, frequency, and midline? Write the equation describing the relationship you graphed. Explain.

   Part C

   From Part A, what is the average rate of change of a car from 0 to 5 s? What does the rate of change mean in this context? Show your work.

Name _____

7 Performance Assessment Form B

Mercedes is doing research on ocean navigation and wave phenomena for a school presentation. She studies some basics such as how to determine distance, direction, and wave activity. She gathers the information shown below.

- $1°$ is $\frac{1}{360}$ of a full 360° rotation. You can divide 1° into 60 equal parts called minutes, where 1 minute is denoted 1'. So $1' = \frac{1}{60}$ of a degree.

- If a central angle with its vertex at the center of the Earth has a measure of 1', then the arc on the surface of the Earth that is cut off by this angle has a measure of 1 nautical mile (NM).

- Compass bearing is the direction measured clockwise from north. An object moving due east would have a bearing of 90 degrees.

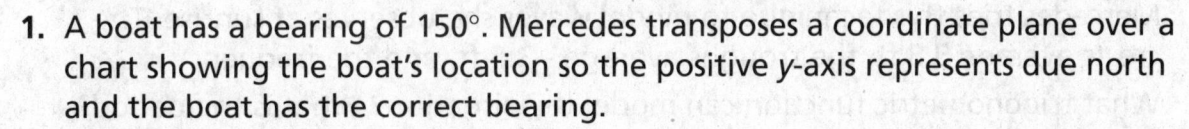

1. A boat has a bearing of 150°. Mercedes transposes a coordinate plane over a chart showing the boat's location so the positive y-axis represents due north and the boat has the correct bearing.

   Part A

   What quadrant is the boat in? What is the reference angle (θ) of the direction of the boat in radians? What is the measure, in radians, of the angle (β) in Quadrant II where $\sin \beta = \sin \theta$? What is the compass bearing of β in degrees?

   Part B

   Each unit on the coordinate plane represents 1 NM. If the boat is 10 NM east of the y-axis, what are its coordinates to the nearest tenth? Explain.

2. Use 4000 land miles for the radius of the Earth. Find the number of land miles in 1 NM to the nearest hundredth of a mile. Explain.

3. Two ships are 450 land miles apart on the ocean. About how many nautical miles apart are the ships? Using your answer from Item 2, find the measure of the central angle (in radians) which has its vertex at the center of the Earth, one ray that passes through ship, and another ray that passes through the second ship. Show your work.

4. Scientists on one of the ships write periodic functions to model waves in the ocean. A crest is considered a maximum and a trough is considered a minimum. Values for y represent the vertical position, in feet, above or below the line of equilibrium (midline) and values for x represent the distance, in feet, from a fixed point.

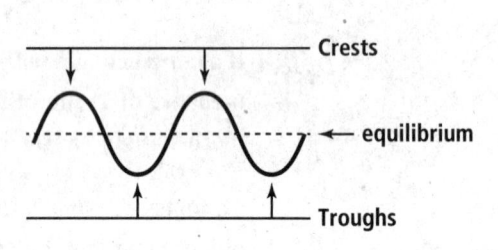

Part A

Mercedes tries this technique to model waves she observes at sunrise. The crests average 3.8 ft, the troughs average −3.8 ft, and the frequency is $\frac{1}{20}$. What trigonometric function can model this situation? What is the period? amplitude? Determine a function that could represent this situation. Explain.

Part B

At sunset, Mercedes observes a series of ocean waves modeled by $y = 4.2 \sin\left(\frac{\pi}{5}x\right)$. How do the period and amplitude of the function in Part A compare to those of the function at sunset? Explain.

8 Readiness Assessment

1. Convert 150° to radians.
   - Ⓐ $\pi - 30$
   - Ⓑ $\frac{5\pi}{6}$
   - Ⓒ 3π
   - Ⓓ $\frac{\pi}{3}$

2. Convert $\frac{4\pi}{3}$ radians to degrees.
   - Ⓐ 60°
   - Ⓑ 240°
   - Ⓒ 420°
   - Ⓓ 480°

3. The hypotenuse of a right triangle is 11 units long, and one leg of the triangle is 5 units long. How long is the third side of the triangle?
   - Ⓐ 6 units
   - Ⓑ $4\sqrt{6}$ units
   - Ⓒ $\sqrt{146}$ units
   - Ⓓ 96 units

4. Find the exact value of cos θ.

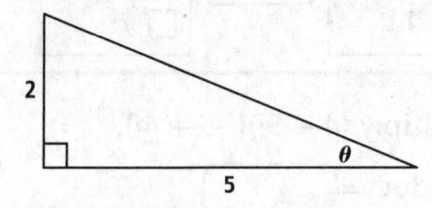

   (right triangle with legs 2 and 5, angle θ opposite side 2)

   - Ⓐ 29
   - Ⓑ $\frac{5}{29}$
   - Ⓒ $\frac{5\sqrt{7}}{7}$
   - Ⓓ $\frac{5\sqrt{29}}{29}$

5. Given $\tan \theta = \frac{3}{4}$ for acute angle θ, find the value of a and b for the statement $\cos \theta = \frac{a}{b}$.

   a = ☐
   b = ☐

6. Which of the following has a value of 1? Select all that apply.
   - ☐ A. sin 0°
   - ☐ B. cos 0°
   - ☐ C. tan 0°
   - ☐ D. cos 45°
   - ☐ E. sin 90°
   - ☐ F. cos 90°
   - ☐ G. tan 90°
   - ☐ H. tan 45°

7. Which of the following has a value of 0? Select all that apply.
   - ☐ A. sin 0°
   - ☐ B. cos 0°
   - ☐ C. tan 0°
   - ☐ D. sin 90°
   - ☐ E. cos 90°
   - ☐ F. tan 90°

8. Use the following choices to fill in each blank. Numbers may be used once, more than once, or not at all.

   $\frac{1}{2}$ $\frac{\sqrt{3}}{3}$ $\frac{\sqrt{3}}{2}$ $\sqrt{3}$

   $\frac{2\sqrt{3}}{3}$ 2

   $\sin \frac{\pi}{6} = $ ☐ $\sin \frac{\pi}{3} = $ ☐

   $\cos \frac{\pi}{6} = $ ☐ $\cos \frac{\pi}{3} = $ ☐

   $\tan \frac{\pi}{6} = $ ☐ $\tan \frac{\pi}{3} = $ ☐

9. Which of the following has the same value as cos 50°? Select all that apply.
- ☐ A. sin 40°
- ☐ B. sin 130°
- ☐ C. cos 130°
- ☐ D. cos 140°
- ☐ E. sin 220°
- ☐ F. cos 230°
- ☐ G. cos 310°
- ☐ H. sin 320°

10. If $\sin\theta = \frac{4}{5}$ and $\frac{\pi}{2} < \theta < \frac{3\pi}{2}$, what is the value of $\tan\theta$?
- Ⓐ $\frac{3}{4}$
- Ⓑ $\frac{4}{3}$
- Ⓒ $-\frac{3}{4}$
- Ⓓ $-\frac{4}{3}$

11. Solve for x.
$\frac{8}{3x} = \frac{2}{9}$
- Ⓐ 3
- Ⓑ 12
- Ⓒ 36
- Ⓓ 72

12. Solve for x.
$\frac{6}{7} = \frac{4x}{3}$
- Ⓐ $\frac{2}{3}$
- Ⓑ $\frac{3}{7}$
- Ⓒ $\frac{9}{14}$
- Ⓓ $2\frac{1}{7}$

13. Find the distance between the points (−2, 6) and (4, −2).
- Ⓐ $2\sqrt{5}$
- Ⓑ $\sqrt{14}$
- Ⓒ 10
- Ⓓ 14

14. Find the length of the segment with endpoints (3, −8) and (−3, −12).
- Ⓐ 2
- Ⓑ $2\sqrt{5}$
- Ⓒ $2\sqrt{13}$
- Ⓓ 52

15. What is the complex conjugate of 4 − 7i?
- Ⓐ 4 + 7i
- Ⓑ −4 + 7i
- Ⓒ 7 − 4i
- Ⓓ −7 + 4i

16. Add (−1 − 6i) + (13 + 9i).
- Ⓐ 12 + 3i
- Ⓑ 12 + 15i
- Ⓒ 14 + 3i
- Ⓓ 14 + 15i

17. Subtract (8 − i) − (−5 − 11i).
Difference =

☐ 13		☐ 3i
☐ 5	☐ +	☐ 10i
☐ 8	☐ −	☐ 12i
☐ 11		☐ i

18. Multiply (4 − 5i)(−5 + 4i).
product = ☐

Name _____

8-1 Lesson Quiz

Solving Trigonometric Equations Using Inverses

1. Which of these is necessary to define the inverse cosine function?
   Ⓐ The cosine function must be always increasing.
   Ⓑ The range of the cosine function must be $y \mid y \geq 0$.
   Ⓒ The domain of the cosine function must be restricted to $0 \leq x \leq \pi$.
   Ⓓ The cosine function must be periodic.

2. What is $\sin^{-1}\left(-\frac{\sqrt{2}}{2}\right)$? Select all that apply.
   ☐ A. $-\frac{\pi}{4}$
   ☐ B. $-\frac{\pi}{2}$
   ☐ C. $-45°$
   ☐ D. $-60°$

3. What are the measures of all of the angles that have a tangent value of 1.99? Give the answer in degrees rounded to the nearest tenth. Choose the numbers to finish the sentence.

   The measures of all the anges are
   ☐ 63.3° ☐ 180°
   ☐ 55.2° ☐ 90°
   ☐ 143.2° ☐ 270°
   ☐ 137.5° ☐ 45°
   + k, where k

   is
   ☐ a multiple of 45
   ☐ an integer
   ☐ a multiple of 10
   ☐ a whole number

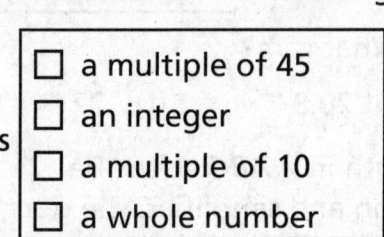

4. Solve $3\sin\theta + 2 = \sin\theta + 1$ for values between 0 and 2π.
   Ⓐ $\frac{2\pi}{3}$ and $\frac{4\pi}{3}$
   Ⓑ $\frac{7\pi}{6}$ and $\frac{11\pi}{6}$
   Ⓒ $\frac{\pi}{6}$ and $-\frac{\pi}{6}$
   Ⓓ $\frac{\pi}{6}$ and $\frac{5\pi}{6}$

5. The average daily high temperature in Seattle is modeled by the function $T = -15\cos\left(\frac{\pi m}{6}\right) + 61$, where T is the temperature in °F, and m is the number of months since the beginning of the year. What is the value of m when the average daily high temperature T is 76°F?

   $m = \boxed{}$

Name _____

8-2 Lesson Quiz

Law of Sines and Law of Cosines

1. In △PQR, the length of the altitude from Q is x. Complete the derivation of the Law of Sines for △PQR.

   | $\frac{x}{r}$ | $r \sin P$ | $\frac{x}{p}$ |
   | $p \sin R$ | $r \sin P = p \sin R$ | $\frac{\sin P}{p} = \frac{\sin R}{r}$ |

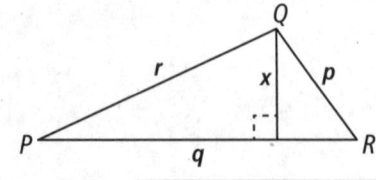

   sin P = [ ]   so x = [ ]

   sin R = [ ]   so x = [ ]

   Setting the two expressions equal to each other gives the equation [ ].

   Divide both sides of the equation by pr to give the result: [ ].

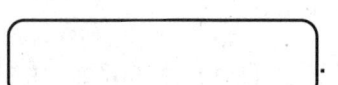

2. In △LMN, m∠L = 108°, m∠M = 25°, and ℓ = 12. What is m?

   Ⓐ about 0.19   Ⓑ about 5.3   Ⓒ about 20.8   Ⓓ 27

3. Tia uses the Law of Cosines to find a missing length in △ABC. After Tia substitutes the values she knows into the equation and simplifies, she gets −23.26 cos A = 0. What does this tell you about △ABC?

   Ⓐ There are two possible triangles that match the information Tia is using.

   Ⓑ The triangle is a right triangle.

   Ⓒ There is no triangle that matches the information Tia is using.

   Ⓓ The triangle is an obtuse triangle.

4. What is the length y? Round to the nearest tenth.

   y ≈ [ ]

5. A path in a park forms a triangle as shown. What is the measure of angle A? Round to the nearest tenth of a degree.

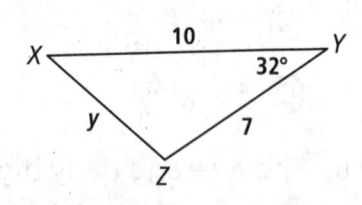

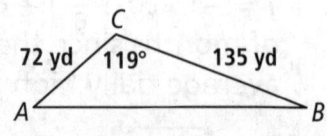

   m∠A ≈ [ ]°

enVision® Algebra 2 • Assessment Sourcebook

8-3 Lesson Quiz

Trigonometric Identities

1. What does the relationship between $\cos(-\theta)$ and $\cos\theta$ tell you about the function $f(x) = \cos x$?

   $\cos(-\theta) = \begin{array}{l} \square \ -\cos\theta \\ \square \ \cos\theta \end{array}$

   The function $f(x) = \cos x$ is $\begin{array}{l} \square \ \text{odd} \\ \square \ \text{even} \end{array}$.

2. A simplified form of the expression $1 - (\cot^2 x)(\sin^2 x)$ is $\begin{array}{l} \square \ \sin^2 x \\ \square \ \cos^2 x \\ \square \ \tan^2 x \\ \square \ \cot^2 x \end{array}$.

3. Complete the proof of the sine sum formula, $\sin(x + y) = \sin x \cos y + \sin y \cos x$.

   $\sin(x + y) = \cos\left[\frac{\pi}{2} - (x + y)\right]$ Cofunction Identity

   $= \cos\left[\left(\frac{\pi}{2} - x\right) - y\right]$ Distributive and Associative Properties

   $= \cos\left(\frac{\pi}{2} - x\right)\cos y + \sin\left(\frac{\pi}{2} - x\right)\sin y$ [____] Difference Formula

   $= \sin x \cos y + \sin y \cos x$ [____] Identities

4. What is the exact value of $\sin 15°$?

   Ⓐ $\frac{\sqrt{6} + \sqrt{2}}{4}$ Ⓑ $\frac{\sqrt{6} - \sqrt{2}}{4}$ Ⓒ $\frac{\sqrt{2} - \sqrt{6}}{4}$ Ⓓ $\frac{\sqrt{2}}{2}$

5. The sound wave for a musical note is modeled by $y = \sin(440\pi x)$. The sound wave for a different note is modeled by $y = \sin\left[440\pi\left(x + \frac{1}{220}\right)\right]$. What is the simplified form of an equation that models the resulting sound wave if the two notes are played at the same time?

   Ⓐ $2\cos(440\pi x)$ Ⓒ $\sin(440\pi x) + \cos(440\pi x)$

   Ⓑ 0 Ⓓ $2\sin(440\pi x)$

Name _____

8-4 Lesson Quiz

The Complex Plane

1. Graph the complex number 2 + 4*i* and its conjugate.

2. What is the midpoint of the segment that joins the complex numbers 7 + 3*i* and −5 − 8*i*?

   Ⓐ $-6 + \frac{11}{2}i$

   Ⓑ $\left(1, \frac{5}{2}\right)$

   Ⓒ $1 - \frac{5}{2}i$

   Ⓓ $\left(-6, \frac{11}{2}\right)$

3. Find the modulus of the complex number 15 − 8*i*.

   modulus = ☐

4. Graph a parallelogram in the complex plane to represent (−3 + *i*) + (−1 − 4*i*).

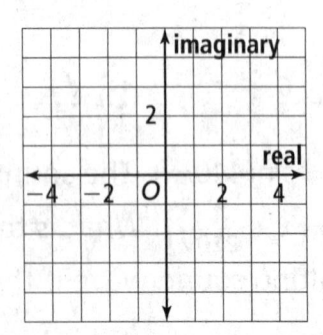

5. Find the distance between the complex numbers −12 + 6*i* and −10 + 5*i*.

   Ⓐ $\sqrt{605} \approx 24.60$

   Ⓑ $\sqrt{5} \approx 2.24$

   Ⓒ $-1 + \frac{11}{2}i$

   Ⓓ $\sqrt{363} \approx 19.05$

8-5 Lesson Quiz

Polar Form of Complex Numbers

1. Graph the complex number $2 \text{ cis } \frac{2\pi}{3}$.

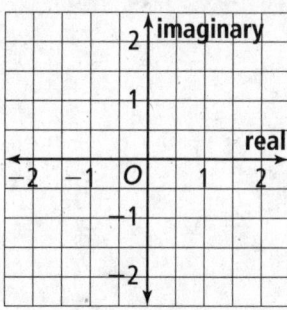

2. Express $4 \text{ cis } \frac{7\pi}{6}$ in rectangular form.

    Ⓐ $-2\sqrt{3} - 2i$ Ⓑ $-\sqrt{3} - i$ Ⓒ $-\frac{\sqrt{3}}{2} - \frac{1}{2}i$ Ⓓ $2 \text{ cis } \frac{14\pi}{3}$

3. **Part A**

    What is the product of $2 \text{ cis } \frac{\pi}{3}$ and $5 \text{ cis } \frac{\pi}{6}$ in polar form?

    Ⓐ $7 \text{ cis}\left(\frac{\pi}{6}\right)$ Ⓑ $10 \text{ cis}\left(\frac{\pi}{6}\right)$ Ⓒ $10 \text{ cis}\left(\frac{\pi}{2}\right)$ Ⓓ $36 \text{ cis}\left(\frac{\pi}{2}\right)$

    Part B

    What is the product of $2 \text{ cis}\left(\frac{\pi}{3}\right)$ and $5 \text{ cis}\left(\frac{\pi}{6}\right)$ in rectangular form?

    product = ☐

4. **Part A**

    What is $-2\sqrt{3} + 2i$ in polar form?

    Ⓐ $4 \text{ cis}\left(\frac{\pi}{3}\right)$ Ⓑ $-4 \text{ cis}\left(\frac{\pi}{3}\right)$ Ⓒ $-4 \text{ cis}\left(\frac{5\pi}{6}\right)$ Ⓓ $4 \text{ cis}\left(\frac{5\pi}{6}\right)$

    Part B

    What is $\sqrt{3} + i$ in polar form?

    Ⓐ $2 \text{ cis}\left(\frac{\pi}{6}\right)$ Ⓑ $2 \text{ cis}\left(\frac{\pi}{3}\right)$ Ⓒ $2 \text{ cis}\left(\frac{\pi}{2}\right)$ Ⓓ $2 \text{ cis}(\pi)$

    Part C

    What is the product of $-2\sqrt{3} + 2i$ and $\sqrt{3} + i$?

    Ⓐ $4 \text{ cis}(\pi)$ Ⓑ $-8 \text{ cis}(\pi)$ Ⓒ $8 \text{ cis}(\pi)$ Ⓓ $-4 \text{ cis}(\pi)$

5. Write the power $(1 - i\sqrt{3})^6$ in rectangular form.

    Ⓐ $64 + 64i$ Ⓑ $64i$ Ⓒ 64 Ⓓ 0

8 Topic Assessment Form A

1. How would you restrict the domain of tan x to define the function $\tan^{-1} x$?

   Ⓐ $-\frac{\pi}{2} < x < \frac{\pi}{2}$ Ⓒ $-\pi < x < 0$

   Ⓑ $0 < x < \pi$ Ⓓ $\frac{\pi}{4} < x < \frac{\pi}{2}$

2. **Part A**

   A model rocket is fired into the air with an initial velocity v of 1,500 ft/s at an angle of elevation x degrees. The height h, in feet, of the rocket at time t seconds after launch, is given by the equation $h = -16t^2 + vt \sin(x)$. Which choice is an equation for x in terms of h when t = 2 s?

   Ⓐ $x = \sin^{-1}\left(\frac{h-64}{3000}\right)$

   Ⓑ $x = \sin^{-1}\left(\frac{h+64}{3000}\right)$

   Ⓒ $x = \sin^{-1}\left(\frac{h-64}{1500}\right)$

   Ⓓ $x = \sin^{-1}\left(\frac{h+64}{1500}\right)$

   Part B

   Find x to the nearest tenth of a degree if h = 750 ft.

   x = ☐ °

3. For △GHJ, $m\angle J = 39°$, h = 36 in., and j = 42 in. Find $m\angle H$ to the nearest tenth of a degree.

   $m\angle H$ = ☐ °

4. For △PQR, p = 7 ft, q = 9 ft, and $m\angle R = 55°$. What is $m\angle Q$?

   Ⓐ 49.0°   Ⓒ 76.0°

   Ⓑ 55.0°   Ⓓ 85.0°

5. What is a simplified form of $1 - \sin^2 \theta$?

   Ⓐ $\cos^2 \theta$ Ⓒ $\tan^2 \theta$

   Ⓑ $-\cos^2 \theta$ Ⓓ $\cos \theta$

6. What is the simplified form of $\frac{\cot \theta \sin \theta}{\cos \theta}$?

   Ⓐ $\frac{\cos \theta}{\sin \theta}$ Ⓒ $\frac{\sin^2 \theta}{\cos^2 \theta}$

   Ⓑ $\frac{1}{\cos \theta}$ Ⓓ 1

7. Find the exact value of tan 135°.

   Ⓐ -1 Ⓒ $-\frac{\sqrt{2}}{2}$

   Ⓑ $\frac{\sqrt{2}}{2}$ Ⓓ $\frac{1}{2}$

8. What is the exact value of $\sin\left(\pi + \frac{\pi}{4}\right)$?

   Ⓐ $\sqrt{3}$ Ⓒ $-\sqrt{3}$

   Ⓑ $-\frac{\sqrt{2}}{2}$ Ⓓ $\frac{\sqrt{2}}{2}$

9. What is the exact value of tan (−75°)?

   Ⓐ $\frac{4}{3} + \frac{\sqrt{3}}{3}$ Ⓒ $-2 - \sqrt{3}$

   Ⓑ -2 Ⓓ $4 + \sqrt{3}$

10. A map of three airports labeled A, B, and C is shown below. How far is airport C from airport A? Round your answer to the nearest tenth of a mile.

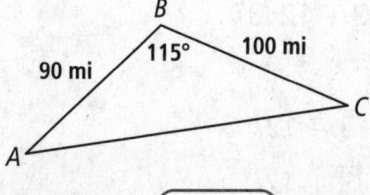

    distance = ☐ miles

11. Which of the following statement(s) are true? Select all that apply.

   ☐ A. sec $(-\theta)$ = sec θ, so sec θ is an odd function.

   ☐ B. csc $(-\theta)$ = −csc θ, so csc θ is an even function.

   ☐ C. csc $(-\theta)$ = −csc θ, so csc θ is an odd function.

   ☐ D. sec $(-\theta)$ = sec θ, so sec θ is an even function.

12. What is the complex number shown on the graph?

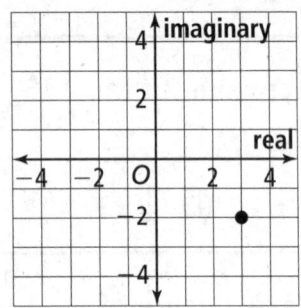

   Ⓐ $-2 - 3i$ Ⓒ $3 - 2i$
   Ⓑ $2 - 3i$ Ⓓ $3 + 2i$

13. What is $5 - 5i$ in polar form?

   Ⓐ $5\sqrt{2}$ cis $\left(\frac{\pi}{4}\right)$
   Ⓑ $5\sqrt{2}$ cis $\left(\frac{7\pi}{4}\right)$
   Ⓒ 10 cis $\left(\frac{\pi}{4}\right)$
   Ⓓ 10 cis $\left(\frac{7\pi}{4}\right)$

14. What is the product of 6 cis $\left(-\frac{\pi}{6}\right)$ and 4 cis $\left(\frac{\pi}{3}\right)$ in rectangular form?

   Ⓐ $-12 + 12\sqrt{3}i$
   Ⓑ $24i$
   Ⓒ $12\sqrt{3} - 12i$
   Ⓓ $12\sqrt{3} + 12i$

15. What is 4 cis $\left(\frac{\pi}{4}\right)$ in rectangular form?

   Ⓐ $2\sqrt{2} + 2\sqrt{2}i$
   Ⓑ $2\sqrt{2} - 2\sqrt{2}i$
   Ⓒ $2\sqrt{3} + 2i$
   Ⓓ $2\sqrt{3} - 2i$

16. What is the midpoint of the segment joining $6 + 6i$ and $12 - 4i$?

   Ⓐ $18 + 2i$
   Ⓑ $\frac{35}{3}$
   Ⓒ $9 + i$
   Ⓓ $9 + 5i$

17. What is the modulus of $39 - 80i$?

   modulus = ⬚

18. Graph $-3 - i$ and its complex conjugate. Label each point.

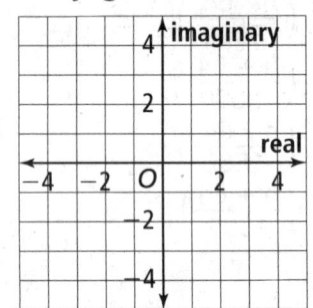

19. Use a parallelogram to represent $(1 - 3i) + (2 + i)$. Label each vertex.

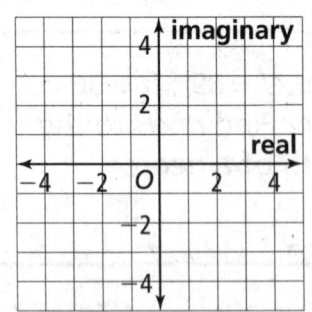

Name _____

8 Topic Assessment Form B

enVision Algebra 2
SavvasRealize.com

1. How would you restrict the domain of cos x to define the function $\cos^{-1} x$?
   Ⓐ $-\pi \le x \le \pi$
   Ⓑ $0 \le x \le \pi$
   Ⓒ $-\frac{\pi}{2} \le x \le \frac{\pi}{2}$
   Ⓓ $\frac{\pi}{2} \le x \le \frac{3\pi}{2}$

2. **Part A**

   A model rocket is fired into the air with an initial velocity v of 600 ft/s at an angle of elevation x degrees. The height h, in feet, of the rocket at time t seconds after launch, is given by the equation $h = -16t^2 + vt \sin(x)$. Which choice is an equation for x in terms of h when t = 3?
   Ⓐ $x = \sin^{-1}\left(\frac{h+144}{1800}\right)$
   Ⓑ $x = \sin^{-1}\left(\frac{h-144}{1800}\right)$
   Ⓒ $x = \sin^{-1}\left(\frac{h+144}{600}\right)$
   Ⓓ $x = \sin^{-1}\left(\frac{h-144}{600}\right)$

   Part B

   Find x to the nearest tenth of a degree if h = 400 ft.

   x = ☐ °

3. For △GHJ, m∠G = 25°, h = 18 in., g = 8 in., with ∠H acute. Find m∠H to the nearest tenth of a degree.
   m∠H = ☐ °

4. For △ABC, a = 12 ft, b = 15 ft, and m∠C = 35°. What is m∠B?
   Ⓐ 91.9°
   Ⓑ 88.0°
   Ⓒ 34.9°
   Ⓓ 53.1°

5. What is a simplified form of $\frac{\tan\theta}{\sec\theta}$?
   Ⓐ $\cot\theta$
   Ⓑ $\sec\theta$
   Ⓒ $\csc\theta$
   Ⓓ $\sin\theta$

6. What is the simplified form of $\frac{\cot\theta}{\csc\theta}$?
   Ⓐ $\cos\theta$
   Ⓑ $\sec\theta$
   Ⓒ $1 + \sec^2\theta$
   Ⓓ $\tan\theta$

7. Find the exact value of sec 120°.
   Ⓐ -2
   Ⓑ $\sqrt{2}$
   Ⓒ $-\sqrt{2}$
   Ⓓ 2

8. What is the exact value of $\tan\left(\frac{2\pi}{3} - \frac{\pi}{4}\right)$?
   Ⓐ $2 + \sqrt{3}$
   Ⓑ $\frac{5 + 2\sqrt{3}}{2}$
   Ⓒ $2 + 2\sqrt{3}$
   Ⓓ $\frac{4 + \sqrt{3}}{2}$

9. Find the exact value of tan (−15°).
   Ⓐ $\frac{\sqrt{2}+1}{-\sqrt{2}+\sqrt{3}}$
   Ⓑ $-2 + \sqrt{3}$
   Ⓒ $\frac{-3+\sqrt{3}}{3}$
   Ⓓ -1

10. A map of three airports labeled A, B, and C is shown below. How far is airport C from airport A? Round your answer to the nearest tenth of a mile.

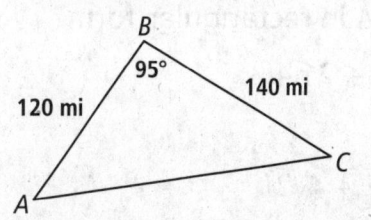

    Triangle with AB = 120 mi, BC = 140 mi, angle B = 95°.

    distance = ☐ miles

11. Which of the following statement(s) are true? Select all that apply.
    - ☐ A. cos (−θ) = cos θ, so cos θ is an odd function.
    - ☐ B. tan (−θ) = −tan θ, so tan θ is an even function.
    - ☐ C. tan (−θ) = −tan θ, so tan θ is an odd function.
    - ☐ D. cos (−θ) = cos θ, so cos θ is an even function.

12. What is the complex number shown on the graph?

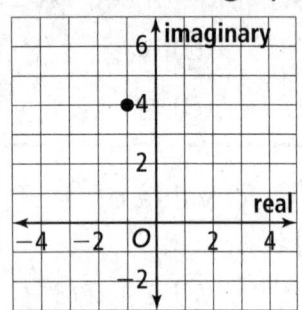

    Ⓐ −1 + 4i
    Ⓑ 1 + 4i
    Ⓒ 4 − i
    Ⓓ −4 − i

13. What is 3 + 12i in polar form?
    Ⓐ 12.4 cis 1.3
    Ⓑ 2.9 cis 0.6
    Ⓒ 12.4 cis 0.2
    Ⓓ 12.0 cis 0.6

14. What is the product of 4 cis $\left(\frac{\pi}{4}\right)$ and 2 cis $\left(\frac{\pi}{4}\right)$ in rectangular form?
    Ⓐ 8.6 + 21.4i
    Ⓑ 8i
    Ⓒ $4\sqrt{2} + 4\sqrt{2}i$
    Ⓓ 6i

15. What is 9 cis $\left(\frac{\pi}{3}\right)$ in rectangular form?
    Ⓐ $\frac{9\sqrt{3}}{2} + \frac{9i}{2}$
    Ⓑ $\frac{9\sqrt{3}}{2} + 9i$
    Ⓒ $\frac{9}{2} + \frac{9\sqrt{3}i}{2}$
    Ⓓ $9 + \frac{9\sqrt{3}i}{2}$

16. What is the midpoint of the segment joining −6 − i and 18 + 4i?
    Ⓐ 14 + 5i
    Ⓑ 24 + 5i
    Ⓒ 6 + 3i
    Ⓓ $6 + \frac{3i}{2}$

17. Write the modulus of −20 − 4i. Round to the nearest tenth.

    modulus = ☐

18. Graph −8 − 2i and its complex conjugate. Label each point.

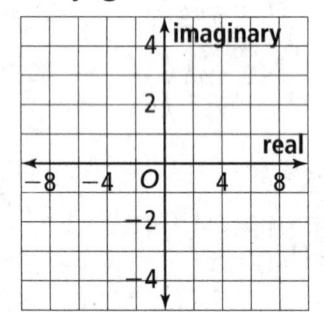

19. Use a parallelogram to represent (−2 − 2i) + (2 − 3i). Label each vertex.

Name _____

8 Performance Assessment Form A

1. Elijah is designing a miniature golf course. One putting green will be shaped as shown.

   a. Find $m\angle C$ to the nearest degree. Explain.

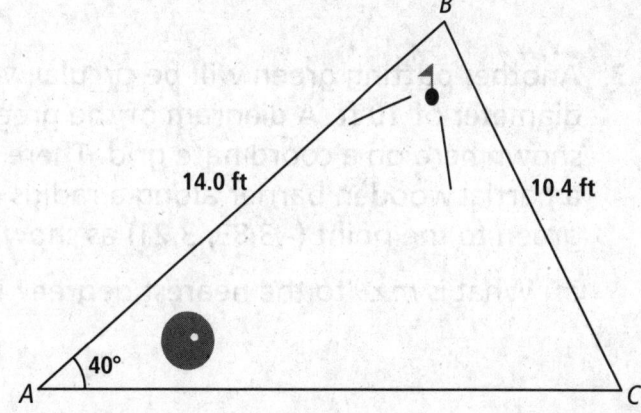

   (Triangle ABC: angle A = 40°, AB = 14.0 ft, BC = 10.4 ft)

   b. To cover the putting green with artificial turf, Elijah needs to know its area. What is the area of triangle ABC in square feet? Explain.

2. Another putting green is to be shaped as shown.

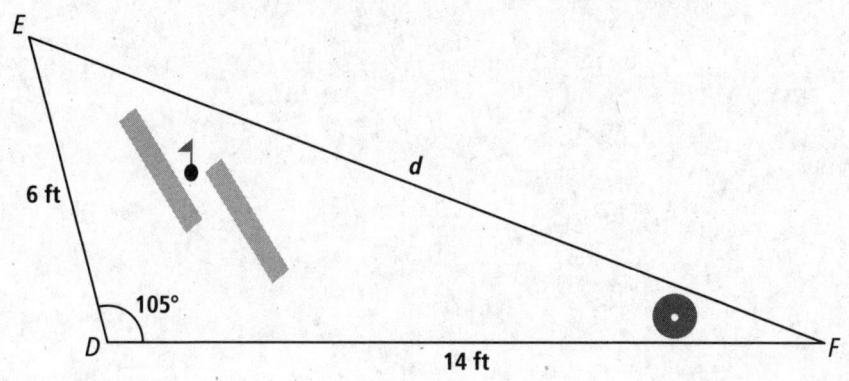

   (Triangle DEF: DE = 6 ft, angle D = 105°, DF = 14 ft, EF = d)

   a. What is the exact value of cos 105°? Explain.

b. What is the length of side d to the nearest tenth of a foot? Explain.

3. Another putting green will be circular, with a diameter of 10 ft. A diagram of the green is shown here on a coordinate grid. There will be a partial wooden barrier along a radius of the green to the point (−3.83, 3.21) as shown.

   a. What is $m\angle\theta$ to the nearest degree? Explain.

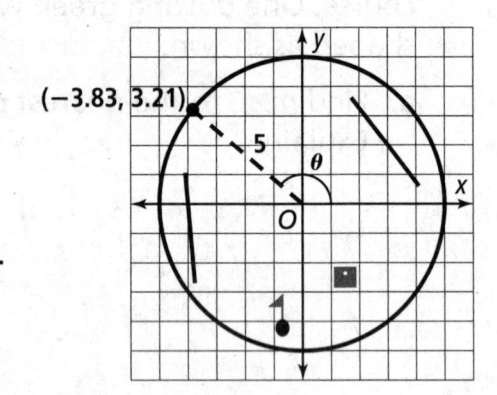

   b. Elijah needs to know the value of $\cos\theta$ to build the barrier; he also needs to identify any other angle(s) with measures between 0 and 360° that have the same cosine. What is $\cos\theta$ to the nearest hundredth? What other angle(s) with measures between 0° and 360° have the same cosine? Explain.

Name _____

8 Performance Assessment Form B

Enrique is practicing with coordinates in the complex plane. He draws a capital italic "E," and uses the coordinates of its vertices to practice.

1. Enrique knows that he will need to be able to convert complex numbers between polar and rectangular form.

   a. Point A is represented by the complex number $2\sqrt{3} + 2i$ in rectangular form. What is this number in polar form? Explain.

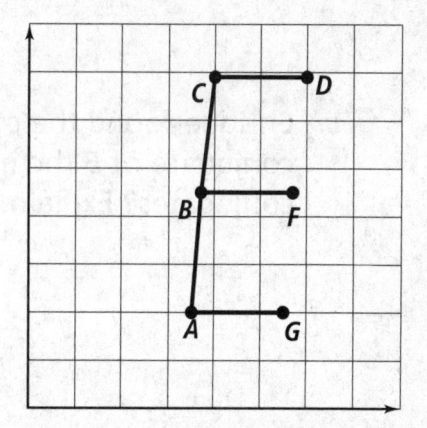

   b. Point C is represented by the complex number $8 \text{ cis } \frac{\pi}{3}$ in polar form. What is this number in rectangular form? Explain.

   c. Each horizontal segment in the drawing of the letter E is 2 units long. What are the coordinates of points D and G? Explain.

2. Enrique wants B to be the midpoint of $\overline{AC}$.

   a. What complex number (in rectangular form) represents point B? Explain.

b. Find the coordinates of point F by finding the midpoint of a segment connecting points D and G. Show your work.

c. Enrique found the complex conjugates of points A, B, and C. Is the conjugate of B the midpoint of the segment formed by the other two conjugates? Explain.

Now Enrique wants to practice multiplying complex numbers using the figure shown at the right. He decides to find the area of the figure in two different ways so he can check his own work.

Labels on figure: P, Q, R, S, T, U; $6 \text{ cis } \frac{\pi}{3}$; $\text{cis } \frac{\pi}{3}$; $2 \text{ cis } \frac{\pi}{4}$; $5 \text{ cis } \frac{\pi}{4}$. Not to scale.

3. What are the lengths PQ and ST? Show your work.

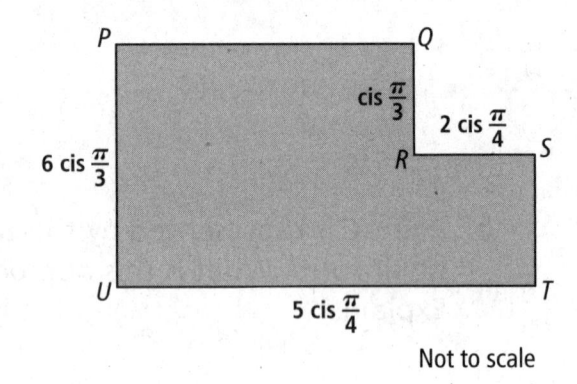

4. Think of the total area as a rectangle having sides $\overline{PU}$ and $\overline{UT}$. A smaller rectangle with sides $\overline{RQ}$ and $\overline{QT}$ is removed from the larger rectangle. Find the area of the large and small rectangles, and then find the area of the figure. Show your work.

5. Think of the figure as being made of a large rectangle with sides $\overline{PU}$ and $\overline{PQ}$, and a small rectangle with sides $\overline{RS}$ and $\overline{ST}$. Find the area of the large and small rectangles, and then find the area of the figure. Show your work.

Name _____

Benchmark Assessment 4

1. Lourdes is filling a 9-gal bucket at a rate of 0.1 gal/s. What is the domain of the function that represents the volume of water in the bucket after x seconds?
   - Ⓐ $0 \geq x \geq 90$
   - Ⓑ $0 \leq x \leq 90$
   - Ⓒ $0 < x < 90$
   - Ⓓ $0 \geq x \geq 90$

2. Solve the equation $x^2 - 23x = 24$.
   $x = \boxed{}$ and $x = \boxed{}$

3. Solve $0 = x^2 + 8x + 64$ by completing the square.
   - Ⓐ $x = -4 + \sqrt{3}i$ and $x = -4 - \sqrt{3}i$
   - Ⓑ $x = -4 + 4\sqrt{3}$ and $x = -4 - 4\sqrt{3}$
   - Ⓒ $x = -4 + 4\sqrt{3}i$ and $x = -4 - 4\sqrt{3}i$
   - Ⓓ $x = -4 + 4\sqrt{5}$ and $x = -4 - 4\sqrt{5}$

4. Find the zeros of the function $f(x) = x^3 - 4x^2 - 51x - 90$, and describe the behavior of the graph at each zero.
   - Ⓐ The graph touches the x-axis at 3 and crosses the x-axis at −10.
   - Ⓑ The graph touches the x-axis at −3 and crosses the x-axis at 3 and 10.
   - Ⓒ The graph touches the x-axis at −3 and crosses the x-axis at −3 and 10.
   - Ⓓ The graph touches the x-axis at −3 and crosses the x-axis at 10.

5. What are the horizontal and vertical asymptotes of the graph of $y = \frac{x+6}{x^3 - 27}$?
   - Ⓐ $y = 0; x = 3$
   - Ⓑ $y = 0; x = -3$
   - Ⓒ $y = 3; x = 0$
   - Ⓓ $y = -3; x = 0$

6. If $t = \frac{2}{x} + \frac{2}{y}$, what is the value of $\frac{1}{t}$?
   - Ⓐ $\frac{xy}{2y + 2x}$
   - Ⓑ $\frac{2xy}{y + x}$
   - Ⓒ $\frac{1}{2y + 2x}$
   - Ⓓ $\frac{xy}{2y + x}$

7. If $a(x) = -9 - 2x$, what is an equation for $a^{-1}(x)$?
   - Ⓐ $a^{-1}(x) = -x - 7$
   - Ⓑ $a^{-1}(x) = \frac{-x}{2} - 9$
   - Ⓒ $a^{-1}(x) = \frac{1}{-9 - 2x}$
   - Ⓓ $a^{-1}(x) = \frac{-x - 9}{2}$

8. If $f(x) = 3 - \sqrt{x}$, which of the following statement(s) are true? Select all that apply.
   - ☐ A. $f^{-1}(0) = -3$
   - ☐ B. $f^{-1}(2) = 1$
   - ☐ C. $f^{-1}(3) = 0$
   - ☐ D. $f \circ f^{-1}(-8) = -8$

9. Which of the following functions has a greater average rate of change on the interval [0, 3] than the function shown in the graph?

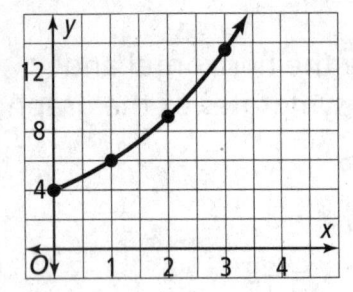

Ⓐ $f(x) = 4(0.5)^x$
Ⓑ $f(x) = 2(1.75)^x$
Ⓒ $f(x) = 3(1.6)^x$
Ⓓ $f(x) = 4(1.75)^x$

10. **Part A**

There is a population of 60 grey seals on an island. The population is increasing at a rate of 15% per year. Write an exponential growth function showing the number of seals y after t months.

Ⓐ $y \approx 60(1.012)^{12t}$
Ⓑ $y \approx 60(1.012)^{13t}$
Ⓒ $y \approx 60(1.012)^{11t}$
Ⓓ $y \approx 60(1.012)^{6t}$

Part B
What is the monthly growth rate?

☐ %

11. High tides at a beach occur at intervals of about 12.5 h. Today, high tide measured 8.5 ft and low tide measured 2.5 ft. What is the amplitude of a cosine function modeling the depth of the water in feet as a function of time in hours? Round to the nearest tenth.

amplitude of a cosine function = ☐ ft

12. What are the sine and cosine of $\frac{5\pi}{4}$?

$\sqrt{2}$ $-\frac{\sqrt{2}}{2}$ $-\frac{\sqrt{3}}{2}$ $\frac{\sqrt{3}}{2}$ $\sqrt{3}$

$\sin \frac{5\pi}{4} = $ ☐ $\cos \frac{5\pi}{4} = $ ☐

13. The graph of f is given. How do the period and the amplitude of f and $g(x) = \sin\left(\frac{\pi}{2}x\right)$ compare?

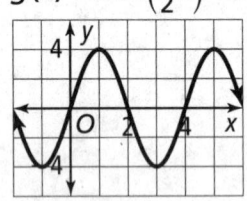

Ⓐ The amplitudes are the same, but the period of f is half as long as the period of g.

Ⓑ The amplitudes are the same, but the period of f is 4 times as long as the period of g.

Ⓒ The periods are the same, but the amplitude of f is 4 times as great as the amplitude of g.

Ⓓ The periods are the same, but the amplitude of f is twice as great as the amplitude of g.

14. Write a trigonometric function that best models the average low temperatures shown in the graph.

Average Low Temperatures (°C)

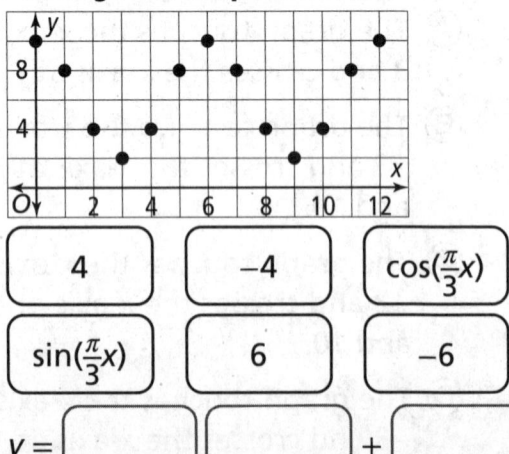

| 4 | −4 | $\cos\left(\frac{\pi}{3}x\right)$ |
| $\sin\left(\frac{\pi}{3}x\right)$ | 6 | −6 |

$y = $ ☐ ☐ $ + $ ☐

15. Which statements about the graph of $y = \cos x$ are true? Select all that apply.

☐ A. The period of the function is π.

☐ B. The range of the function is $[-1, 1]$.

☐ C. The function has vertical asymptotes whenever $\sin x = 0$.

☐ D. The function has zeros whenever $\sin x = -1$ or 1.

☐ E. The function is increasing when $0 < x < \pi$.

16. Which of the following are measures of the angle shown? Select all that apply.

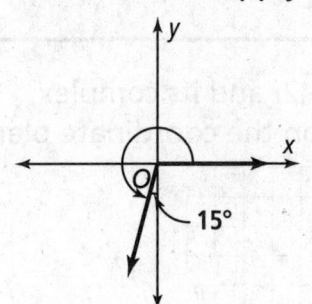

☐ A. 195°

☐ B. −105°

☐ C. 255°

☐ D. −195°

17. An angle has a reference angle of 40° and its terminal side lies in Quadrant III. What are a possible positive measure and a negative measure for the angle?

Ⓐ 220°, −140°

Ⓑ 240°, −120°

Ⓒ 140°, −220°

Ⓓ 200°, −140°

18. Latoya walks in a straight line from the trailhead at (0, 0). She travels at an average rate of 4 mi/h in the direction 60° east of north. What are the coordinates of her location, relative to the trailhead, after 5 h?

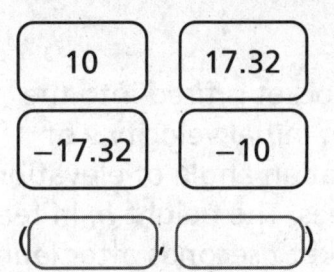

| 10 | 17.32 |
| −17.32 | −10 |

(⬚ , ⬚)

19. What is an equation represented by the graph?

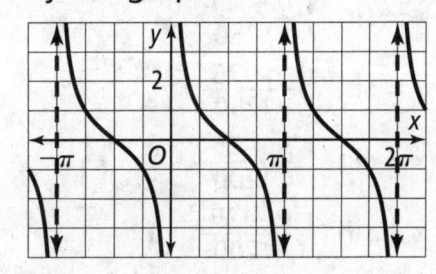

Ⓐ $y = \tan x$

Ⓑ $y = \frac{1}{2} \cot x$

Ⓒ $y = \tan \frac{1}{2} x$

Ⓓ $y = \cot x$

20. What is $\sin \theta$ if $\cos \theta = \frac{20}{29}$ and θ is in Quadrant IV?

Ⓐ $-\frac{21}{29}$

Ⓑ $\frac{21}{29}$

Ⓒ $-\frac{9}{29}$

Ⓓ $-\frac{20}{29}$

21. How would you restrict the domain of sec x to define the function $\sec^{-1} x$?

Ⓐ Domain: $0 \geq x \geq \pi$, $x \neq \frac{\pi}{2}$

Ⓑ $y =$ Domain: $0 \leq x \leq \pi$, $x \neq \frac{\pi}{2}$

Ⓒ $y =$ Domain: $x \leq 0 \leq \pi$, $x \neq \frac{\pi}{2}$

Ⓓ $y =$ Domain: $x \leq \pi \leq 0$, $x \neq \frac{\pi}{2}$

22. For △ABC, m∠A = 42°, a = 24 in., and b = 21 in. Find m∠B to the nearest tenth of a degree.

m∠B = ☐°

23. **Part A**

A model rocket is fired into the air with an initial velocity v of 1,000 ft/s at an angle of elevation of x degrees. The height h, in feet, of the rocket t seconds after launch is given by $h = -16t^2 + vt[\sin(x)]$. Which choice is an equation for x when t = 1.25 s?

Ⓐ $x = \sin^{-1} \frac{h + 25}{1250}$

Ⓑ $x = \sin^{-1} \frac{h - 25}{1250}$

Ⓒ $x = \sin^{-1} \frac{h + 25}{1200}$

Ⓓ $x = \sin^{-1} \frac{h - 25}{1200}$

Part B

Find x to the nearest degree if h = 300 ft.

x = ☐°

24. What is the exact value of $\sin\left(2\pi - \frac{\pi}{3}\right)$?

Ⓐ $-\sqrt{3}$ Ⓒ -0.5

Ⓑ $-\frac{\sqrt{3}}{2}$ Ⓓ $\frac{\sqrt{3}}{2}$

25. A map of three airstrips labeled A, B, and C is shown below. About how far is airstrip C from airstrip A?

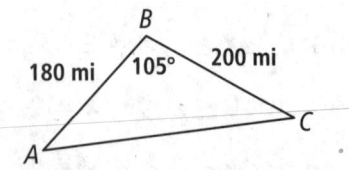

[Triangle diagram: B at top with 105° angle, AB = 180 mi, BC = 200 mi, with vertex A at bottom left and C at bottom right]

Ⓐ 380 mi   Ⓒ 302 mi
Ⓑ 317 mi   Ⓓ 269 mi

26. In △ABC, find the length of an altitude drawn from ∠C to its opposite side. Then use that altitude to find the area of △ABC. Round values to the nearest tenth.

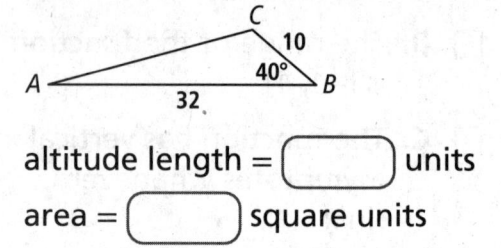

[Triangle diagram: C at top, CB = 10, angle at B = 40°, AB = 32]

altitude length = ☐ units

area = ☐ square units

27. The function sec x is an even function, so sec(−x) = _____.

Ⓐ csc x

Ⓑ −sec x

Ⓒ sec x

Ⓓ −csc x

28. Graph −2 + 2i and its complex conjugate on the coordinate plane.

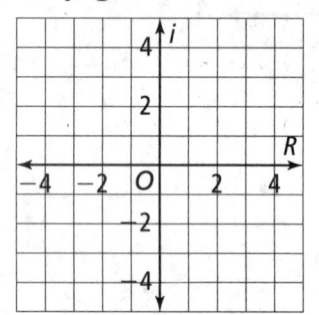

[Coordinate plane with point R marked near (3, 0)]

29. What is the midpoint of the segment joining 12 + 12i and 24 − 8i?

Ⓐ 18 + 2i

Ⓑ 18 + 10i

Ⓒ 36 + 4i

Ⓓ 18 + 4i

30. What is the modulus of 8 − 6i?

modulus: ☐

31. The principal of an elementary school put $1.50 into a barrel on the first day of a fund-raiser. She challenged the students, as a collective body, to put in exactly 20% more each day. The students did so for the next 25 days. The total amount of money was d dollars. Which is the best estimate of d?

Ⓐ 79

Ⓑ 567

Ⓒ 708

Ⓓ 851

32. The amount of oxygen in an adult male's lungs is measured during a deep breathing experiment. The data is recorded starting after the male has fully exhaled. The graph below gives the volume in liters, y, of oxygen in the male's lungs x seconds after the experiment began.

Oxygen in a Male's Lungs

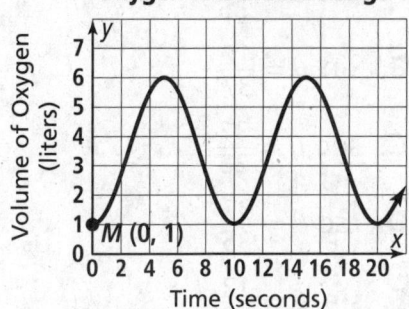

Point M is a minimum value of the function. What is the equation of a cosine function, using radians, that gives the volume as a function of time? Enter your numbers in the boxes to complete the equation.

$y = \boxed{} + \boxed{} \cos(\boxed{} \pi x)$

33. **Part A**
An expression for the surface area of a rectangular prism is $2lw + 2lh + 2wh$, where l, w, and h represent the length, width and height respectively. How many terms are in the expression?

$\boxed{}$ terms

Part B
Which term of this formula is not dependent on the width?

Ⓐ $2lh$

Ⓑ $2lw$

Ⓒ $2wh$

Ⓓ all of the terms are dependent on the width

34. In the expression shown $a \neq b$.
$$\frac{(3a - 3b)^2 + (a - b)}{b - a}$$
When x replaces $(a - b)$, which expression is equivalent to the expression shown? Select all that apply.

☐ A. $\dfrac{9x^2 + x}{-x}$

☐ B. $\dfrac{-3x^2 + x}{x}$

☐ C. $\dfrac{-9x^2 - x}{x}$

☐ D. $\dfrac{(9x)^2 + x}{x}$

☐ E. $\dfrac{(3x)^2 + x}{x}$

35. The exponential function $y = 12{,}000(1 + 0.03)^t$ has an initial value of ☐ 12,000. / ☐ 12,360.

The function represents exponential ☐ growth / ☐ decay with a rate of ☐ 1.03% / ☐ 3%.

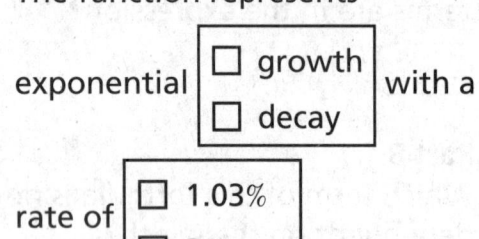

36. Solve $x^2 - 2x + 7 = 0$.
Complete the solution using the choices provided.

(1) (-1) (2) (-2)
($\sqrt{6}$) ($i\sqrt{6}$) ($2i\sqrt{2}$) ($2\sqrt{2}$)

$x =$ ☐ $\pm$ ☐

37. Find the zeros of the function $f(x) = x^3 + 3x^2 - 16x + 12$ and describe the behavior of the graph at each zero.

Ⓐ The graph touches the x-axis at −6 and 2, and it crosses the x-axis at 1.

Ⓑ The graph crosses the x-axis at −2, −1, and 6.

Ⓒ The graph touches the x-axis at −6, and it crosses the x-axis at 1 and 2.

Ⓓ The graph crosses the x-axis at −6, 1, and 2.

38. If $b = \frac{1}{2x} - \frac{1}{y}$, then what is an expression for $\frac{2}{b}$ in terms of x and y?

Ⓐ $\dfrac{4xy}{y - 2x}$

Ⓑ $\dfrac{2xy}{y - 4x}$

Ⓒ $\dfrac{4xy}{y + 2x}$

Ⓓ $\dfrac{2x - y}{2}$

39. Which of the following is equivalent to $\dfrac{6}{2 - \sqrt{5}}$?

Ⓐ $\dfrac{2\sqrt{5} - 4}{3}$

Ⓑ $-6\sqrt{5} + 12$

Ⓒ $6\sqrt{5} + 12$

Ⓓ $-6\sqrt{5} - 12$

40. Given $\tan \theta = \frac{12}{35}$, and $0 \leq \theta \leq 90°$, which of the following are other trigonometric ratios for θ? Select all that apply.

☐ A. $\cot \theta = \frac{12}{35}$

☐ B. $\sin \theta = \frac{12}{37}$

☐ C. $\sec \theta = \frac{37}{35}$

☐ D. $\csc \theta = \frac{37}{35}$

☐ E. $\sin \theta = \frac{12}{35}$

☐ F. $\cot \theta = \frac{35}{12}$

Name _____

9 Readiness Assessment

1. Find the distance between the points (4, −1) and (−3, 23).
   - Ⓐ 5
   - Ⓑ 25
   - Ⓒ 31
   - Ⓓ 625

2. Which two points are equidistant from the point (6, 4)?
   - Ⓐ (1, 3) and (−1, −3)
   - Ⓑ (6, −4) and (−6, 4)
   - Ⓒ (9, 7) and (2, 0)
   - Ⓓ (10, 2) and (8, 8)

3. Which point is 20 units from (−3, −1)?
   - Ⓐ (1, 1)
   - Ⓑ (9, −9)
   - Ⓒ (−15, 15)
   - Ⓓ (17, 19)

4. What is the perimeter of the triangle with vertices at (−7, 2), (−2, 2), and (−2, 14)?

   perimeter = ◯ units

5. What value of c will make the expression $x^2 + 6x + c$ a perfect square trinomial?
   - Ⓐ 3
   - Ⓑ 6
   - Ⓒ 9
   - Ⓓ 36

6. Rewrite the equation $x^2 - 10x + 14 = 0$ in the form $(x - p)^2 = q$.

   $(x - ◯)^2 = ◯$

7. Solve the equation $x^2 + 8x - 9 = 0$ by completing the square.

   $x = ◯$ or $x = ◯$

8. Identify the vertex of the parabola given by the equation $y = -4(x + 7)^2 - 11$.
   - Ⓐ (7, 11)
   - Ⓑ (7, −11)
   - Ⓒ (−7, 11)
   - Ⓓ (−7, −11)

9. Graph $y = \frac{1}{2}(x - 1)^2 - 3$.

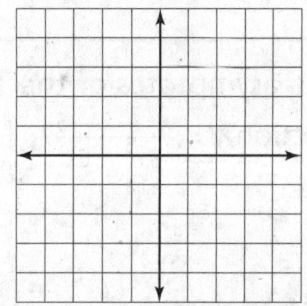

10. Rewrite the equation $y = 3x^2 + 30x + 34$ in vertex form.

    $y = ◯(x + ◯)^2 - ◯$

11. Identify the vertex of the parabola given by the equation $y = 2x^2 - 12x + 26$.
    - Ⓐ (3, 8)
    - Ⓑ (3, 17)
    - Ⓒ (6, −10)
    - Ⓓ (6, −46)

12. Write the vertex form of the equation of the parabola that has vertex (−2, 1) and passes through (0, 13).
    - Ⓐ $y = 3(x + 2)^2 + 1$
    - Ⓑ $y = 3(x + 2)^2 + 13$
    - Ⓒ $y = 3(x - 2)^2 + 1$
    - Ⓓ $y = 3(x - 2)^2 + 13$

13. Write equations for the asymptotes of the graph.

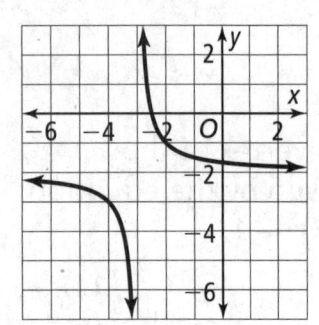

    $x = $ ⬚

    $y = $ ⬚

14. What are the asymptotes of the rational function $y = \dfrac{x^2 + x - 6}{3x^2 - 6x}$?

    Ⓐ $x = 0, y = \dfrac{1}{3}$

    Ⓑ $x = 0, y = 1$

    Ⓒ $x = 0, x = 2, y = \dfrac{1}{3}$

    Ⓓ $x = 0, x = 2, y = 1$

15. Which of the following are asymptote(s) of the rational function $y = \dfrac{x - 5}{x^2 - 25}$?
    Select all that apply.

    ☐ A. $y = 0$
    ☐ B. $y = 1$
    ☐ C. $x = 5$
    ☐ D. $x = -5$
    ☐ E. $x = 25$
    ☐ F. $x = -25$

16. **Part A**

    Find the vertical asymptote(s) and horizontal asymptote(s) of the rational function

    $y = \dfrac{2x^2 - 12x + 16}{x^2 - 5x + 4}$.

    $x = $ ⬚

    $y = $ ⬚

    Part B Graph the function.

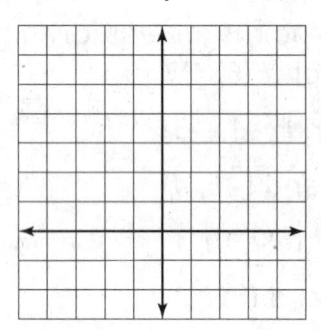

17. What are the vertex and the equation of the line of symmetry for the graph of the parabola with equation $y = x^2 + 5x + 5$?

    vertex:

    Ⓐ $\left(-\dfrac{5}{2}, -\dfrac{5}{4}\right)$

    Ⓑ $\left(-\dfrac{5}{2}, 5\right)$

    Ⓒ $\left(\dfrac{5}{2}, \dfrac{5}{4}\right)$

    Ⓓ $\left(\dfrac{5}{2}, -5\right)$

    line of symmetry:

    Ⓐ $x = -\dfrac{5}{4}$

    Ⓑ $x = -\dfrac{5}{2}$

    Ⓒ $x = \dfrac{5}{2}$

    Ⓓ $x = -5$

Name _____

enVision Algebra 2

SavvasRealize.com

9-1 Lesson Quiz

Parabolas

1. What is the equation of a parabola with focus (0, −8) and directrix $y = 8$?
   - Ⓐ $x = \frac{1}{32}y^2$
   - Ⓑ $x = -\frac{1}{32}y^2$
   - Ⓒ $y = \frac{1}{32}x^2$
   - Ⓓ $y = -\frac{1}{32}x^2$

2. What is the equation of the parabola with vertex (0, 0) and directrix $x = -\frac{1}{2}$?
   - Ⓐ $x = -\frac{1}{2}y^2$
   - Ⓑ $x = \frac{1}{2}y^2$
   - Ⓒ $x = 2y^2$
   - Ⓓ $x = -2y^2$

3. What is the equation of the parabola shown in the graph?
   - Ⓐ $x = -\frac{3}{2}y^2$
   - Ⓑ $x = -\frac{1}{4}y^2$
   - Ⓒ $x = \frac{1}{6}y^2$
   - Ⓓ $x = -\frac{1}{16}y^2$

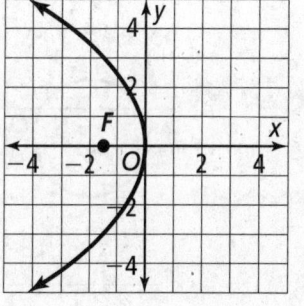

4. Which statement is true about the parabola with equation $y = \frac{1}{4}(x - 3)^2 - 6$?
   - Ⓐ The focus is (3, −5).
   - Ⓑ The vertex is (−3, −6).
   - Ⓒ The directrix is $y = -5$.
   - Ⓓ It opens to the right.

5. Identify the vertex, focus, and directrix of the parabola with equation $x + y^2 + 4y - 1 = 0$. (Hint: Complete the square to find the vertex form of the equation.)

   vertex: (⬚), (⬚)

   focus:
   - Ⓐ $(3\frac{3}{4}, -2)$
   - Ⓑ $(4\frac{3}{4}, -2)$
   - Ⓒ $(5\frac{1}{4}, -2)$
   - Ⓓ $(4\frac{1}{4}, -2)$

   directrix:
   - Ⓐ $x = 4\frac{1}{4}$
   - Ⓑ $y = 4\frac{1}{2}$
   - Ⓒ $x = 5\frac{1}{4}$
   - Ⓓ $y = 5\frac{1}{2}$

enVision® Algebra 2 • Assessment Sourcebook

9-2 Lesson Quiz

Circles

1. Write the equation of a circle with radius 9 and center (6, −4) in standard form.
   - Ⓐ $(x + 6)^2 + (y − 4)^2 = 9$
   - Ⓑ $(x − 6)^2 + (y + 4)^2 = 9$
   - Ⓒ $(x + 6)^2 + (y − 4)^2 = 81$
   - Ⓓ $(x − 6)^2 + (y + 4)^2 = 81$

2. Write the equation of a circle with radius 10 and center (−7, 9) in standard form.
   $(x − \boxed{})^2 + (y − \boxed{})^2 = \boxed{}$

3. Which of these could be the graph of the equation $(x − 3)^2 + (y − 1)^2 = 4$?

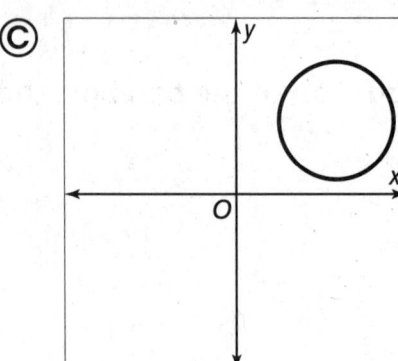

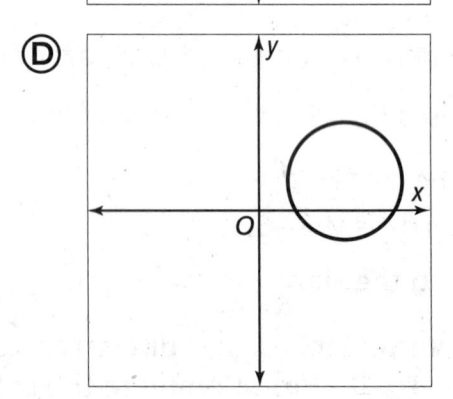

   Ⓐ Ⓒ

   Ⓑ Ⓓ

4. Identify the center and radius of the circle with equation $x^2 + y^2 − 8x − 4y − 5 = 0$.
   center: ($\boxed{}$, $\boxed{}$), radius: $\boxed{}$

5. Solve the system of equations.

   $x^2 + y^2 = 26$

   $y = 5x$

   - Ⓐ (−1, 5) and (1, −5)
   - Ⓑ (1, 5) and (−1, 5)
   - Ⓒ (1, −5) and (1, 5)
   - Ⓓ (1, 5) and (−1, −5)

Name _____

9-3 Lesson Quiz

Ellipses

1. Which ellipse has a major axis that is vertical?
   - Ⓐ $\dfrac{(x+1)^2}{20} + \dfrac{(y+12)^2}{6} = 1$
   - Ⓑ $3x^2 + 7y^2 - 21 = 0$
   - Ⓒ An ellipse with foci (0, 15) and (0, −15) and co-vertices (4, 0) and (−4, 0)
   - Ⓓ An ellipse with vertices (0, 4) and (30, 4) and co-vertices (15, 3) and (15, 5)

2. An elliptical-shaped whispering gallery has two chairs positioned at the foci of the ellipse, 6 meters apart. The width of the room, measured along its minor axis, is 8 meters. Find an equation of the ellipse representing the floor of the room if its center is at the origin and its major axis is horizontal. What is the length of the room measured along its major axis?

   equation:
   - Ⓐ $\dfrac{x^2}{9} + \dfrac{y^2}{16} = 1$
   - Ⓑ $\dfrac{x^2}{36} + \dfrac{y^2}{64} = 1$
   - Ⓒ $\dfrac{x^2}{2} + \dfrac{y^2}{64} = 1$
   - Ⓓ $\dfrac{x^2}{25} + \dfrac{y^2}{16} = 1$

   length of room: ☐ m

3. Which of the following is true about the graph of $\dfrac{(x-3)^2}{25} + \dfrac{(y+1)^2}{49} = 1$?
   - Ⓐ The center is (−3, 1).
   - Ⓑ The foci are (3, −1 + 2√6) and (3, −1 − 2√6).
   - Ⓒ The vertices are (−2, −1) and (8, −1).
   - Ⓓ The co-vertices are (−5, −1) and (5, −1).

4. Graph the ellipse represented by $\dfrac{(x+5)^2}{9} + \dfrac{(y+2)^2}{4} = 1$.

5. Identify the center, foci, vertices, and co-vertices of the ellipse represented by $4x^2 - 16x + y^2 - 6y + 21 = 0$.

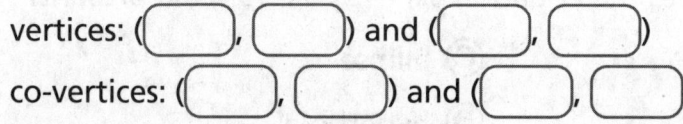

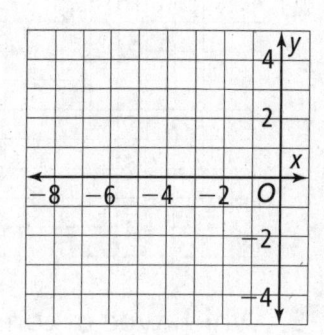

   center: (☐, ☐)

   vertices: (☐, ☐) and (☐, ☐)

   co-vertices: (☐, ☐) and (☐, ☐)

   foci::
   - Ⓐ (1, 2 + √3) and (1, 2 − √3)
   - Ⓑ (2, 3 + √3) and (2, 3 − √3)
   - Ⓒ (1, 3 + √3) and (1, 3 − √3)
   - Ⓓ (3, 2 + √3) and (3, 2 − √3)

9-4 Lesson Quiz

Hyperbolas

1. Which statement is true for the hyperbola represented by the equation $\frac{y^2}{25} - \frac{x^2}{75} = 1$?

    Ⓐ The vertices are $(5\sqrt{3}, 0)$ and $(-5\sqrt{3}, 0)$.

    Ⓑ The foci are $(0, 5\sqrt{2})$ and $(0, -5\sqrt{2})$.

    Ⓒ The asymptotes are $y = \pm\frac{\sqrt{3}}{3}x$.

    Ⓓ It opens left and right.

2. Write an equation for the hyperbola with foci $(0, 6)$ and $(0, -6)$ and a constant difference of 8.

    Ⓐ $\frac{y^2}{4} - \frac{x^2}{9} = 1$　　　Ⓒ $\frac{y^2}{16} + \frac{x^2}{20} = 1$

    Ⓑ $\frac{y^2}{4} + \frac{x^2}{9} = 1$　　　Ⓓ $\frac{y^2}{16} - \frac{x^2}{20} = 1$

3. Write an equation for the hyperbola with vertices $(9, 0)$ and $(-9, 0)$ and asymptotes $y = \pm\frac{2}{3}x$.

    Ⓐ $\frac{y^2}{81} - \frac{x^2}{36} = 1$　　　Ⓒ $\frac{x^2}{9} - \frac{y^2}{4} = 1$

    Ⓑ $\frac{x^2}{81} - \frac{y^2}{36} = 1$　　　Ⓓ $\frac{y^2}{9} - \frac{x^2}{4} = 1$

4. Graph the hyperbola represented by the equation $9x^2 - 4y^2 - 36 = 0$.

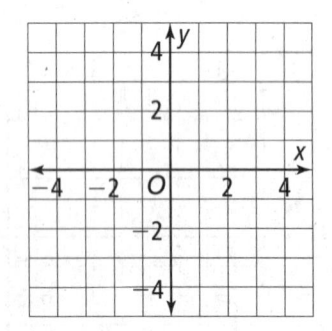

5. Which type of conic section does the equation $3x^2 - 3y^2 + 15 = 0$ represent?

    Ⓐ parabola　　　Ⓒ ellipse

    Ⓑ circle　　　Ⓓ hyperbola

Name _____

9 Topic Assessment Form A

1. Which of the statements about the parabola represented by $x = -\frac{1}{28}(y-5)^2 + 1$ are true? Select all that apply.
   - ☐ A. The focus is (−6, 5).
   - ☐ B. The vertex is (5, 1).
   - ☐ C. The directrix is $y = 8$.
   - ☐ D. The focal length is 7.

2. The cross-section of a flashlight's mirror is a parabola modeled by the equation $y = \frac{1}{12}x^2$ with x and y measured in centimeters. The light bulb is located at the focus of the parabola. How many centimeters from the vertex of the mirror is the light bulb?
   - Ⓐ $\frac{1}{3}$
   - Ⓑ $\frac{1}{12}$
   - Ⓒ 3
   - Ⓓ 12

3. Complete the square to find the vertex form of the equation $y + x^2 + 6x + 13 = 0$. Identify the vertex, focus, and directrix of the parabola.

   vertex: (☐ , ☐)

   focus:
   - Ⓐ $(-3\frac{1}{4}, -4)$
   - Ⓑ $(-2\frac{3}{4}, -4)$
   - Ⓒ $(-3, -3\frac{3}{4})$
   - Ⓓ $(-3, -4\frac{1}{4})$

   vertex:
   - Ⓐ $y = -4\frac{1}{4}$
   - Ⓑ $y = -3\frac{3}{4}$
   - Ⓒ $y = -3\frac{1}{4}$
   - Ⓓ $y = -3$

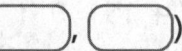

4. What is an equation for the parabola with focus (2, 0) and directrix $x = -2$?
   - Ⓐ $x = \frac{1}{8}y^2$
   - Ⓑ $x = -\frac{1}{8}y^2$
   - Ⓒ $x = \frac{1}{4}y^2$
   - Ⓓ $x = -\frac{1}{4}y^2$

5. What is an equation for the parabola with vertex (0, 0) and directrix $y = -8$?
   - Ⓐ $y = \frac{1}{2}x^2$
   - Ⓑ $y = \frac{1}{4}x^2$
   - Ⓒ $y = \frac{1}{8}x^2$
   - Ⓓ $y = \frac{1}{32}x^2$

6. What is an equation for the circle with radius 7 and center (0, 0)?
   - Ⓐ $x + y = 7$
   - Ⓑ $x^2 + y^2 = 7$
   - Ⓒ $x + y = 49$
   - Ⓓ $x^2 + y^2 = 49$

7. What is the equation in standard form for the circle with radius 6 and center (2, 10)?

   $(x - \boxed{})^2 + (y - \boxed{})^2 = \boxed{}$

8. The center of the circle with equation
   $x^2 + y^2 - 2x + 10y + 17 = 0$ is
   - ☐ (−1, −5)
   - ☐ (−1, 5)
   - ☐ (1, −5)
   - ☐ (1, 5)

   and the radius is
   - ☐ 3
   - ☐ 10
   - ☐ 4
   - ☐ 9

9. Which of the statements about the ellipse represented by the equation $\frac{(x-5)^2}{9} + \frac{(y+2)^2}{16} = 1$ are true? Select all that apply.

☐ A. The center is (5, −2).
☐ B. The foci are (5, √7) and (5, −√7).
☐ C. The vertices are (2, −2) and (8, −2).
☐ D. The major axis is 8 units long.

10. Graph the ellipse represented by $\frac{(x-3)^2}{1} + \frac{(y-2)^2}{9} = 1$.

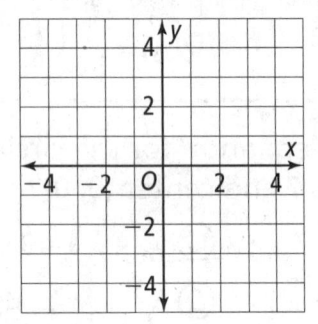

11. Identify the center, foci, and vertices of the ellipse represented by $x^2 - 2x + 4y^2 + 16y + 1 = 0$.

center: (⬚, ⬚)
vertices: (⬚, ⬚) and (⬚, ⬚)
foci:
Ⓐ $(1 \pm \sqrt{3}, 2)$ Ⓒ $(1 \pm 2\sqrt{3}, 2)$
Ⓑ $(1 \pm \sqrt{3}, -2)$ Ⓓ $(1 \pm 2\sqrt{3}, -2)$

12. What are the asymptotes of the hyperbola with vertices (±9, 0) and foci (±15, 0)?
Ⓐ $y = \pm \frac{3}{5}x$ Ⓒ $y = \pm \frac{4}{3}x$
Ⓑ $y = \pm \frac{3}{4}x$ Ⓓ $y = \pm \frac{5}{3}x$

13. Write an equation for the hyperbola with foci (0, 8) and (0, −8) and constant difference of 14.
Ⓐ $\frac{x^2}{49} - \frac{y^2}{15} = 1$ Ⓒ $\frac{x^2}{49} - \frac{y^2}{64} = 1$
Ⓑ $\frac{y^2}{49} - \frac{x^2}{15} = 1$ Ⓓ $\frac{y^2}{49} - \frac{x^2}{64} = 1$

14. Graph $\frac{y^2}{1} - \frac{x^2}{4} = 1$.

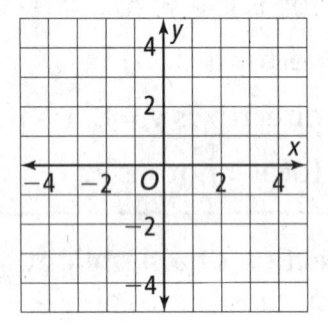

15. For which value of A does the equation $Ax^2 - 10y^2 + 90 = 0$ represent a circle?
Ⓐ 0   Ⓒ −10
Ⓑ 10   Ⓓ −90

16. Match the type of conic with each equation.

(ellipse)   (circle)
(hyperbola) (parabola)

$9x^2 - 9y^2 + 9 = 0$ ⬚
$-3x^2 - 5y^2 + 15 = 0$ ⬚
$5x^2 + x - 6y + 30 = 0$ ⬚
$x^2 - 5x + y^2 - 15 = 0$ ⬚

17. Which type of conic section does the equation $8x^2 + 8y + 2 = 0$ represent?
Ⓐ parabola   Ⓒ ellipse
Ⓑ circle   Ⓓ hyperbola

Name _____

9 Topic Assessment Form B

1. Which of the statements about the parabola represented by $x = \frac{1}{20}(y-1)^2 + 3$ are true? Select all that apply.
   - ☐ A. The focus is (8, 1).
   - ☐ B. The vertex is (3, 1).
   - ☐ C. The directrix is $x = -5$.
   - ☐ D. The focal length is 7.

2. The cross-section of a telescope's lens is a parabola modeled by the equation $y = \frac{1}{24}x^2$, with x and y measured in inches. A mirror is located at the focus of the parabola. How many inches from the vertex of the lens is the mirror?
   - Ⓐ $\frac{1}{6}$
   - Ⓑ $\frac{1}{24}$
   - Ⓒ 6
   - Ⓓ 24

3. Complete the square to find the vertex form of the equation $-x + y^2 - 10y + 26 = 0$. Identify the vertex, focus, and directrix of the parabola.
   vertex: (☐, ☐)
   focus: (☐, ☐)
   directrix: $x = $ ☐

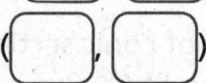

4. What is an equation for the parabola with focus (0, −10) and directrix $y = 10$?
   - Ⓐ $y = \frac{1}{40}x^2$
   - Ⓒ $y = \frac{1}{20}x^2$
   - Ⓑ $y = -\frac{1}{40}x^2$
   - Ⓓ $y = -\frac{1}{20}x^2$

5. What is an equation for the parabola with vertex (0, 0) and directrix $x = 4$?
   - Ⓐ $x = y^2$
   - Ⓒ $x = \frac{1}{16}y^2$
   - Ⓑ $x = -y^2$
   - Ⓓ $x = -\frac{1}{16}y^2$

6. What is an equation for the circle with radius 4 and center (0, 0)?
   - Ⓐ $x^2 + y^2 = 2$
   - Ⓑ $x^2 + y^2 = 4$
   - Ⓒ $x^2 + y^2 = 8$
   - Ⓓ $x^2 + y^2 = 16$

7. What is the equation in standard form for the circle with radius 2 and center (−9, −1)?
   $(x - ☐)^2 + (y - ☐)^2 = ☐$

8. What are the center and radius of the circle with the equation $x^2 + y^2 + 6x - 20y + 60 = 0$?
   center: (☐, ☐)
   radius: ☐

9. Which of the statements about the ellipse represented by the equation $\frac{(x+6)^2}{36} + \frac{(y+8)^2}{4} = 1$ are true? Select all that apply.

☐ A. The center is (6, 8).

☐ B. The vertices are (±6, −8).

☐ C. The co-vertices are (−6, −10) and (−6, −6).

☐ D. The horizontal axis is 12 units long.

10. Graph the ellipse represented by $\frac{(x+1)^2}{16} + \frac{(y-6)^2}{4} = 1$.

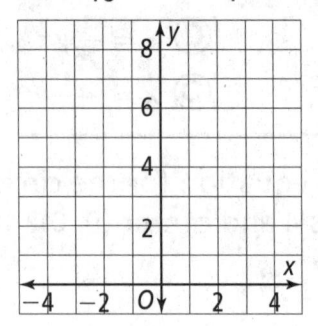

11. Identify the center, foci, and vertices of the ellipse represented by $25x^2 - 100x + y^2 - 2y + 76 = 0$.

center: (☐, ☐)

vertices: (☐, ☐) and (☐, ☐)

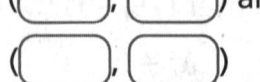

foci:

Ⓐ $(2, 1 \pm \sqrt{6})$　　Ⓒ $(2, 1 \pm 2\sqrt{6})$

Ⓑ $(-2, 1 \pm \sqrt{6})$　Ⓓ $(-2, 1 \pm 2\sqrt{6})$

12. What are the asymptotes of the hyperbola with vertices (±3, 0) and foci (±6, 0)?

Ⓐ $y = \pm\frac{1}{2}x$　　Ⓒ $y = \pm\sqrt{3}x$

Ⓑ $y = \pm\frac{\sqrt{3}}{3}x$　Ⓓ $y = \pm 2x$

13. Write an equation for the hyperbola with foci (9, 0) and (−9, 0) and constant difference of 14.

Ⓐ $\frac{x^2}{7} - \frac{y^2}{4\sqrt{2}} = 1$　Ⓒ $\frac{x^2}{49} - \frac{y^2}{32} = 1$

Ⓑ $\frac{x^2}{7} - \frac{y^2}{9} = 1$　Ⓓ $\frac{x^2}{49} - \frac{y^2}{81} = 1$

14. Graph $\frac{x^2}{9} - \frac{y^2}{16} = 1$.

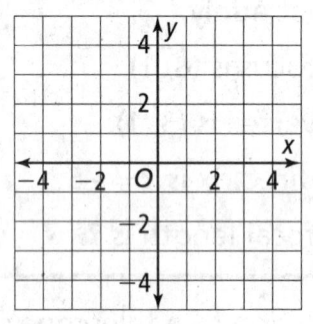

15. For which value of A does the equation $Ax^2 - 4x + 4y^2 + 7y - 100 = 0$ represent an ellipse?

Ⓐ 0　　Ⓒ 25

Ⓑ 4　　Ⓓ −25

16. Match the type of conic with each equation.

[ellipse]　[circle]

[hyperbola]　[parabola]

$-9x^2 - 3y^2 + 18 = 0$ ☐

$4x^2 + 4x + 4y^2 - 1 = 0$ ☐

$-2x^2 + 12y^2 + 1 = 0$ ☐

$6x - 5y^2 - 2y + 9 = 0$ ☐

17. Which type of conic section does the equation $5x^2 - 9y^2 + 3 = 0$ represent?

Ⓐ parabola　　Ⓒ ellipse

Ⓑ circle　　Ⓓ hyperbola

9 Performance Assessment Form A

An entertainment corporation is planning a multi-themed park in a resort. Several features of the park will use shapes that are conic sections. When the planners and architects look at different aspects of the park, they analyze equations and graphs of conic shapes to get a sense of shape and scale.

1. An architect sketches a section of a roller coaster. The shape is a parabola with a focus of (0, 20) and directrix $y = -20$, with lengths measured in meters. Derive the equation of the parabola. Then graph the equation. Show your work.

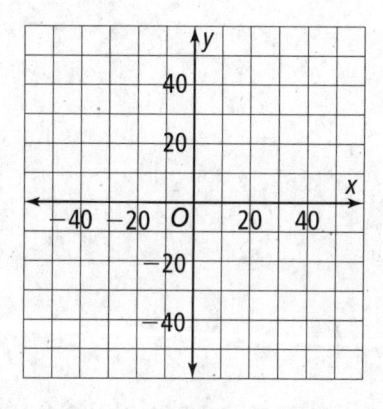

2. A circular-shaped fresh water pool is proposed in the resort water park.

   Part A

   The graph of the circle that represents the pool has a center of (50, −25) and a radius of 125 ft. Use the Pythagorean Theorem to write an equation in standard form that describes the circle. Then graph the circle.

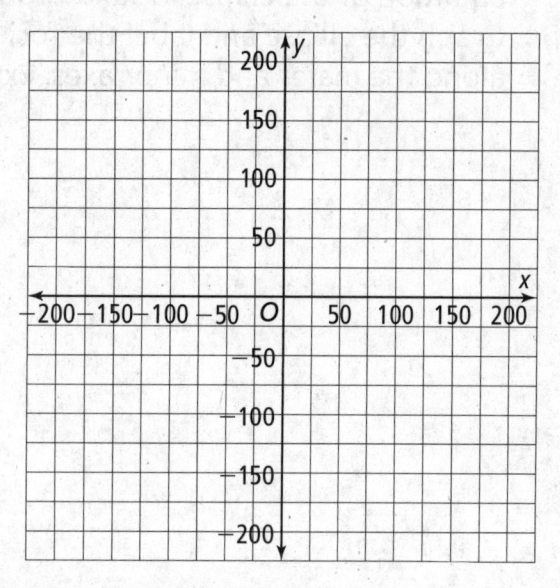

   Part B

   A different plan for the pool is modeled by the equation $x^2 + y^2 + 160x - 200y + 775 = 0$.

   Rewrite the equation by completing the square to identify its center and radius. What are the center and radius, in feet, for this pool design?

Part C

The planner wants to find the point(s) of intersection between the line represented by the equation $y = -x$ and the proposed pool represented in Part B. These will be the entry point(s) to the pool. What are their coordinates? Round to the nearest tenth. Explain.

3. From an aerial viewpoint, the shape of the theme park resembles an ellipse. The foci of this ellipse are 600 ft from its center at (0, 0). The sum of the distances from the foci to any point on the ellipse is 2,000 ft. What is the equation of the ellipse in standard form? Graph the ellipse and label the foci and vertices along the major and minor axes. Explain.

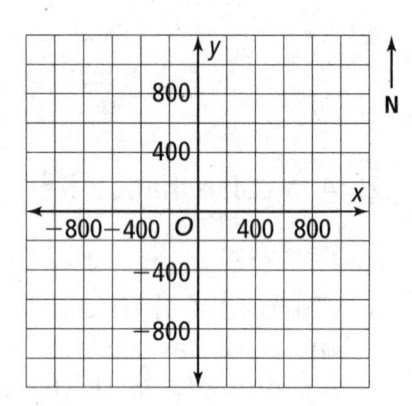

Name _____

9 Performance Assessment Form B

Malia wants to design an interesting layout for a natural history museum. She wants the animal exhibits to have conic shapes. She will analyze equations and graphs of conic sections to get a better idea of the sizes and layouts of different exhibits.

1. The diagram at the right is an overhead sketch of the exhibit for the herbivores, which are plant-eating animals, such as antelopes and zebras. Malia wants to design this section as a hyperbola where the walking paths for visitors are the asymptotes represented by dashed lines in the sketch.

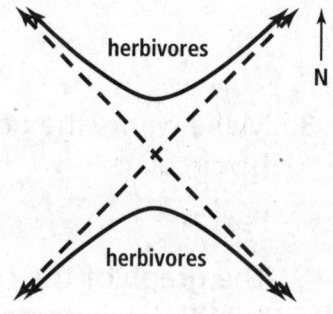

   Part A

   The foci of the hyperbola are located 150 ft north and south from its center at (0,0). The constant difference between the distances from a point on the hyperbola to each focus is 100 ft. Derive the equation for the hyperbola.

   Part B

   Find the equation of the hyperbola in Part A if Malia needs to redesign the exhibit so that the foci are located to the east and west of the center instead. To check your work, use a graphing calculator to compare your graph with the graph of the equation from Part A.

2. The waterfowl lake exhibit will be shaped like an ellipse. Malia chooses an ellipse with foci that are 40 m east and west of the lake's center at (0, 0). The sum of the distances from the foci to any point on the ellipse is 110 m. What is an equation for the ellipse in standard form? Graph and label the foci, vertices, and co-vertices along the major and minor axes.

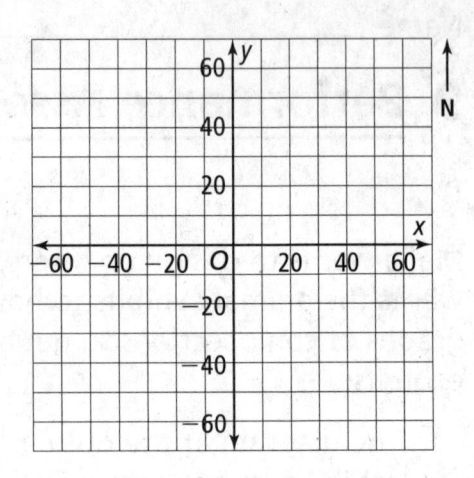

3. Malia wants the gorilla and panda exhibits to be circular.

   Part A

   The graph of the circle that represents the gorilla exhibit has a center, in feet, of (−40, −40) and a radius of 40 ft. Use the Pythagorean Theorem to write an equation in standard form that describes the circle. Then graph the circle.

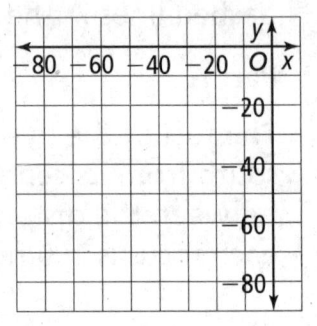

   Part B

   The equation of the circle that represents the panda exhibit is

   $x^2 + y^2 - 100x - 60y + 3175 = 0$.

   Complete the square to identify the center and radius of the circle. What are the center and radius, in feet, of the exhibit?

4. The wide entrance of the bird aviary exhibit extends out to a path in the main hall of the museum and is shaped like a parabola with a focus, in feet, of (60, 0) and directrix $x = -60$. Derive the equation of the parabola. Show your work.

Name _____

10 Readiness Assessment

1. Sketch the image of quadrilateral PQRS after it has been rotated 90° clockwise around the origin.

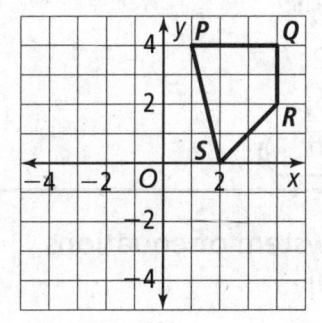

2. What are the coordinates of quadrilateral PQRS from Item 1 after a reflection across the y-axis?

   P'(___), (___),
   Q'(___), (___)
   R'(___), (___),
   S'(___), (___)

3. What are the coordinates of the image of a triangle with vertices A(2, 3), B(4, −5), C(0, −1) after a translation 3 units left and 5 up?

   A'(___, ___),
   B'(___, ___),
   C'(___, ___)

4. Triangle JKL is the image of a dilation, centered at the origin, of triangle DEF. Given points D(0, 3) and J(0, 9), what is the scale factor of the dilation?

   Ⓐ $\frac{1}{3}$ Ⓑ 2   Ⓒ 3   Ⓓ 6

5. Given A(x, y), match the coordinates of A' with the corresponding transformation.

	Dilation	Translation	Reflection	Rotation
A'(y, x)	☐	☐	☐	☐
A'(−x, y)	☐	☐	☐	☐
A'(4x, 4y)	☐	☐	☐	☐
A'(x + 3, y − 1)	☐	☐	☐	☐

6. Which of the following describes the transformation (x, y) → (2x, −2y)?

   Ⓐ dilation and reflection
   Ⓑ dilation and rotation
   Ⓒ translation and reflection
   Ⓓ translation and rotation

7. A triangle has vertices at (−3, 2), (4, 2), and (−3, −22). What is the length of the longest side of the triangle?

   (___) units

8. What is the length of the hypotenuse of the triangle?

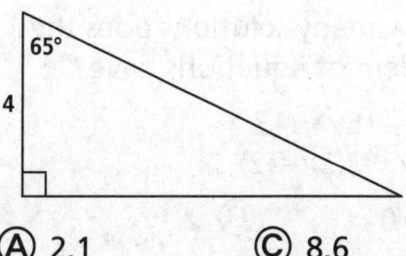

   Ⓐ 2.1   Ⓒ 8.6
   Ⓑ 4.4   Ⓓ 9.5

9. What is the length of the segment with one endpoint at the origin and the other endpoint at (12, −5)?

   Ⓐ $\sqrt{17}$ units
   Ⓑ 13 units
   Ⓒ 17 units
   Ⓓ 169 units

10. What is the acute angle formed by the segment in Item 9 and the x-axis?

    Ⓐ 21°
    Ⓑ 22.6°
    Ⓒ 67.4°
    Ⓓ 69°

11. A right triangle has hypotenuse of length 14 and a leg of length 7. What is the measure of the angle formed by these sides?

    Ⓐ 0.5°
    Ⓑ 2°
    Ⓒ 30°
    Ⓓ 60°

12. Find the measure of the smallest angle of a right triangle with leg lengths of 2 and 9, to the nearest tenth of a degree.

    ( )

13. How many solutions does the system of equations have?

    $6x - 15y = -3$
    $10y = 2(2x + 2)$

    Ⓐ 0   Ⓒ 2
    Ⓑ 1   Ⓓ infinitely many

14. Use elimination to solve the system of equations.

    $3x - 2y = 10$
    $5x + 3y = -15$

    (,)

15. Use substitution to solve the system of equations.

    $4x + y = -2$
    $3x + 2y = 6$

    (,)

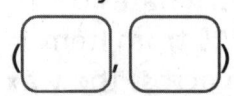

16. Solve the system of equations algebraically.

    $-4x + 8 = 3y$
    $7x + 4y = 12$

    (,)

17. Solve the system of equations algebraically.

    $4x + 9y = 9$
    $2y = 14$

    (,)

18. Solve the system of equations algebraically.

    $7y + 4x = 10$
    $9y - 12x = 0$

    (,)

Name _____

10-1 Lesson Quiz

Operations With Matrices

1. In matrix C, the entries are the numbers of students in a chess club at a high school. Column 1 lists boys, column 2 lists girls, row 1 lists juniors, and row 2 lists seniors. What does the number in position c_{21} represent?

$C = \begin{bmatrix} 5 & 6 \\ 4 & 3 \end{bmatrix}$

Ⓐ 4 girls who are juniors   Ⓒ 6 girls who are seniors

Ⓑ 4 boys who are seniors   Ⓓ 6 boys who are juniors

2. The rows in matrix A represent the prices of long-sleeved and short-sleeved shirts. The columns represent the fabrics: cotton, linen, and silk. If the sales tax rate is 5%, use scalar multiplication to list the sales tax for each shirt in matrix S. Express each entry as a decimal to the nearest hundredth.

$A = \begin{bmatrix} 25 & 40 & 50 \\ 20 & 35 & 45 \end{bmatrix}$ $S = \begin{bmatrix} \square & \square & \square \\ \square & \square & \square \end{bmatrix}$

3. Given matrices $X = \begin{bmatrix} 2 & -3 \\ -1 & 4 \end{bmatrix}$ and $Y = \begin{bmatrix} -4 & 1 \\ 3 & -2 \end{bmatrix}$, complete the matrix for each sum or difference.

$X + Y = \begin{bmatrix} \square & \square \\ \square & \square \end{bmatrix}$ $X - Y = \begin{bmatrix} \square & \square \\ \square & \square \end{bmatrix}$ $Y - X = \begin{bmatrix} \square & \square \\ \square & \square \end{bmatrix}$

4. What are the values of the variables in the matrix equation? $\begin{bmatrix} 9 & 3x \\ 18 & 16 \end{bmatrix} = \begin{bmatrix} 9 & 6 \\ 2y & 16 \end{bmatrix}$

Ⓐ $x = 5, y = 8$ Ⓒ $x = 3, y = 6$

Ⓑ $x = 6, y = 3$ Ⓓ $x = 2, y = 9$

5. If $A = \begin{bmatrix} 2 & 1 & -3 \\ 5 & -4 & -6 \end{bmatrix}$, $B = \begin{bmatrix} -2 & -1 & 3 \\ -5 & 4 & 6 \end{bmatrix}$, and $C = \begin{bmatrix} -2 & -5 \\ -1 & 4 \\ 3 & 6 \end{bmatrix}$, which statements about matrices A, B, and C are true? Select all that apply.

☐ A. Matrices A and B are additive inverses.

☐ B. Matrices A and C are additive inverses.

☐ C. Matrices B and C cannot be combined using addition or subtraction.

☐ D. Matrices A and B cannot be combined using addition or subtraction.

☐ E. $A + B = B + A$

☐ F. $A - B = B - A$

Name _____

10-2 Lesson Quiz

Matrix Multiplication

1. In a weighted grading system, students are graded on quizzes, tests, and a project, each with a different weight. Matrix W represents the weights for each kind of work, and matrix G represents the grades for two students, Felipe and Helena.

$$W = \begin{matrix} Q & T & P \\ [0.40 & 0.50 & 0.10] \end{matrix} \qquad G = \begin{matrix} & \text{Felipe} & \text{Helena} \\ Q & \begin{bmatrix} 80 & 70 \\ 60 & 80 \\ 90 & 60 \end{bmatrix} \end{matrix}$$

Final grades are represented in a matrix F. If F = WG, what is F?

Ⓐ $\begin{bmatrix} 71 \\ 74 \end{bmatrix}$ Ⓑ $[71 \ 74]$ Ⓒ $[74 \ 71]$ Ⓓ $\begin{bmatrix} 74 \\ 71 \end{bmatrix}$

2. Given matrices $X = \begin{bmatrix} -2 & 2 \\ 1 & -3 \end{bmatrix}$ and $Y = \begin{bmatrix} 4 & -1 \\ -3 & 2 \end{bmatrix}$, find the product XY.

$XY = \begin{bmatrix} \Box & \Box \\ \Box & \Box \end{bmatrix}$

3. For a 4 × 4 matrix, what is the multiplicative identity matrix I?

Ⓐ $\begin{bmatrix} 1 & 0 & 0 & 0 \\ 0 & 1 & 0 & 0 \\ 0 & 0 & 1 & 0 \\ 0 & 0 & 0 & 1 \end{bmatrix}$ Ⓑ $\begin{bmatrix} 0 & 0 & 0 & 1 \\ 0 & 0 & 1 & 0 \\ 0 & 1 & 0 & 0 \\ 1 & 0 & 0 & 0 \end{bmatrix}$ Ⓒ $\begin{bmatrix} 1 & 1 & 1 & 1 \\ 1 & 1 & 1 & 1 \\ 1 & 1 & 1 & 1 \\ 1 & 1 & 1 & 1 \end{bmatrix}$ Ⓓ $\begin{bmatrix} 1 \\ 1 \\ 1 \\ 1 \end{bmatrix}$

4. Matrices A, B, and C are all 2 × 2 matrices. Which statements about A, B, and C are true? Select all that apply.

☐ A. AB = BA
☐ B. (AB)C = A(BC)
☐ C. (AB)C = (BA)C
☐ D. AA + AB = A(A + B)
☐ E. C(A + B) = CA + CB
☐ F. (A + B)B = AB + BA

5. Complete the matrix that represents a reflection over the x-axis in the coordinate plane.

$\begin{bmatrix} 1 & \Box \\ \Box & \Box \end{bmatrix}$

enVision® Algebra 2 • Assessment Sourcebook

Name _____

10-3 Lesson Quiz

Vectors

1. A vector has an initial point at (2.1, 2.1) and a terminal point at (4.5, 7.8). Complete the statements below with the correct numbers. Express your answers to the nearest tenth of a unit.

   The component form of the vector is ⟨☐, ☐⟩.

   The magnitude of the vector is about ☐.

   The direction of the vector is about ☐°.

2. Consider the vectors $\vec{v} = \langle 1, 6 \rangle$ and $\vec{w} = \langle 0, -4 \rangle$. What is the magnitude of $\vec{v} + \vec{w}$ expressed to the nearest tenth of a unit?

   Ⓐ 10.1   Ⓒ 4.0

   Ⓑ 6.1   Ⓓ 2.2

3. The vector $\vec{r} = \langle 2, 3 \rangle$ is multiplied by the scalar −4. Which statements about the components, magnitude, and direction of the scalar product $-4\vec{r}$ are true? Select all that apply.

   ☐ A. The component form of $-4\vec{r}$ is $\langle -8, -12 \rangle$.

   ☐ B. The magnitude of $-4\vec{r}$ is 4 times the magnitude of $\vec{r}$.

   ☐ C. The direction of $-4\vec{r}$ is the same as the direction of $\vec{r}$.

   ☐ D. The vector $-4\vec{r}$ is in the fourth quadrant.

   ☐ E. The direction of $-4\vec{r}$ is 180° greater than the inverse tangent of its components.

4. Consider the vectors $\vec{v} = \langle 3, -2 \rangle$ and $\vec{w} = \langle -6, 10 \rangle$. What is $\vec{v} - \vec{w}$?

   $\vec{v} - \vec{w} = \langle ☐, ☐ \rangle$

5. A plane is set to fly due north, but it is pushed off course by a crosswind blowing west. At 1 P.M. the plane is located at point A and at 2 P.M. the plane is located at point C, as shown in the diagram. In what direction and at what speed is the plane traveling?

   Ⓐ about 5.7° west of north at approximately 500.1 mph

   Ⓑ about 5.7° west of north at approximately 502.5 mph

   Ⓒ about 84.3° west of north at approximately 500.1 mph

   Ⓓ about 84.3° west of north at approximately 502.5 mph

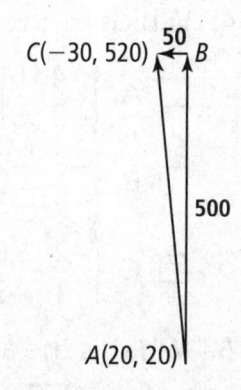

Name _____

10-4 Lesson Quiz

Inverses and Determinants

1. What is the inverse matrix of $\begin{bmatrix} 3 & 2 \\ 4 & 1 \end{bmatrix}$?

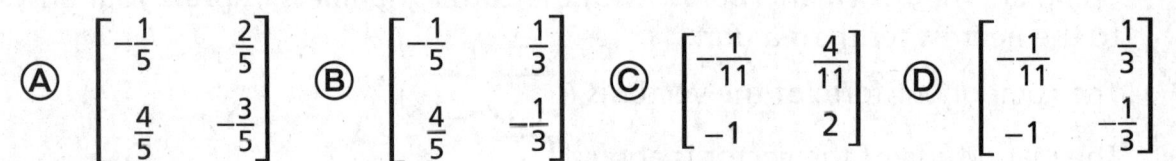

   Ⓐ $\begin{bmatrix} -\frac{1}{5} & \frac{2}{5} \\ \frac{4}{5} & -\frac{3}{5} \end{bmatrix}$
   Ⓑ $\begin{bmatrix} -\frac{1}{5} & \frac{1}{3} \\ \frac{4}{5} & -\frac{1}{3} \end{bmatrix}$
   Ⓒ $\begin{bmatrix} -\frac{1}{11} & \frac{4}{11} \\ -1 & 2 \end{bmatrix}$
   Ⓓ $\begin{bmatrix} -\frac{1}{11} & \frac{1}{3} \\ -1 & -\frac{1}{3} \end{bmatrix}$

2. The graph shows the location of a triangle to be painted on a wall mural, where each unit on the grid represents 1 foot. What is the area of the triangle in ft²?

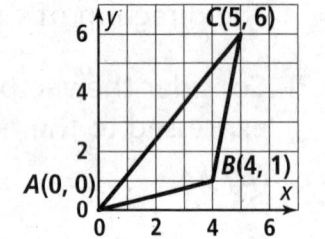

   Ⓐ 2.5 ft²

   Ⓑ 5 ft²

   Ⓒ 9.5 ft²

   Ⓒ 18 ft²

3. A parallelogram that has one vertex at the origin, is defined by the vectors ⟨4, 6⟩ and ⟨−3, a⟩, and has an area of 6 square units. What are the possible values of a? Select all that apply.

   ☐ A. −6

   ☐ B. −3

   ☐ C. 0

   ☐ D. 3

   ☐ E. 6

4. Which of the given matrices has an inverse? Select all that apply.

   ☐ A. $\begin{bmatrix} 4 & 6 \\ -2 & 3 \end{bmatrix}$ 　　　☐ D. $\begin{bmatrix} 4 & 6 \\ -2 & -3 \end{bmatrix}$

   ☐ B. $\begin{bmatrix} -6 & -2 \\ 9 & -3 \end{bmatrix}$ 　　☐ E. $\begin{bmatrix} -2 & 6 \\ 9 & -3 \end{bmatrix}$

   ☐ C. $\begin{bmatrix} -2 & 6 \\ 1 & -3 \end{bmatrix}$ 　　☐ F. $\begin{bmatrix} -2 & -6 \\ 1 & -3 \end{bmatrix}$

5. What is the area of the triangle defined by the vectors ⟨2, 4⟩ and ⟨−1, 6⟩?

   area = ◯ square units

Name _____

10-5 Lesson Quiz

Inverse Matrices and Systems of Equations

1. What is a matrix equation for the system of linear equations $\begin{cases} 2x + 3y = 8 \\ 4x - y = 5 \end{cases}$?

   Complete the equation with the correct numbers.

   $\begin{bmatrix} 2 & \boxed{} \\ \boxed{} & \boxed{} \end{bmatrix} \begin{bmatrix} x \\ y \end{bmatrix} = \begin{bmatrix} \boxed{} \\ \boxed{} \end{bmatrix}$

2. Which statements about the system $\begin{cases} 4x + 3y = 12 \\ 8x + 6y = 4 \end{cases}$ are true? Select all that apply.
   - ☐ A. The coefficient matrix is $\begin{bmatrix} 4 & 3 \\ 8 & 6 \end{bmatrix}$.
   - ☐ B. The determinant of the coefficient matrix is 8.
   - ☐ C. The coefficient matrix is not invertible.
   - ☐ D. The system can be solved using a matrix inverse.
   - ☐ E. The solution of the system is (2, −2).

3. A company makes short boots and tall boots. Last week, the company spent $855 on labor and $1,150 on materials. Let s represent the number of pairs of short boots produced and t represent the number of pairs of tall boots produced. Which matrix equation models the situation?

Manufacturing Costs per Pair ($)		
Boot Style	Labor	Materials
Short	15	22
Tall	24	30

   Ⓐ $\begin{bmatrix} 15 & 22 \\ 24 & 30 \end{bmatrix} \begin{bmatrix} s \\ t \end{bmatrix} = \begin{bmatrix} 855 \\ 1150 \end{bmatrix}$

   Ⓒ $\begin{bmatrix} 15 & 24 \\ 22 & 30 \end{bmatrix} \begin{bmatrix} s \\ t \end{bmatrix} = \begin{bmatrix} 855 \\ 1150 \end{bmatrix}$

   Ⓑ $\begin{bmatrix} 15 & 22 \\ 24 & 30 \end{bmatrix} \begin{bmatrix} s \\ t \end{bmatrix} = \begin{bmatrix} 1150 \\ 855 \end{bmatrix}$

   Ⓓ $\begin{bmatrix} 15 & 24 \\ 22 & 30 \end{bmatrix} \begin{bmatrix} s \\ t \end{bmatrix} = \begin{bmatrix} 1150 \\ 855 \end{bmatrix}$

4. The coordinates (x, y) of a point in a plane are the solution of the matrix equation $\begin{bmatrix} -1 & 2 \\ 2 & -1 \end{bmatrix} \begin{bmatrix} x \\ y \end{bmatrix} = \begin{bmatrix} 11 \\ -10 \end{bmatrix}$. In which quadrant is the point located?

   Ⓐ I   Ⓑ II   Ⓒ III   Ⓓ IV

5. What is the solution of the matrix equation $\begin{bmatrix} 5 & 3 \\ 2 & 1 \end{bmatrix} \begin{bmatrix} x \\ y \end{bmatrix} = \begin{bmatrix} -5 \\ -1 \end{bmatrix}$?

   $\begin{bmatrix} x \\ y \end{bmatrix} = \begin{bmatrix} \boxed{} \\ \boxed{} \end{bmatrix}$

Name _____

10 Topic Assessment Form A

1. Matrices X, Y, and Z are all 2 × 2 matrices. Which statements are true? Select all that apply.
   - ☐ A. $(XY)Z = X(YZ)$
   - ☐ B. $(XY)Z = (YX)Z$
   - ☐ C. $XX + XZ = X(X + Z)$
   - ☐ D. $Z(X + Y) = ZX + ZY$

2. The rows in matrix H represent the prices in dollars of regular hats and monogrammed hats. The columns represent the sizes small, medium, and large. If the sales tax rate is 6%, use scalar multiplication to list the sales tax for each hat in matrix S.

   $H = \begin{bmatrix} 10 & 12 & 14 \\ 13 & 15 & 16 \end{bmatrix} \quad S = \begin{bmatrix} a & b & c \\ d & e & f \end{bmatrix}$

   a = ☐ b = ☐ c = ☐
   d = ☐ e = ☐ f = ☐

3. Given vectors $\vec{v} = \langle 1, 6 \rangle$ and $\vec{w} = \langle 0, -4 \rangle$. What are the component form, magnitude and direction of $\vec{v} + \vec{w}$? Round to the nearest tenth of a unit.

   component form: ⟨☐, ☐⟩
   magnitude: ☐
   direction: ☐°

4. What is the area in square units of the triangle with one vertex at the origin and defined by the vectors ⟨3, 5⟩ and ⟨−2, 4⟩?
   - Ⓐ 6
   - Ⓑ 11
   - Ⓒ 12
   - Ⓓ 22

5. A plane is set to head due east, but it is being pushed off course by a crosswind blowing south. At 9 A.M. the plane is located at point A and at 10 A.M. the plane is located at point C, as shown in the diagram. In what direction and at what speed is the plane traveling? Round to the nearest tenth of a unit.

   A(10, 70)   300   B
                     60
               C(310, 10)

   direction: ☐° south of east
   speed: ☐ mph

6. In matrix V, the entries are the numbers of cans of vegetables in a market. Column 1 lists peas, column 2 lists corn, row 1 lists small cans, and row 2 lists large cans. What does the number in position v_{12} represent?

   $V = \begin{bmatrix} 22 & 15 \\ 10 & 9 \end{bmatrix}$

   - Ⓐ 10 large cans of peas
   - Ⓑ 15 small cans of peas
   - Ⓒ 15 small cans of corn
   - Ⓓ 10 large cans of corn

7. Select all the equations that are represented by the matrix equation.

   $\begin{bmatrix} 2 & -4 \\ 1 & 6 \end{bmatrix} \begin{bmatrix} x \\ y \end{bmatrix} = \begin{bmatrix} 8 \\ -1 \end{bmatrix}$

   - ☐ A. $2x - 4y = 8$
   - ☐ B. $2x + y = -1$
   - ☐ C. $-4x + 6y = -1$
   - ☐ D. $2x + y = 8$
   - ☐ E. $x + 6y = -1$
   - ☐ F. $-4x + 6y = 8$

8. Consider matrices
$X = \begin{bmatrix} 3 & 7 \\ -2 & 6 \end{bmatrix}$ and $Y = \begin{bmatrix} -5 & 1 \\ -4 & 2 \end{bmatrix}$.

Part A

What is $X - Y$? $X - Y = [2 \times 2]\begin{bmatrix} a & b \\ c & d \end{bmatrix}$

a = ☐   b = ☐
c = ☐   d = ☐

Part B

What is XY? $XY = [2 \times 2]\begin{bmatrix} e & f \\ g & h \end{bmatrix}$

e = ☐   f = ☐
g = ☐   h = ☐

9. Which transformation in the coordinate plane is represented by the matrix $\begin{bmatrix} 0 & -1 \\ 1 & 0 \end{bmatrix}$?

Ⓐ reflection over the x-axis
Ⓑ reflection over the y-axis
Ⓒ rotation 90° clockwise
Ⓓ rotation 90° counterclockwise

10. Consider the vector $\vec{a} = \langle 4, 6 \rangle$. Which statements about the scalar product $2\vec{a}$ are true? Select all that apply.

☐ A. The component form of $2\vec{a}$ is $\langle 6, 8 \rangle$.

☐ B. The magnitude of $2\vec{a}$ is 2 times the magnitude of $\vec{a}$.

☐ C. The direction of $2\vec{a}$ is the same as the direction of $\vec{a}$.

☐ D. The vector $2\vec{a}$ is in the first quadrant.

11. Matrix $X = \begin{bmatrix} -6 & -1 \\ 3 & 2 \end{bmatrix}$ and $Y = \begin{bmatrix} 0 & 0 \\ 0 & 0 \end{bmatrix}$.

Find $X + Y$.

$X + Y = \begin{bmatrix} a & b \\ c & d \end{bmatrix}$

a = ☐   b = ☐
c = ☐   d = ☐

12. A parallelogram has vertices at the origin, (2, 5), and (−2, y), and has an area of 12 square units. Select all the possible values of y.

☐ A. 11   ☐ D. 1
☐ B. −11   ☐ E. −1
☐ C. 0   ☐ F. 2

13. Which matrix has an inverse?

Ⓐ $\begin{bmatrix} 6 & -9 \\ -2 & 3 \end{bmatrix}$ Ⓒ $\begin{bmatrix} 1 & 3 \\ 3 & 9 \end{bmatrix}$

Ⓑ $\begin{bmatrix} -4 & -3 \\ 8 & 6 \end{bmatrix}$ Ⓓ $\begin{bmatrix} 1 & 4 \\ -2 & 8 \end{bmatrix}$

14. A company makes long scarves and short scarves. Last week, the company spent $19,500 on labor and $25,000 on materials.

| Manufacturing Costs per Scarf ($) |||
Scarf Style	Labor	Materials
Long	4	5
Short	3	4

Let x represent the number of long scarves produced and y represent the number of short scarves produced. Complete the matrix equation to model the situation, then solve for x and y.

$\begin{bmatrix} 4 & a \\ b & c \end{bmatrix}\begin{bmatrix} x \\ y \end{bmatrix} = \begin{bmatrix} d \\ e \end{bmatrix}$

a = ☐   b = ☐   c = ☐
d = ☐   e = ☐
x = ☐   y = ☐

Name _____

10 Topic Assessment Form B

1. Matrices R, S, and T are all 3×3 matrices. Which statements are true? Select all that apply.
   - ☐ A. $ST + TT = S(T + T)$
   - ☐ B. $T(R + S) = TR + TS$
   - ☐ C. $(RS)T = T(RS)$
   - ☐ D. $(RS)T = R(ST)$

2. The rows in matrix B represent the prices in dollars of small flower bouquets and large flower bouquets. The columns represent tulips, roses, and daisies. If the sales tax rate is 4%, use scalar multiplication to list the sales tax for each bouquet in matrix S.
   $B = \begin{bmatrix} 15 & 30 & 20 \\ 25 & 50 & 35 \end{bmatrix}$ $S = \begin{bmatrix} a & b & c \\ d & e & f \end{bmatrix}$
   $a = \boxed{}$ $b = \boxed{}$ $c = \boxed{}$
   $d = \boxed{}$ $e = \boxed{}$ $f = \boxed{}$

3. Given vectors $\vec{v} = \langle 2, 8 \rangle$ and $\vec{w} = \langle 0, -2 \rangle$. What are the component form, magnitude and direction of $\vec{v} + \vec{w}$? Round to the nearest tenth of a unit.
   component form: $\langle \boxed{}, \boxed{} \rangle$
   magnitude: $\boxed{}$
   direction: $\boxed{}°$

4. What is the area in square units of the triangle defined by the vectors $\langle -3, -5 \rangle$ and $\langle 2, -4 \rangle$?
   - Ⓐ 3
   - Ⓑ 6
   - Ⓒ 7
   - Ⓓ 11

5. A plane is set to head due east, but it is pushed off course by a crosswind blowing south. At 8 P.M. the plane is located at point A and at 9 P.M. the plane is located at point C, as shown in the diagram. In what direction and at what speed is the plane traveling? Round to the nearest tenth of a unit.

   $A(30, 140)$ — 400 — B
   110
   $C(430, 30)$

   direction: $\boxed{}°$ south of east
   speed: $\boxed{}$ mph

6. In matrix V, the entries are the numbers of loaves of bread at a bakery. Column 1 lists wheat bread, column 2 lists rye bread, row 1 lists small loaves, and row 2 lists large loaves. What does the number in position v_{22} represent?
   $V = \begin{bmatrix} 22 & 15 \\ 10 & 9 \end{bmatrix}$
   - Ⓐ 9 large rye loaves
   - Ⓑ 10 large wheat loaves
   - Ⓒ 10 large rye loaves
   - Ⓓ 9 large wheat loaves

7. Select all the equations that are represented by the matrix equation.
   $\begin{bmatrix} 3 & 5 \\ 2 & -2 \end{bmatrix} \begin{bmatrix} x \\ y \end{bmatrix} = \begin{bmatrix} 13 \\ -2 \end{bmatrix}$
   - ☐ A. $3x + 5y = 13$
   - ☐ B. $2x - 2y = -2$
   - ☐ C. $5x - 2y = -2$
   - ☐ D. $3x + 2y = 13$
   - ☐ E. $2x - 2y = -2$
   - ☐ F. $5x - 2y = 13$

8. Consider matrices
$X = \begin{bmatrix} 2 & 6 \\ -5 & -1 \end{bmatrix}$ and $Y = \begin{bmatrix} 3 & -1 \\ 4 & 6 \end{bmatrix}$.

Part A

What is $Y - X$? $Y - X = [2 \times 2] \begin{bmatrix} a & b \\ c & d \end{bmatrix}$

$a = \boxed{}$ $b = \boxed{}$
$c = \boxed{}$ $d = \boxed{}$

Part B

What is XY? $XY = [2 \times 2] \begin{bmatrix} e & f \\ g & h \end{bmatrix}$

$e = \boxed{}$ $f = \boxed{}$
$g = \boxed{}$ $h = \boxed{}$

9. Which transformation in the coordinate plane is represented by the matrix $\begin{bmatrix} -1 & 0 \\ 0 & 1 \end{bmatrix}$?

Ⓐ reflection over the x-axis
Ⓑ reflection over the y-axis
Ⓒ rotation 90° clockwise
Ⓓ rotation 90° counterclockwise

10. Consider the vector $\vec{v} = \langle 1, 2 \rangle$. Which statements about the scalar product $-2\vec{v}$ are true? Select all that apply.

☐ A. The component form of $-2\vec{v}$ is $\langle -2, -4 \rangle$.

☐ B. The magnitude of $-2\vec{v}$ is 2 times the magnitude of $\vec{v}$.

☐ C. The direction of $-2\vec{v}$ is the opposite of the direction of $\vec{v}$.

☐ D. The vector $-2\vec{v}$ is in the first quadrant.

11. Matrix $X = \begin{bmatrix} -1 & 1 \\ 2 & 4 \end{bmatrix}$ and $Y = \begin{bmatrix} 0 & 0 \\ 0 & 0 \end{bmatrix}$.
Find $X + Y$.

$X + Y = \begin{bmatrix} a & b \\ c & d \end{bmatrix}$

$a = \boxed{}$ $b = \boxed{}$
$c = \boxed{}$ $d = \boxed{}$

12. A parallelogram has vertices at the origin, (2, 5), and (−2, y), and has an area of 10 square units. Select all the possible values of y.

☐ A. 9   ☐ D. 1
☐ B. −9   ☐ E. −1
☐ C. 0   ☐ F. 3

13. Which matrix has an inverse?

Ⓐ $\begin{bmatrix} 6 & -9 \\ -4 & -6 \end{bmatrix}$ Ⓒ $\begin{bmatrix} 4 & 2 \\ 8 & 4 \end{bmatrix}$

Ⓑ $\begin{bmatrix} -4 & 8 \\ -3 & 6 \end{bmatrix}$ Ⓓ $\begin{bmatrix} 3 & -3 \\ 7 & -7 \end{bmatrix}$

14. A company makes cardigan and pullover sweaters. Last week, the company spent $18,500 on labor and $16,000 on materials.

| Manufacturing Costs per Sweater ($) |||
Sweater Style	Labor	Materials
Cardigan	15	12
Pullover	11	10

Let c represent the number of cardigans produced and p represent the number of pullovers produced. Complete the matrix equation to model the situation, then solve for c and p.

$\begin{bmatrix} 15 & a \\ b & d \end{bmatrix} \begin{bmatrix} c \\ p \end{bmatrix} = \begin{bmatrix} e \\ f \end{bmatrix}$

$a = \boxed{}$ $b = \boxed{}$ $d = \boxed{}$

$e = \boxed{}$ $f = \boxed{}$

$c = \boxed{}$ $p = \boxed{}$

Name _____

10 Performance Assessment Form A

enVision Algebra 2
SavvasRealize.com

Oil spills and chemical contamination of groundwater are modern environmental hazards. The field of bioremediation uses bacteria that occur naturally in the environment to decompose hazardous wastes.

1. The table shows data from an aboveground biotreatment project. Scientists analyzed five samples from different areas of soil for the presence of hazardous components of petroleum products. They found benzene (B), toluene (T), ethylbenzene (E), and xylene (X). A finding of 0.06 mg/kg for benzene means in Sample 1 in 1 kilogram of soil there is about 0.06 mg of benzene present.

Component Levels in Soil (mg/kg)

Area	B	T	E	X
1	0.06	0.95	0.9	18.5
2	0.06	1.05	0.73	13.5
3	0.35	6	5.6	49
4	0.22	0.19	2	19.5
5	0.11	0.82	2.5	26a

Part A

Present the data in the table as matrix C where the five sampling areas are the rows of matrix C and the four components are the columns of matrix C.

Part B

From Part A, an engineer uses 20% of each sample in matrix C for error analysis. Use a matrix operation to find the matrix P (mg/kg) whose elements are each 20% of the corresponding element of matrix C. Round to the nearest hundredth.

Part C

From Part A, create two matrices labeled R and S where R is a 5 × 2 matrix that represents the samples for benzene and toluene. Matrix S is a 5 × 2 matrix that represents the samples for ethylbenzene and xylene. Then find the sum R + S.

2. Bioengineers decide to treat Areas 3 and 5 for toluene and xylene. Refer to Item 1 to create a square matrix F with the estimated contamination levels, again using the different sampling areas as the rows and the contaminants for the columns. Matrix G represents the treatment costs, where g_{11} is the cost in cents per kilogram for treating 1 mg of toluene, and g_{21} is the cost in cents per kilogram for treating 1 mg of xylene.

$$G = \begin{bmatrix} .07 \\ .22 \end{bmatrix}$$

Does $FG = GF$? Explain the meaning of any product you compute. Round to the nearest hundredth of a cent.

3. An engineer wants to predict the flow rates (L/s) of two streams A and B that are near an oil spill to design remediation plans if the oil reaches either stream. The system of equations below represents the situation. Represent the system of linear equations as a matrix equation. Then solve the system using an inverse matrix to find the flow rate for each stream. Round to the nearest tenth. Explain.

$$\begin{cases} 30A + 28B = 680 \\ 36A + 36B = 840 \end{cases}$$

10 Performance Assessment Form B

A group of math students go camping. During their trip, their teacher asks them to interpret their movements in the woods using vectors and determinants.

1. The students want to find a water source. They analyze their trip using a coordinate plane where each unit represents one mile. They start a search from their campsite at point A(2, 2).

   ### Part A

   The students end their search at point B(3.5, 4.9). What is the vector, in component form, that represents the total change in position due to their trip? What are its magnitude and direction? Round values to the nearest tenth.

   ### Part B

   The next day, the students try a different path from the campsite to find a water source. The vector $\vec{AC} = \langle 3.1, -2 \rangle$ represents this trip. Using $\vec{AB}$ from part A, find $\vec{AB} + \vec{AC}$ graphically and algebraically. Explain.

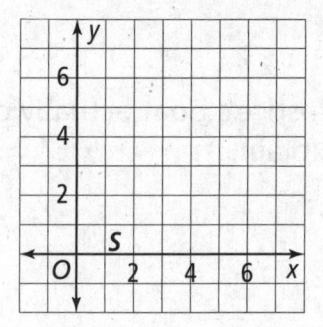

   ### Part C

   From Part B, let the vector $\vec{r}$ represent the sum of $\vec{AB}$ and $\vec{AC}$. On the third day, the students plan to travel from the campsite on a vector of $1.5 \cdot \vec{r}$. Find $1.5 \cdot \vec{r}$. How do the magnitude and direction of $1.5 \cdot \vec{r}$ compare to those of $\vec{r}$? Round values to the nearest hundredth. Explain.

2. The students find a canyon that is roughly the shape of a triangle. The triangle can be arranged on the coordinate plane so that one vertex is at the origin and the other two vertices are at points (−1, 5) and (−3, 10). Use a vector matrix T and its determinant to estimate the area of the canyon in square miles. Explain.

3. Justice, a few students, and a teacher, pilot a boat across a river with the engine set at speed and direction $\vec{s}$, 10 mph headed 30° north of west. The current of the river is $\vec{c}$, 4 mph in a direction 45° east of south.

   Part A

   What are the component forms of $\vec{s}$ and $\vec{c}$? Explain.

   Part B

   If you include the effect of the current, how fast does Justice's boat actually go, and in what direction, as he pilots it across the river? Explain.

Name _____

Benchmark Assessment 5

1. Use a graph to solve $|x + 4| - 2 < \frac{1}{3}x + 2$.

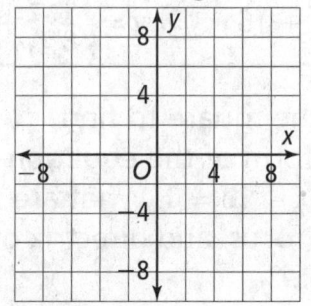

   Ⓐ $6 < x < 0$
   Ⓑ $-6 < x < 0$
   Ⓒ $-6 > x > 0$
   Ⓓ $6 > x > 0$

2. The path of a projectile launched from a 20-ft-tall tower is modeled by the equation $y = -5x^2 + 40x + 20$. Graph the equation. What is the maximum height, in meters, reached by the projectile?

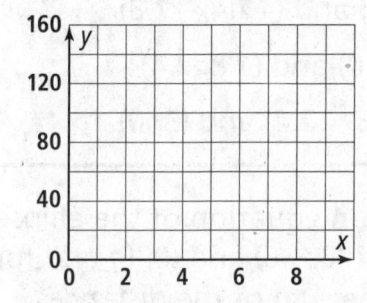

   The maximum height is ⬚ m.

3. Solve $x^2 + 4x + 43 = 0$ by using the Quadratic Formula.

   Ⓐ $x = -2 + \sqrt{39}$ and $x = -2 - \sqrt{39}$
   Ⓑ $x = -4 + \sqrt{43}i$ and $x = -4 - \sqrt{43}i$
   Ⓒ $x = -2 + \sqrt{55}i$ and $x = -2 - \sqrt{55}i$
   Ⓓ $x = -2 + \sqrt{39}i$ and $x = -2 - \sqrt{39}i$

4. For the graph of $f(x) = x^3 - 8x^2 + 7x$,

   f is [ ] increasing [ ] negative [ ] positive [ ] decreasing on the intervals $(-\infty, 0)$ and $(1, 7)$.

   f is [ ] increasing [ ] negative [ ] positive [ ] decreasing on the intervals $(0, 1)$ and $(7, \infty)$.

5. Solve $1 = \frac{4}{x^2 - 1} - \frac{2}{x - 1}$. State any restrictions on the variables.

   Ⓐ $-3, x \neq -1, 1$
   Ⓑ $1, x \neq 1$
   Ⓒ $-3, 1$
   Ⓓ $3, x \neq -1, 1$

6. Simplify $\sqrt[3]{64x^{18}y^6}$.

   Ⓐ $8x^9y^3$
   Ⓑ $4x^6y^2$
   Ⓒ $4x^9y^3$
   Ⓓ $2x^6y^2\sqrt[3]{2}$

7. A store offers a $25-off sale on cell phones. Registered customers can also get a 5% discount on the sale price. Let x represent the price in dollars, and let $f(x) = x - 25$ and $g(x) = 0.90x$ represent the discounts. Which function can the store manager use to find the final price for a registered customer?

   Ⓐ $f \circ g$
   Ⓑ $f + g$
   Ⓒ $g \circ f$
   Ⓓ $\frac{f}{g}$

8. Estimate the solution of the equation $4\log_2(2x) = x + 4$ by graphing. Select all that apply.

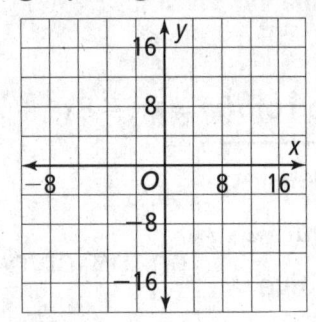

- [ ] A. $x = 1$
- [ ] B. $x = 2$
- [ ] C. $x = 4$
- [ ] D. $x = 5$
- [ ] E. $x = 8$
- [ ] F. $x = 16$

9. What is the frequency of the graph of $y = \frac{1}{3}\sin(2x)$?

Ⓐ 4π
Ⓑ 3
Ⓒ $\frac{1}{2}$
Ⓓ $\frac{1}{\pi}$

10. Use a parallelogram to represent $(2 + 4i) + (3 - 3i)$. Label each vertex.

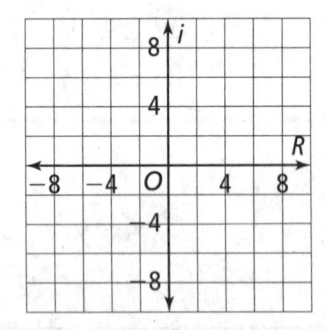

11. What are the center and radius of a circle with the equation $x^2 + y^2 + 4x + 20y + 40 = 0$?

Ⓐ $(-2, -10)$, 8
Ⓑ $(2, -10)$, 8
Ⓒ $(10, 2)$, 16
Ⓓ $(-10, -2)$, 16

12. A theme park has an arch at its entrance in the shape of a parabola. The focus of the arch, in feet, is $(0, 14)$ and directrix is $y = 18$. Use the definition of a parabola to write its equation.

Ⓐ $y = -\frac{1}{8}x^2 + 18$
Ⓑ $y = \frac{1}{8}x^2 + 16$
Ⓒ $y = \frac{1}{8}x^2 - 16$
Ⓓ $y = -\frac{1}{8}x^2 + 16$

13. Complete the square to find the vertex form of the equation $4y - x^2 - 8x - 16 = 0$. What are the vertex, focus, and directrix of the parabola?

Ⓐ $(-4, 0)$, $\left(-4, \frac{1}{4}\right)$, $y = -\frac{1}{4}$
Ⓑ $(-1, 1)$, $\left(-1, \frac{5}{4}\right)$, $y = \frac{3}{4}$
Ⓒ $(-4, 0)$, $(-4, 1)$, $y = -1$
Ⓓ $(-4, 0)$, $(4, 1)$, $y = 1$

14. Solve the system of equations.

$x^2 + y^2 = 9$
$2y = -4x + 6$

Ⓐ $(0, 3)$ and $(2.4, -1.8)$
Ⓑ $(0, 3)$ and $(-2.4, -1.8)$
Ⓒ $(-3, 0)$ and $(1.8, 2.4)$
Ⓓ $(-1.8, -2.4)$ and $(3, 0)$

15. What is an equation of the ellipse with foci $(0, -6)$ and $(0, 6)$ and for which the sum of the distances from the foci to any point on the ellipse is 16?

Ⓐ $\frac{x^2}{36} + \frac{y^2}{16} = 1$
Ⓑ $\frac{x^2}{28} + \frac{y^2}{64} = 1$
Ⓒ $\frac{x^2}{12} + \frac{y^2}{16} = 1$
Ⓓ $\frac{x^2}{64} + \frac{y^2}{28} = 1$

16. Which of the statements about the ellipse represented by the equation $\frac{(x+1)^2}{36} + \frac{(y-6)^2}{25} = 1$ are true? Select all that apply.

☐ A. The center is (–6, 1).

☐ B. The foci are $(-1 - \sqrt{11}, 6)$ and $(-1 + \sqrt{11}, 6)$.

☐ C. The vertices are (–7, 6) and (5, 6).

☐ D. The minor axis is 6 units long.

17. Graph $\frac{(x+3)^2}{81} + \frac{(y+2)^2}{100} = 1$.

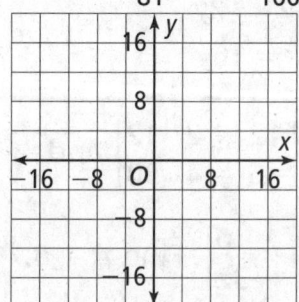

18. Write an equation for the hyperbola with foci (0, 8) and (0, –8) and constant difference of 8.

Ⓐ $\frac{y^2}{16} - \frac{x^2}{32} = 2$

Ⓑ $\frac{y^2}{16} - \frac{x^2}{64} = 3$

Ⓒ $\frac{y^2}{16} - \frac{x^2}{48} = 1$

Ⓓ $\frac{y^2}{16} - \frac{x^2}{64} = 1$

19. Graph $\frac{x^2}{64} - \frac{y^2}{25} = 1$.

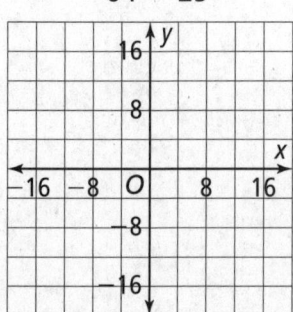

20. Match each equation with the type of conic section it represents.

parabola   circle   ellipse   hyperbola

$\frac{y^2}{48} - x^2 = 1$ ☐

$x = \frac{1}{48}y^2$ circle ☐

$\frac{x^2}{48} + \frac{y^2}{48} = 1$ ☐

$x^2 + \frac{y^2}{48} = 1$ ☐

21. Matrices P and Q are both 3 × 3 matrices. Which statement about P and Q is always true?

Ⓐ $PQ = QP$ Ⓒ $(Q + P)P = QP^2$

Ⓑ $PQ = P + Q$ Ⓓ $P + Q = Q + P$

22. The rows in matrix D represent the prices in dollars of regular hockey shirts and custom hockey shirts. The columns represent the sizes small, medium, and large. If the sales tax rate is 9%, use scalar multiplication to show matrix T, which represents the sales tax for each type of shirt.

$D = \begin{bmatrix} 20 & 24 & 28 \\ 26 & 30 & 32 \end{bmatrix}$ $T = \begin{bmatrix} a & b & c \\ d & e & f \end{bmatrix}$

a = ☐   b = ☐   c = ☐
d = ☐   e = ☐   f = ☐

23. Consider the vectors $\vec{v} = \langle 5, 2 \rangle$ and $\vec{w} = \langle 3, -1 \rangle$. What is the approximate direction of $\vec{v} + \vec{w}$?

Ⓐ 82.9°   Ⓒ 33.7°

Ⓑ 56.3°   Ⓓ 7.1°

24. In matrix G, the entries are the numbers of types of video games in a tech store. Column 1 lists action, column 2 lists racing, row 1 lists beginner, and row 2 lists expert. What does the number in position g_{21} represent?

$$G = \begin{bmatrix} 44 & 30 \\ 20 & 18 \end{bmatrix}$$

Ⓐ 20 beginner action games
Ⓑ 30 expert racing games
Ⓒ 30 beginner racing games
Ⓓ 20 expert action games

25. What transformation in the coordinate plane is represented by the matrix $\begin{bmatrix} -1 & 0 \\ 0 & -1 \end{bmatrix}$?

Ⓐ reflection over the x-axis
Ⓑ reflection over the y-axis
Ⓒ rotation 180° around the origin
Ⓓ rotation 90° counterclockwise

26. Consider the vector $\vec{b} = \langle 12, -8 \rangle$. Which statement is true?

Ⓐ $3\vec{b} = \langle 15, -5 \rangle$
Ⓑ Vectors $\vec{b}$ and $3\vec{b}$ have the same direction.
Ⓒ $|3\vec{b}| \approx 8.94$
Ⓓ $3\vec{b} - \vec{b} = \langle 24, 16 \rangle$

27. What is the system of equations represented by the matrix equation?

$$\begin{bmatrix} 4 & 6 \\ -2 & -8 \end{bmatrix} \begin{bmatrix} x \\ y \end{bmatrix} = \begin{bmatrix} -2 \\ 16 \end{bmatrix}$$

Ⓐ $\begin{cases} 4x + 6y = -2 \\ -2x - 8y = 16 \end{cases}$

Ⓑ $\begin{cases} 4x + 6y = -2 \\ -2x - 8y = 16 \end{cases}$

Ⓒ $\begin{cases} 10x = -2 \\ -10y = 16 \end{cases}$

Ⓓ $\begin{cases} 4 + 6y = -2y \\ -2 - 8x = 16y \end{cases}$

28. Matrix $A = \begin{bmatrix} 12 & 2 & 12 \\ -6 & -4 & 30 \end{bmatrix}$ and

$B = \begin{bmatrix} 7 & -9 & 0 \\ 18 & 19 & -32 \end{bmatrix}$. Find $A - B$.

$A - B = \begin{bmatrix} a & b & c \\ d & e & f \end{bmatrix}$

a = ☐   b = ☐   c = ☐
d = ☐   e = ☐   f = ☐

29. What is the solution of the matrix equation below?

$$\begin{bmatrix} -6 & 3 \\ 10 & -2 \end{bmatrix} \begin{bmatrix} x \\ y \end{bmatrix} = \begin{bmatrix} 60 \\ -22 \end{bmatrix}$$

$$\begin{bmatrix} x \\ y \end{bmatrix} = \begin{bmatrix} a \\ b \end{bmatrix}$$

a = ☐
b = ☐

30. A company makes golf clubs for adults and juniors. Last month, the company spent $38,000 on labor and $60,000 on materials.

Manufacturing Costs per Golf Club ($)		
Club Length	Labor	Material
Adult (x)	30	35
Junior (y)	40	60

Let x represent the number of clubs made for adults and y the number of clubs made for juniors. Complete the matrix equation to model the situation.

$$\begin{bmatrix} 30 & a \\ b & c \end{bmatrix} \begin{bmatrix} x \\ y \end{bmatrix} = \begin{bmatrix} d \\ e \end{bmatrix}$$

a = ☐ b = ☐ c = ☐
d = ☐ e = ☐

---

31. Part A The standard form for a quadratic equation is $ax^2 + bx + c$ where a, b, and c represent constants. How many terms are in the formula?

☐ terms

Part B Select all of the terms that are dependent on x.

☐ A. a
☐ B. b
☐ C. c
☐ D. ax^2
☐ E. bx

---

32. The exponential function $y = 9{,}000(0.97)^t$ has an initial value

of ☐ 9,000
   ☐ 9,360

The function represents

exponential ☐ growth   with a
            ☐ decay

rate of ☐ 97%
        ☐ 3%

---

33. Part A If $\vec{s} = \langle 4, 5 \rangle$ and the scalar is −2. Find the new vector components.

⟨☐ , ☐⟩

Part B Reflect $\vec{s}$ over the y-axis using matrices.

⟨☐ , ☐⟩

34. What is the average rate of change of the function $y = 3\cos x$ on the interval $\left[-\frac{\pi}{2}, \pi\right]$?

   Ⓐ $-\frac{\pi}{2}$
   Ⓑ $\frac{4}{\pi}$
   Ⓒ $-\frac{2}{\pi}$
   Ⓓ $\frac{2}{\pi}$

35. What is the value of b? Round to the nearest tenth.

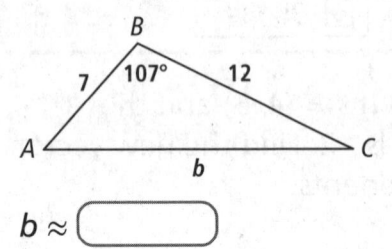

   Triangle with vertices A, B, C; angle at B = 107°, side from A to B = 7, side from B to C = 12, side b from A to C.

   $b \approx$ ⬚

36. What is an equation of the parabola with vertex $(0, 3)$ and directrix $y = 1$?

   Ⓐ $y = \frac{1}{8}x^2 + 3$
   Ⓑ $y = \frac{1}{4}x^2 + 3$
   Ⓒ $y = \frac{1}{4}x^2 + 2$
   Ⓓ $y = \frac{1}{3}x^2 + 8$

37. Identify the center, foci, and vertices of the ellipse represented by $9x^2 + 54x + 4y^2 - 8y + 49 = 0$.

   center: (⬚, ⬚)
   foci: (⬚, $1 - \sqrt{5}$),
   (⬚, $1 + \sqrt{5}$)
   vertices: (⬚, ⬚),
   (⬚, ⬚)

38. There are 50 deer in a particular forest. The population is increasing at a rate of 15% per year. Write an exponential growth function that represents the number of deer, y, in that forest after x months. Round to the nearest thousandth.

   $f(x) =$ ⬚ (⬚)^x

39. Select all equations that are represented by the matrix equation.

   $\begin{bmatrix} 4 & -1 \\ 2 & 3 \end{bmatrix} \begin{bmatrix} x \\ y \end{bmatrix} = \begin{bmatrix} 0 \\ 2 \end{bmatrix}$

   ☐ A. $4x + 2y = 0$
   ☐ B. $2x + 3y = 2$
   ☐ C. $4x - y = 0$
   ☐ D. $2x - y = 2$
   ☐ E. $4x + 2y = 2$
   ☐ F. $-x + 3y = 0$
   ☐ G. $-x + 3y = 2$
   ☐ H. $2x - y = 0$

40. A vector has an initial point at $(2, 5)$ and a terminal point at $(5, 7)$. Complete the statements below with the correct numbers rounded to the nearest tenth of a unit.

   The component form of the vector is $\langle$ ⬚ , ⬚ $\rangle$.

   The magnitude of the vector is about ⬚ .

   The direction of the vector is about ⬚ °.

Name _____

11 Readiness Assessment

enVision Algebra 2
SavvasRealize.com

1. **Part A**
   Jack recorded the number of lawns he mowed per week over 13 weeks.

   12, 15, 10, 22, 7, 12, 18, 14, 9, 11, 5, 14, 19

   Fill in the table with the frequencies for a histogram plot that displays the data.

Lawns mowed	5–9	10–14	15–19	20–24
Frequencies				

   Part B
   In Part A, in what percent of the weeks were more than 9 lawns mowed?

   Ⓐ 79.62% Ⓒ 23.08%
   Ⓑ 76.92% Ⓓ 0.77%

2. **Part A**
   The test scores of a group of 14 students in their math midterm exam are shown.

   99, 72, 65, 83, 87, 76, 94, 80, 67, 59, 73, 91, 70, 82

   Fill in the table with the frequencies for a histogram plot that displays the data.

Test Scores	50–59	60–69	70–79	80–89	90–99
Frequenci					

   Part B
   In Part A, what percent of test scores range from 70 to 79? Round to the nearest hundredth of a percent.

   percent = ☐ %

3. Find e using the equation $e = \frac{2p}{\sqrt{n}}$ where $p = 2.2$ and $n = 100$.

   Ⓐ 0.022 Ⓒ 0.044
   Ⓑ 0.22   Ⓓ 0.44

4. Find m using the equation $m = \frac{2s}{\sqrt{n}}$ where $s = 20.5$ and $n = 4$.

   Ⓐ 10.25 Ⓒ 20.5
   Ⓑ 11.25 Ⓓ 41

5. Kaitlyn makes 65% of her free throws on the basketball court. If she attempts 50 free throws in practice, about how many would you expect her to make?

   Ⓐ 17 Ⓒ 27
   Ⓑ 23 Ⓓ 33

6. Consider two sets of data.

   Set A: 14, 10, 17, 9, 20, 22, 9, 6, 11, 2
   Set B: 15, 12, 18, 10, 21, 25, 11

   Calculate the mean for both data sets. Which data set has a greater mean?

   mean of set A = ☐

   mean of set B = ☐

   Set ☐ A / ☐ B has the greater mean.

7. Find the value of x so that the data set has a mean of 93.

   101, 92, 76, 88, x

   $x =$ ☐

8. Find the value of x so that the data set has a mean of 26.5.

   22.6, 32.9, 29.7, 19.8, x

   x = ☐

9. Consider two sets of data.

   Set M: 4, 24, 12, 6, 24, 2, 74, 8, 24

   Set N: 23, 4, 29, 12, 6, 27, 74

   Calculate the median for both data sets. Which is greater?

   M: ☐   N: = ☐

   Set ☐ has the greater median.

10. In the data set, which is greater, the mean or the median?

    14.5, 10, 7, 14, 26, 11, 8.5

    mean = ☐   median = ☐

    The ☐ median / ☐ mean is greater.

11. Use the data to make a dot plot.

    24, 22, 19, 21, 24, 23, 24, 18, 19, 23, 18, 21, 22, 19

    18 19 20 21 22 23 24

12. Use the data to make a dot plot.

    106, 102, 104, 106, 101, 106, 104, 105, 101, 104, 102, 104, 106, 101

    101 102 103 104 105 106

13. Given the dot plot shown below, what is the median value?

    200 201 202 203 204 205

    median = ☐

14. Select all the data displays in which the exact median of a data set can be determined.

    ☐ A. box plot   ☐ D. scatter plot
    ☐ B. dot plot   ☐ E. bar plot
    ☐ C. histogram

15. Select all the statements that appear to be true about the box plot shown below.

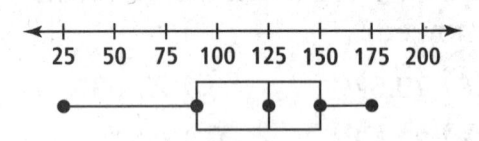

    25 50 75 100 125 150 175 200

    ☐ A. The median is about 125.
    ☐ B. The interquartile range is about 60.
    ☐ C. The first quartile is about 90 and the third quartile is about 150.
    ☐ D. The mean is about 125.
    ☐ E. The range is about 175.
    ☐ F. The maximum is about 175.

16. What appears to be the median of the data represented by the box plot below?

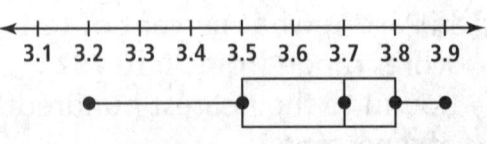

    3.1 3.2 3.3 3.4 3.5 3.6 3.7 3.8 3.9

    Ⓐ 3.2   Ⓑ 3.5   Ⓒ 3.7   Ⓓ 3.8

Name _____

11-1 Lesson Quiz

Statistical Questions and Variables

1. Select the type of variable of each quantity.

	Quantitative	Categorical	Neither
The distance from your home to your school in miles	☐	☐	☐
The types of cars owned by families in your neighborhood	☐	☐	☐
The number of hours veterinarians work in a week	☐	☐	☐
The number of ingredients in your family cheese cake recipe	☐	☐	☐

2. A veterinarian polled her clients who own dogs as to whether or not they used dry food only for their dogs. Which of the following describes the population of this survey?

   Ⓐ pet owners
   Ⓑ dog owners
   Ⓒ this veterinarian's clients
   Ⓓ this veterinarian's dog-owning clients

3. A survey question is conducted on all high school students in Miami. Select the type of variable that will result from each survey question.

	Quantitative	Categorical
Do you have any siblings?	☐	☐
What is your eye color?	☐	☐
How old are you?	☐	☐
What was your grade in the last math exam?	☐	☐
How many languages do you speak?	☐	☐

4. Select all the statements that are parameters.

   ☐ A. 75% of the students at North High School voted for Lucy.
   ☐ B. The total collected at a fund-raiser was $5,281.
   ☐ C. The mean height of students at one table in the cafeteria is 1.3 m.
   ☐ D. Ten out of 25 people surveyed chose "red."
   ☐ E. 78% of science students said they got a fair grade on an assessment.

5. From a population of 1,600 cars, a dealer chooses a sample of 25 cars and calculates their mean weight. Is this mean weight a *statistic* or a *parameter*?

   This mean weight is an example of a ☐ statistic
                                         ☐ parameter

Name _____

11-2 Lesson Quiz

Statistical Studies and Sampling Methods

1. Which of the following is an example of a statistical experiment?

   Ⓐ Twenty people in a neighborhood are asked if they want more streetlights on the street.

   Ⓑ More streetlights are installed on one street and people are then asked if they like the change.

   Ⓒ The number of accidents on the street is compared to last year's rate.

   Ⓓ People are asked to call a number to say if they want more streetlights.

2. Choose the sampling method that best describes each example.

	Convenience	Systematic	Self-selected
The first ten people who show up for class are asked to fill out a form.	☐	☐	☐
All students whose ID numbers are divisible by 5 are asked about what music they like.	☐	☐	☐
Students participate in a voluntary on-line survey conducted by your school cafeteria.	☐	☐	☐

3. A lawyer reviews a sample of his past cases to find his success rate. What type of study is this?

   Ⓐ experiment   Ⓑ survey   Ⓒ observational study   Ⓓ biased study

4. A student wants to study the effect of meditation on the time a person is able to balance on one leg. She finds 40 volunteers who have never meditated, and records their balance times. She selects 20 of them at random, and instructs them to practice meditation daily for two weeks. In two weeks, she records the balance times for all 40 volunteers again.

   The 40 volunteers are the
   ☐ control
   ☐ sample   group.
   ☐ experimental
   ☐ study

   The 20 mediators are the
   ☐ sample
   ☐ experimental   group.
   ☐ control
   ☐ study

5. Select all the sampling methods that would bias the set of responses.

   ☐ A. asking people to return a mail-in card
   ☐ B. tossing a chipped number cube
   ☐ C. calling people between 3:00 P.M. and 4:00 P.M.
   ☐ D. interviewing pet owners about their pet's health
   ☐ E. asking the first 50 people who enter a food store about their shopping habits

enVision® Algebra 2 • Assessment Sourcebook

Name _____

11-3 Lesson Quiz

Data Distributions

Use the following data sets for Items 1–2.

Data Set A	24, 31, 30, 32, 23, 25, 34, 32, 25, 21, 22, 29
Data Set B	35, 33, 32, 21, 22, 23, 24, 25, 24, 22, 25, 25

1. Identify the five-number summary for each data set.

	Minimum	1st Quartile	Median	3rd Quartile	Maximum
Data Set A					
Data Set B					

2. Describe each data set as *skewed left*, *skewed right*, or *symmetrical*.

   Data Set A is ☐ skewed left ☐ symmetrical ☐ skewed right. Data Set B is ☐ skewed right ☐ skewed left ☐ symmetrical.

3. Use the following data set.

   35, 22, 20, 22, 16, 24, 25, 24, 23, 25, 25, 19, 15, 28, 32, 37, 40

   How would you classify the data set? What statistics should you use to describe the center and spread of data?

   It is ☐ symmetrical ☐ skewed right ☐ skewed left. The ☐ median ☐ mean ☐ mode ☐ average and ☐ range ☐ variance ☐ standard deviation ☐ quartiles should be used in this case.

4. Which of the following is likely to be an example of a normal distribution?

   Ⓐ the last digits of the street addresses in your contacts

   Ⓑ the number of bicycles owned by people who live in a particular city

   Ⓒ the scores on a nationwide math test

   Ⓓ the value of a card drawn at random from a stack of cards numbered from 1 to 10

5. In a data distribution that is skewed left, the ☐ median ☐ mean will be greater.

enVision® Algebra 2 • Assessment Sourcebook

11-4 Lesson Quiz

Normal Distributions

A data set with a mean of 34 and a standard deviation of 2.5 is normally distributed. Use this information for Items 1–2.

1. According to the Empirical Rule, what percent of the data is in each of the following ranges? Round to the nearest tenth of a percent if necessary.

    Between 34 and 39: [ ] %

    Less than 31.5: [ ] %

    Between 29 and 36.5: [ ] %

2. Select the data value that best matches each statement.

	−36.1	36.1	34.5	40.0
Greater than approximately 80% of the distribution	☐	☐	☐	☐
Greater than approximately 97.6% of the distribution	☐	☐	☐	☐

3. Find the percent of all values in a normal distribution for which $z \leq 1.00$, to the nearest tenth of a percent.

    percent = [ ] %

    Keenan scored 80 points on an exam with a mean of 77 points and a standard deviation of 4.9 points. Rachel scored 78 points on an exam with a mean of 75 points and a standard deviation of 3.7 points. Use this information for Items 4–5.

4. Kennan's z-score = [ ]; Rachel's z-score = [ ].

5. It is meaningless to compare Keenan's and Rachel's scores directly, because they each took a different exam. Which of the following describes a valid way to use statistics to compare Keenan's score on his exam with Rachel's score on her exam?

    Ⓐ Keenan did equally as well as Rachel because each of them scored 3 points above the mean for their exam.

    Ⓑ Keenan did better than Rachel because his exam had a greater standard deviation than Rachel's had.

    Ⓒ Rachel did better than Keenan because her z-score was greater than Keenan's.

    Ⓓ Rachel did better than Keenan because the mean for her exam was less than the mean for Keenan's exam.

enVision® Algebra 2 • Assessment Sourcebook

Name _____

11-5 Lesson Quiz
Margin of Error

1. A poll reports that 23% of students have at least one pet at home. The margin of error is 5%. Estimate the number of students polled.

    Ⓐ 500

    Ⓑ 400

    Ⓒ 40

    Ⓓ 25

2. Malia found the margin of error for the percent of lengths of 100 willow leaves greater than 5 cm. If she increases her sample to 400, how will this affect her margin of error?

    Ⓐ It will not change the margin of error.

    Ⓑ It will double the margin of error.

    Ⓒ It will reduce the margin of error by one-half.

    Ⓓ It will reduce the margin of error by one-fourth.

3. A random sample of 2,000 driver's license applications found that 17% reported their eye color as blue. What is the margin of error for the sample? Round to the nearest tenth of a percent.

    margin of error = ☐ %

4. A brand of light bulbs has a mean lifetime of 1,500 hours and a standard deviation of 150 hours. A sample of 100 light bulbs gave a mean lifetime of 1,400 hours. What is the margin of error for the sample?

    Ⓐ 30

    Ⓑ 15

    Ⓒ 3

    Ⓓ 1

5. A survey of 120 twelfth-graders finds that 36% were carrying more than $15 on the day of the survey. Use the margin of error to complete the following. Round to the nearest whole percent.

    An interval that will likely include the proportion of students in the population of twelfth-graders who carry more than $15 is ☐ % to ☐ %.

enVision® Algebra 2 • Assessment Sourcebook

Name _____

11-6 Lesson Quiz

Testing Hypotheses From Experiments

1. Before a high-school football game the footballs were inflated to $p = 13$ psi (pounds per square inch). After the game the mean inflation was 12.5 psi. Select the null hypothesis H_0.

   Ⓐ $H_0: p = 13$ Ⓑ $H_0: p = 12.5$ Ⓒ $H_0: p < 13$ Ⓓ $H_0: p > 12.5$

Use the following information for Items 2–4.

Stacy recorded the number of minutes she used her smartphone each day for one week before using an app that awards points for decreased phone usage, and for one week after using the app. Stacy's alternative hypothesis is $H_a: x < 114.6$.

Before	103	127	87	124	95	136	130
After	83	94	120	105	75	98	96

2. What is the difference in the sample means? Round to the nearest tenth of a minute.   difference in sample means = ☐ minutes

3. Stacy randomly sorted her data into two new groups. The first is randomly sorted, as shown. Fill in the table with the rest of the data in ascending order.

New Group 1	83	94	96	105	124	130	136
New Group 2							

What is the new difference between the sample means? Round your answer to the nearest tenth of a minute.   new difference = ☐ minutes

4. Stacy used a simulation to randomize her data 200 times. She found that the difference between sample means over 200 trials is approximately normally-distributed, with a mean of −0.2 and a standard deviation of 9.1. Which of the following conclusions is most appropriate?

   Ⓐ Phone use did not change.   Ⓒ Phone use increased.
   Ⓑ Phone use increased and then decreased.   Ⓓ Phone use decreased.

5. A car manufacturer claims that the gas mileage for an SUV is at least m miles per gallon (mi/gal). A national sample finds that the mileage for that model SUV is 37.8 ± 2.1 mi/gal. Write an inequality to represent the values of m that would lead to a conclusion that the company's claim is false.

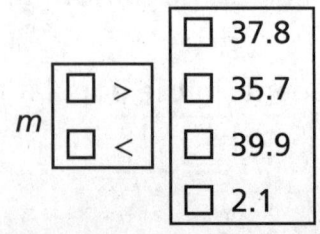

   m ☐ >   ☐ 37.8
       ☐ <   ☐ 35.7
             ☐ 39.9
             ☐ 2.1

enVision® Algebra 2 • Assessment Sourcebook

Name _____

11 Topic Assessment Form A

1. A poll of voters showed Candidate X is preferred by 53% of those polled, while Candidate Y is preferred by 47%. The margin of error was 5%. Select all the true statements that apply.
   - ☐ A. Candidate X could have as little as 48% of voter support.
   - ☐ B. Candidate Y could have as little as 42% of voter support.
   - ☐ C. Candidate X could have as much as 63% of voter support.
   - ☐ D. Candidate Y could have as much as 52% of voter support.
   - ☐ E. There is a 5% chance that Candidate X will win the election.
   - ☐ F. There is a 95% chance that Candidate X will win the election.

2. A census reports that the mean retirement age is 68.3 years. In a random sample, the mean retirement age is 65.8 years. What is the mean of 68.3 years?
   - Ⓐ a parameter   Ⓒ a statistic
   - Ⓑ a variable   Ⓓ a sample

3. In order to make valid statistical conclusions from data, which type of research needs to have randomization as part of its design? Select all the types of research that apply.
   - ☐ A. sample survey
   - ☐ B. population census
   - ☐ C. observational study
   - ☐ D. double-blind experiment
   - ☐ E. comparative experiment

4. Every third person on a list of soccer players is selected for a survey. What kind of sampling method is used?
   - Ⓐ convenience   Ⓒ cluster
   - Ⓑ systematic   Ⓓ stratified

5. **Part A**
   A data set is normally distributed with a mean of 27 and a standard deviation of 3.5. Find the z-score for a value of 25, to the nearest hundredth. ☐

   Part B
   In Part A, about what percent of the data is greater than 35?
   - Ⓐ 2.5% Ⓑ 1% Ⓒ 2% Ⓓ 0.11%

6. Use the data sets.

   A: 1 3 3 2 4 0 4 3 3 5 2

   B: 3 5 5 4 6 1 6 6 6 6 5

	Skewed right	Skewed left	Symmetrical
Data Set A	☐	☐	☐
Data Set B	☐	☐	☐

7. Which five-number summary is most likely to represent a normal distribution?

   Ⓐ 4; 4; 4; 12; 30

   Ⓑ 4; 5; 7.8; 10.1; 11.3

   Ⓒ 8; 8; 8; 8.1; 19

   Ⓓ 1; 3; 4; 59.5; 61.3

8. Select all the statistical variables that are likely to be normally distributed.

   ☐ A. height of a sunflower plant 12 weeks after planting

   ☐ B. distance between parking meters along a city street

   ☐ C. number of seconds a person can exhale continuously

   ☐ D. length of earthworms found in a soybean field

   ☐ E. weight, of newborns in the United States

9. A student wants to know the average age of teachers at her high school. She records the ages of 15 randomly selected teachers at the school. This sampling method is

   ☐ biased

   ☐ unbiased

10. The mean on a statewide geography test was 74 with a standard deviation of 12. West County sampled the scores of some of its students and reported a mean of 79 with a margin of error of ±1.9.

    Part A

    To the nearest whole number, how many students were in West County's sample? ☐

    Part B

    What is the range of reasonable means for a sample of this size?

    ☐ or ☐

11. A company claims their new battery lasts longer than their original battery in a gaming device. Data Set A shows times for the original battery, and Data Set B shows times for the new battery.

A	3.1 h	3.3 h	3.6 h	3.2 h	3.1 h
B	3.5 h	3.4 h	3.7 h	3.9 h	4.0 h

    Part A

    Calculate the difference of the sample means to the nearest hundredth. ☐ h

    Part B

    The company used a simulation to randomize the data, sorting it into two new groups 1000 times. The difference of the means in this simulation was normally distributed with mean −0.011 and standard deviation 0.203. Does the simulation allow you to reject the null hypothesis that there is no difference in battery life?

    ☐ yes

    ☐ no

Name _____

11 Topic Assessment Form B

1. A poll of voters showed Candidate X is preferred by 56% of those polled, while Candidate Y is preferred by 44%. The margin of error was 5%. Select all the true statements that apply.
   - ☐ A. Candidate Y could have as little as 39% of voter support.
   - ☐ B. Candidate X could have as little as 45% of voter support.
   - ☐ C. Candidate X could have as much as 66% of voter support.
   - ☐ D. Candidate Y could have as much as 55% of voter support.
   - ☐ E. There is a 95% chance that Candidate X will win the election.
   - ☐ F. There is a 5% chance that Candidate X will win the election.

2. A census reports that the mean retirement age is 68.3 years. In a random sample, the mean retirement age is 65.8 years. What is the mean of 65.8 years?
   - Ⓐ a parameter   Ⓒ a variable
   - Ⓑ a statistic   Ⓓ a sample

3. In order to make valid statistical conclusions from data, which type of research does NOT need to have randomization as part of its design? Select all the types of research that apply.
   - ☐ A. observational study
   - ☐ B. sample survey
   - ☐ C. population census
   - ☐ D. comparative experiment
   - ☐ E. double-blind experiment

4. A list of basketball players is divided into groups by the alphabetical order of the players' last names, and then one group is used as a sample for a survey. What kind of sampling method is used?
   - Ⓐ convenience   Ⓒ cluster
   - Ⓑ systematic   Ⓓ stratified

5. **Part A**
   A data set is normally distributed with a mean of 25 and a standard deviation of 1.5. Find the z-score for a value of 20, to the nearest hundredth. ☐

   Part B
   In Part A, about what percent of the data is greater than 26?
   - Ⓐ 28% Ⓑ 25% Ⓒ 0.4% Ⓓ 0.23%

6. Use the data sets.

    A: 1 1 3 5 0 0 4 1 0 1 4

    B: 2 1 4 5 1 1 3 6 5 3 1

	Skewed right	Skewed left	Symmetrical
Data Set A	☐	☐	☐
Data Set B	☐	☐	☐

7. Which five-number summary is most likely to represent a normal distribution?

    Ⓐ 4; 4; 4; 4; 6.7

    Ⓑ 4; 5; 5; 20.6; 30.9

    Ⓒ 8; 9; 12; 14; 16.1

    Ⓓ 1; 1; 1; 2; 3

8. Select all the statistical variables that are likely to be normally distributed.

    ☐ A. heights of children in an elementary school class

    ☐ B. number of apples per tree in an orchard

    ☐ C. number of pets per household

    ☐ D. weight of fish caught in a net

    ☐ E. number of days that a bridge is closed due to bad weather

9. A student wants to know the average height of students in his high school. He records the heights of all ninth graders. This sampling method is ☐ biased ☐ unbiased

10. The mean on a statewide geography test was 76 with a standard deviation of 11. West County sampled the scores of some of its students and reported a mean of 75 with a margin of error of ±2.2.

    Part A

    To the nearest whole number, how many students were in West County's sample? ☐

    Part B

    What is the range of reasonable means for a sample of this size?

    ☐ or ☐

11. A company claims their new battery lasts longer than their original battery in a gaming device. Data Set A shows times for the new battery, and Data Set B shows times for the original battery.

A	4.3 h	4.7 h	3.9 h	4.1 h	4.3 h
B	3.3 h	4.2 h	3.9 h	3.7 h	3.2 h

    Part A

    Calculate the difference of the sample means to the nearest hundredth. ☐ h

    Part B

    The company used a simulation to randomize the data, sorting it into two new groups 1000 times. The difference of the means in this simulation was normally distributed with mean 0.014 and standard deviation 0.283. Does the simulation allow you to reject the null hypothesis that there is no difference in battery life? ☐ yes ☐ no

11 Performance Assessment Form A

The stock market is an electronic market where stocks and bonds are bought and sold. Usually the goal of a person who buys stock is to hold shares of stock for a period of time and then sell them for more than the purchase price. You can use statistics to analyze stock prices and make decisions based on your findings.

1. The tables below show the closing price (in dollars) per share of stock in XYZ Company for the first 12 weeks of two successive years.

   - Last year

Week	1	2	3	4	5	6	7	8	9	10	11	12
Stock Price ($)	5.34	5.40	5.41	5.42	5.50	5.55	5.55	5.57	5.70	5.65	5.66	5.68

   - This year

Week	1	2	3	4	5	6	7	8	9	10	11	12
Stock Price ($)	6.00	5.95	5.92	5.80	5.81	5.75	5.75	5.75	5.64	5.52	5.40	5.03

Part A

What is a statistical question you could ask that could be used to compare the data? What is a statistical variable that is common between both data sets? Is that variable categorical or quantitative? Explain.

Part B

Determine the type of distribution, center, and spread of both data sets using the mean and five-number summaries (minimum, 1st quartile, median, 3rd quartile, maximum). Round to the nearest hundredth, if necessary. Then compare each type of distribution based on your results.

Part C

Use the stock prices per share from last year. Calculate a z-score for a price of 5.65 to determine whether 5.65 is a high or low price for this stock. Use this score to estimate the percentage of prices that were below 5.65. Round to the nearest hundredth, if necessary. Explain.

Part D

Based on the results this year, do you think a stock analyst would suggest that people invest money in this stock during week 13? Explain.

2. Which of the three main types of studies are shown in each example below? Explain your answers.

Study 1	A fund manager studies whether the values of her clients' investments increase, decrease, or stay the same based on applying her normal investment strategy or using a more aggressive strategy.
Study 2	An investment company polls randomly selected business-school students about which industry they would most likely invest their money in.
Study 3	A firm tests how much attention their website gets using a less formal design. An intern determines the number of times each visitor stays on the site for more than ten seconds using the new design and then using the old design.

3. An investment firm claims that the mean increase in price per share of companies it invests in is $1.95 per share every year. A national sample of 100 companies shows that the mean increase in price per share is $1.82 per year. The standard deviation of share prices nationally is $0.30. Would you be skeptical of this claim? Explain.

11 Performance Assessment Form B

Helena gathers data about the music preferences of users of a social media application. She gathers information on music events (MEs). In her study, a music event is defined as a posting that has a hashtag or is linked to other video-sharing websites.

1. From her data, Helena claims that about 15% of MEs on the application are hip hop/rap. Juan wants more proof of her claim.

    - Juan uses technology to determine the genres of music of 100 MEs he chooses at random. He determines that 9 were hip hop/rap.

    - Juan points out the 9% rate to Helena.

    Part A

    Assume Helena is correct and 15% of MEs on the app are hip hop/rap. Use random numbers and a simulated sampling distribution to simulate the outcome of several trials, in which each trial samples 100 MEs from the app and counts the number of hip hop/rap MEs. Make a histogram for your data. Is the model consistent with what you would expect? Explain.

Part B

Helena tells Juan that even though he found a rate of 9% hip hop/rap MEs, this doesn't contradict her assessment that 15% of MEs as a whole are hip hop/rap. Juan's result could be due to natural variability. Use your sampling distribution from Part A to find a range of values centered on the mean that includes 95% of the samples. Use this to determine whether Juan's result contradicts Helena's assessment.

2. The application claims that 30% (0.30) of the MEs are pop music. Helena does 50 trials in which she selects 100 MEs at random. She determines that 25 out of every 100 MEs are pop music, with a standard deviation among the trials of about 5 MEs. Does Helena's research provide strong evidence that the social media app's claim of 30% pop music MEs is false? Explain.

3. Among all users on the app, 20% of MEs are rock music. The app makers want to know what percentage of MEs from users under 18 years old are rock music. From a sample of 200 MEs from users under 18 years old, 15% of those users' MEs turn out to be rock music.

   The app makers want to know if the percent of rock MEs coming from all users under 18 is really less than it is for users of all age groups combined. Write hypotheses for this situation and run a simulation to test the hypotheses. Make a histogram for your data. What hypothesis does the simulation support? Show your work.

Name _____

12 Readiness Assessment

1. What is the value of p in the proportion?
   $\frac{8.7}{1,160} = \frac{p}{100}$
   - Ⓐ 0.0075
   - Ⓑ 0.75
   - Ⓒ 0.029
   - Ⓓ 0.0029

2. What is the value of the expression $100 \cdot (p)^r \cdot \frac{(1-p)^n}{(1-p)^r}$ for $p = 0.7$, $r = 3$, and $n = 5$?

   [_____]

3. What proportion of the surface area is on each face of the shape, to the nearest percent?

	Cube	Tetrahedron (Triangular Pyramid)
Percentage	[ ]%	[ ]%

4. Match the probabilities with the appropriate event.

Event\Probability	0.15	0.5	1	0	0.78
Impossible	☐	☐	☐	☐	☐
Unlikely	☐	☐	☐	☐	☐
Neither likely nor unlikely	☐	☐	☐	☐	☐
Likely	☐	☐	☐	☐	☐
Certain	☐	☐	☐	☐	☐

5. What is the probability that the spinner lands on the letter A?
   - Ⓐ $\frac{1}{4}$
   - Ⓑ $\frac{1}{3}$
   - Ⓒ $\frac{1}{2}$
   - Ⓓ $\frac{2}{3}$

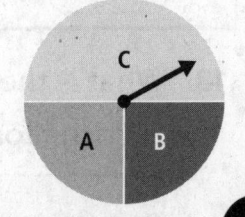

6. A quarter is tossed four times. If heads is worth $0.25 and tails is worth nothing, what is the probability that you end up with exactly $0.50?
   - Ⓐ $\frac{7}{16}$
   - Ⓑ $\frac{1}{2}$
   - Ⓒ $\frac{11}{16}$
   - Ⓓ $\frac{3}{8}$

7. A restaurant owner wants to survey customers. Which method produces a random representative sample?
   - Ⓐ Survey the first 20 people that come in after opening.
   - Ⓑ Survey every 20th person that comes in after opening.
   - Ⓒ Survey 20 customers who leave large tips.
   - Ⓓ Survey 20 people on the sidewalk in front of the restaurant.

8. A fair coin is tossed n times. For which value of n is the experimental probability of tossing tails most likely to equal the theoretical probability?
   - Ⓐ 5
   - Ⓑ 25
   - Ⓒ 33
   - Ⓓ 42

9. The number of miles Sheena ran each day since she started her training program are shown.

   {3, 4, 6, 2x, 7, 10, 8, 2x − 1, 6, 7}

   What is the value of x if she ran an average of 2x miles each day during this period?

   x = [_____]

10. Two standard number cubes are rolled, one red and one blue. How many different sums are possible?

    ☐

11. In 20 free throw attempts, Raul made 8. Based on this data, what is a reasonable estimate of the probability that Raul will make his next free throw?

    Ⓐ 8%   Ⓒ 20%
    Ⓑ 30%   Ⓓ 40%

12. A bag has 2 red, 3 blue, and 5 green marbles. A marble is randomly drawn from the bag. Select all the correct probabilities.

    ☐ A. $P(red) = \frac{1}{4}$
    ☐ B. $P(blue\ or\ green) = \frac{3}{7}$
    ☐ C. $P(green) = \frac{1}{2}$
    ☐ D. $P(not\ red) = \frac{4}{5}$
    ☐ E. $P(not\ green) = P(green)$

13. Solve $p(1 - p) = 0.24$ for p. Enter the answers in ascending order.

    $p = $ ☐ or $p = $ ☐

14. The data set {80, 85, 85, 80, 85} gives James' scores on 5 math tests. What is his mean score?

    ☐

15. Select all the game moves that are best represented by a negative integer in a game of chance.

    ☐ A. Moving ahead 2 spaces
    ☐ B. Moving back 2 spaces
    ☐ C. A loss of 2 points
    ☐ D. A gain of 2 points
    ☐ E. A drop of 2 points

16. A circular target has a radius of 9 inches. At the center is a red circle with a diameter of 9 inches. Select all the true statements.

    ☐ A. The ratio of the area of the red circle to the remaining target area is 1:3.
    ☐ B. The circumference of the target is double the circumference of the red circle.
    ☐ C. The area of the target not covered by the red circle is $\pi \cdot 9^2$ square inches.
    ☐ D. Doubling both the radius of the target and the diameter of the red circle doubles the ratio of their circumferences.
    ☐ E. Doubling both the radius of the target and the diameter of the red circle doubles the ratio of their areas.

17. A sample of 200 students were surveyed about whether or not they walk to school.

    Part A

    Complete the frequency table.

	Walk	Don't Walk	Total
Grade 10	☐	40	100
Grade 11	70	☐	☐
Total	☐	70	200

    Part B

    Of all the students surveyed, what percent walk to school?

    ☐ %

18. What is the value of the expression $200p^2q^3$ for $p = \frac{2}{5}$ and $q = \frac{3}{5}$?

    ☐

Name _____

12-1 Lesson Quiz

Probability Events

1. A rectangular piece of stained glass has the dimensions shown in the diagram. What is the probability that a random leaf that lands on the rectangle lands within either section shaped like a right triangle?

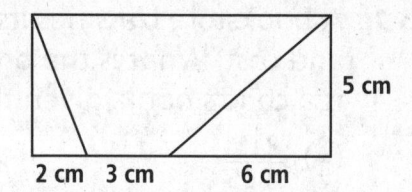

   (2) (3) (4) (5) (6) (8)
   (9) (10) (11) (12) (14) (16)

   $\dfrac{\boxed{}}{\boxed{}}$

   5 cm
   2 cm   3 cm   6 cm

2. There are 5 red tiles and 5 blue tiles with the letter A in a bag. There are also 6 red tiles and 4 blue tiles with the letter B in the bag. What is the probability that a randomly selected tile is blue or has the letter B?

   Ⓐ $\dfrac{9}{20}$ Ⓑ $\dfrac{1}{2}$ Ⓒ $\dfrac{3}{4}$ Ⓓ $\dfrac{19}{20}$

3. Select from the following pairs of events all the pairs that are independent.

   ☐ A. Draw a 2 of clubs from a standard deck of 52 cards, keep it, then draw a 2 of diamonds.

   ☐ B. Draw a 3 of spades from a standard deck of 52 cards, replace it, then draw a 5 of hearts.

   ☐ C. Roll a number cube. Then roll again if the first roll is a 6.

   ☐ D. Roll a 2 on a number cube and spin a 3 on a spinner.

   ☐ E. Events A and B, where $P(A) = 0.4$, $P(B) = 0.2$, and $P(A \text{ and } B) = 0.8$

   ☐ F. Events A and B, where $P(A) = 0.1$, $P(B) = 0.5$, and $P(A \text{ and } B) = 0.05$

4. On a track and field team, 8% of the members run only long-distance, 32% compete only in field events, and 12% are sprinters only. Find the probability that a randomly chosen team member runs only long-distance or competes only in field events. Write the probability as a decimal.

   [_____]

5. The probability that Yuri will make a free throw is 0.3. The probability that he will make two consecutive free throws is [____]. The probability that he will make the first and not the second in two free throws is [____]. The probability that he will make neither of the two free throws is [____].

enVision® Algebra 2 • Assessment Sourcebook

Name _____

12-2 Lesson Quiz
Conditional Probability

1. A bookstore classifies its books by reader group, type of book, and cost. What is the probability that a book selected at random is a child's book, given that it costs more than $10?

   Ⓐ $\frac{315}{1005}$ Ⓒ $\frac{315}{575}$

   Ⓑ $\frac{470}{1005}$ Ⓓ $\frac{470}{575}$

		<$10	>$10
Child	Fiction	120	255
	Nonfiction	35	60
Adult	Fiction	200	110
	Nonfiction	75	150

2. Half of a class took Form A of a test and half took Form B. Of the students who took Form B, 39% passed. What is the probability that a randomly chosen student took Form B and did not pass?

   Ⓐ 0.055   Ⓑ 0.195   Ⓒ 0.305   Ⓓ 0.390

3. Select all the pairs of independent events.

   ☐ A. A student selected at random has black hair. A student selected at random drives to school.

   ☐ B. Events A and B where $P(A|B) = \frac{8}{9}$, $P(A) = \frac{3}{4}$, and $P(B) = \frac{2}{3}$

   ☐ C. A student selected at random is in middle school. A student selected at random is in high school.

   ☐ D. Events A and B where $P(B|A) = 0.9$, $P(A \text{ and } B) = 0.45$, and $P(A) = 0.5$

   ☐ E. Events A and B where $P(B) = 0.15$, $P(A) = 0.25$, and $P(A|B) = 0.15$

4. Three-fourths of a research team worked in a lab while one-fourth of the team worked near a pond. Of the researchers who worked near the pond, 14% collected insects. What is the probability that a randomly chosen researcher worked near the pond and collected insects?

   [ ] %

5. A bag contains 4 blue and 6 green marbles. Two marbles are selected at random from the bag.

   Find each probability. Round to two decimal places if needed.

	With replacement	Without replacement
P(blue second | green first)	[ ] %	[ ] %
P(green second | blue first)	[ ] %	[ ] %

enVision® Algebra 2 • Assessment Sourcebook

Name _____

12-3 Lesson Quiz

Permutations and Combinations

1. A chef randomly chooses 5 apples from a case of 24 apples. In how many ways can the chef make the selection?

   Ⓐ 11,628   Ⓑ 42,504   Ⓒ 5,100,480   Ⓓ 1,395,360

2. A game at the fair involves balls numbered 1 to 18. You can win a prize if you correctly choose the 5 numbers that are randomly drawn. What are your approximate chances of winning?

   Ⓐ 0.0001   Ⓑ 0.056   Ⓒ 0.078   Ⓓ 0.278

3. Identify each situation as a permutation or a combination. Then find the number of possible arrangements.

   6 books are placed from left to right on a bookshelf.

   This is a ☐ permutation.   There are ( ) possible arrangements.
              ☐ combination.

   4 goldfish are selected from a tank containing 8 goldfish.

   This is a ☐ permutation.   There are ( ) possible arrangements.
              ☐ combination.

   3 class representatives are chosen from 25 students.

   This is a ☐ permutation.   There are ( ) possible arrangements.
              ☐ combination.

4. A bag contains 7 marbles; one each of red, orange, yellow, green, blue, violet and white. A child randomly pulls 4 marbles from the bag. What is the probability that the marbles chosen are green, blue, red, and yellow? Round your answer to the nearest hundredth?

   ( )

5. Serena has a playlist of 10 songs. She plays 2 songs. What is the approximate probability in each case?

	45%	2.2%	1.1%	90%
She hears her 2 favorite songs.	☐	☐	☐	☐
She hears her favorite song first and her next-favorite song second.	☐	☐	☐	☐

enVision® Algebra 2 • Assessment Sourcebook

Name _____

12-4 Lesson Quiz

Probability Distributions

1. The probability that a machine part is defective is 0.1. Find the probability that no more than 2 out of 12 parts tested are defective.

   Ⓐ 0.23   Ⓒ 0.89

   Ⓑ 0.66   Ⓓ 0.61

2. The probability that a newborn baby at a certain hospital is male is 50%. Find the probability that 7 or 8 out of 10 babies born in the hospital on any day are male. Round to the nearest hundreth.

   [ ]

3. Select all the statements that are conditions for a binomial experiment.

   ☐ A. There is a fixed number of trials.
   ☐ B. Each trial has two possible outcomes.
   ☐ C. The trials are dependent.
   ☐ D. The trials are independent.
   ☐ E. The probability is constant throughout the trials.
   ☐ F. The probability may vary throughout the trials.

4. A tile is chosen at random from a bag containing the following tiles: 7 blue, 3 green, and 6 yellow. You select with replacement two tiles at random from the bag. Define the theoretical probability distribution for selecting a number of yellow marbles on the sample space {0, 1, 2}.

   Write each probability rounded to the nearest hundredth.

   $P(0) =$ [ ]

   $P(1) =$ [ ]

   $P(2) =$ [ ]

5. In an experiment with 50 trials, the number 5 occurred 17 times, the number 6 occurred 8 times, the number 7 occurred 13 times and the number 8 occurred 12 times.

   Let p be defined on the set {5, 6, 7, 8}. Find each of the following. Write each probability rounded to the nearest hundredth.

P(5)	P(6)	P(7)	P(8)	P(6 or less)

enVision® Algebra 2 • Assessment Sourcebook

Name _____

12-5 Lesson Quiz

Expected Value

1. What is the expected value when rolling a fair die in each of the following cases?

   A 6-sided die with the numbers 2 twice, 4 twice, and 6 twice on its six faces. ( )

   An 8-sided die with the numbers 1 twice, 5 twice, 7 three times, and 8 once on its eight faces. ( )

2. The chance of rain is forecast to be 20% each day over the next 7 days. How many rainy days should be expected?

   Ⓐ 0.7

   Ⓑ 1.4

   Ⓒ 2

   Ⓓ 2.7

3. A bag has 8 red tiles and 2 green tiles. In a charity carnival game, you pay $5 to randomly pull a tile from the bag. The payout for pulling a red tile is $1 and the payout for pulling a green tile is $10. Find each of the following.

   The expected payoff per game for the charity is $( ).

   In 20 games, the charity can expect to make $( ).

4. A spinner with 20 equal-sized sections has 5 red, 10 blue, 3 green, and 2 yellow sections. Ann pays $10 to spin the spinner. If she spins a yellow, she wins $20; if she spins green, she wins $15; otherwise, she loses.

   She plays the game twice. The expected payoff for her games is $( ).

5. An insurance company offers two accident policies. Policy A has a premium of $2,000 with a deductible of $800. Policy B has a premium of $2,400 with a deductible of $200. The probability of an accident costing more than $800 in a given year is 15%. Assume a person has at most one accident a year and no accidents costing less than $800. Complete each statement.

   The annual expected cost to the owner for Policy A is $( ).

   The annual expected cost to the owner for Policy B is $( ).

   Policy ( ) has the lesser annual expected total cost to the owner.

12-6 Lesson Quiz

Probability and Decision Making

1. Students from 4 towns attend a conference. Each town is assigned a number 1 to 4.

   A number is drawn and replaced 6 times. Is this a fair way to pick 6 members to give each town representation? ☐

   What is the probability that Town 1 will have at least 1 representative after 6 number draws, to the nearest percent? ☐ %

2. In a two-player game, five cards, numbered 1 through 5, are placed in a bag. A card is drawn at random, and the players look at the number. Which of the following scoring rules makes a fair game?

   Ⓐ If it is greater than 2, Player 1 earns 2 points. If not, Player 2 earns 2 points.

   Ⓑ If it is less than 2, Player 1 earns 3 points. If not, Player 2 earns 2 points.

   Ⓒ If it is greater than 3, Player 1 earns 2 points. If not, Player 2 earns 2 points.

   Ⓓ If it is less than 3, Player 1 earns 3 points. If not, Player 2 earns 2 points.

3. Do the rules described result in a fair situation? Select Yes or No for each rule.

	Yes	No
Roll a 1 through 6 number cube. If the result is 1 or 2, Joel walks the dog. If the result is 3 or 4, Kyle walks the dog. If the result is 5 or 6, Mindy walks the dog.	☐	☐
Write the names of 5 participants on identical index cards. Put the names in a hat and draw a name at random.	☐	☐
Assign each of 10 players a number from 0 to 9. Use a random number generator to select the first 4 to play.	☐	☐
One-half of a spinner is green. The other two quarters are yellow and purple. Spin green and pay $1. Spin yellow or purple and win $2.	☐	☐

4. A caterer needs 12 workers for an event, but each worker has a 5% chance of not showing up. The caterer wants at least a 90% probability that enough workers show up, so she hires 13 workers.

   The caterer's strategy ☐ is ☐ is not effective because the probability that enough workers show up is ☐ 0.14 ☐ 0.65 ☐ 0.86 ☐ 0.95.

5. At a concert hall, seats are reserved for 10 VIPs. For each VIP, the probability that they will attend is 0.8. The probability that 6 VIPs attend is ☐.

   The probability that 10 VIPs attend is ☐.

   The probability that more than 6 VIPs attend is ☐.

Name _____

12 Topic Assessment Form A

1. A card is selected at random from the set of cards below.

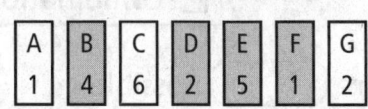

A	B	C	D	E	F	G
1	4	6	2	5	1	2

(B, C, D, E, F are shaded)

A sample space for the experiment is {A, B, C, D, E, F, G}. Let W represent the event "the card is white", let S represent "the card is shaded", and let L represent "the number is less than 3".

Part A

Select all the correct statements.

☐ A. The event W is {A, C, G}.
☐ B. The event W or L is {A, D, F, G}.
☐ C. The event W and L is {A, G}.
☐ D. The event not L is {B, C, E, F}.
☐ E. P(W or S) = 1
☐ F. P(W and S) = 0

Part B

What is P(S or L)?

Ⓐ 0.23   Ⓒ 0.80
Ⓑ 0.57   Ⓓ 0.91

2. The local sandwich shop is running a promotion where customers can win $500 worth of free sandwiches. The first 25 customers to buy a $7.99 sandwich are entered into the drawing. What is the expected payoff of the promotion for each customer? $ ☐

3. Two-thirds of the juniors at a local high school volunteer in their community. Of the juniors who volunteer, 45% volunteer at least twice a week. What is the probability that a randomly chosen junior volunteers in the community at least twice a week? ☐ %

4. If events A and B are independent with P(A) = 0.86 and P(B) = 0.52, what is P(A|B)?

☐

5. Seventy-five percent of students are eligible to participate in a school-wide fundraiser. Of the students who participate, 10% earn a prize for their sales. What is the probability that a student who is eligible to participate in the fundraiser will earn a prize for sales? ☐ %

6. Collision insurance with a $500 deductible costs $310 per year. With a $1,000 deductible, it costs $255 a year. The table shows the average cost of repairs for two types of accidents and the probability of each type.

	Avg. Cost	Probability
Minor Accident	$683	9%
Major Accident	$4,612	6%

Which option has the least expected cost for one year?

$ ☐ deductible

What is that cost? $ ☐

7. A sample of juniors and seniors were asked if they plan to attend college.

	Plan to Attend	Do Not Plan to Attend	Totals
Juniors	288	134	422
Seniors	279	107	386
Totals	567	241	808

One surveyed student is chosen at random. Select all the true statements. Percents are rounded.

☐ A. The probability the student is a junior is 52%.

☐ B. The probability the student plans to attend college is 70%.

☐ C. Given the student plans to attend college, the probability the student is a junior is 68%.

☐ D. Given the student is a junior, the probability the student plans to attend college is 68%.

☐ E. Events "is a junior" and "plans to attend" are independent.

☐ F. Events "is a senior" and "plans to attend" are independent.

8. The table shows data for bus arrivals at one stop. By how many minutes can you expect a bus to be late?

Minutes Late	0	1	2	3	4	5
Number of Days	8	7	3	4	2	1

9. Part A

In how many ways can 12 gymnasts be awarded first, second, and third place?

This represents a ☐ permutation.
☐ combination.

There are (_____) possible arrangements.

Part B

In how many ways can 3 teachers out of 12 be selected for a committee?

This represents a ☐ permutation.
☐ combination.

There are (_____) possible arrangements.

10. Margo has a bag containing 12 yellow stars and 8 blue stars.

Part A

She randomly selects 6 stars. How many ways can her selection contain 4 yellow stars?

Part B

Margo replaces each star after recording what she draws. What is the probability that she chooses 4 yellow stars and 2 blue stars in 6 draws? Round the answer to three decimal places.

11. There are 3 white marbles and 4 striped marbles in a bag. A marble is selected at random from the bag, and a coin is flipped. Let S represent "the marble is striped", and let H represent "the coin shows heads". Select all the statements that can be used to show that events S and H are independent.

☐ **A.** $P(S) = \frac{4}{7}$

☐ **B.** $P(H) = \frac{1}{2}$

☐ **C.** $P(S \text{ and } H) = \frac{2}{7}$

☐ **D.** $P(S \text{ or } H) = \frac{11}{14}$

☐ **E.** $\frac{4}{7} \times \frac{1}{2} = \frac{2}{7}$

☐ **F.** $\frac{4}{7} \times \frac{1}{2} \neq \frac{2}{7}$

---

12. Select all of the following equations that are true.

☐ **A.** $P(A) \times P(B|A) = P(B) \times P(A|B)$

☐ **B.** $P(A \text{ and } B) = P(A) \times P(A|B)$

☐ **C.** $P(B \text{ and } A) = P(B) \times P(A|B)$

☐ **D.** $P(A|B) = \frac{P(A \text{ and } B)}{P(A)}$

☐ **E.** $P(B|A) = \frac{P(A|B)}{P(B)}$

---

13. Ten percent of the students at Memorial High School buy a salad, 18% buy a hot lunch, and 1% buy both. If a student is selected at random, what is the probability that the student buys a salad or a hot lunch?

Ⓐ 10%

Ⓑ 19%

Ⓒ 27%

Ⓓ 28%

---

14. A bag has 9 striped marbles, 6 clear marbles, and 5 solid marbles. You draw one marble, report its color, and return it to the bag. You draw another marble and report its color.

Part A

Find the probabilities of the following events. Round to the nearest hundredth.

Event	Probability
You have a striped marble in both draws.	⬭
You have a solid marble in the first draw and not a clear marble in the second draw.	⬭
You have a clear marble in the first draw and a striped or solid marble in the second draw.	⬭
You don't have a solid marble in the first draw, and you have a clear marble in the second draw.	⬭

Part B

The color of the first marble

☐ does
☐ does not

affect the color of the second marble so the events are

☐ independent
☐ dependent

15. A restaurant gave each customer one free dessert to try, either pie or ice cream. Customers sampled the desserts and then decided if they would recommend the restaurant to a friend.

	Pie	Ice Cream
Would Recommend	36	43
Would Not Recommend	8	13

Part A

What is the probability that a customer who recommended the dessert tried the pie? Round to the nearest whole percent. ( ) %

Part B

Recommending pie is

☐ independent
☐ not independent

from recommending ice cream because the probability of recommending

pie is
☐ greater than
☐ less than
☐ equal to

the probability of recommending ice cream.

---

16. A town lottery sells 1,000 tickets for $5 a piece. There is a grand prize of $800, two second place prizes of $250, and four third place prizes of $50. The expected value of the game is ( ).

The lottery
☐ is
☐ is not
fair.

---

17. Chen is going on vacation and packed an orange shirt, a red shirt, a blue shirt, and a yellow shirt. She also packed one pair of pants and one pair of shorts. If she chooses a top and bottom at random, what is the probability that she will wear a red shirt and shorts?

Ⓐ $\frac{1}{3}$

Ⓑ $\frac{1}{6}$

Ⓒ $\frac{1}{8}$

Ⓓ $\frac{1}{12}$

---

18. Hilaria has a bag of coins, labeled 1 through 20. Her friend draws a coin from the bag at random. What is the probability that the coin shows a number that is even or a multiple of 3?

( ) %

---

19. Carolina is organizing flowers for her community garden. She purchases a random assortment of flowers from the local nursery, which contains gardenias, pansies, and sunflowers in multiple colors.

	Gardenia	Pansy	Sunflower
Purple	0	12	0
Yellow	16	12	10
White	12	18	0

Carolina will choose one plant at random to plant in her personal garden. What is the probability that she selects a yellow pansy?

( ) %

12 Topic Assessment Form B

1. A card is selected at random from the set of cards below.

Q	R	S	T	U	V	X
7	4	5	7	10	9	4

   (Cards Q, S, U, V, X are shaded; R, T are white.)

   A sample space for the experiment is {Q, R, S, T, U, V, X}. Let W represent the event "the card is white", let H represent "the card is shaded", and let M represent "the number is greater than 6".

   Part A

   Select all the correct statements.

   ☐ A. The event H is {Q, S, U, V, X}.
   ☐ B. The event H and M is {Q, S, U, V}.
   ☐ C. The event H or M is {Q, S, T, U, V, X}.
   ☐ D. The event not M is {R, S, X}.
   ☐ E. $P(W \text{ and } H) = 0$
   ☐ F. $P(W \text{ or } H) = 0$

   Part B

   What is $P(W \text{ or } M)$?

   Ⓐ 1   Ⓒ 0.57
   Ⓑ 0.86 Ⓓ 0.29

2. A car dealership is running a promotion where customers can win 10 years of free oil changes, valued at $600. The first 10 customers to buy a $15 carwash will be entered into the drawing. What is the expected payoff of the promotion for each customer?

   $ _____

3. One-third of the sophomores at a local high school participate in school clubs. Of the sophomores who participate, 54% participate in at least 2 clubs. What is the probability that a randomly chosen sophomore participates in at least 2 school clubs? _____ %

4. If events A and B are independent with $P(B) = 0.64$ and $P(A) = 0.58$, what is $P(B|A)$?

   _____

5. Data show 62% of students at a local school buy lunch in the cafeteria. Of the students who buy lunch, 15% buy milk. What is the probability that a student in the school will buy lunch, including milk?

   _____ %

6. Collision insurance with a $250 deductible costs $150 per year. With a $500 deductible, it costs $210 a year. The table shows the average cost of repairs for two types of accidents and the probability of each type.

	Avg. Cost	Probability
Minor Accident	$542	10%
Major Accident	$6,104	4%

   Which option has the least expected cost for one year?

   $ _____ deductible

   What is that cost? $ _____

7. A random sample of voters were asked whether they plan to vote for Doris Brown for mayor.

Plans to vote for Doris Brown

	Yes	No	Totals
Men	246	237	483
Women	288	236	524
Totals	543	464	1,007

One surveyed voter is chosen at random. Select all the true statements. Percents are rounded.

☐ A. The probability the person is a man is 48%.

☐ B. The probability the person plans to vote for Doris Brown is 54%.

☐ C. Given the person plans to vote for Doris Brown, the probability the person is a man is 51%.

☐ D. Given the person is a man, the probability the person plans to vote for Doris Brown is 51%.

☐ E. The events "is a man" and "plans to vote for Doris Brown" are independent.

☐ F. The events "is a woman" and "plans to vote for Doris Brown" are independent.

---

8. The table shows data for ferry arrivals at a port. By how many minutes can you expect the ferry to be late?

Minutes Late	0	1	2	3	4	5
Number of Days	10	4	6	7	2	1

☐

---

9. Part A

In how many ways can 5 bottles out of a crate containing 10 be randomly selected?

This represents a ☐ permutation.
                  ☐ combination.

There are ⬚ possible arrangements.

Part B

In how many ways can 14 science fair participants be awarded first, second, third, and fourth place?

This represents a ☐ permutation.
                  ☐ combination.

There are ⬚ possible arrangements.

---

10. Jonathon has a bag containing 14 red circles and 8 green circles.

Part A

He randomly selects 7 circles. How many ways can his selection contain 3 green circles?

⬚

Part B

Jonathon replaces each circle after recording what he draws. What is the probability that he choses 3 green circles and 4 red circles in 7 draws? Round the answer to three decimal places.

⬚

11. There are 2 white marbles and 5 striped marbles in a bag. A marble is selected at random from the bag, and a coin is flipped. Let W represent "the marble is white", and let H represent "the coin shows heads". Select all the statements that can be used to show that events W and H are independent.

☐ **A.** $P(W) = \frac{2}{7}$

☐ **B.** $P(H) = \frac{1}{2}$

☐ **C.** $P(W \text{ or } H) = \frac{11}{14}$

☐ **D.** $P(W \text{ and } H) = \frac{1}{7}$

☐ **E.** $\frac{2}{7} + \frac{1}{2} = \frac{11}{14}$

☐ **F.** $\frac{2}{7} \times \frac{1}{2} = \frac{1}{7}$

---

12. Select all of the following equations that are true.

☐ **A.** $P(A \text{ or } B) = P(A) \div P(B)$

☐ **B.** $P(B \mid A) = \frac{P(B \text{ and } A)}{P(A)}$

☐ **C.** $P(B \text{ and } A) = P(B) \times P(A)$

☐ **D.** $P(A \mid B) = \frac{P(A \text{ or } B)}{P(A)}$

☐ **E.** $P(B) \times P(A \mid B) = P(A) \times P(B \mid A)$

---

13. Thirty-eight percent of the patrons at a local water park on a specific day use only the Lazy River, 49% use the only the water slides, and 74% use both. If a patron is selected at random, what is the probability the patron uses the Lazy River or the water slides?

Ⓐ 13%

Ⓑ 25%

Ⓒ 35%

Ⓓ 36%

---

14. A deck of playing cards has some cards missing. There are 13 hearts, 8 clubs, 12 spades, and 6 diamonds. You draw one card at random, record the suit and return it to the deck. You draw another card and record its suit.

Part A

Find the probabilities of the following events. Round to the nearest hundredth.

Event	Probability
You draw a heart in both draws.	
You draw a club for the first draw and not a spade for the second.	
You draw a heart in the first draw and a diamond or club in the second.	
You don't draw a diamond in the first draw, and you draw a spade in the second.	

Part B

The suit of the first card

☐ does
☐ does not

affect the suit of the second, so the events are

☐ independent
☐ dependent

15. A bookstore gave customers a free book to read, either fiction or nonfiction. Customers read the book and then decided if they would recommend the bookstore to a friend.

	Non-Fiction	Fiction
Would Recommend	27	61
Would Not Recommend	17	21

Part A

What is the probability that a customer who would not recommend the bookstore read a fiction book? Round to the nearest whole percent. ( ) %

Part B

Recommending a non-fiction book is [☐ independent / ☐ not independent] from recommending a fiction book because the probability of recommending non-fiction is

[☐ greater than / ☐ less than / ☐ equal to] the

probability of recommending fiction.

16. A school fundraiser is selling 700 tickets for a raffle. Tickets are $3 a piece. There is a grand prize of $500, two second place prizes of $100, and five third place prizes of $25. The expected value of the raffle is ( ).

The raffle [☐ is / ☐ is not] fair.

17. Stefano is buying breakfast for his brothers. He buys 2 poppyseed bagels, 3 egg bagels, and 1 plain bagel. He also buys veggie cream cheese and plain cream cheese. If Stefano chooses one bagel and one topping at random, what is the probability that he will eat an egg bagel with plain cream cheese?

Ⓐ $\frac{1}{3}$

Ⓑ $\frac{1}{4}$

Ⓒ $\frac{1}{6}$

Ⓓ $\frac{1}{12}$

18. Micki has a bag of coins, labeled 1 through 30. She draws a coin from the bag at random. What is the probability that the coin shows a number that is odd or a multiple of 5?

( ) %

19. Shreya is making sandwiches for her coworkers. She uses three different types of bread and three different types of sandwich fillings.

	White	Wheat	Sourdough
Turkey	10	7	4
Ham	8	4	10
Veggie	5	9	3

Shreya will choose one sandwich at random for herself. What is the probability that she chooses a veggie sandwich on white bread? Round to the nearest percent.

( ) %

Name _____

12 Performance Assessment Form A

A company is trying to reduce the cost of producing one of its tools. It comes up with a much cheaper new method of production. A large box of tools produced by both methods is examined by testers.

	Acceptable	Defective
Old Method	1,640	23
New Method	328	9

1. One tool is selected at random. What is the probability of drawing a defective tool, or one produced by the new method? Explain.

2. Two tools are selected at random, one at a time.

   Part A

   One tool is chosen at random from the box. It is then replaced. A tool is selected again. What is the probability that both selections were acceptable? Are the events dependent or independent events? Explain.

   Part B

   One tool is chosen at random from the box. It is *not* replaced. A tool is selected again. What is the probability that the first one was produced by the old method and the second one by the new method? Are the events dependent or independent events? Explain.

3. Two tools are selected at random from the box, one at a time.

   Part A

   What is the probability that a tool selected at random is defective given that the tool was produced by the new method?

Part B

Is P(defective | new) the same as P(new | defective)? Explain.

Part C

Are the events "select a defective tool" and "select a tool produced by the new method" dependent or independent events? Use conditional probability to support your answer.

4. The company produces 12 different types of tools. Three types will be selected to create a tool set.

Part A

How many ways can the set of 3 tools be selected? Explain.

Part B

Suppose 4 of the 12 types of tools are different types of screwdrivers. If 3 tools are selected at random, what is the probability that they are all screwdrivers? Explain.

Part C

A machine puts one of 12 sticker codes on each tool after it is produced. If the stickers were placed on the 3 tools randomly, what is the probability that each sticker would be on the correct tool? Explain.

12 Performance Assessment Form B

1. Your family is packing for a 4-day trip to another city. The forecast is shown below. Assume that whether it rains on each day is independent of whether it rains on any other day.

	Thu	Fri	Sat	Sun
high	80°	77°	79°	83°
low	54°	50°	52°	60°
rain	30%	40%	20%	60%

   ### Part A
   What is the probability it will not rain on either of the first two days to the nearest percent? Explain.

   ### Part B
   What is the probability it will rain on both Thursday and Friday to the nearest percent? Does this adding this probability to your answer from Part A total 100%? Explain.

   ### Part C
   What is the probability it will not rain on any of the four days to the nearest percent?

   ### Part D
   What is the probability it will rain on at least three of the four days to the nearest percent? Explain.

2. For a school project you complete a survey of 50 high school students and 50 adults. Of the 100 people surveyed, 72 said they owned an umbrella, of those, 44 were adults.

Part A

Use the data to make a two way frequency table.

	Student	Adult

Part B

What is the probability that a surveyed person who owns an umbrella is a student? What is the probability that a surveyed person who owns an umbrella is an adult? Round to the nearest percent. Explain.

Part C

Based on the results from Part B, what could you conclude about the relationship between age and umbrella ownership? Explain.

Part D

What is the probability that a person owns an umbrella, given that they are a high school student? Are being a high school student and owning an umbrella independent, based on the survey? Explain.

Benchmark Assessment 6

1. Kyle is filling a 25-gal gas tank at a rate of 10 gal per minute. What is the domain of the function that represents the volume of gas y in the tank after x minutes?

   Ⓐ $0 \le x \le 2.5$
   Ⓑ $0 < x < 2.5$
   Ⓒ $0 < x < 25$
   Ⓓ $0 < y < 25$

2. Write the explicit formula for the sequence defined by
   $a_n = \begin{cases} 9, n = 1 \\ a_{n-1} - 4, n > 1 \end{cases}$

   Ⓐ $a_n = 9 + 4n$
   Ⓑ $a_n = 9 - 4n$
   Ⓒ $a_n = 13 - 4n$
   Ⓓ $a_n = 4 + 9n$

3. Solve the system of equations.
   $\begin{cases} 6x + 3y = 9 \\ x - 7y = 9 \end{cases}$

   $x = \boxed{}$
   $y = \boxed{}$

4. What is the equation in vertex form of a parabola with vertex $(-2, 6)$ that passes through $(1, -3)$?

   Ⓐ $y = -(x - 2)^2 - 6$
   Ⓑ $y = -(x + 2)^2 + 6$
   Ⓒ $y = -(x + 2)^2 - 6$
   Ⓓ $y = -(x - 2)^2 + 6$

5. Write the quotient $\frac{26}{-2 + 3i}$ in the form $a + bi$.

   Ⓐ $-4 - 5i$
   Ⓑ $-4 - 3i$
   Ⓒ $-4 - 6i$
   Ⓓ $-4 - 2i$

6. Evaluate $64^{\frac{2}{3}}$.

   Ⓐ 4   Ⓑ 8   Ⓒ 16   Ⓓ 512

7. Use polynomial identities to factor $27 + 125y^3$. Select all factors.

   ☐ A. $(3 + 5y)$
   ☐ B. $(9 + 15y + 5y^2)$
   ☐ C. $(9 - 15y + 5y^2)$
   ☐ D. $(3 - 5y)$
   ☐ E. $(9 + 15y + 25y^2)$
   ☐ F. $(9 - 15y + 25y^2)$

8. A school is holding a $10000 raffle and each ticket has the odds of 1:1550 odds of being the winner. Which of the following best represents the price where tickets would start costing too much to play and expect to make money in the long run?

   Ⓐ $6.45
   Ⓑ $6.00
   Ⓒ $6.75
   Ⓓ $6.50

9. What are all the real and complex solutions of
   $a^3 - 22a^2 + 154a - 160 = 168$?

   Ⓐ $4, -9 + i, -9 - i$
   Ⓑ $-9, 1, 4$
   Ⓒ $4, 9 + i, 9 - i$
   Ⓓ 4

10. Q varies inversely with x. If $Q = 12$ when $x = 5$, find the value of Q when $x = 12$.

Ⓐ 4
Ⓑ 5
Ⓒ 19
Ⓓ 28.8

11. Solve $\frac{3(2+x)}{2x} = -\frac{1}{x} + 2$. Identify any extraneous solutions.

$x = \boxed{}$

There are $\boxed{}$ extraneous solutions.

12. The formula for an arithmetic sequence is $a_1 + (n-1)d$ where a_1, n, and d represent constants. How many terms are in the formula?

$\boxed{}$ terms

13. Given the sequence

1, 4, 7, 10, ...

What is the 8th term?

Ⓐ 13   Ⓑ 3   Ⓒ 21   Ⓓ 24

14. Solve $\sqrt{2x + 12} = 2 + \sqrt{4 + x}$.

Part A

Select all viable solutions.

☐ A. $x = -4$
☐ B. $x = 12$
☐ C. $x = 4$
☐ D. $x = -6$
☐ E. $x = 0$

Part B

Complete the sentence.

There are $\boxed{}$ extraneous solutions.

15. Graph the function $4 - \sqrt{x}$.

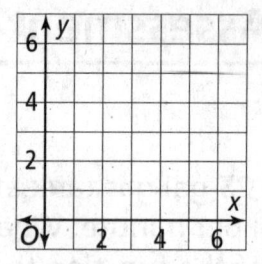

16. There are 50 deer in a particular forest. The population is increasing at a rate of 15% per year. Write an exponential growth function that represents the number of deer, y, in that forest after x months. Round to the nearest thousandth.

$f(x) = \boxed{}(\boxed{})^x$

17. Find the equation of the inverse of the function $f(x) = \log(5x)$. Write values as decimals when necessary.

$f^{-1}(x) = \boxed{}(\boxed{})^x$

18. Solve for x: $3^{x+4} = 9^{x-1}$.

$x = \boxed{}$

19. Use the frequency table below to find the P(A). Round to the nearest hundredth.

	Ripe (R)	Unripe (U)	Total
Apples (A)	15	18	33
Bananas (B)	25	22	47
Total	40	40	80

$P(A) = \boxed{}$

20. When the sun shines at a 30° angle to the ground, Manuel casts a 109-in. shadow when he is standing. To the nearest inch, how tall is Manuel?

Manuel's height = $\boxed{}$ in.

21. A deck of 36 cards consists of 12 red cards, 12 white cards, and 12 blue cards.

    - Of the red cards, 2 are blank and the rest have a number on them.
    - Of the white cards, 4 are blank and the rest have a number on them.
    - Of the blue cards, 6 are blank and the rest have a number on them.

    The deck of 36 cards is shuffled and one card is selected at random. If the selected card is either white or red, what is the probability that it is blank? Enter your answer in the box.

    The probability that the card is blank is ☐ %.

22. Find the components of a vector with an initial point at (1, 6) and terminal point at (2, −5).

    Ⓐ ⟨1, −11⟩
    Ⓑ ⟨−1, 11⟩
    Ⓒ ⟨3, 1⟩
    Ⓓ ⟨−3, −1⟩

23. Find the exact value of cos 75°.

    Ⓐ $\frac{\sqrt{6} - \sqrt{2}}{4}$
    Ⓑ $\frac{\sqrt{6} + \sqrt{2}}{4}$
    Ⓒ $\frac{-\sqrt{6} - \sqrt{2}}{4}$
    Ⓓ $\frac{-\sqrt{6} + \sqrt{2}}{4}$

24. What is 6 cis $\frac{3\pi}{4}$ in rectangular form?

    Ⓐ $3\sqrt{2} - 3i\sqrt{2}$
    Ⓑ $2 - i\sqrt{3}$
    Ⓒ $-2\sqrt{3} + 2i\sqrt{3}$
    Ⓓ $-3\sqrt{2} + 3i\sqrt{2}$

25. A vector has an initial point at (−1, 3) and a terminal point at (2, 4). Complete the statements below with the correct numbers rounded to the nearest tenth of a unit.

    The component form of the vector is ⟨☐, ☐⟩

    The magnitude of the vector is about ☐

    The direction of the vector is about ☐°.

26. A company claims that its cell phone's battery life is longer than that of its competitor. Data Set A shows times for the original battery, and Data Set B shows times for the new battery.

    | A | 19.2 h | 19.5 h | 18.9 h | 20.2 h | 18.9 h |
    | B | 18.9 h | 20.0 h | 17.9 h | 18.1 h | 17.5 h |

    Part A Calculate the difference of the sample means to the nearest hundredth.

    difference of means = ☐ h

    Do the data support the company's claim? ☐ yes ☐ no

    Part B The data are resampled so that Data Set A is now 20.2 18.1 18.9 17.9 18.9.

    difference of means = ☐ h

    Do the resampled data support the company's claim? ☐ yes ☐ no

27. Write an equation for the hyperbola with foci (−6, 0) and (6, 0) and constant difference of 4.

   Ⓐ $\frac{y^2}{36} - \frac{x^2}{32} = 1$

   Ⓑ $\frac{x^2}{16} - \frac{y^2}{20} = 1$

   Ⓒ $\frac{x^2}{36} - \frac{y^2}{32} = 1$

   Ⓓ $\frac{y^2}{16} - \frac{x^2}{20} = 1$

28. Which matrix has an inverse?

   Ⓐ $\begin{bmatrix} -9 & 6 \\ 3 & -2 \end{bmatrix}$

   Ⓑ $\begin{bmatrix} -4 & 3 \\ 4 & 3 \end{bmatrix}$

   Ⓒ $\begin{bmatrix} 1 & 2 \\ 4 & 8 \end{bmatrix}$

   Ⓓ $\begin{bmatrix} -1 & 3 \\ -2 & 6 \end{bmatrix}$

29. Marta surveyed her classmates to find out how many movies they had seen in the last month. Complete the probability distribution table. Round to the nearest whole percent.

Number of Movies Seen in Past Month				
Number	0	1	2	3+
Frequency	3	9	15	6
Relative Frequency (%)	◯%	◯%	◯%	◯%

30. There are 12 marbles in a bag. Of these, Four of them are blue and the rest are green. You reach into the bag and take out two marbles without looking. What is the probability that both marbles are blue? Round to the nearest whole percent.

   probability = ◯ %

31. A student watches the patrons in a supermarket, and counts how many pay for their groceries with cash and how many use a debit or credit card. What type of study is described?

   Ⓐ observational study

   Ⓑ cluster study

   Ⓒ sample survey

   Ⓓ experiment

32. A data set is normally distributed with mean 18 and standard deviation 2.7. Approximately what percent of the data are greater than 14?

   Ⓐ 0.7%

   Ⓑ 6.9%

   Ⓒ 0.9%

   Ⓓ 93.1%

33. Which are the best measures of center and spread to use to describe the data set?

   2 5 9 5 1 3 4 3 6 5 8

   Ⓐ mean and standard deviation

   Ⓑ mode and range

   Ⓒ mean and variance

   Ⓓ median and quartiles

34. The mean on a statewide biology test was 76 with a standard deviation of 11. One county within the state sampled the scores of some of its students and reported a mean of 80 with a margin of error of ±2.3. What is the range of reasonable means for the county's sample?

   range: ◯ to ◯

35. A game company gave customers one game to test and asked whether they would recommend the game. What is the probability that a customer who recommended their game tested Game A? Round to the nearest whole percent.

	Game A	Game B
Would Recommend	43	38
Would Not Recommend	7	12

P(tested Game A | reommended their game) = ☐ %

36. Libby eats oatmeal, pancakes, or eggs, and she drinks apple juice or orange juice. If she picks a food and a drink at random, what is the probability that she will have oatmeal and apple juice?

Ⓐ $\frac{1}{3}$

Ⓑ $\frac{1}{5}$

Ⓒ $\frac{1}{6}$

Ⓓ $\frac{1}{8}$

---

37. Students took a pretest at the beginning of a program. After six weeks of instruction, they took a posttest. The teacher had evidence that over the years the mean change of the scores was normally distributed. The teacher randomly selected ten students to analyze the effectiveness of the program.

Students' Pretest and Posttet Scores

Student	1	2	3	4	5	6	7	8	9	10
Pretest	58	60	70	50	66	60	42	58	72	74
Posttest	68	80	68	60	74	50	50	60	80	68

Which statements are true? Select all the statements that apply.

☐ A. There were many outliers in the mean change of the scores for these ten students.

☐ B. The mean change of the scores for these ten students was at least 4 points.

☐ C. All of the students showed an increase from their pretest score to their posttest score.

☐ D. The teacher's study could be improved if only the scores of the highest-performing students were analyzed.

☐ E. The teacher's study could be improved if only the scores of the lowest-performing students were analyzed.

☐ F. The teacher's methodology for this study validates that the mean change of the scores for these ten students is a good indicator of the mean change of all students.

38. The diagram shows a normal distribution with dotted segments marking 1, 2, and 3 standard deviations on either side of the mean. The mean of this distribution is 8.6. Select the correct values that correspond to points P and Q. Drag and drop the two correct numbers into the boxes under the number line in the diagram.

(7.4) (7.8) (8.0) (9.2) (9.4) (9.6) (10.2)

Normal Distribution

6.2 P 8.6 Q

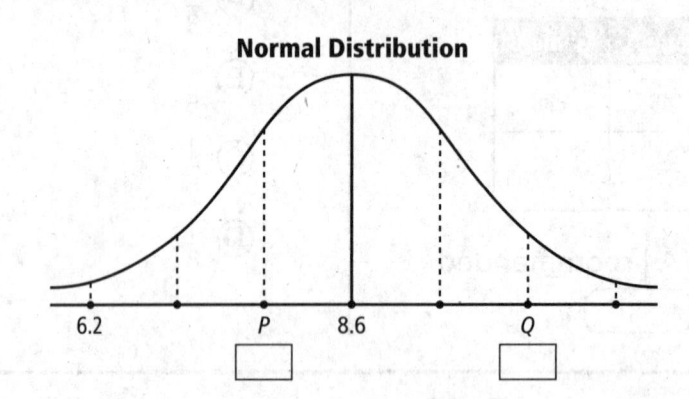

39. A quality control specialist for a printing company took a random sample of 40 ink cartridges from Company A and a random sample of 40 ink cartridges from Company B. In the experiment, $\bar{x}_A$ represents the mean maximum number of pages printed using Company A's cartridge, and $\bar{x}_B$ represents Company B's cartridge. Here is part of her report:

> The mean difference $(\bar{x}_A - \bar{x}_B)$ is -28.6 pages with a standard deviation of 4.2 pages. The results are statistically significant ($p < 0.001$).

Complete each sentence.

The ink cartridge from ☐ Company A / ☐ Company B

will make more copies than the ink cartridge from ☐ Company A / ☐ Company B

The data suggests that the results of this experiment are

☐ very likely
☐ rather likely
☐ rather unlikely
☐ very unlikely

due to chance.